THE PRICE OF LIFE

THE TRUE STORY OF AN AUSTRALIAN HELD TO RANSOM FOR 462 DAYS

Nigel Brennan
Nicole Bonney & Kellie Brennan

PENGUIN BOOKS

PENGUIN BOOKS

UK | USA | Canada | Ireland | Australia
India | New Zealand | South Africa | China

Penguin Books is part of the Penguin Random House group of companies
whose addresses can be found at global.penguinrandomhouse.com.

Penguin
Random House
Australia

First published by Penguin Books Australia Ltd, 2011
This edition published by Penguin Group (Australia), 2012

Text and illustrations copyright © The Dirty Hostage 2011

The moral right of the authors has been asserted

Cover design by Adam Laszczuk © Penguin Group (Australia)
Text design by Karen Scott © Penguin Group (Australia)
Front cover images: cell © Shutterstock; figure © Ojo Images / Getty Images
Typeset in Fairfield by Post Pre-press Group, Brisbane, Queensland
Printed and bound in Australia by Griffin Press, an accredited ISO AS/NZS 14001
Environmental Management Systems printer.

National Library of Australia
Cataloguing-in-Publication data:

Brennan, Nigel, Kellie; Bonney, Nicole
Price of life
2nd ed.
9780143567332 (pbk.)
Prev. ed. 2011
Brennan, Nigel – Kidnapping, August 2008
Lindhout, Amanda – Kidnapping, August 2008
Kidnapping victims – Biography
Photographers – Australia – Biography
Kidnapping – Somalia
Ransom – Australia – Political aspects
International offences

364.154

penguin.com.au

MIX
Paper | Supporting
responsible forestry
FSC® C018684
www.fsc.org

To those who love us:
our families, and our friends,
who are the family we choose

The events in this book are true to our experiences and have been recorded as we remember them. The content has been derived from conversations, meetings, diaries, emails and other correspondence, both official and personal. As such, it is a subjective account, and thus is susceptible to the vagaries and elisions of memory.

In the process of writing we have altered minor facts, condensed time lines and simplified events to help make the narrative more understandable. In order to maintain their anonymity in some instances we have changed the names and identifiable characteristics of individuals.

CONTENTS

Prologue   1

August 2008: Hanging on the telephone   7
2006–August 2008: Into Africa   46
September 2008: Bring Blackie back   56
October 2008: Team Brennan   105
November 2008: It's kidnap month in Somalia   135
December 2008: Walking on eggshells   152
January 2009: A very dirty business   170
February 2009: Back-pocket strategies   205
March 2009: What if?   216
April 2009: Stuck in Groundhog Day   238
May 2009: All pitch in   257
June 2009: Limbo   279
July 2009: Blink and you'll miss Vancouver   287
August 2009: Keep calm and carry on   309
September 2009: Big squabbling families   330
October 2009: Trust   347
November 2009: Sometimes you just have
to take a chance   377

Epilogue   455
Acknowledgments   463

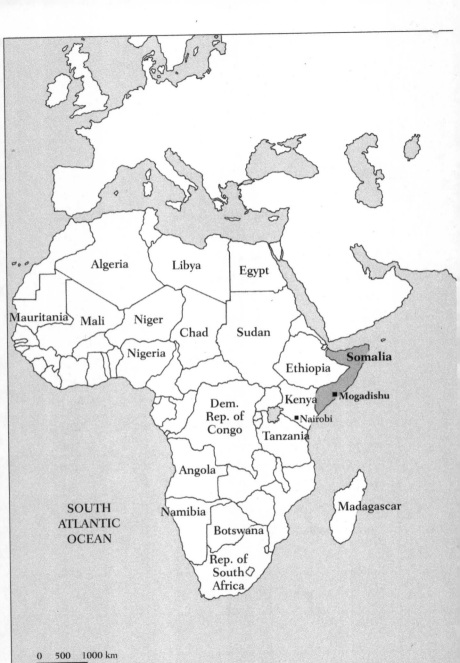

Algeria

Libya

Egypt

Mauritania

Mali

Niger

Chad

Sudan

Nigeria

Ethiopia

Somalia

Kenya

■Mogadishu

Dem. Rep. of Congo

■Nairobi

Tanzania

Angola

Madagascar

SOUTH ATLANTIC OCEAN

Namibia

Botswana

Rep. of South Africa

0   500   1000 km

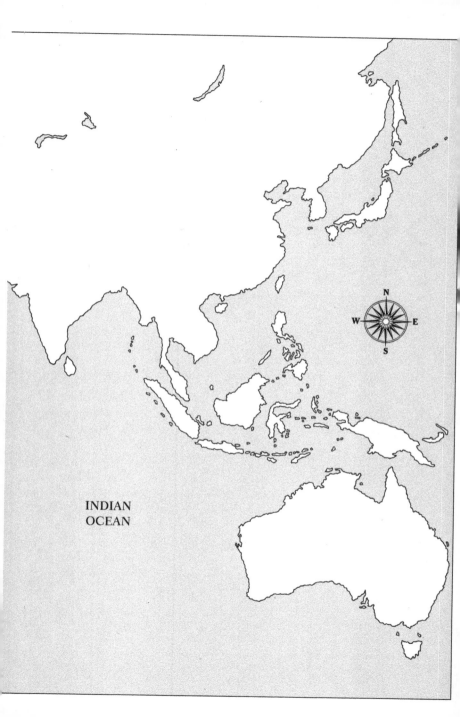

INDIAN
OCEAN

PROLOGUE

Kellie
Newcastle, NSW
Sunday, 24 August 2008

Oh god, I missed the phone. I hate clients calling on a Sunday. It's around 10.30 a.m., and I think to myself, *If it's important, they'll call back*, just as the home phone starts ringing. *Arrrgh.*

'Hello, Kellie speaking.'

'Hi, Kellie, I'm sorry to call you on a Sunday morning.'

'Yeah, right,' I say. I'm curt but not rude. I just don't like discussing work on a Sunday – it's the only day my family spends time together without any interruptions. Besides, I'm a little hung-over and I haven't yet had the caffeine fix I need to get me going.

The woman on the end of the line has an Asian accent. She doesn't sound like a regular client who wants my time; she sounds genuinely apologetic for calling me, yet probing, wanting something.

'My name is Glenda Kwek and I'm from the *Sydney Morning*

Herald. I'm sorry to call you about this as I realise it must be a terribly distressing time for the family but . . .'

But *what*? What the hell is she talking about? She must have the wrong number.

'. . . but can you confirm the kidnapping of Nigel Brennan in Somalia?'

'*What?!* Are you serious?' I ask. She must be having a laugh.

'Yes, I am very serious. There are reports that an Australian man called Nigel Brennan has been kidnapped in Somalia with Canadian journalist Amanda Lindhout.'

Oh, holy crap.

There is a long pause.

I feel the blood drain from all parts of my body; my knees buckle underneath me and I slump into a nearby chair. My armpits start to prickle and I can feel the adrenaline building in my body.

Matt is looking at me, questioning me with his eyes. On a nearby notepad I scrawl the words 'Nigel and Amanda have been kidnapped in Somalia' and pass it to him. He disappears.

I am numb to what Glenda is saying so I ask her to tell me exactly what she knows.

She does so, and it all becomes a bit too real. As Glenda repeats Amanda's name, I know it's true, even though I hadn't heard that Nige had hooked up with her again.

My mouth is dry and as I go to talk, I have to try a couple of times before I can peel my tongue from the roof of my mouth.

'Look, all I can confirm is yes, Nigel Brennan is my brother-in-law; he was going to Kenya last I heard. And yes, I know Amanda Lindhout.'

'Is this the first time you have heard this?' she asks, sounding more shocked than I am.

2

'Yes. I have no idea what you're talking about.'

The penny drops for her. Glenda has just realised that she, a journalist from a major daily newspaper, has informed our family of their son and brother's kidnapping. Not the cops, not the Australian Federal Police, not the Department of Foreign Affairs and Trade, but a journalist.

Matt appears in front of me with a map, showing me that Somalia is next to Kenya.

Oh my god, this is really happening. Matt starts to pace the room and I can see what he's thinking. *How? Why? When? By whom?*

Glenda informs me that it happened yesterday, 23 August. Nigel and Amanda were reported missing when they didn't return to their hotel after a day out taking photographs of refugee camps. DFAT is presently unable to confirm exactly what's happened to them.

She asks if she can speak with Nigel's mother.

'Ah, no,' I say. 'I will take your number and get her to call you.' Glenda gives me her number and we say goodbye.

I have never forgotten the sound of Glenda Kwek's voice.

I'm not sure whether it is adrenaline or instinct, or both, that takes over at this moment, but I turn to Matt and say, 'Right, I need to call your parents to let them know. Your mum needs to phone Glenda Kwek, and we'll go from there.' I feel like I could run a marathon, yet my legs are like jelly.

The knot in my stomach feels as big as those in the fastening ropes of an ocean liner and my head is starting to pound. I dial the number and wait.

Part of me is hoping Matt's mum, Heather, won't pick up because then she will have just a few more minutes of normality before I turn her and Geoff's life to shit. Another part of me is willing them

3

both to the phone so that we can find out exactly where Nigel is and whether he is okay.

Why did he go to Somalia? This question keeps going over and over in my head.

Heather answers the phone in a bright, cheery voice, a voice that sounds like a beautiful sunny Queensland morning. I am about to deliver a cyclone right into her house.

'Hi,' I say, trying to sound like my usual self. 'Is Geoff with you?'

'No, he's outside. How are you?'

'Ah, good. Can you do me a favour and go and get him? I've got some news to tell you both.'

'What's wrong?'

'Oh, nothing. I just need you both to be there together.'

The last time I did this I told them I was having another baby. How do I tell my in-laws this kind of news? And why does it have to be me? I figure it's best that it comes from a family member and not the press, as I have just experienced. And it's too much for Matt to handle.

'He's here,' she says. 'Now what's wrong?'

'I need you to sit down.'

'I don't need to sit down. What is it?' Her tone is anxious.

'I've just had a phone call from Glenda Kwek. She's a journalist with the *Sydney Morning Herald*, and she told me that Nigel has been kidnapped in Somalia with Amanda Lindhout.'

'Don't be ridiculous! He's in Kenya,' she says.

'Heather, Kenya is next to Somalia. Glenda said they haven't returned to their hotel and are feared kidnapped.'

'Oh, that's ridiculous. He wasn't going to Somalia.'

'Look, here's her number. You need to ask her all the details. She's waiting for your call.'

4

'You're serious about this, then?'

'Yeah, I am. Just call her and find out as much as you can and we'll talk again soon.'

Matt and I stare at each other in silence, and then he starts ranting.

'The stupid little fucker!'

I let Matt continue for a bit as I can't seem to move. All I can feel are vibrations through the chair legs as Matt stomps around on the floorboards. He continues to pace.

'Matt, we don't know anything yet. We need to wait for your mum to call back to see if she can confirm if it's Nigel or not.'

'I don't need it confirmed. How many other Nigels do you think Amanda knows who would do something this fucking stupid?'

What happens next can only be described as a barrage. I hear my mobile first and when I don't answer it, the home phone starts ringing off the hook. On the other end are journalists who've just discovered the news on the wire, and are desperate for a comment. If you look up 'Nigel Brennan' on Facebook, you find me. My mobile number is listed on my profile, along with my business details and email address.

I have never been involved with the press in any way. I am a media virgin. As the day unfolds, I learn very quickly that nothing is private, especially when there's a story in it.

The phone is ringing again and thank god for caller ID – it's Heather and Geoff's number.

I pick up the phone, still hoping that it's all just a horrible misunderstanding. Heather tells me she can't get hold of Nigel's girlfriend in Scotland to find out where he was going, as it's the middle of the night there, and that DFAT cannot confirm what's happened to Nigel at this stage, only that he is missing. Heather gives me a number for DFAT so I can call someone called Emily, our newly appointed media liaison officer. Emily will provide me with a blanket statement that family and friends – anyone who might be contacted for a comment or background information – can give to the press.

So while Heather calls Nigel's friends to see if he told anyone where he was going, I set out to phone people to give them the official statement, just as the 11 a.m. news has the first hint of the story.

By 3 p.m. I'm still on the phone, calling everyone I can think of to warn them about what they will see in full detail on the 6 p.m. news. The phone is ringing again and I pick it up.

It's the phone call Matt and I have been dreading. Confirmation.

To the world this is just another news report about some unknown people in a dangerous country. Most are immune to this sort of story. The war in Afghanistan has been raging for years, and images of men in jeeps with machine-guns are disturbingly familiar. But the gunmen's home country is different this time.

In the news story there are no US troops, no villages are annihilated by rogue bombs. This story involves us, the Brennans, and a member of our family. This story is about to become our entire world.

AUGUST 2008

Hanging on the telephone

Nicky
Moore Park, 23 kilometres north of Bundaberg, Queensland
Sunday, 24 August

Sunday afternoon is marching on normally enough. My husband, Simon, and I are clearing out weeds and cutting back shrubs for some farming neighbours, who have gone to Malta for a few months. The kids are spread all over the local community: Jacinta is with my best friend, Ange; Monty is with his best mate from primary school; Atti is with Dylan, who has been his negative-image twin since they were three.

Work done, we head off to collect the kids, starting with Jacinta. When we get to Ange's, she asks straightaway if we've seen my dad.

'No. Why?'

Ange takes a deep breath. 'Okay. Geoff has been here looking for you. It appears – and we don't know if this is definitely the case yet – that Nigel has been kidnapped.'

'What? Nige? Don't be ridiculous.'

Ange goes on to tell me that it seems my youngest brother has been kidnapped in Somalia, which hits me as unlikely enough to dismiss, until she says the words 'with Amanda'.

Then my blood runs cold and in my heart I need no further confirmation.

Ange knows what she's told me will send me into a spin. She'd met Amanda briefly when she visited here from Canada, and Ange has about the same level of tolerance for cheerleaders as I do – that's just one of the reasons we have been best friends since our uni days.

'Nic,' she tells me, 'just go and see your folks. They should have more information by now.'

So with that, Si and I head over to Mum and Dad's place. Ange lives two blocks away from me, and my parents are less than a kilometre down the road.

We arrive to find the oldies looking shell-shocked. They have been talking to DFAT, who still can't confirm the story. There is some confusion: it has come down the wire that 'Michael' Brennan has been kidnapped.

We are all at a loss – Nige had told Mum he was going to Kenya on his way to Australia from Scotland. He was coming home to photograph the weddings of a couple of his mates.

Mum has been trying to get hold of Nigel's girlfriend in Scotland to establish exactly where he is. Eventually someone tracks her down and she confirms that Nige had flown into Somalia with Amanda, from Kenya. All the pieces are clicking into place.

Shortly after we arrive, a James from DFAT calls. I explain that Nige's girlfriend has established he is in Somalia with Amanda. James's response is that DFAT has not yet received confirmation that Nigel has been kidnapped. I wonder what it takes to get confirmation. A dead body?

Si heads home because the kids have school tomorrow. We decide that I will sleep over with the folks – we both want to support them as best we can. James has given me his private mobile number, saying I can call any time if something happens.

By the time it gets dark, DFAT has confirmed that Nigel has been kidnapped and told us they believe he and Amanda are being held somewhere near the animal markets, in what used to be the Italian sector to the north of Mogadishu, the capital city.

I want to be near Mum and Dad so I fold out the lounge in the office opposite their bedroom. That's where I sleep until the call comes in.

Kellie
Newcastle
Monday, 25 August

I wake on Monday morning with a throbbing headache. Actually, I don't think I even slept, only dozed between thoughts of Nigel being tortured or executed at the hands of his captors. I look at the clock: 5:33 a.m. I turn to look at Matt – he is staring at the ceiling. I reach over to hold his hand and he turns to look at me. I start crying.

'I'm sorry, I'm so sorry this has happened to you and your family – our family. I don't know what to do next. I feel so helpless.'

He pulls me closer and kisses my forehead, and I snuggle into him, trying not to choke on his chest hair. He holds me there for a while, squeezing me tighter and tighter.

'Honey, you're going to suffocate me.'

As Matt lets me go, the phone next to the bed rings. We both jump. Matt grabs it and I can just hear that it's my father-in-law, Geoff, on the other end. I watch Matt, hoping that he will give me some sort of clue as to what's being said, but he just keeps saying 'Right' and 'Okay'.

'Did she get a chance to talk to Nige?' Matt asks.

Wow, sounds like something has happened. Maybe he's been released and it's all over.

No such luck.

Matt hangs up and tells me that the hostage takers have rung and asked for a ransom payment of US$3 million for both of their captives. That's US$1.5 million for Nigel.

'Who took the call?' I ask.

'Nic.'

'Did they say anything to her about Nige?'

'No, they said, "We have Nigel Brennan; he has given us this number and this is a ransom call and we want three million dollars."'

Three million! Where does a family like ours find that sort of money?

We both lie there without talking, staring at nothing. I turn on the TV at the end of our bed to drown out the white noise in my head. Eventually the 6.30 a.m. news bulletin starts and there is Nigel on screen. They're using his Facebook profile photo, and he looks like a drunken idiot; he's at the races, his arms thrown around two girls.

Matt and I both break into laughter.

'Your mum would hate that photo,' I say.

'I know.' Matt's still chuckling. 'So would Nige. It's one thing to have it on Facebook but another to have it all over the news.'

I get out of bed and throw back the curtains. It is a beautiful winter's day. *This is what it must feel like after someone gets sick or dies*, I think to myself. *The world still goes on.*

Over breakfast Matt and I discuss Nigel with the kids – I need to make sure they are okay to go to school today. I want to protect them from this as much as I can. Gigi keeps asking questions about Nige. Callaghan doesn't really understand and Stirling is too young to realise that anything has happened at all.

Matt and I tell them that some very bad men have taken Uncle Nigel to their house to stay.

'Like a sleepover?' Cal asks.

'Sort of, but without the lollies and all the fun,' I reply.

'Do they have guns, Mummy?' Gigi asks.

'Yes, sweetheart, they have guns.'

'Will they shoot him?' she asks.

'No, no, darling. They won't shoot him; the guns are for protection against other bad men, not to shoot Uncle Nigel.'

Oh, crap, how would I know if they are going to shoot him or not? DFAT told us last night that Nigel and Amanda were kidnapped on the road to Afgooye, about 26 kilometres south of Mogadishu. The information was all technical and factual, and no one even said anything about whether they would still be alive. In the phone call to Nic the kidnappers said they had Nigel, but we didn't get what the police are calling a 'proof of life', some statement that confirms beyond doubt he is alive.

I pile the kids into the car. My mum rings me just as I'm about to get in the driver's seat.

'It's everywhere, Kel, all over the papers and on the news.'

'Yes, Mum, I know.'

'Where are the kids?'

'They're here with me in the car, on the way to school.'

'Don't you think they should stay at home?'

'No. Matt and I will be on the phone all day, finding out stuff that may not be fantastic news, and I would rather filter what I pass on to them.'

'Okay. Are you all right?' I can tell by her voice that she is worried.

'Yeah, fine,' I say with a laugh before I hang up.

I'm not really fine – I am just numb.

I walk Gigi and Cal into school and on the lunch table is the pile of today's newspapers that the school gets. The children discuss the news in the paper each day in class.

There on the front page is Nigel, with a caption that reads 'Aussie journalist kidnapped'.

Heather must have supplied the media with a pic. In this one he looks so happy and handsome. It's much better than the photo on the telly this morning.

Well, at least the kids will know all about this news story.

I explain the situation to the principal. She looks at me in disbelief and as I continue, her expression turns to shock and, finally, concern.

As I leave her office, I hear her tell another teacher what I have just told her. The school is tiny, with just thirty-six students, so everyone knows everyone else's business, and if they don't, they soon find out.

Here goes, I think to myself, *this is the start of the bush telegraph. Hold on tight, Kellie.*

I get home to find Matt packing his bags. 'I'm going up to Moore Park – will you be right if I go?'

'Oh my god, of course! The kids and I will be fine. Mum and Dad are around if I need them, and if you want me to come up, I can be there in a few hours. If I wasn't working this weekend, I'd go with you.'

Matt and I left the Brennan family farm near Moree in New South Wales in 2005. If it hadn't have been sold, we would probably still be there, right in the middle of this whole ordeal. Heather and Geoff are very special to me; I have a great relationship with my in-laws. I suppose that happens when you all live together for eight and a half years. Right now, I just want to be there, to help and to comfort them and have them do the same for me. Family should gather round in stressful times, band together and support each other. And that's what I want to do for all the family – Heather and Geoff, Matt, and Nigel's other siblings, Nicky and Hamilton.

I walk into my office and find my brother-in-law on my home-page as one of the day's top headlines. I Google 'Nigel Brennan' and thousands of stories come up. Feared kidnapped, car hijacked, taken at gunpoint, held for ransom – the list of headlines goes on and on.

I set up a Google alert, which means I'll get an email every time 'Nigel Brennan' or 'Amanda Lindhout' are written, spoken or blogged about. Information overload is exactly what I need right now.

Nicky
Moore Park
Monday, 25 August

As twenty-year-olds my uni mates and I found it nothing short of hilarious to ring friends (usually sober and interstate) at ungodly hours. It goes without saying we were blind-rotten drunk. Invariably a parent would answer the phone, always in a breathless state of trepidation. Once I became a parent myself, I realised that the middle-of-the-night phone call is the bogeyman for grown-ups. No Stephen King novel can induce nightmares quite like the prospect of hearing the phone ring in the dead of night.

Subconsciously, I'm half expecting it; we all are, I suppose. Nevertheless, on 25 August at 1.40 a.m. I surge forth from the fold-out lounge in my folks' office to grab the phone. I pick up on the second ring, before I have to hear any more of the creepy carnival merry-go-round music that for some bizarre reason has been made the ringtone. That sound will give me a start for the rest of my life.

With the phone in hand, I sit in the swivel chair next to the desk at the end of the lounge.

'Hello, Nicky speaking.' There is the same quaver in my voice that I'd heard from those parents years ago.

'Who is this?' It's a slightly accented voice, but understandable. 'Do you know Nigel?'

Oh my god, oh my god, oh my god, oh my god.

'Yes, I am Nigel's sister. My name is Nicky. Is Nigel with you? Is he all right?'

'My name is Adam, you understand?' the voice continues. 'This is a ransom call. We have Nigel and Amanda. We are demanding a price of $1.5 million US per head.'

I knock the keyboard on the desk and Mum's computer springs to life. The azure blue of a South Pacific beach, her screensaver, bathes me in light. I grab a pencil and a piece of paper on the desk. In the half light I scrawl down as much information as I can. My fear for Nigel's safety has ramped right up.

'Do you have a phone number so I can contact you?' I ask.

I am surprised that Adam obliges. There are a couple of digits that I have some difficulty understanding because of his accent, but after some back and forth I get it down correctly.

Adam says something like, '. . . Call back in four hours.'

Who? Him or me? I think he said he'll call me back. I can't hear even though he is speaking loudly. Inside my head is only fuzz. My hearing has checked out and it feels as if my bladder is not going to be far behind.

'You understand this is a ransom call?' This is not a movie; it is happening right here and right now – at my parents' home, for Chrissake.

'Yes.'

And that is it. The call is over.

Shit, shit, shit, shit, shit. The mantra in my head has ramped up as well.

I scramble for the bit of paper near the computer with James's mobile number on it. Right now, in the middle of the night, I want him to make this better.

'So let me get this straight: the kidnappers have contacted you directly?' he says, sounding sleepy.

'Yes, I've just finished talking to him. I rang you straightaway.'

'That's unusual.'

You're not making this better, James.

Mum has come in from her bedroom across the hallway. Her arms are crossed tightly across her chest. It's cold even in Bundaberg at this time of the year. She is wearing the famous Sutherland family frown, a look of consternation that pushes her left eye down into a squint. My grandad had it and so does my younger brother, Matthew. My middle child, Monty, will too one day, once he's old enough to have wrinkles and creases.

I go through the whole conversation with James while Mum listens on. Later she will tell me I looked grey. By the time I relay the story to James, I am seriously bloody scared. I have indigestion thrashing around in my belly and acid burning its way up my throat. My mouth tastes of aluminium. I pat down my inner thighs just to make sure I haven't wet myself.

'Will they ring me back in four hours? That's 5:30 a.m. – not so long away. I don't want to take another phone call. What if they are doing something really awful to Nige? I hate guns; I don't want to hear them going off in the background. One and a half million dollars is a ridiculous amount of money. When do they want it by? Surely not in four hours?'

I'm not sure if I've said all of this aloud to James or whether they are just thoughts.

The phone is beeping in my ear. *Oh god. Is that Adam again?*

James tells me to see if there's a voicemail message and says he'll call me back. He sounds calm, and adds that he needs to ring a few people to organise something in case there's another call in the morning.

There have, in fact, been two missed calls. One was a hang-up and the other was some muttering that I later suspect is '*inshallah*'. Its literal translation is 'God willing', but my sister-in-law Kellie would claim it to be the Somali equivalent of 'what*evah*'. Three fingers of your left hand up in the air (to make a W) then swung clockwise (to make an E) would become our standard sign whenever we heard '*inshallah*'. It'd provide levity in some stressful situations.

Dad is sleeping, unaware of the phone call. Mum and I let him slumber and it's a wise decision. For the next four days he won't sleep a wink.

I don't hear anything for half an hour. As this stretches out to forty-five minutes, I can't stand it any longer. I ring James to see what is going on.

'It's okay,' he tells me. 'The Australian Federal Police (AFP) is arranging someone to be there before the next call comes in.'

So Mum and I wait it out. By four o'clock we are pacing the floor. Mum and Dad's place is tucked away. *God, I hope they don't get lost. If it's someone from out of town, they won't find the place.* I can't take the tension. I want them here now, set up and ready to go. They can't miss the next call. Deep down what I really want is for someone else to take the call, explain that it's all a mistake and it's not really Nigel this is happening to but someone else far away.

Dad gets up with the sun. There's a pink glow peeking over the horizon on this cool and crisp winter's morning. Fear glues the inside of my upper lip to my gums. I pry them apart with my tongue. Will Nigel's beaten and broken body be dragged through the streets of Mogadishu like the American soldiers in *Black Hawk Down*? It can't be happening, not when the day is so clear and typically Queensland perfect. I try to think rationally. *Nah, he's an Aussie; everyone loves us.* It settles down my fear. Just.

Finally, lights swing into the driveway. Here they are. The boys in blue, QPol – Queensland Police. Relief instantly comes over me. I fill my lungs with what feels like the most oxygen I've inhaled for hours.

The officers introduce themselves as they make their way into the living room. There are big burly men everywhere, some are in uniform, others in plain clothes. This feels right, like how it should be. They are here to take care of things, to get my brother back. They are all locals except for one fellow. Kevin and Ross are our negotiators.

The Bundy boys go through the family demographics. There has been lots of communication between us and my brothers Matt and Hamilton – Ham – as well as my aunts. The cops catch on pretty quickly that we're a clanny lot.

They position the phone upstairs on the kitchen island bench. It now has two headsets attached – one for us and another for them so they can listen to the call – and a recording device.

Kev asks me to write down the conversation with Adam as I remember it, while it's still fresh in my mind. I remember more of the conversation as I put it to paper. All of them shower me with praise for jotting down notes while I was talking and especially for getting Adam's phone number. It gives me enough confidence that I feel ready to take the next call.

We hunker down and wait. Five-thirty comes and goes.

It's gut-wrenching when the call doesn't come. Doubt creeps in. Did I get the time wrong? Have I cocked it up? It fills me with a greater fear because I have the resources of a nation here at my parents' house and maybe I got the details wrong. This is way worse than that bad dream you have where you're back at school, walking into the dining room with shoes, socks, shirt and tie, 6-inch Bondi bloomers, but no tunic.

While we're watching the clock, Kev again goes over the list of what I should say. I need to talk to Nigel and if I can't, I have to ask a simple question that only Nige can answer. The first proof-of-life question. There are laptops set up on the kitchen table. There are calls going from QPol to the AFP.

After breakfast, the phone rings. *Shit.* Deep breaths. I answer it. False alarm – it's Mum and Dad's old neighbour. I ask Peggy to call back on the mobile. My heart rate settles down and moisture returns to my mouth.

The day passes slowly. Nigel is splashed all over the newspapers and TV news bulletins; it's right in our faces but weirdly that doesn't make it feel any more real.

At 9 p.m., sixteen long hours after I expected the call, Adam rings back. Kev's next to me, coaching me through the call. My vision closes to a tunnel; my eyes swing from six lines of tight writing on an A4 sheet of paper to his face, and back to the paper again. I don't see or hear anything but the phone, the paper, and Kev. Nothing exists outside this.

'Is this Nicky, Nigel's sister?'

'Yes, it's Nicky. Adam, can I speak to Nigel? I need to know he is with you. Can you ask him a question for me?'

'Yes. What is the question?'

I look at Kev. He is nodding, thumbs up, the classic gesture.

'Okay. Can you ask him what was the name of the property that Mum and Dad lived at?'

'What is property?'

'Yeah, that's right. What is the name of the property?'

'What is this? I do not know.'

'Um, yeah, you don't know. That's why I'm asking you to ask Nigel.' Then it hits me. Oh god, 'property' is an Aussie word. I go blank trying to think of an alternative. *Duh!*

'Farm. Farm,' I finally get out. 'What is the name of the *farm* they lived on?' Instinctively, I want to keep well away from any mention of ownership. I'm trying to imply they lived there rather than owned it – avoiding any suggestion that our family is wealthy. Can Adam detect this emphasis? I swap to another question.

'What is the name of my dog? I have a pet dog; what is its name?'

'What is the name of Nigel's dog?'

'No, *my* dog. What is the name of *my* dog?'

'Okay. I will ask him and will call back.'

Did he get that I was talking about Zeke, my dog? Nige doesn't have a dog. I'm not sure Adam got it.

Adam hangs up. No 'bye' or any social niceties. Kev gives a whoop and wraps his arms around me; both of us are grinning like idiots. My legs are jelly and I'm glad he's holding me, otherwise I might just fall in a slow gelatinous slide to the floor. I am glowing, so pleased I've done him and his training proud.

There's a flurry of activity – calls to QPol and the AFP. Kev's out on the verandah, phoning the Canadian cops to see if they have had any similar contact with the kidnappers.

It feels as if we've barely had time to draw breath when the next call comes in at 11 p.m. No, I can't speak to Nigel. 'Perhaps later,' I am told by Adam.

'Nigel's father, his name is Geoffrey Kevin Brennan. Nigel's mother, her name is Heather Joy Brennan. This is correct?'

'Yes,' spills out before I remember I'm not supposed to prompt him.

'The farm, the place they lived, it is called M-A-R-L-O-W.' Adam spells it out to me; he wants to make sure he is getting it right.

'Nigel says he has no dog now, but when he was young he has a dog. It is called Gopher.' The pronunciation is slightly off but I completely get what he is saying. The answer to the dog question isn't correct. The answer – 'Zeke' – is written on Kev's negotiator notes next to the phone. But Nige's childhood dog was called Gopher. No one else would know that.

I'm madly nodding my head and giving Kev the thumbs up, trying to keep as quiet as possible so Adam doesn't catch on that I'm not alone.

Then, suddenly, the conversation is over. No mention of the money this time.

'It's okay; he's establishing rapport with you,' Kev tells me, aware of my confusion.

More people arrive. This time they are from the AFP: intelligence officers and a woman named Gayle, who is our family liaison officer (FLO). She'll live with us for a couple of weeks. There are more AFP negotiators due to arrive later. I don't really understand the difference between the two police forces. The house is overflowing but the vibe is positive as we fall into bed. I am exhausted and sleep surprisingly soundly.

Over the next few days we start gathering information like nesting magpies. None of us likes to sit still. We track down family friends who worked in Somalia before it completely turned to shit but no one has contacts left in the country. We ring Bill, Nigel's ex father-in-law. He is really upset. This is way bigger than any grudge his ex in-laws could bear. Bill tracks down someone who works for the UN; he's a guru on Somalia and, the best bit of all, he's Canadian. We call him and then pass on his details to the AFP. We pat each other on the back. We might be a bunch of farmers from central Queensland but we know how to put the feelers out. *Oh, we are so clever.*

Then nothing. No feedback whatsoever.

Kellie
Newcastle
Thursday, 28 August

I took Matt to the airport on Tuesday morning after I dropped the kids at school, and he has been calling me regularly with updates. With each phone call he sounds more and more stressed out, and I am starting to worry about him.

Matt will be finding it difficult up there right now; he gets very frustrated if he can't figure out exactly what is going on and this is what I fear is happening now. If everyone is under strain and things are happening quickly, no one is going to be able to give Matt the time he needs to process what is going on.

Sure enough, I get a phone call from Heather telling me that Matt is extremely aggro and agitated and that she and Gayle are going to give him a sleeping tablet to help him get a full night's sleep. I book my ticket to Bundaberg straight away.

Nicky
Moore Park
Thursday, 28 August

The first of the federal negotiators have turned up. Yesterday DFAT's James and Emily arrived as well as Catherine, who was introduced as an expert on Somalia.

'So how did you come to know so much about Somalia?' Mum asked her. 'Did you speak the language when were you there?'

'No, I studied Somalia while I was at university,' she replied.

The look on Mum's face was priceless, and the DFAT crowd saw the faux pas they made. We don't hear from Catherine again after that meeting.

The calls are infrequent. By now, all of the immediate family are at Mum and Dad's too. Si, the three kids and I are camped in the one room. The AFP is a bit wary of this – there are too many people around. But I'm completely fine with it; it's tight and unified and we are together when we need to be. I want the kids close by so we can be as honest as possible with them about what is going on. Ignorance is not bliss in our household.

The school and our community are being amazing. One of Ham's old neighbours drops food in every day to feed the masses.

He makes the most delicious bread. 'Figure you have to be able to cook bread if your name is Fred,' he tells us.

Mum finds it gratifying to cook for large numbers. It's reminiscent of harvest days when she used to feed a cast of thousands in the paddocks. She would pack up two separate casseroles, chat potatoes and bread rolls, along with card tables and cutlery and crockery, for Dad and all the others contracted to get the wheat off as soon as possible – before it rained and turned it from premium-grade to chook feed.

I am on a knife's edge, always waiting for the next call. I hold off to pee for as long as possible so I'll be spared the indignity of bolting from the bathroom, strides around my ankles, if the phone rings. Likewise showers: in and out, with an emergency extra-long sloppy joe kept nearby to pull on if necessary. I can't even finish my meals, and that's unheard of for a tuckerbag like me. My stomach has no room left. It's all devoted to knots.

By day five I am starting to clue in to the major differences between the AFP and QPol. They are completely separate entities and it seems to be difficult for them to work in each other's jurisdictions. They can't access the same information on their computers. To me it seems as if there's poor communication between the forces. I keep overhearing phrases like 'lack of security clearance'. Mum and I madly try to eavesdrop. We regroup in her room and swap the stories we've heard.

On Thursday the two AFP negotiators, Adrian and Dave, head off towards the beach for a chat. While they're out, Ross and Kev sit us down to tell us they are being pulled from our case. I am shocked. Dad looks dumbfounded and Mum is incredulous. These guys are crying – they want to work on this case to see it through, and I desperately don't want them to go. Adrian and Dave arrive back and can see instantly what's gone on, and they are not happy. I suspect that if Ross and Kev hadn't told us, they would have just been rostered off, never to appear again.

I'm pissed off and having trouble understanding the reasoning behind the move. A cop is a cop is a cop, surely? Adrian's trying to talk me through it: the QPol guys just don't have the security clearance to work the case. Everything I've learnt so far about negotiating has come from Kev and Ross, and they can't help us any more because of some piece of paper? All my ideas about the boys in blue swooping in to save the day are crushed. It'll be like I'm doing this on my own.

Friday is Ross's last day. He brings his wife out to meet us. This is the personal touch I need to get through this. In the meantime I know I need to have Adrian and Dave on my side so they can help me and direct me through future calls.

Sunday, 31 August

Having my family nearby now feels as if it's a physical need. And it's just too hard relaying messages back and forwards to everyone.

Kev has called in to wish us well. We are sitting, talking away from the others, in the upstairs kitchen over near the next-of-kin (NOK) phone (we call it the bat phone), which is all hooked up like a piece of medical equipment with wires and lights. I am twitching all over. Every time I sit, my right knee jiggles up and down; the water in the glass on the bench ripples with the vibrations. I quiz him.

'Kev, what's going to happen when I get a bad phone call?' This has not been discussed before. I know I'm probably jumping the gun, but I can't help thinking of a call where Nige is screaming incoherently down the line or I hear the sound of automatic gunfire.

'Nic, you're getting ahead of yourself.'

'I know but . . .' I want Kev to give me as much good advice as he can before he goes. I'm cramming for my dealing-with-kidnappers exam.

'Nic, if – and it may never come to that – *if* you get a call like that, these guys will be prepared for it and they will go through this with you. Don't work yourself up about something that in all probability may not happen.'

I've stopped the leg jiggles and am now rapping at my sternum. Short sharp staccato taps. After tonight I will have a deep purple bruise there – a 50-cent-sized piece of tenderness. From this point on, every time I tap there the memory of that stressful time comes flooding back.

Now the AFP has fully shifted into the house, the NOK phone unit is moved downstairs. It'll be better for me when calls come in the middle of the night. And with all the family staying upstairs, it'll give the Feds an area slightly removed from us.

That night after Kev leaves we're asked our first really ugly question – but it comes from the cops, not the kidnappers. What is our family's collective net worth? *What the fuck?* We have been told all week that the government doesn't pay or facilitate ransoms, yet here are the AFP asking about how cashed up we are. Don't they get how conflicting this is? All the Brennans are sitting in the same room. We glance at each other, trying to read each other's minds. Ham jacks up first.

'Where is this coming from?'

'Higher up.'

Adrian asks us how much money we can have available in

twenty-four hours. There's a collective realisation that this could get Nige out. Yep, we would be paying a ransom but it could all be over quickly. But 'instantly available' money? That is a bit tricky. We are all mortgaged up to the eyeballs. After putting our heads together, a bit of redraw here and busting out of a fixed-term deposit there, we figure out we have twenty-five grand.

'So how much are the Lindhouts putting up?' It was an off-the-cuff question from Dad, a throwaway line.

'Nothing.'

We all stare at Adrian.

'So this $25 000 is for Nigel, right? What are they going to do about getting Amanda out?' I say.

'These two cases – Nigel and Amanda's – are joined at the hip. We are negotiating for their joint release,' Adrian replies.

'Let me get this straight,' I say. 'Our $25K is for both Nigel and Amanda? The Canadian family aren't putting anything into the pot?'

'That's correct.'

'Well, we don't have anything either,' says Dad, sitting back in his chair, folding his arms across his chest. We nod in agreement.

There's a bad feeling in my gut.

'Geoff, they have no money,' says Adrian.

'What, they can't even scrape up twenty bucks to chip in? That's a couple of days' worth of durry money, boys.' This is Ham's response.

Adrian and Ham lock eyes.

'No. And we are asking all of you not to have any contact with the Canadian family, and in particular not to discuss money with them.'

My sinking feeling gets a whole lot deeper. I can't absorb what is being said.

Ham is on to it pretty quickly.

'So, boys.' *God, he can make 'boys' sound so condescending.* 'To sum it up: you're asking us to cough up twenty-five thou for both Nige and Amanda. And because we are such nice guys it's a prezzie from us, but we are not even allowed to contact Amanda's parents to tell them what nice guys we are?' Ham is bristling with sarcasm.

How do you answer that?

'Perhaps it's something as simple as the RCMP [Royal Canadian Mounted Police] not having had this depth of discussion with Amanda's parents yet. They may not be in the same place as you are. But it has been clearly requested that you do not contact Jon and Lorinda,' Adrian says.

This placates us enough for now. Once again we huddle for a group discussion. The majority decision, which is our basis for working through this entire ordeal, is that we'll pay. If we have to pay for Amanda as well, so be it.

Nigel
Mogadishu, Somalia
Saturday, 23 August

It's our fourth day in Mogadishu, and I've organised to go on patrol with the Ugandan AMISOM (African Union Mission in Somalia) troops this morning. I'm really looking forward to it as it's going to be just Abdifatah Elmi, the local cameraman Amanda has hired, and me. Amanda has decided not to go on this early-morning trip; she just wants Abdi to get shots for her. He's a bit nervous about going out with the troops – the ongoing political situation means he could be compromised if he's seen in their vehicles. Abdi is a lovely guy, married with kids. He's pretty keen to know whether

27

Amanda and I are married, though, and I just keep ducking the question. He's also commented that Amanda is 'very strong' and that this can create problems in his country.

I get up at six and go downstairs. I make a coffee and sit in front of the TV while I wait for Abdi; I watch as Steve Hooper wins gold in the pole vault at the Olympics. When Abdi finally arrives, he tells me there has been a mortar attack near the Ugandan base and he can't get on to the major who was going to take us out with his troops. The plan has fallen over. It's a bit disappointing but I know that today's other scheduled visit – to the Internally Displaced Persons (IDP) camps just outside Mogadishu on the road to Afgooye – is going to be well worth it. Amanda's keen to join us for this trip.

When you enter a country in conflict, you virtually put your life in the hands of a fixer, someone who knows what's happening on the ground and has contacts so that you can cover certain stories. They also take care of accommodation, transport and the security detail. Amanda found Ajoos Sanura using her contacts in Iraq. He comes highly recommended and is also working with a team from *National Geographic*.

I talk to Ajoos and he says that everything has been sorted for our trip to the camps, including the extra security detail we've paid for because we're going into a militia-run area.

Just before nine, Ajoos introduces Amanda and me to a new driver. Wary of last-minute changes, I pull Ajoos aside to question him about this, and he explains that this driver knows the people we will be meeting – he's from that area. Pascal, the *National Geographic* photographer, tells me to take care; they have been out to the camps before and while it is reasonably safe, we should keep our wits about us.

About forty minutes before we leave, I start to get a queasy gut. Is it the food or just nerves? Something just doesn't feel right but I try to ignore it. I leave my wallet and passport in the hotel owner's room, under the bottom draw of the filing cabinet, the same place the two *National Geographic* guys have put theirs. Back downstairs I listen as Amanda calls her dad, asking him to transfer funds into the country, as the work money she has been counting on has yet to come through.

Ajoos and the *National Geographic* pair leave about ten minutes before we do, heading to Merca, a port city, but starting out on the same route as we'll be taking. Everyone piles into the four-wheel drive, Abdi between Amanda and me, the new driver and our old driver in the front and the two security boys in the back.

Just as we reach the city limits we come to a halt, and the boys in the back jump out. I ask Abdi what's going on. He says they have to stay here, that it's not safe for them to go any further because they are seen as part of the Transitional Federal Government (TFG).

He says, 'They will wait here until we come back.'

Ajoos hadn't told us this part of the plan and it doesn't sit well with me. 'Hang on, Abdi. I don't understand.'

'Because we go into a militia area they cannot come, otherwise they will be killed,' he says.

My gut's telling me to get out of the car right then and there, but instead I ask him, 'Where is our security then?'

'We have to travel a short distance to where we will meet them.'

We had organised for three extra security personnel today, believing we would have five in total. To now travel unprotected seems like madness. Abdi assures me that this is the only way we'll be able to go into the militia area. I look at Amanda, and we decide to continue, both keen to make it to the IDP camps since the first few days here have not been that fruitful, work-wise. I look over my shoulder as our two guards disappear in a cloud of dust.

The four-wheel drive hurtles down the bitumen road, and the arid African bush flies past us. I haven't yet had a good look at the photos I took yesterday; now is my chance. My attention flips between the scenery and the viewfinder on my camera.

Abdi and Amanda are talking; he's asking again if we are married. She changes the subject and starts to sing Ace of Base's 'All That She Wants'. This is Abdi's ringtone, and he quickly joins in. It's nice that he's so friendly, relaxed and comfortable with us. Our two drivers don't speak English.

As I'm deleting images from my camera, I think I hear Abdi say, 'This could be a problem,' but I don't really register it. I look up to see a little Suzuki Vitara parked on the left-hand side of the road ahead, its lights flashing. *Our security detail*, I think. Our vehicle slows down but my focus is still on my camera. We pull up on the opposite side of the road to the Suzuki. I put my camera away and look up. We are completely surrounded by gunmen. My heart skips a beat.

At my window is a big guy pointing an AK47 straight in my face, only the window between us. All of the gunmen are in civilian clothing. Muslim head cloths cover their faces so that we can see only their eyes. Fear floods my entire body.

'What's going on?' I ask Abdi.

He manages to reply, 'I don't know,' just before the car doors are swung open. Everything happens in slow motion. We're pulled out of the car, pushed to the ground, arms and legs spread, kissing the dirt before being yanked back to our feet. All five of us are forced into the backseat of our car with the big guy. Completely numb,

I can't breathe. My brain is unable to register what's taking place. Amanda is on my knee as we're jammed in like sardines. The big guy has both of our bags and I'm more concerned about my camera gear than anything.

Amanda asks Abdi, 'What's going on?' but before he has a chance to reply one of the guys barks, 'No talking.' Amanda again asks Abdi what's happening to which he replies, 'Don't talk, don't talk.' I can't see much as everyone's packed in on top of me. The car lurches forward, following the Suzuki, and we peel off from the main road onto a dirt track, travelling at high speed as we weave through the rough terrain. I'm trying to brace myself with my arms on the roof so as not to get thrown around. My heart hammers away. The big guy demands everyone's mobile phones and switches them off. I can't reach mine.

There are two guys behind us, AK47s pointed directly at our skulls. I'm terrified each time we slam over a bump that a gun will go off.

Suddenly we come to a stop in the middle of desolate scrub. Amanda is ripped from the car and ordered into the Suzuki. I feel like I'm in quicksand, alarmed that we've been separated. I start to ask a question but am again ordered not to talk. The big guy gets in beside me and slams the door as we take off in hot pursuit of the Suzuki. *Fuck, fuck, fuck, fuck* keeps rattling around my head, and I'm trying to calm myself and ride the adrenaline hit.

We are now following something like a goat track as we drive cross-country over the top of bushes, swerving and accelerating. After five or ten minutes we again come to a screaming halt, and this time I'm pulled from the car and thrown into the back of the Suzuki with Amanda. I'm relieved to be next to her but seriously worried about what will happen to Abdi and our drivers. There are five guys in the car with us, two behind with AK47s pointed at our heads, one next to Amanda and two up front. The guy in the front passenger seat is the only one who doesn't have his face covered, and I'm wishing that he did. I'm sure that being able to identify him is going to get us killed.

Amanda tells me that this guy's name is Ahmed and that he speaks English. He has already asked who we are, what we are doing in the country and said they are going to hold us and take us to their commanders. At least they are not going to kill us immediately. We ask the guys behind us to stop aiming their guns at our heads but they ignore us. Amanda then forcefully asks Ahmed to order them to lower their weapons as it's not safe. She tells him we are not going to try to do anything. Ahmed complies. He is very calm.

I'm cold with fear, unsure what has become of our colleagues. We hit a bitumen road then hurtle through a small town, the main street lined with rustic tin-shack shops and a market area flooded with locals.

We turn off onto another dirt track; IDP camp–style structured housing lines both sides of the road, along with the signs of foreign non-government organisations (NGOs). About forty-five minutes after we were picked up, we zigzag through a tiny village and finally stop between two walled compounds.

As the guy next to Amanda gets out, the gates of the compound on the left-hand side swing open. *They have been waiting for us. This has all been planned.* Our vehicle darts into the courtyard and the gates slam behind us.

We are ordered from the car, and Amanda asks if she can go to the toilet, which is just to the left. In the courtyard there is a lean-to corrugated-iron shed, and a bigger building. I'm marched into the building, which has three rooms running from right to left across the back wall, and placed in the far left room while Amanda does her thing. There are a number of dirty mattresses on the floor and I'm ordered to sit on one up against the right-hand wall.

Amanda is escorted into the room by a guy who was seated beside her in the car. We would later know him as 'Ali'. He scared the shit out of me from the moment I saw him in the Suzuki – his is quite a solid build for a Somali and his eyes are pure hate. He orders Amanda to sit against the back wall.

He leaves Amanda and me alone. In a wave of panic we discuss what the hell's going on. She is calm, believing that we are going to be all right – she points out that the room is pink, a good omen as it's her safe colour. We both have an almost-drunk hysterical moment, laughing as we confirm what's just happened: *Holy shit, we've just been kidnapped.*

Everything feels warped. The room is dirty and littered with pieces of electrical wire – I wonder if they have been making some sort of bomb in here. Through the open door I can see guys walking around with their guns. We don't get long to talk before Ali comes back in, demanding to know where Amanda's mobile phone is. She replies that they took it from her in the car. My phone's still in my pocket, and for whatever reason he hasn't asked me about it. I'm too terrified to tell him that I have it and I don't want to let it go – I might get the chance to use it.

I ask about my camera bag, having not seen it since we were first taken. He brings it back moments later, tossing it at my feet. I open it; they have been rifling through it, but to my surprise the cameras are still there.

Ali then snaps, 'Passports! Money!' Amanda opens her bag and hands over $211 in US currency. He then looks at me. 'You!'

I reply, 'I don't have any money on me, only these coins.'

'Passports!' he barks again. We explain that they're at the hotel, along with the rest of our money. I'm quietly thankful that mine isn't here; its Ethiopian stamp wouldn't have gone down well in this situation. Ali seems agitated, and zeros in on me.

'You have phone?' he asks. I weigh up the odds of getting away with lying before I picture his mate's AK47. I nod as I pull my mobile from my jeans pocket, kicking myself for not using it sooner to notify someone. Remembering a US$100 bill folded up tightly in my coin pocket, I also hand this over. I'm certain they'll search us sooner rather than later. He places it in Amanda's wallet which he throws back into her bag, along with our phones. He keeps these items but strangely leaves us the camera bag.

He then orders Amanda to stand up. He motions for me to close my eyes, before frisking her. She is visibly shaken by having his hands all over her body.

Ali pulls Amanda out of the room and takes her next door. I believe she is about to be raped and I can do nothing to help her. My skin shrinks tight when I hear her scream.

She is brought back into the room several minutes later, shaking. I ask, 'Are you okay?'

'He's just put his hands all over my breasts and down my pants.' Wiping the tears from her face, she says that he accused her of trying to hide something when she went to the toilet.

Ahmed and Ali come into the room, both carrying weapons. They begin interrogating us: *Who are you? What are you doing in Somalia? Are you religious?* I stupidly almost tell them that I lean towards Buddhism if anything, but instead we both say that we're Christian. Ahmed tells us they are not going to hurt us. They are waiting for the arrival of their commanders, who will question us further.

They leave the room and we both start smoking cigarettes like fiends. Ali comes in on a regular basis to survey the room. At one point I see Abdi and our drivers being marched across the dirt courtyard, looking very timid. Soon after, we hear them being shepherded into the room beside ours. I'm so relieved they haven't been executed, but I don't really understand why they've been abducted as well.

In the afternoon Amanda and I are let outside for about fifteen minutes. We sit under a tree in the middle of the yard, playing noughts and crosses in the dirt, but frankly our thoughts are elsewhere. We reassure ourselves that Ajoos and the *Geographic* team will certainly know we are missing and contact the appropriate people.

Back in our room, the heat from the tin roof makes it stifling. They won't open the window in here and when they close the door, it's like a pressure-cooker.

That evening we're again granted time outside. We sit on a rattan mat up against the wall, eavesdropping as our guards listen to the BBC Somali service. We hear Amanda's name mentioned. The realisation dawns on me: my family will soon know about this. Their world is about to be turned upside down.

Later that evening we are confronted by four of them. Ahmed and Ali are joined by a much older man called Yahya, who doesn't speak much English. He was the guy driving our vehicle when we were first picked up. From his age and bearing, he seems like the elder of the group. The other guy is introduced to us as Adam. He wasn't part of the team this morning. He's over six foot tall, speaks with an American accent and is missing a front tooth. I have a sudden flash of the scene from the movie *Harlem Nights* where

Eddie Murphy says to the guy shooting craps, 'Throw the dice, you snaggle-toothed motherfucker,' and the thought almost makes me laugh hysterically. Mostly I'm relieved that the commanders have finally turned up so we can explain ourselves and get out of here.

Adam asks the usual questions: our names, where we're from and what we are doing in Somalia. We explain that we're journalists and that we were on our way to the IDP camps this morning. He accuses us of being spies and working with the government – he doesn't identify which one. I suggest they do a simple internet search to see that we're telling the truth, and then they get up and leave.

Ten minutes later they all file in again, and Adam punches a hole in life as we knew it.

'Okay, we believe that you are not spies but we are going to hold you for ransom.'

We tell them our governments have treaties that mean they won't pay ransoms. It's as though Adam doesn't even hear. He says, 'What do you think is a fair ransom for you?' We plead with them not to go down this path, telling them we are good people. Then the old guy finally says something in Somali.

Adam translates his words: 'No money, no life.'

There's a sick, hollow feeling now at the bottom of my stomach. I've heard of cases like this in Iraq and Afghanistan. The price on people's heads is around a million dollars US.

Even so, Amanda and I try to remain optimistic. I have to hand it to her: she is fantastic, teaching me how to light up my chakras, with both of us thinking positively and comforting each other. Amanda suggests we delete our camera memory cards as they have pictures of the Ugandan troops from yesterday's trip – she's worried we'll be seen as collaborators.

Ali has been keeping a watchful eye on us; he's constantly

walking in and out of the room. As I'm unzipping my bag in the dark, he bursts in, demanding to know what I'm doing. Blood pumping, I tell him I'm just making sure everything is in my bag, and he shines his torch around suspiciously before leaving. I manage to get rid of all my image files, but I'm terrified the whole time.

Soon after, sleep rips me away from this nightmare and I don't care about the filthy mattress or pillow.

Sunday, 24 August

Amanda and I are woken early, surrounded by four of the gang.

Adam is there, demanding our parents' names and phone numbers. As we scribble them down, he informs us in a businesslike way that there will be a deadline for the ransom payment.

He makes himself very clear: 'If they do not pay within twenty-four hours, we will kill you.'

I tell him that it's against the law for our governments to pay a ransom but Adam argues back – governments do it all the time for their citizens. It will fall to our families, and I know they won't be able to do anything in the time frame. I ask him why they are doing this.

'Because your governments are at war with Islam; they fight in Iraq, Afghanistan and Pakistan.' Adam reiterates: 'If there is no money in twenty-four hours, you will be killed.' Then they leave.

We have no idea who they are or what price they've put on our heads.

Yesterday I'd hoped they might be bluffing, boys playing at being men, but things have escalated beyond that now. It's difficult to stay positive when someone puts a time limit on your life. To make matters worse Ali starts taunting us.

'How do you feel? Are you ready to die? If there is no money, then we will kill you.' He does this every few hours, counting down: 'In twenty hours we will kill you.'

Finally Amanda snaps back at him. 'You may as well kill me now because there's no money for me. My family don't have anything and the Canadian government won't pay a ransom.'

His eyes narrow, a viper about to strike, and he says coldly, 'Are you prepared to die now? I will kill you now; do you want to die?'

Amanda realises her mistake in being outspoken and quickly back-pedals.

'I don't want to die, but this is ridiculous. How do you expect my family to have money here in twenty-four hours? It's impossible.'

'If they have no money, you will be killed.' His grin is callous.

The day drags on. We smoke fags like there's no tomorrow. Which there may well not be. The deadline draws nearer with nightfall, and the darkness brings with it fear. We both jump when we are again confronted by Adam and his entourage.

Adam informs us that he has spoken with our families and that it is going to take some time to organise the ransom. They are not going to kill us. It's a relief to hear this but I'm unsure whether I can believe him.

He tells me he has spoken to my sister, Nicky. I can't imagine how my family is dealing with this – I hadn't told any of them what my plans were, so to have some complete stranger call them and say, 'We have kidnapped Nigel in Somalia' would be a complete headfuck. Guilt chews away at me.

Adam tells us that we're being taken to another house tonight. I ask where we are going and what they are planning to do with our three colleagues. Adam tells us not worry about them: they're next door and will be taken care of. He says they want to move us to a place where it will be 'more comfortable'. His hospitable gesture is beyond me, as I know that what they're doing is all part of some plan but I have no idea what that plan actually is.

We're ushered out of the house and into the back of an old station wagon. Amanda is beside me, and we're hanging onto each other's hand for dear life; both Adam and Ahmed join us for the ride. We travel through the small streets, the car struggling at times with the sand under its tyres. Eventually we stop in a built-up area. There are tall compound walls that tower over the car. We are ordered out into the middle of the street. My nerves are raw as we are quickly pushed through a small metal gate, across a courtyard and marched into the deserted house.

We're placed in a small room at the back, and I note with relief that this place has electricity. I survey our new digs. There is a small window on the side wall that looks onto another house; I can see a narrow alleyway running between the two buildings. Off to the side of our room is a tiny bathroom with a toilet and shower. It's filthy, with cockroaches congregating in the dark corners. In our room two dirty mattresses lean against the wall and there are some mosquito nets lying on the ground. A crystallised fungus is growing 3 feet up the back wall. We position ourselves as far away from it as possible: Amanda against the side wall opposite the window and me next to the wall adjoining the bathroom. We are only a few metres apart.

Adam and Ahmed come in; they seem quite solicitous. This makes me think this new abode will be our jail for the foreseeable future. Adam tells us he will come to talk with us in the morning, then we're left alone. I feel like I have cheated death.

Later that night I'm relieved to hear Adbi and our drivers being moved into the room next door to ours. They are okay for now. And I'm hoping there's safety in numbers.

The Filthy House
Sunday, 25 August

In the morning Adam, Ahmed and Ali come to talk with us, and it seems awkwardly civilised. I watch Adam peeling a grapefruit.

'Everything is okay,' he says. 'It will take some time for the ransom. Maybe you will stay here for one or two months.' This is crushing. I think of the financial ruin and stress my family will face. We go around in the same old circles, with Amanda and I reiterating our governments' policies on ransoms. I feel like banging my head against the wall; it'd feel more productive.

They talk to us about our religious beliefs and ask for more background about what we do. Amanda explains she has been living in Iraq, working for Press TV and that she was held captive in Sadr City in 2008 but was released after a few hours. Jon, her father, is terminally ill and her mum, Lorinda, has a low-paid job. I tell them I'm self-employed and have no insurance, and that I've been living in Scotland with my girlfriend. That my folks are old retired farmers, and are not wealthy; and Nicky and Simon, my sister and brother-in-law, are horticulturists.

After what seems like hours, they ask us if we need anything. We request some basics: bottled water, so we don't get sick, cigarettes, soap and shampoo – things that will make life more comfortable. We haven't showered since we were captured, but they've been bringing us cans of tuna and some cold pasta.

We're allowed outside a few times. We sit in the courtyard, checking out our new surrounds. It's a proper house, with four rooms and a rustic old kitchen leading off the hallway. There's a small verandah, where the guards all sit. An outside toilet that they use is in the corner of the courtyard. The high perimeter wall is hedged with razor wire.

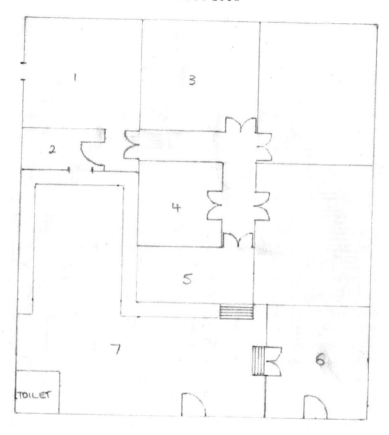

The Filthy House

1. Amanda and Nigel's room
2. Bathroom
3. Abdi and the drivers' room
4. Kitchen
5. Verandah
6. Captain Yahya's room and weapons hold
7. Courtyard

There are ten guards hanging around and I recognise some of them from the day before. All of them now have their faces uncovered, apart from Ali. Constantly being watched by a bunch of boys with AK47s strapped to them squashes any pleasure I'd otherwise get from sitting in the sun under the green trees.

We get the first of a series of phone calls. Surrounded by Ahmed, Ali and Yahya, Amanda is handed the phone. She answers some questions before passing it over to me. I press the receiver to my ear, saying, 'Hello, Nigel Brennan speaking.' The guy on the other end identifies himself as Gary from the AFP; he's calling from South Africa but his accent is clearly Australian. Amanda says to Ahmed that he's from the Associated French Press, assuming that's what 'AFP' stands for. I ask Gary which organisation he is from and he replies, 'the Australian Federal Police'. I'm so relieved that he's a cop rather than a journalist – it means my government is on the case.

Gary asks if we are all right.

'Yeah, we're okay,' I say. 'They're giving us food and water and we have a mosquito net.'

He wraps things up by telling me my family loves me and the government is doing everything they can. Gary then gives Adam his phone number. I tell Ahmed they will have to call Gary back so that the negotiations can begin. I feel calmer after the call, knowing that the wheels have started to turn back in Australia, but most importantly that my family will soon know that I am alive.

Over the coming days they bring us a few things: underpants, toothbrushes and toothpaste and bottles of aftershave and perfume, which seems strange. Amanda and I discuss asking for two English-language Qur'ans. She thinks we might have to convert to get out of this mess. She's got a point. I tell Ali we want to understand Islam better. At first he seems suspicious. I ask him a few questions about religion to loosen him up. Ali says they believe the Bible and Torah were books of God, but that they had been corrupted by priests and rabbis. After we talk for a while, he gets excited that we're keen and tells us he will look for English Qur'ans at Bakaara market.

I know I'm in for a religious re-education. I'll be a complete non-believer pretending to be interested in the faith. This is dangerous territory.

Wednesday, 27 August

Amanda speaks to her mother for the first time, and it feels like a breakthrough. I'm sure that soon I'll get to speak to one of my family members as well. Amanda assures her mum that we are okay before asking how much the group wants.

Her face drops when she hears the reply. Amanda turns to Ahmed, stammering, 'The Canadian government doesn't pay ransoms and my family are trying to raise the money.' Before she gets the chance to say anything else to Lorinda, the phone is disconnected.

Amanda tells me the price for our release is US$1.5 million each.

Numb with disbelief, I can't get my head around how enormous this is. It's as if they've just plucked a figure from the air. Amanda's family doesn't have a chance in hell of ever being able to come up with that sort of coin.

I think of my parents' retirement, how hard they've worked all their lives to get to where they are — it's meant to be a joyous time.

They could never scrape together that sum, but I know in my heart they'll be selling off everything to get me out.

Amanda is a powerhouse in that first week. She does most of the talking when the head guys come to speak with us. She has the greater knowledge of Islam and they seem more accommodating to her than me. I'm happy to let her be our mouthpiece; I'm still struggling to come to terms with what's happening.

The curiosity of some of the boys works to our advantage. Jamal and Abdullah, two of our younger guys, start asking us questions when they bring in our food and water. They look no older than twenty. Jamal is six foot tall and slender; he's got a huge bright smile. Abdullah is shorter and stockier, and, like Ali, scared the bejesus out of me from the moment I set eyes on him. He comes in with his face covered but his eyes are intense.

Jamal always speaks with me and Abdullah with Amanda. In fact he seems fixated on her. But both Amanda and I know we have to jump at the chance to build rapport with them, not only so they will see us as human beings, but to better get a handle on what's going on.

I actually enjoy my talks with Jamal; they take my mind off things; we speak about football, surfing, driving cars and Australia. He seems like a kid caught up in a bad crowd. When he explains that the occupying forces have killed his entire family, I feel sorry for him, and ask him what he wants to do with his life. His aspirations are like those of anyone his age: he wants to go abroad – to India – to study IT then come back and start his own business, to get married and have children.

He says to me at one point, 'I don't want to be a soldier, I don't like being a soldier; I want to go to university.'

Abdullah, on the other hand, seems past the point of no return. He's filled with anger and hatred, constantly talking about slaying infidels and fighting Jihad. His parents have also lost their lives in the war, and he seems driven by revenge. Abdullah tells us in great detail how he has killed Ethiopian soldiers – he's like a schoolboy boasting about getting laid. Sure, he's probably all talk but he still scares me.

Jamal is a good ally; one of his duties is going to the market to buy our food, and we ask him to buy us cigarettes. While telling us that they are bad for our health, he sneaks them in, our little secret. In the first week the two of us bond. Even though we are captor and hostage, he shows me some respect.

The stress is starting to wear. But Amanda and I are sure there's a mountain of people working behind the scenes back in our countries, trying to do everything they can to get us out of here alive.

2006-AUGUST 2008

Into Africa

Nigel
The Filthy House

In our first week of being held captive I spend a lot of time thinking about how I ended up in such a mess. The idea of going to a conflict zone to take photographs had been kicking around for a while, and Amanda and I talked about Somalia when we first met in 2006 in Ethiopia. Amanda was backpacking her way through East Africa and I was on a photography assignment for the International Rescue Committee. We hit it off from the moment we met and ended up having an affair. I guess I was running away from responsibilities at the time, having had a major meltdown with my then-wife before I left England for Ethiopia.

We kept in contact over the next six months and Amanda eventually came to Australia for a short visit in early 2007. The relationship fizzled out when she moved to Afghanistan to kickstart her career in journalism – she wanted me to join her but I was helping to build a retirement house for my parents. I was also working as a photojournalist for the local newspaper and didn't want to leave.

We kept in touch sporadically over the year, and just before Christmas 2007 she called to say she was moving to Baghdad to work for Press TV. I was surprised as she had no formal training, but I knew she was passionate about getting into the industry and loved a challenge.

By the start of 2008 I was living in Scotland with my new girl-friend, AJ, an executive chef on a shooting estate on the west coast near Dunoon. It was a beautiful part of the world but I began to feel very isolated. Cracks started appearing in the relationship. It felt like I was just treading water, not doing what I truly wanted.

I had been drawn to war photography when I was studying photojournalism at Griffith University in Brisbane, and I'd always been a devotee of *Four Corners, Foreign Correspondent* and *Time* magazine. For me, it wasn't the adrenaline rush; I wanted to capture the futility of war and what happens to the innocents who are caught in the crossfire.

I was planning to come home in September 2008 because I'd been asked to photograph the weddings of two very close friends, and I was looking forward to catching up with the family. I already knew I wouldn't be going back to Scotland after this visit home. I was planning to base myself in either India or China, where I'd start the hard graft of trying to make it as a freelance journalist.

Amanda contacted me again in July, wondering what I was up to. We talked about what she was doing in Iraq and it sounded like she had fallen on her feet – she was now working for France 24 as their freelance Baghdad correspondent. Of course I was happy for her, but I had a slight twinge of jealously. When Amanda suggested

I come to Iraq to cover some stories with her, I began to think about it seriously.

Over the next week we talked several times about the prospect of me going to Baghdad, but in the end I couldn't afford the huge cost. Paying for security was going to be the killer; I knew this was essential when working in a war-ravaged country. I decided to drop the idea, to Amanda's disappointment.

It was no longer than a week after this that Amanda contacted me again, suggesting a trip into Africa, and that piqued my interest. She was thinking of going to Kenya, Ethiopia and Somalia. I knew the first two countries were relatively safe but the third was a different story.

Somalia is one of the most dangerous countries in the world. Anarchy has basically reigned there unchecked since January 1991, when Mohamed Siad Barre's government fell. After that, Somalia imploded with civil war as clans fought to gain control and usurp what little government there was left.

The Islam Courts Union is made up of the heads of the major clans, and they formed a government. This was a time of relative peace under Sharia law. Western countries didn't like the situation, however, and the American government destabilised the Sharia-ruled government. With the downfall of the ruling Islam Courts Union in 1996, the power of a group known as Al-Shabaab ('the youth') rose, creating havoc for the African Union troops trying to support the Transitional Federal Government of Somalia, which was backed heavily from Ethiopia.

Amanda and I discussed at length the cost of going for three or four weeks and exactly what would be required to get in and out of Somalia safely. I started researching all three countries.

Kenya was still recovering after the election riots in early 2008, and I wanted to not only focus on this but also to photograph the slums in Nairobi, the capital. Ethiopia was by far the safest option; the drought in the southern part of the country was causing massive problems for aid organisations dealing with children suffering from malnutrition.

In Somalia the drought and food crisis was just part of the story – the war that was ravaging Mogadishu was by far the bigger one. Most NGOs had pulled out of the country due to serious threats to the safety of their staff. I was well aware that being a western journalist would put me in an extremely vulnerable position and that there was the threat of kidnapping – and being killed. We were going to need good security and a fixer we could trust.

Amanda and I decided to spend up to ten days in Somalia. Any longer than that and we would be pushing our luck. It was going to cost a pretty penny just for this leg of the trip and I questioned whether the money would be worth it, but sometimes in life you have to overcome your fear and let go of the rope. I had always landed on my feet and I didn't think this time would be any different.

I rang Mum, telling her I was thinking about going to Kenya, leaving out the Somalia bit because I knew she'd freak out. I didn't want to worry her unnecessarily. It was exciting to finally book my plane tickets: I would be flying out of London on 16 August and into Nairobi the same day to meet Amanda.

In retrospect it was unsurprising that AJ didn't share my enthusiasm, and we had a massive argument as she dropped me at the airport. She accused me of not going for work purposes but for a fling. I would be lying if I didn't say that I was curious to see if there was still something between Amanda and me, but I also thought I was doing the right thing in terms of my career.

Nairobi
Saturday, 16 August

Amanda met me at the airport in Nairobi. It was great to see her after so long. At twenty-seven, she was as beautiful as I remembered, and we were both excited about the possibilities ahead of us. We drove to a hotel in town where I dumped my stuff, and headed straight back out to celebrate with a few drinks. It felt amazing to be back in Africa – to experience the vibrancy, colour, sounds and smells that all developing nations seem to have; life at its rawest. The place felt so alive. We found a seedy little bar and sat out on the balcony, just watching people go about their day.

We got quite drunk, catching up on what the other had been doing. We met a guy called Rich from South Carolina, with the quintessential southern accent, who was working as a doctor for Médecins Sans Frontières (MSF).

My ears pricked up as he explained that he was working in one of the smaller slums in Nairobi. I asked if I could come to photograph the work he was doing at his clinic. He seemed genuinely happy to help me and thought that it wouldn't be a problem with his organisation. I couldn't believe my luck – everything seemed to be falling into place.

We kicked on till 1 a.m., drinking beer and slamming tequila shots before making our way back to the hotel. The karaoke bar across the road made it impossible to sleep, the music blaring and the singing atrocious.

Amanda and I decided to slip across the road for a few nightcaps, and, pretty smashed by this point, we did a rendition of George Michael's 'Faith'.

We were both still in stitches when we finally fell into our beds.

Sunday, 17 August

I woke up feeling like I'd been kicked by a mule.

We spent the day wandering around the city. It being a Sunday, the place was a ghost town. We ended up at the beautiful old Sarova Stanley Hotel in the city centre, where we bumped into Rich again and organised to go to dinner that night at a well-known Italian restaurant, Trattoria, just around the corner.

That night Rich told me he had spoken with MSF to arrange everything for when I got back from Mogadishu. We were all in good spirits and again ended the night on the balcony of a bar in the downtown area.

Monday, 18 August

I spent the morning organising my visa to get into Somalia. I needed a letter of support from a media organisation and I ended up knocking one off. I used a logo from a website and typed up a letter saying that I was an employee on assignment covering a story in Somalia. I got Amanda to forge the signature, not wanting to do it myself in case it looked too much like my writing.

We headed off to the Somali consulate, nervous about how long it would take them to process the visa application – we were due to fly to Mogadishu in two days' time. Amanda and I persuaded the woman processing it to push it through by the next day.

I ran into a major problem later that afternoon; I couldn't change any of my Scottish pounds. Every money changer I went to treated it like Monopoly money. I had close to a thousand pounds of the stuff and I realised I was going to have to call the old girl. I had to do a cash advance on my credit card to cover the costs for Somalia.

I called Mum, told her the situation and she was happy to help. I didn't mention Somalia to her then either.

Tuesday, 19 August

I returned to the consulate. My lucky streak continued: they had processed my visa, so all that was left to do was purchase the plane tickets to Mogadishu. Amanda had booked seats for both of us on Daallo Airlines.

We arrived at the airline office to be informed that the booking had been cancelled as the tickets were due to be paid for the day before. Amanda tried to argue the point but the guy politely informed her that the flight was now completely booked. Maybe the universe was trying to tell us something. I was beginning to feel nervous about the trip: I had told virtually no one what I had planned and suddenly the whole thing seemed a little rushed.

Amanda threw around some ideas. Maybe we could go to Ethiopia, head down south to cover the drought then enter Somalia via Hargeisa in Somaliland. I didn't like that plan; it'd blow my budget. I was more than happy to wait for next week's flight and spend the extra time in Nairobi photographing Rich's clinic. But Amanda went back to the airline office to ask them to double-check if there were seats available. After several minutes, the assistant said that now there were in fact two seats free.

We took the tickets and later that afternoon Amanda contacted our fixer, Ajoos, in Mogadishu to confirm that everything was set for our arrival. That night we celebrated, going to Trattoria again because we knew the food in Somalia would be pretty basic. My worries vanished and both of us were excited that we would be in Mogadishu by noon the next day.

Mogadishu
Wednesday, 20 August

It was an early start, arriving at Nairobi International Airport around five in the morning. Fate nearly intervened again – we were daydreaming and almost missed the flight, making it to the gate just before it closed.

From the tarmac, the plane looked like a second-hand Aeroflot rust bucket. Suddenly I was more nervous about getting on the plane than reaching our destination. The inside looked more like that of a local bus; we were certainly flying African style, with broken seats and a toilet door that could only be opened from the outside.

I tried to get some sleep while Amanda talked to an Italian contractor en route to Hargeisa, and I heard him say that we would have to be very careful in Mogadishu. As we descended, I got my first look at the city and the beautiful coastline bordering it, the scars of the last seventeen years clearly visible. Coming through customs, I had to laugh at the entry card – it had a large space for declaring weapons. We had just walked into the Wild West.

The arrivals lounge was absolute chaos, and I felt like an alien as I watched AMISOM (African Union Mission in Somalia) troops walking around with massive machine-guns in hand. We were met by Abdifatah Elmi, who would be Amanda's cameraman while we were in the country. He would also work as our sub-fixer while Ajoos was working with the *National Geographic* team.

Before we'd left the airport, a guy tried to bribe us for an entry visa, which we fobbed off but took as a good indication that money is the main language here. We were met at the car by the driver and our security detail, both packing AK47s, before making the short trip to our hotel.

Hotel Shamo was a nice enough place considering we were in Mogadishu; the staff were friendly and we met the owner, who was kind enough to allow us to share a room. This would save us $125 a night, but I knew he was uncomfortable about it. He asked if we would tell the staff we were married so they wouldn't be offended.

We spent the afternoon at the United Nations World Food Programme, making contacts and organising our plan for the next day, then drove around the port area of Mogadishu. It was easy to see that it had once been a magnificent city. We headed back to the hotel before the 5 p.m. curfew – it wasn't safe on the street after that. There we met with Ajoos, Robert Draper and Pascal Maître from *National Geographic*.

Ajoos seemed a bit aloof and quickly pointed out it would be impossible to cover some of the things we wanted to as the fighting in Mogadishu had kicked up a notch. This seemed fair enough but it was hard work getting information out of him.

That first night Amanda and I were unable to sleep so we went up to the top of the hotel to have a cigarette. It was beautiful up there. It is one of the most dangerous places in the world yet from the roof of the hotel it all seemed so tranquil. It was a city asleep, no sounds of war.

Thursday, 21–Friday, 22 August

Over the next two days we spent time in different areas of Mogadishu. I photographed Ugandan troops, as well as a number of IDP camps within the city, the Medina Hospital, around Villa Somalia and the port area. It was a struggle to get stuff done; we could only operate between the hours of nine and five, and Ajoos was being uncommunicative.

By the evening of the twenty-second, both of us were fed up with Ajoos' lack of information. We felt like we were getting the scraps, and that his attention was firmly focused on the *National Geographic* team. Amanda asked me to confront him. I was happy enough to do it if it meant getting what I came for, so I met with Ajoos. He seemed detached, as though he wasn't even listening. I made it clear that he was getting paid well for his time, considering he wasn't even with us during the day.

Before returning to the room I sent some emails. The first was a chain email, one of those ones that if you send it to ten people within a certain time frame something good will happen. It's not something I would normally do but given where I was, I thought I could do with all the help I could get. I then emailed a mate in Bundaberg, explaining what I was up to but asking him not to tell Mum and Dad. Finally, I emailed my girlfriend in Scotland. I told her that I was sorry for the way things went before I left and that everything had gone smoothly so far.

When I got back to the room, Amanda suggested we should try to get some booze. She called the owner's nephew and asked what was available. The choice was whisky or gin but I killed the idea – alcohol and Islam just don't mix.

Now, sitting in our filthy room, I wish I'd just had that fucking drink. I didn't know it then but my luck was just about to run out.

SEPTEMBER 2008

Bring Blackie back

Kellie
Moore Park
Monday, 1 September

Matt meets me at Bundaberg Airport. He looks tired and he hasn't shaved. Gayle Judd, our family liaison officer, is there too and it's nice to finally put a face to the name. The three of us walk out to the car; it's an AFP one, a blue Commodore or something like that, fitted out with all the police gear, lights, sirens and so on. Matt lets me sit in the front so Gayle can give me the run-down on what to expect when I get to the house.

'How is everyone?' I ask tentatively.

'You'll be a better judge than I am – I've just met them, but on the whole they seem pretty good,' Gayle answers.

I ask her for all the info they have to date on Nige – what we know, what they know in Nairobi. Gayle starts on a long spiel about Nic training as the next-of-kin (NOK) negotiator, and how the phones are all hooked up to answering machines so that the conversations can be recorded when the hostage takers phone. She explains that the downstairs area has been taken over by the AFP, allowing the family a little bit of normality and privacy upstairs.

We pull up outside Heather and Geoff's place, the house that Nigel built for them with Geoff and Ham, their retirement home. Heather always wanted to live on the coast and after so many years on the farm in inland New South Wales, she finally got her wish. The house was designed to fit everyone in – all the kids, partners and grandkids. Downstairs is fitted with an open-plan kitchen, dining and lounge room, a huge kid-friendly bathroom, laundry and three bedrooms. Upstairs is designed around the view; all rooms look towards the ocean over Moore Park Beach. I am almost certain, though, that when Heather decided the house needed to be big enough to fit everyone in, she wasn't thinking of her present AFP guests.

There are about seven cars parked out the front, some I recognise and some I assume belong to the AFP as they are very similar to Gayle's. I am so nervous about going in – the Brennans are my family, but even so I'm unsure what to say to them.

I walk in the front door, and I can see from the passageway that the lounge room-cum-dining room is set up with clocks, computers, printers and phones. Butcher's paper covers the walls, and written on it are the prompt questions for Nicky to ask the kidnappers. There are also proof-of-life questions and, at the very top, the instruction KEEP CALM in big red lettering. I wonder if that is really possible.

I see a large map of Somalia on the wall, with Mogadishu highlighted in yellow. On the opposite wall are four clocks with time zones set for Moore Park, Mogadishu, Nairobi and Red Deer in

Canada, where Amanda's parents live. Dave from the AFP starts explaining everything in front of me, but I'm too distracted by the official-ness of the room and the people in it to actually hear anything he's saying.

This is feeling unreal, like I'm in an episode of 24. All I need is for Kiefer Sutherland to burst through the door.

'Thanks for explaining all that, Dave, but I think I'll come back a bit later and go through it all again. It's all a bit much to take in at the moment.'

Dave understands and invites me back whenever I'm ready to do it all again.

I walk up the stairs to find the rest of the family. Nic is standing in the breezeway, waiting for me.

'Hi, kiddo,' she says, smiling.

We hug, holding each other longer than we normally would.

I can hear Heather in the background saying, 'No tears, no tears.'

Nic and I let go and laugh as we look at each other; our eyes are wet but we are not crying.

I hug Heather, squeezing her tight, and ask her if she is okay.

'We're all fine, but thank you for coming.'

I see Geoff coming towards me; he looks very fragile and older all of a sudden. Poppy, as everyone calls him, gives me a giant bear hug and I can feel his body start to shake around me.

'It's okay. Everything's going to be fine,' I tell him.

'I know, but, god, it's good to see you,' he says, wiping his eyes.

'It's good to be here.' I look at everyone in the room and then quote Hamilton. 'Well, this is a bit of a shit sandwich, isn't it?'

The whole family is here: Heather and Geoff, Nic and Si, all the kids, Jacinta, Monty and Atti, and Ham and Amy. Adrian from the AFP heads downstairs to give us some privacy. AJ has arrived from

Scotland too. It was her idea to come – going it alone over there would be even harder than this. We welcome her into the family.

A lamb roast is cooking and smells amazing. I have arrived right on wine o'clock and start on my first glass of chilled sauvignon blanc. We all start talking. Gayle is with us, though not drinking because she is working. It is so nice to sit with loved ones, to just see their faces and know that they are doing okay.

The house feels different. It's not sterile or hospital-like; it has a sense of anticipation about it, like something unexpected could happen at any minute. It takes longer than usual to feel comfortable in a house where I am always very relaxed.

Maybe it has something to do with the way everyone is talking. It's like someone came in and taught my family a new language, and I missed the lesson. They're all speaking in acronyms that I don't understand. I wasn't aware that any of my family were members of the Australian Federal Police, but that's what it sounds like now. Nicky is the NOK negotiator, downstairs is the NOK cell (I also hear of a 'Nairobi cell'), all the negotiators are being referred to by their initials, and the kidnappers are now the HTs (hostage takers).

I try to pick up what I can of the new lingo. As the night progresses, I learn that the boys, Dave and Adrian, come upstairs every evening to give the family a progress report. I wonder how tonight's will go: we're all starting to get a bit jolly with the consumption of good food and alcohol, and there's plenty of family banter. It actually feels good to have a few drinks; I can feel the tension that I have been holding in my shoulders for the last nine days start to slide away.

After dinner is finished, we stay sitting at the dining table and start telling stories about Nige, funny stories about him as a kid. The pitch-black humour of the Brennan family comes out. It's great to have a laugh about the ridiculousness of what has happened – only Nigel would get himself into something like this. We laugh at his vanity, how worried he'll be without his toothbrush to keep his teeth white. How he got himself kidnapped by chasing a bit of skirt into a dangerous country.

The night turns into an absolute piss-take of Nige, his life, his failed marriage. We laugh at how he has a great house but even if we sell it, it won't get his sorry arse home because he owes too much on it. He had to pay out the ex-wife he cheated on with Amanda. We're all yelling over each other to tell yet another tale about the black dog Nigel, so called because you can't trust a black dog. You turn your back on them and they will bite you on the leg.

This starts Ham singing falsetto.

Black dog, black dog, where'd you park your bone?
Black dog, black dog, now you've lost your home.

Of course, the conversation turns to money and how we could ever get our hands on such an extraordinary amount. Ham suggests we sell T-shirts with the phrase 'Bring Blackie back' on the front and 'He still owes me money' on the back. We talk about sending him one in Somalia so he can get a laugh out of it too, but decide it could be taken as being racist and might in fact get him killed.

The laughter is raucous and I wonder what on earth they are thinking downstairs. I don't really care because for the first time since we heard the news everyone around me is smiling and enjoying themselves. I am so pleased I came.

Tuesday, 2 September

I wake up early and walk into the negotiation room; it's unnerving that the officers close their laptops as I approach. I wonder if the information is that sensitive or whether they're just killing time on Facebook or playing solitaire. I decide to go back upstairs.

I sit down to eat breakfast and the phone rings. *The* phone.

Nic starts running downstairs, yelling, 'I'm coming! I'm coming!' Everyone else in the room has frozen. Nic takes the stairs three at a time. Then the ringing stops as she picks up the receiver.

The rest of us just sit or stand in silence. I can feel my heart pounding.

'False alarm!' she yells.

Everyone around me exhales.

Later in the day I find Gayle working on her laptop in the negotiation room and we start chatting about her real job, when she is not being an FLO, and some of the places she has been. I like Gayle; she seems like a straight shooter and is very easy to talk to.

She asks me about the family, how we all fit together and which kids belong to whom. She asks me about Geoff's family's farming partnership and Geoff and Heather's families and about Matt's accident and what side effects still linger. She then asks me if I know whether Nigel has ever been involved in any criminal activity. The only thing I can think of is his growing marijuana plants in Heather's garden a few years back, and Heather trying to hide them from the local Tulloona Ladies one Melbourne Cup Day.

I'm sure she is not referring to this sort of indiscretion – I think she wants to know if he entered Somalia on false documentation, but I say nothing.

All of the family members have already been interviewed about Nigel, his travel plans, his last known contact, his relationship with Amanda and so on. Now it is my turn.

I know Nigel has had his fair share of life experiences and was always quite 'resourceful', but what country boy who's been sent away to boarding school isn't? He has travelled the world and been to many places off the regular tourist track. He is a typical type O personality – a nomad – so he gets antsy easily. He always needs a plan to move on to the next thing, to get to the next destination.

I answer Gayle's questions as honestly as I can, and tell her about our family.

Heather and Geoff have four children. Nicole is the oldest at forty-one and she's married to Simon; they have three children: Jacinta (twelve), Monty (eleven) and Atticus (nine) and they live in Moore Park Beach, down the road from Heather and Geoff. Next is Matthew, my husband, who is forty, and we also have three children: Gigi (seven), Callaghan (five) and Stirling (two). We moved to Clarence Town in the Hunter Valley when the family farm was sold. Hamilton (thirty-nine) is married to Amy and they also have three children: Oscar (six), Izzy (four) and Mac (two). Ham and Amy have lived everywhere from Karratha to Cairns and Darwin but have settled in Grafton. And then there is Nigel, the baby, at thirty-six.

When I married Matt, I basically married his family too, which was fine by me as I get along exceptionally well with all of them. Nicky is like the sister I never had, and she and Matt have a very special bond because of their horror accident.

Back in 1985 on the way home from a New Year's Eve party, about 350 kilometres from home, Matt and Nicky were involved in a terrible car crash. Matt was sixteen and Nic was seventeen. She was driving and swerved to miss a roo and landed in a ditch. They were on a gravel back road and there was no sign of any neighbours or help. Matt wasn't wearing a seatbelt and had been flung 30 metres from the car. He'd landed on his head and split his skull open in not one place but two. He had massive internal injuries and was bleeding from his ears.

When Nic found him he was dead, but she revived him and then lit a fire to attract attention. On a flat open plain there is nothing that raises the alarm better than a single spire of smoke.

Matt was airlifted to Sydney but was in a deep coma. The Brennans were told not to expect too much in terms of his recovery; while he would wake up, it was more than likely that due to brain damage he would never walk or talk again.

'We'll see about that,' the family said.

Six weeks later he woke up from the coma with no movement on his right side and no memory of the crash. He had to learn to walk and talk again, starting from scratch. He was incredibly determined. As he got better, he would wait outside the rehab room, and if patients didn't turn up for their session, he would take it.

His family was with him the whole time. They never gave up; they were always questioning the doctors and specialists, wanting more answers, doing their own research. They were not going to just sit there and let this happen to them; they were going to get in there and fight this battle with Matt.

I met Matt ten years after his accident, when I was at uni studying agricultural science. I had no idea what he'd been through; he was just a regular guy. He had completed his HSC, gone to uni, played rugby, travelled the world, and he was currently working at the family property, Marlow, in Moree. It wasn't until I got to know him better that I discovered what an extraordinary person he was.

The legacy of Matt's accident is paralysis on his right side, but it's so slight that if you met him, you would never know it was there. And he takes a little longer to process some of his thoughts than other people. That said, I've met people without a brain injury who are a lot slower than he is.

I married Matt Brennan in October 1999; we had been living

together for two years prior to that at Marlow, down the road from Heather and Geoff's place. When I first moved to the farm, Heather was the only woman I knew within 50 kilometres, so you can imagine we became quite good friends. She was, and still is, a very stoic woman – she needed to be, out there. She raised those four kids 70 kilometres from anything, while Geoff ran the farm.

Heather is blessed with amazing skin; she goes the most beautiful golden colour in the sun. In her younger days she was a stunner and one you could imagine men admiring from afar.

Geoff is like a mad professor, with this wild, woolly hair and a shaggy beard. He smokes a pipe, and in the old days he'd wear Volley sandshoes the colour of the black soil plains, stubbies and a ripped T-shirt come rain, hail or shine. I remember winters being quite cold at Marlow. I would be huddled in front of the fire and Geoff would rock up in his Volleys and shorts like the sun was shining. These days he still wears the same thing but manages to drag on some good shoes and a shirt when he goes out.

Geoff is soft and at times can be a bit of a pushover. But if something goes against his principles, he's at it like a dog with a bone, not letting it go until it's over. Heather also always fights for what is right, but she just does it in a different way. Teachers' college and Matt's accident have made her the tough woman she is, one who will take on anything or anyone for her family. She is strong enough for all of them. Their marriage looks tumultuous; they bicker often, yet I know they couldn't live without each other. What seems like a bit of a disaster on the surface is actually a solid relationship built on mutual respect.

I ask Gayle if this is enough information. I actually feel like I am dobbing on my family. I respect authority and the role it plays in the community. I've always been one to fall into line, right from the time I was at school. I wasn't a rebellious teen: I did what I was told. However, now, as we talk, I feel like I'm doing something wrong. I'm divulging all of this information about my family, and I'm not sure for what purpose. I wonder if what I say will be crosschecked.

The idea that the justice system in this country seems to rely on most citizens conforming starts to make me wonder. What if I keep travelling down this path and put all my trust in authority, and this situation ends up in a red-tape bungle? Perhaps it's time for me, as an adult who knows my own mind, to start asking a few questions myself.

I learn that every person who comes in or out of the house must be identified and logged because the information contained in the negotiation cell downstairs is highly confidential. When I leave the house two days later, I am asked to write down all the phone numbers and birthdates of each family member, including kids and partners. I'm driven to Brisbane Airport by someone from the AFP, who has also booked my return tickets. As I sit in the airport waiting lounge, I spot a number of AFP staff nearby. I am now in tune with the activities of the Australian Federal Police.

Nicky
Moore Park
Friday, 5 September

It's 4 a.m., still night-time by my definition, when once again the ringing of the phone pulls me from my sleep. As I open the door of the spare room downstairs, I almost collide with Adrian, who is running down the hallway to wake me.

'I'm awake, I'm awake,' I mumble through sleep-numbed lips before picking up the phone.

'Hello, Adam.'

'Ah, Nicky.'

'Adam, is Nigel there with you? Can I talk to him?'

'Yes, one minute, but first we talk. Nigel. He has something to say, yes?'

'Um, okay.'

I stand rigid against the small table on which the NOK phone sits. My headset isn't a little Madonna number. It's got a big ear-muff on one side only, so I'm lopsided. I squeeze my eyes shut in the vain hope that if I take away one of my senses, another – my hearing – will be enhanced.

'Your family is very brave and I ask you to be brave and will think . . . to have him understand . . .' *Nope, the eyes-shut thing is not working.*

'Slow down,' I say to Adam. It sounds like his lips are pressed against the mouthpiece.

'. . . want to say to Australian government, understand . . .' Adam continues.

'You don't want the family to pay?' Is that what he's saying? He wants the government to pay the ransom not us?

'Yes, yes,' says Adam. *Good guess,* I think to myself.

I try to clarify. 'Nigel doesn't want the family to pay?'

'Nigel, yes,' Adam responds. 'We are sorry about the money . . . we want . . . he is . . . worried about the . . . ticket . . . wants you to know about the ticket . . .'

What bloody ticket? Where is this going?

'It's a lot of money, you understand?' Adam continues.

'Okay,' I say. *No, I don't understand any of this but let's try to work it out.* I look across to Adrian. He's got the second headset on so he can hear the conversation and direct me if need be. He shrugs.

The line is silent. *Oh no, it's cut out.*

'Adam? Adam?' I call out.

'Yes.'

Okay, good. He's still there.

'He is wanting to come to you to ask, how is family at this time? Are they fine, are they good?'

Is he kidding?

'Our family is worried about Nigel.' What an understatement. Terror and shock are still our reigning emotions.

'Okay, okay. I will connect to you on the line,' Adam says.

'Thank you,' I reply, trying not to sound fawning. Am I going to speak to Nige? My heart is thumping in my chest, adrenaline pumping into my core.

'Please hold on.'

My god, what is that?! I pull back from the table and almost rip off the headset. The feedback is ear-piercing – no, it's *not* feedback; it almost sounds like a bird song, a butcher bird warble on a continuous loop, combined with the *Dr Who* theme.

'Hello, hello?'

We're talking over each other, neither pausing long enough for the time delay, when I realise I can hear Nige.

'Hello, Nic?'

'Nigel! Nigel, how are you?'

'Fine.'

Relief washes over me. It's Nige and I can hear him. His voice is nice and clear, so I assume he doesn't have a split lip from being smacked in the mouth by a semiautomatic or even a plain old fist. I'm starting to tick off my intel points to glean info, whether Amanda and Nige are together and if they're all right.

'Is Amanda with you?'

'Yep, and we're physically okay, actually okay,' *Oh, good boy, Nige*, I think, *you're giving me all the right answers.*

'I just obviously wanted to talk to you or Mum or Dad, probably better to talk to you because if I talk to Mum . . .' Nigel's voice quavers.

'She'll go to water,' I finish the sentence for him. *Hell, I have.*

Now is the time for reassurance. 'Nige, we're doing everything we can to get you home.'

'Yeah, I know that. I know they've asked for, I think it is . . . I've spoken to a guy in Nairobi, he works for the Australian government . . .' He's trying to give as much information as he can. I'm being trained in all these negotiation techniques and Nige is doing it all off his own bat.

'We spoke to him too.' Well, I haven't directly but I am aware that there is an AFP officer over in Nairobi.

'He sort of said to me that, that Australia's not paying for a ransom, and I said yes, I've explained that to Adam. But Adam has assured us that he doesn't want money from our families; he's interested in money from the governments. And then they will let us go.'

'Okay.' I feel a wild surge of hope. Then I wonder if that really will be the case.

'So that's what we are being told here. Not sure what the government is telling you, and I don't know what Mum and Dad are doing, whether they are selling whatever they've got to get me out of here. But from what I'm being told, they're not interested in Mum and Dad's money or the families' money whatsoever . . .'

'This is huge,' I tell him. 'Mum and Dad are doing everything they can, okay? And I do understand what you're saying so be strong. You've made that really clear, Nige, what you want and what the kidnappers want.'

'It's fine . . .' He sounds teary.

I don't want to upset him and have him fall in a heap. I tell him, 'Be calm, be strong.' Then I move off script a little and tell him that AJ is here in Australia. I want to let him know she's here with us, with the rest of his family. I know it will be important for him to know she is okay. In fact she is right beside me; she came running down the stairs when the action started.

Adam hears that Nige is distressed and he interjects, talking over both of us. 'Let me ask you, is there a problem?'

Can Adam see if Nige is upset or just hear? Is he there with Nige or not? Adam gets distracted by this 'girlfriend' conversation and wants to talk to AJ, but I quickly tell him she's asleep and get the dialogue back on track. I tell him everything is fine.

Adam continues, 'We should be friendly after this time, sister. Understand?'

Rightio. Now's the time to slap on the praise; he's let me talk to Nige and I want this to keep going. 'Thank you, Adam. Thanks for looking after Nigel and Amanda.'

Nige says, 'Yeah.' He doesn't have the suck-up down pat like I do.

'It's time to call Amanda . . . this time to call her family . . .' *Adam is winding us up.*

Nige recognises this too. 'Can I just say . . . Nic? I've actually got plane tickets booked. One is for Swiss Air going to London. I'm not even sure if it matters; it's Swiss Air. I have a ticket on 1 October, coming back to Australia with Qantas. I know that ticket can be changed. I don't know what you can do or when we'll be out of here . . .'

What? Oh my god, he wants me to change his flight details. He's kidnapped in Somalia and the tight-arse is fretting about losing money on his tickets. I'm gunna kill him!

'. . . just tell Mum and Dad I love them very much. I love you guys; tell Matt and Kel and Ham and Amy . . .' *Okay,* I reassess, *I'm not going to kill him.*

'They all love you too,' I say, starting to tear up myself. We're both trying to suck it up and not cry, reassuring each other across the massive distance between us.

Nige repeats where the money must come from: 'I think they have to talk to the AFP because they're only interested in money from the government. I'm not going to take Mum and Dad's money away from them; they've worked so hard for it,' he blurts out.

I scramble to think how to keep the conversation going.

'Nige, is Amanda with you right now? Can we speak to her?'

'Yeah, I'll put her on.'

'Hi, Nicky.' Nige has passed the phone straight to her.

'We're doing everything we can over here to get you home, okay?'

'Thank you, thank you so much.' Her voice is starting to waver. 'Have you been talking to my parents?'

'We've been speaking to your mum and dad.' This isn't strictly true, but we need to emphasise that we're working as a team.

'Yes, I think it's better if both families keep in touch with each other about what's going on,' Amanda says.

I think she's got it but go on to tell her, 'Both the Australians and the Canadians are working on this together.' The only word I've omitted is 'government' but I'm sure she can read between the lines. 'As far as your family and our family are concerned, we're in this together.'

'Thank you so much, thank you.'

'That's okay,' I tell her. 'Chin up.'

'Thank you, Adam,' I say, meaning for letting me speak to

Amanda, but just as I say it the line is disconnected. And with that, it's over.

I'm in a pair of boxers and a T-shirt and although I have some-how, somewhere acquired a jumper, I'm still cold. The massive dump of adrenaline is long gone and I'm left feeling fatigued and quivery. I look down at the strategies, the priorities and techniques that are written on a sheet of butcher's paper sticky-taped to the wall by the phone.

Adrian sees me scanning them. 'That was a great call; we said just about everything we needed to. We pretty much exhausted all the conversation topics there.'

I like Adrian and I've worked really hard at doing so since the QPol removal saga – he's big and loud and rambunctious and a lot like Ham – and then he says something dumb like that. I wouldn't have cared if every single thing on the strategy sheet had been said, I'd have stayed on the phone to Nige for hours if given the chance.

We go over the call, recapping what I thought I'd said and what I thought Nige and Amanda had said. I can hardly keep my eyes open.

'Go to bed,' Adrian says. 'We'll try to decipher it.'

Nigel
The Filthy House
Early September

With September comes the start of Ramadan – the month in which all Muslims fast from sunrise to sunset. This practice of refraining from eating, drinking and sexual intercourse is intended to teach patience, humility and spirituality – all of which are a bit lost on me at the moment.

I'm feeling as defenceless as a baby, unable to do anything to change the circumstances. My head is flooded with images of Daniel Pearl, the American journalist beheaded in Pakistan, and thoughts that my life could end the same way.

At the beginning of the month Ali presents us both with English-language Qur'ans, as we requested. With great excitement he explains how this holy book must be handled – it should never be placed on the floor and always picked up with the right hand. His index finger raised to enforce the point, Ali says, 'You can ask me anything about the Qur'an that you don't understand.' It's like listening to the school suck-up.

After Ali leaves, we amuse ourselves by mimicking him and his high-pitched voice.

Ahmed has explained that if we convert, they can neither harm us nor take our money. He's made it very clear that our being non-Muslim means they could very easily take the ransom money and then kill us anyway. He reiterates this point several times. He tells us that to become Muslim is the best thing we could do, but that it would have to come from our hearts.

Knowing all this, for the next few days I immerse myself in the Qur'an, having never even read the Bible. My state of mind being what it is, it's like trying to wade through mud. I am shocked by some of the passages, especially those about women and their second-class status. The pages on Jihad and fighting I find just as difficult, but I'm intrigued by the passages that state non-believers have the right to live in peace if they choose not to become Muslim.

When my head isn't buried in the Qur'an, I start a diary as a way of keeping track of time and events, not that there's a lot going on. It's a small leather-bound travel diary that I'd been using to take note of what I'd photographed and which people I'd met.

Wednesday, 3 September

We take another phone call. I speak with a man named Mark, who is a negotiator from the AFP based in Nairobi. To hear an Australian accent is comforting but what he has to say doesn't ease my mind.

He asks if we are okay and if they are taking care of us. I say that thus far they have treated us fairly and provided us with water, food, bedding, some personal effects and we've been allowed outside.

He asks me a POL question: 'Who did you used to go skiing with?'

'Sandy Goddard. He is an old family friend,' I reply.

Mark then tells me that the ransom price is $US1.5 million each. Amanda had already told me this after her call to her mother, but to now hear it officially is something else. I'm hit with a giddy sensation like I'm about to vomit. Mark goes on to ask me if I understand the government's stance on the payment of ransoms.

'Yes,' I say. 'We have explained to the kidnappers that the government will not pay.'

'That's correct.'

I knew well before I came to Somalia that Australia and Canada had signed a treaty forbidding the payment of ransoms for their citizens. Mark tells me that the government is working with my family to negotiate our release. I thank him, and then I hand the phone over to Amanda.

After the call we talk with Adan – not Adam as I had first misheard his name. He has been designated the communications expert and spokesman for the group. He's based in another location, and sets up and listens in on all the conference calls we take. I explain what Mark has told me but he won't listen. 'Mark is trying to corrupt your mind. Allah will open his heart and your government will pay the money.' *Is he on crack?* It's like trying to reason with a spoilt child.

'Your government will pay; they always pay,' he says.

Thursday, 4 September

In the morning Amanda is once again put on the phone to Lorinda, her mother.

I have no idea why I have not been granted a single call. I just want the comfort of listening to the voice of someone in my family, and I'm desperate to ask their forgiveness for what I'm putting them through.

Whenever I ask to make a call, the answer is always '*inshallah*', which I know means 'God willing', but reminds me of when I was a kid and my mother would say, 'Let me think about it.' That's when I knew I had bugger-all chance.

Amanda tells her mum we are okay. She tells Lorinda to stop trying to raise money for us as the group will not accept one dollar from our families. I leave the room to give her some privacy. I talk to Ahmed briefly outside the room. He says, 'What Amanda told her mother just now is very bad. She should not have said this.' I can't understand what his problem is; isn't that exactly what he's been telling us? The contradiction is confusing and frustrating, but I can't get any more information out of him.

Later that afternoon Amanda and I are talking about our families. She stands and says, 'You should demand to call them.' I don't want to be too confrontational as it seems like the quickest way to get ourselves killed. Still, I can't let go of the idea.

We are allowed outside, and I sit at the back of the courtyard under the trees, formulating a plan, and working myself up into a near-hysterical state. I'm in tears as I approach Captain Yahya, begging him to allow me a phone call. The boys translate. I can see he's uncomfortable by the way he tries to fob me off, but I keep at him until he finally capitulates, putting me on the phone to Ahmed.

Ahmed asks me why I'm so upset, and I tell him that I need to speak with my family so they'll know I'm still alive.

'*Inshallah*. I will organise it tomorrow,' he replies.

'No, I need to call them today,' I snap without thinking. I take a breath and a different tack. 'Please. Amanda has spoken to her family; I need to do the same.'

'It is not possible today. *Inshallah* tomorrow. I will talk to Adan and arrange it.'

There's no point in continuing to hammer him so I let it go. It's not yet a victory but I've made my intentions clear.

In the evening, to my surprise, Ahmed turns up, telling me that I will talk to Nicky shortly. Jubilance is quickly followed by a nauseating thought about how furious my family must be. I try to keep it in check.

Adan puts through the conference call. The sound of squawking birds fills my ear before the phone finally connects. Just hearing Nic's voice almost makes me lose it.

I try to stay composed as I tell her we are both okay and we haven't been harmed. In some respects I'm happy it's her on the other end and not Mum or Dad – I don't think I could have got through it otherwise. I manage to keep it together during the phone call but as I hand over the phone to Amanda, I start to sob uncontrollably.

Ahmed seems perturbed by my tears.

'Why do you cry? You should be happy to speak with your family. It is a sign of weakness for a man to cry; only women cry.'

Suddenly I want to jump on this arsehole and punch his buck-teeth into the back of his throat. I explain once again that my family believes we will be killed if there is no money. He seems to find this funny.

Both Amanda and I know we have to make these people like us. We have countless discussions with Ahmed, Adan, Ali and some of the younger boys.

The main theme of our talks is our governments' 'war with Islam'. Ahmed keeps pointing out the fact that both our countries had troops in Iraq, Afghanistan and Pakistan and that they are fighting a crusade against the Muslim world. Neither of us even lives in our country of birth but this makes no difference to them. Ahmed states again they are only interested in our governments' money. He argues that Australia *will* pay a ransom for one of its citizens. These conversations are infuriating. Telling them that their beliefs are bullshit just isn't an option; we can't do anything other than sit here and take the barrage of insults.

Friday, 5 September

Today seems like just another day, but I can feel depression taking hold, squeezing the lifeblood from me.

I'm angry at myself, and at Amanda for having suggested coming to this godforsaken country in the first place. I find myself withdrawing from her to spend the morning trying to read the Qur'an. I can tell she is unhappy about this, and she asks one of the boys for permission to go out into the courtyard. I'm still struggling to read as Amanda comes back into the room.

'I've told them that we are going to convert to Islam at eleven o'clock today,' she says.

I can't believe my ears.

'Hang on, *what*?!'

We have talked about the possibility of converting as a survival technique, but she's just gone and made the decision for us. I haven't even got all the way through the Qur'an and I'm battling to comprehend a fair slab of what I have read. This is not a game.

'Well, I have told them we will. We have to do this,' Amanda argues.

'Are we actually going to discuss this first?'

'What is there to discuss? At the end of the day it's something we're going to have to do to stay alive.'

I don't have a religious bone in my body. Religion, to my mind, is the root of a lot of the pain and suffering that has occurred over history. Now I'm going to have to immerse myself in, perform the rituals of, and follow something that I don't even understand. I'm not sure I can pull this off; it will be the biggest bluff of my life and if they ever find out it's a sham, they will butcher us like animals. But she's right: we don't have a choice.

Muslims are not allowed to smoke, as it's classed as a drug and therefore forbidden. We've been chain-smoking a pack a day. I'd begun to hoard them as Amanda was smoking my share. They haven't brought us our daily packet yet and I have two hidden away. I ask if Amanda wants a final cigarette and the look on her face tells me she is desperate. How will we be able to give this up? I slowly pull two from my camera bag and hand her one.

Both of us sit there, doing what it seems will be our last

pleasurable activity for a while. We slowly smoke our last coffin nails, having no idea what the future holds.

Ali comes into the room, excited that we are willing to convert. He asks me firstly why I want to do it. I pull the answer out of my arse: after reading the Qur'an, I know in my heart being a Muslim is something I want to do and that Islam is the true way. He seems to swallow it but surely he must suspect we're not doing this for the right reasons.

He teaches us some Arabic words so that we'll be able to recite the declaration of faith, Shahadah, the oath one takes to become Muslim.

There's no turning back now. I can't quite believe what I have got myself into; I imagine the looks on my family's faces if they could witness this farce. Struggling with every word, I try to practise the two short sentences. Ali thankfully walks us through it when the time comes. Surrounded by several of the boys and Captain Yahya, I stammer out the words, feeling their eyes burning into me. They must know I'm an impostor.

As soon as we finish showering and completing our ablutions, we perform two Raka'ah, the prayer movements. I have no clue what I'm meant to do. I stand there as Ali recites the first Surah of the Qur'an; being a woman, Amanda has to stand behind me and to the right. Following the movements of Ali, I prostrate myself, stand up then kneel before finally touching my forehead to the ground. I'm in way over my head.

The whole thing is over in a matter of minutes; we are then given our Muslim names. Mine is Mohammad and Amanda's is Mary. Our Muslim brothers embrace us, and, feeling like I have just entered a cult, I shake the hand of each of the boys. I can't believe it's that easy to convert.

Now we are Muslim we get to see Ali's face. The first thing I notice is a mouth full of jagged teeth. He seems older than the other guys, maybe late twenties or early thirties, but his eyes are just as intense as when his face was covered. He says to us that he will soon be leaving the house and going to another group. I can't say I'll miss him.

Our religious education starts. It is a steep learning curve and I know we can't stuff this up. From here on in we will have to pray five times daily, and perform the fasting rules of Ramadan and the rituals of ablution.

Just before midday prayer we are brought out of our room to join the group. Jamal teaches me how to do ablution properly: first washing the hands then the face while snorting water up the nostrils, next the forearms and then the feet, finishing by running water over the top of the head.

Amanda is only able to watch all of this. She's not allowed to pray with us as there is not enough space on the small verandah. I pray with all the boys for the first time. Standing toe to toe between two of them, I am uncomfortable. I feel like a fraud; I *am* a fraud.

Being male is a clear advantage here. Amanda is isolated. She's completely surrounded by men, unable to participate in the same rituals, certainly not seen as an equal. I'm grateful we are being held in the same room, as I think this will stop any sexual advances. A voice at the back of my mind tells me this is a false sense of security: they really have carte blanche.

Sunday, 7 September

A few days after our conversion Ahmed introduces us to two more players in the group; they are brought in under the guise of being our religious teachers. Both speak fluent English and appear to be well educated. Mohammad – 'Old Mohammad' as we call him – sweats profusely and is plump for a Somali, which suggests he's wealthy. Abdullah – our second one – is no older than twenty-five, a runt really, with scrappy facial hair. He distances himself from the group from the get-go, explaining he has nothing to do with the kidnapping. When the others are not around, he whispers to us that the gang is extremely dangerous.

These two act as middlemen, pretending to be interested in our religious education, asking if we need anything but generally trying to squeeze more information from us. We ask if we can change our Muslim names, as I keep forgetting to answer to 'Mohammad' whenever anyone tries to get my attention. Having been called 'Nigel' for the last thirty-six years, I am now going to need something that at least partway resembles it. They concede the point: my new Muslim name is 'Noah' and Amanda's is 'Amina'.

That evening I ask Ahmed how long they intend to hold us. He has said they'll release us if the government doesn't cough up so I'm sure they have some sort of plan in place. He says that it will be 'finished' within six weeks. I ask him to promise this, knowing that it states in the Qur'an that a Muslim must keep their word. He seems happy to give me this reassurance. Whether he is just blowing smoke up my arse or telling the truth I have no idea, but it gives me something to hold on to and a date to work towards.

Over the next little while our discussions with the younger guys go some way to distracting me. We slowly get to know each of them. One day Abdullah our guard comes in with Ismail, who up to this point has had little to do with us, most likely because he speaks no English. His features are very feminine and he is incredibly shy. Abdullah does the talking.

It's all pleasant enough to begin with. Noticing the massive scar on Ismail's leg, I ask him how he got it. Through Abdullah he explains it is a war wound – a result of a close call with a mortar. Abdullah starts up on his favourite subject, killing infidels, and the conversation suddenly goes downhill. He begins taunting us.

'I think you will be here for one or two years.'

I lose my temper – standing up and walking to the door, I bang on it furiously to get the attention of one of the older guys.

Abdullah gets up and pushes me, asking me what I am doing. I keep banging on the door. He brushes past me, leaving with Ismail, but turns back to face me from the hallway. He's a smiling assassin, letting me know I've overstepped the mark.

Amanda asks if I'm crazy, telling me to calm down. 'Nige, don't make enemies with these guys.' She's completely right. Now fear wells up as I wonder how I'll pay for my outburst. Tail between my legs, I apologise to Abdullah the next time he comes into the room. I say I was upset because I want to go to a Mosque to be able to learn my religion, which he seems to accept. I'll make damn sure that I don't cross him again.

One or two years. Not even having passed the one-month mark yet I don't know if I have the mental strength to do this.

Nicky
Moore Park
Saturday, 6 September

In the morning we call Mum. She is over in WA for a conference with the crankies (our term of endearment for her beloved Country

Women's Association). Interestingly enough, Stephen Smith, the foreign affairs minister, asks her if she would like to meet his mother, who is also over there. Mum thinks his time would be better suited to getting her son home rather than introducing her to his family members. Mum has her own friends, who scrum around her in support.

The AFP sends a psych up to Moore Park, and we assume this is for our benefit. At the end of the first week DFAT provided a psychologist and she was brilliant, spending time with each of us, including an entire day with my kids to see how they were coping. She went through how we would likely respond to Nigel's absence, drawing up a chart with the emotions we would experience if this took a month, six months, a year. We scoffed at that. There's no way this could go on for that long. But it was very sobering when she discussed how we'd feel if he *never* came home. Silence fell on the room, broken by Mum. 'Well, I am completely optimistic. Nigel will come home.'

This AFP psych, however, is awful. It's like having a creeping Jesus in the house. She watches us all the time and closes her laptop quickly whenever any of us go downstairs, like a nerdy kid in an exam, preventing the rest of us dunces from cheating. It makes us feel like we are doing something wrong. It turns out she's primarily here to assess the mental health of the AFP staff but she's also clinically appraising us as NOK negotiators.

Since I'd taken the first call from Adam and hadn't cracked under the pressure, the QPol guys were happy to have me continue in the NOK negotiator role. Mum and Dad suffered pretty badly in the first few days so the two things together appeared to make me better qualified for the role. As I understand it, QPol did a quick assessment when they got in the door and were happy with me taking calls, and so started going over negotiator strategies straightaway.

The AFP psych completes her critical assessment, and I get the gig officially. We've also discussed this among ourselves. Ham's name was thrown in the ring but we decided against this because he's a bit of a hot-head. Matt knocked back the role – he felt he wouldn't be able to answer the questions quickly enough as he is a write-things-down-and-ponder kind of person. Over time Mum probably could have done it, but she was too upset at first and thought she would likely abuse the captors. Dad couldn't do it; he's just a basket case at the moment.

Time becomes very fluid. There is one week that feels like three but then whole passages of time will disappear quick as a wink. The AFP negotiators are on a fortnightly rotation. I ring an AFP contact high up the chain to ask if certain negs could be rotated back after they have had a spell away from us. I've had to tell so many newbies about our family tree, repeating the same information over and over, and it takes at least a week for the freshly arrived negotiator to assess my ability. By now I know what I'm capable of and it shits me that every two weeks I have to prove myself all over again.

The officious woman on the other end of the line says that this would be very difficult because they don't have a 'negotiators division'; the negotiators come from all different areas of the force. They have other workplace commitments so can't be moved up here on my request. As well as that, they have families and lives. *Yeah, well, so did I, once upon a time.*

The woman tells me my concerns have been duly noted, and

says that if they can rotate previous negotiators back on the job, they will.

Around this time it is decided that Adam's name is actually 'Adan'. Someone higher up must have figured this out, and the negs pass it on to me. This is what I'm to call him from now on. 'Adam' is not a Somali name, so I must have misheard him.

Not long after this happens, the AFP guys move from Bundaberg to the Villas, the local holiday accommodation units at the northern end of Moore Park, about a kilometre from Mum and Dad's place. Initially, we had two negotiators and two intelligence officers here in the house. After the Creeping Jesus leaves us, the intel guys are rostered down to the Major Incident Room (MIR) at Brisbane. It seems they don't need to be up here at the house, and that we really shouldn't have been getting wind of the intelligence coming in anyway.

The two negs remain our conduit to the action, but our calls from the HTs are less frequent than Lorinda's. They are now coming in between five days and a week apart. The contact is painfully sporadic, and one of the negs suggests I call Adan to speed things up.

'What? No! I can't do that!' I am so terrified at the thought my gag reflex starts going. Bile fills my mouth. My skin feels prickly all over. *Oh no, I'm going to vomit all over Mum's kitchen bench in front of a federal cop.*

I know it makes no sense to be this terrified at the mere thought of phoning Adan, but the calls are shit-scary. It's not so much what's said, more that it's so alien to me that I'm dealing with someone like Adan in the first place. For some reason, calling him is one step more frightening. I just don't want to make a decisions for fear it is the wrong one.

In the end I don't have to make that call because Adan rings me.

Every call follows a structure: I try to obtain a proof of life, then I establish if Nige and Amanda are still being held together, and follow this up with a question about their welfare. Finally, I defer all money discussions to Nairobi, telling Adan, 'You need to talk to Mark; he is organising the money for both our families.'

As time goes on my strategy document gets longer. It's a case of having a response ready for anything Adan says to me. I have moved on to 'active-listening techniques', adding to the negotiation 101 course that the Feds ran me through.

As well as this, I need to ask questions to gain intel – probing but not too probing. I need to 'attend': avoiding jumps from one topic to another or interrupting makes Adan believe I am listening to him. This apparently contributes to trust, and allows the negs to collect information about Adan. I have to 'hear' what Adan is saying, recognise what has been said and commit it to memory. This is no easy feat as he talks fast and is quite often completely incomprehensible.

Ideally I should summarise the conversation and repeat the main points back to Adan at the end of the call. This is almost impossible as there is quite a lot I haven't understood, and there's often no warning that the call is ending. As soon as the conversation is over for him, he just hangs up.

There's so much to keep in my head during these conversations. But the loudest thought of all is, *What if I fuck up and say something wrong and Nige ends up dead for it?*

Wednesday, 17 September

Ham rings early in the morning. 'Alley cat, check out your Google alert. There's a video of Nige.'

'Video?'

'Yeah, yeah, video.'

'What, like news footage?' I'm a bit slow as I'm still waking up. Ham's been getting up early for work and has got in the habit of checking out the Google alerts while he's having his morning coffee.

'Nah, there's a video of him and Amanda. She's in a hijab and there's armed gunmen all around them.'

Shit! Now I am hearing him. My mouth turns dry. Horrific images, ones that can never be blotted out, of Daniel Pearl's execution and scenes from *Black Hawk Down* flash to mind. I bolt to the office and switch on Mum's computer. The noise rouses Mum and she comes into the room.

Josh and Ian, our latest negs, can tell something is up and hit Google too. All information the negs pass on to us must first be approved by someone higher up, but our family moves much faster than bureaucratic machinations.

Josh is cluey enough to have picked this up. He's on the phone to Canberra immediately. He's no magic eight ball but is preparing himself for the twenty questions he knows he's going to get from us. Josh is very young and very buff. My kids love him and Jacinta's friends – who are all of thirteen – flirt outrageously with him. Ian is an old-school policeman. He would have been a fantastic small-town cop; he's compassionate and picks up nuances quickly. He's one of the few negs to have worked on an international kidnapping case before this one (in Africa, but unfortunately not in Somalia).

We avidly watch the video. It becomes almost a game to pick out something that no one else has noticed.

'Does anyone recognise the clothes?' Josh asks.

'I don't know, Mum, are they Nigel's clothes?' The hijab isn't nearly stylish enough to be Amanda's own. Her body and feet are covered but we can see Nigel's feet. They're clean; he's either recently had a wash or isn't anywhere with bare earth. He's got his sleeves rolled up and we can see his wrists. We can't spot any ligature marks so he's not been cuffed or cable tied.

Then we pause the video to look at a still of his face. Okay, his head isn't shaved and he's grown a beard – no shock there. He came back from Ethiopia a couple of years ago looking way scruffier than that.

'Can you see his teeth? What's his mouth look like?' asks Mum. Nige has a great smile and has always been vain about his teeth. We all had buckteeth as kids and were subjected to years of orthodontic torture in the form of braces – and not the cute little stick-on coloured ones with attachable diamantes, but the great grey all-encompassing ones that made you look like Jaws from the James Bond movies.

Nige's face looks clear, a bit pale – he hasn't had much sun by the looks – but no split lips, no swelling, and he looks well nourished enough. So does Amanda. Nige actually looks more pissed off than scared; he's picking up small pebbles and flicking them off to one side.

The courtyard looks clean of shrapnel and there are pot plants all around them. Surely this means they are somewhere relatively stable? Who's going to the trouble of looking after house plants if there is constant fighting and mortars going off around them? The dudes with the guns next to Nigel are pretty frightening. It's so hard to watch someone being nonchalant with a gun in their hand.

Growing up on the farm, we had it drummed into us just how dangerous weapons are; we only ever dealt with 22 or 4.10 rifles – relatively genteel ones, with gleaming oiled-timber butts. I wouldn't even use the .303 because the kickback was enormous and would leave me bruised from shoulderblade to armpit. The guns these kids are holding are big ugly automatic uber-scary weapons.

The guys with the guns are all tall and lean and have juvenile physiques, so it looks as though the gang is made up of youths. I can't decide how I feel about them; they look too young to be evil. It's completely outside my realm of understanding that one group of people can potentially do something torturous and hideous to another. I know it happens – I'm not an idiot – it's just that where I live, within my community and my country, this is pretty much unknown. I'm so unprepared for this scenario that I can't condemn the kidnappers.

We ask Josh about Al Jazeera, who broadcast the video. A family friend of ours, Julie, knows a reporter who works for them.

Julie looked after us years ago when Mum had to go into hospital during harvest time, and Dad had four kids under six years of age in the house while he was out working. Julie looked after us for a couple of weeks; she'd only just finished school and we loved her to bits. Mum and Dad have maintained contact even though we have all moved around. The AFP says it's already been in contact with Julie as Dad had put her partner, Madji, up more than once to assist us with translation – he had negotiated the release of one of his family members in a kidnapping in Jordan. He speaks fluent Arabic.

We hear nothing back in regard to this from Canberra for another few weeks.

The video is a mixed blessing. Nigel is alive and neither of them looks any worse for wear. We ask for info about where the video came from and how it was released, but we don't get it. More than this, though, the video puts it all into perspective: Nige is in deep, deep shit.

Nigel
The Filthy House
around Friday, 12 September

Within a week of converting, we get another visit from Old Mohammad and the older Abdullah. It's not to give us religious instruction – they inform us we're going to make a video. Memories surface of Daniel Pearl and Douglas Wood begging for their lives surrounded by armed men. My heart is in my mouth, but I try not to betray any fear.

Amanda asks why they want to do a video. According to Abdullah, it's to document our conversion; in it we will have to answer five questions. They plan to put the video on the internet, as has occurred when other people have converted to Islam. We're taken out into the courtyard, where they have set up a single-seat lounge chair under the tree. Then they dress us up as if we are their dolls. I am in a long-sleeved shirt, with jeans rolled up to my shins and the Muslim headscarf draped over my head. Amanda is in a hijab and abaya.

It turns out to be neither seriously threatening nor objectively documentary – it is pure propaganda. I get to go first. The first question is relatively simple: I'm asked why I became Muslim. I give them a predictable spiel, but each question becomes more difficult. Trying to be natural and sincere, but thinking on my feet, I blurt out each answer.

The final question is: 'What would you say to people who identify Islam as an extremist religion?'

I feel like saying *people misconceive Islam as extremist because of groups like the one we are being held by now, ironically validating that stance.* Instead I say, 'Islam is the religion of peace; it is a simple and easy religion to learn. People who say this are ignorant and don't understand our religion. They are scared by Islam because of their own shortcomings.'

Abdullah seems satisfied with my responses. Amanda swaps places with me and is made to jump through the same hoops.

Though we're happy to get back to the room after it's all done, both of us are dreading the fact that it will hit the internet. Even though I've withdrawn from her recently, Amanda helps to quieten my concerns: these people wouldn't know the first thing about uploading something onto YouTube. We agree that making the video widely known wouldn't help their cause; if it became general knowledge that we'd converted, surely they wouldn't get a cent?

My relief is short-lived. Not long after, the whole gang turns up again. Abdullah, our religious teacher and the bearer of bad news, tells us to prepare a script, though we're told exactly what we should say. We are marched out to the courtyard, and my entire body tightens when I see what they have ready for us. We are forced to sit on a mat while four of the young guys stand behind us, their faces completely obscured by their head scarves, and all of them packing weaponry. I find it cowardly of Ahmed and the other guys in charge. They spout their bullshit about Jihad and honour, yet are obviously too spineless and paranoid to risk being identified – using the grunts to do the dirty work. I feel like slapping the young guys and telling them to wake up. They're being manipulated, just like us.

I suddenly realise what is actually happening. This will be a show of force to terrify our families. Now they're going down this path, there is every chance they'll make a third video, documenting our brutal deaths. I'm trying to stay calm but I feel like a caged animal. With Ahmed and his little posse standing behind the camera, we read our statements: we are being held for ransom as we have been accused of working with the occupying forces; we ask our governments to intervene so that we can be released.

One of the more senior guards, Joseph, talks at the end, reading from a piece of paper in Somali; the only words I can make out are 'Canada' and 'Australia'. Filming the statement takes no longer than a few minutes, but all I want is to get back to our room. They make us wait on the ground while they stand around reviewing their handiwork. Eventually we are allowed to leave. I'm happy to be alone with Amanda, but I know our little cameo is about to hit the news.

Saturday, 13 September

In the evening Jamal walks into our room, AK in hand and his ammo belt across his shoulders. He tells us to pack our things; we are about to be moved.

'What's going on? Is everything okay?'

'No problem, don't worry, quickly, we go in five minutes,' he replies coolly before leaving.

We start throwing our things together. About thirty minutes later we're marched into the courtyard and ordered to sit. All of the young guys are completely kitted out, ready for battle. My mind races off in all directions; I'm trying to divine what's coming next. Amanda and I comfort each other, repeating that we are going to be okay. We watch the almost-full moon slowly rising in the jet-black sky, wishing it were under different circumstances.

It seems to take forever before we are pushed through the front gate into an awaiting car. I'm terrified about being out in the open. I grasp for Amanda's hand as we are pushed into the backseat. A boy sits on either side of us. I'm desperate to believe that we are being moved to another house. Other thoughts crowd in: they could be handing us over to another group or simply going to kill us. The unknown is torturous.

The car moves forward slowly, gathering speed. After a few minutes we travel through a market area full of people. It looks apocalyptic: shanty-style corrugated-rooftopped shops line the road and cooking fires dot the edge of the street.

Amanda's grip tightens every second. Past the built-up area we turn down a sandy track, and after a short distance we come to a stop. Captain Yahya gets out, unlocking two large metal gates so the car can drive into the courtyard of a house. The gates slam closed before we're pulled from the car. We're marched up the stairs of the verandah and into a dark hallway. Our new room is at the back right-hand corner of the house.

There's no electricity so it's hard to get a sense of the surrounds until they bring us a torch. The room is much larger than our last one, maybe 5 by 8 metres, with a window on each of the exterior walls, and a tiled floor. There are two new 4-inch foam mattresses up against the walls, still in their plastic wrap. It will be a relief not to have to sleep on a filthy wafer-thin mattress any more.

The bathroom is at the end of the hallway. There is no door, just a thin curtain, and that first night the bathroom is absolutely crawling with cockroaches. A bonus is that in it is a western-style toilet and shower, but the plumbing doesn't work so we have to use water from a bucket to both flush and wash. There is also a small vanity, and a large window about 6 feet off the ground. The cockroaches have made their way down the hall into our room, much to Amanda's disgust. We're ordered to go to sleep. To fend off more roaches I close the doors and jam the plastic covering from the mattresses under the bottom edge, hoping it will stop them from entering.

The Light House
Sunday, 14 September

In the morning we get a better sense of the house. Both of us are unhappy about our new jail cell, even though it has more space and light. Abdi and the other two have also been moved during the night and are now in the room next to ours, closer to the front door. We start communicating to each other by knocking on our adjoining wall.

When we are allowed outside later that morning into the L-shaped courtyard, there's more disappointment. It's a concrete jungle. Gone are the leafy green trees; now there's only the heat, sun and glare from the whitewashed compound walls.

Both Amanda and I are unsettled by the move, being ripped so suddenly from a place we had become accustomed to, all our small routines thrown out. We set up the room so our mattresses are on opposite walls, about 3 metres apart, both of us using our nets more as a deterrent for the cockroaches than the mozzies.

The window on the back wall of the compound looks out into the yard of another house – well, not a house so much as a tin shack – we occasionally see people come and go. Seditious thoughts cross my mind about trying to contact the neighbours, but these are quickly quashed when the guys explain that we're surrounded by Al-Shabaab. We're told that if anyone tries to take us by force, our captors will kill us.

From our room we have a view out over the tops of rooves and trees, and I can watch birds flying and the sun set every evening. It is a form of escape. The other window looks onto a house that is just over a metre away. Diagonally opposite is the window of the neighbours' house, and the boys are always checking to see if it is locked.

A small alleyway runs between the houses and the light coming in is reflected off the white walls.

We settle in but I can't shake a morbid feeling. Amanda finally pulls me up, giving me a stern talking to – she doesn't remember me ever being this quiet; I've always been a gregarious person. I know in my heart I am blaming her for our situation. I try to fob her off but she won't let it go.

'We're in this together; we have to support each other. You're the only person I can talk to and you are ignoring me.'

It's a hard pill to swallow but I know she has every right to kick me up the arse. I'm being a moody little prick. I have no one to blame but myself for the situation I'm now in; Amanda didn't force me to come here. I apologise, and it's like a dark cloud has been lifted. This is a wake-up call. Wallowing can only lead to despair. We're a team and we need to keep sharp and positive.

Thursday, 18 September

I have been constipated for days and my stomach has started to distend. When I finally force myself to go, it's like I'm tearing myself a new arsehole. Then I notice the blood in the toilet bowl. When Jamal next comes in, I try to explain my problem. We play charades; I slice at my wrist and enact the squirting of blood before pointing to my bum and motioning like I'm taking a crap. He looks completely dumbfounded and tries to leave, but I won't let him go. Amanda now gets in on the act, taking my red sarong – to symbolise blood – and flapping it behind my arse while I make farting noises. Jamal finally clicks and races out of the room, returning with Captain Yahya.

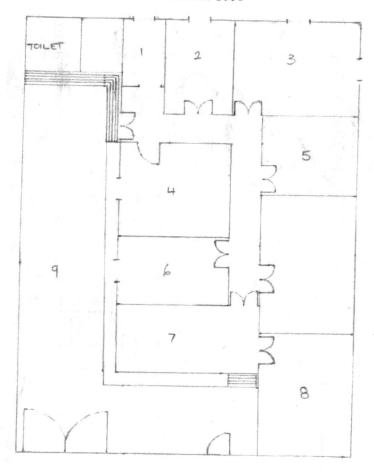

The Light House

1. Bathroom
2. Nigel's room after separation
3. Amanda and Nigel's room
   before separation
4. Kitchen
5. Abdi and the drivers' first room
6. Abdi and the drivers' second
   room
7. Verandah
8. Weapons hold and Captain
   Yahya's room
9. Courtyard

Mistaking my problem for diarrhoea, they bring me a litre and a half bottle of water containing sugar. They force me to skol the whole thing. As soon as I finish, I can tell it's all going to come racing back up. Jamal takes me to the toilet where I throw up the lot.

When I'm brought back to the room, Captain Yahya seems concerned. A thought strikes: *If they believe we're extremely sick, they might let us go.* I lie on the mattress, exaggerating my symptoms. Yahya says in stilted English that they will get medicine from the market. After eating breakfast, I put my fingers down my throat to force myself to vomit but it only makes me gag. Amanda is much more adept at it; she learned how to do it as a teenager. She brings up the contents of her stomach onto the floor next to me.

Lying on the mattress, she bangs furiously on the door to get their attention. While our hope for an early release doesn't pan out, our diet improves. Later that afternoon Old Mohammad arrives with a smorgasbord of food and medicine. There are cans of Coke, pieces of fried fish, a huge bowl of salad, an array of fruit and a mixture of drugs from Panadol to anti-nausea tablets. Amanda is grateful for the tablets, which are basically sedatives and help her to sleep.

The call to prayer is actually useful as it breaks the day into segments. After first prayer at dawn, we sleep more, getting up around nine. Making it to Asr prayer (between mid-afternoon and sunset) is our hump, after that we get a flask of tea and that signals we have made it through another day.

Praying is a chore but we try to time it so someone will see us doing it. Sometimes Amanda just sits back and watches me go through the process. This worries me. We are playing a huge bluff already and if someone were to walk in, there'd be hell to pay.

We've given each of our captors a nickname so that we can talk about them safely. Ahmed becomes 'M&M', not to be confused with the rapper Eminem, even though we're sure he thinks of himself as a gangster. His protruding front teeth and bulbous head lend him his name 'Monkey Man', which we've abbreviated. Adan we call 'Snaggle' in reference to his missing front tooth, and Ali was 'Evil Eyes'. Abdullah, our supposed religious teacher, is 'Romeo' as in *Romeo and Juliet* because he is so captivated by Amanda. Old Mohammad is 'Donald Trump' as we're sure he is the one financing the whole operation. Captain Yahya, having worn the same underpants since the start of Ramadan, we call 'Skids'. It has a double meaning as he is the one who always pulls the brakes and determines what we can and can't do when the head guys aren't around. Joseph, the big guy, exercises every morning, or tries to, by lifting an invisible dumbbell. We call him 'Mr T'. Young Mohammad, all of 5 foot 2 with his small pinched face, is a little dictator so we dub him 'Mao'. Young Abdullah we give the unfortunate name 'Donkey', not only because he is an ass but because this is the worst form of insult for a Muslim. Amanda names Young Yahya, with his good looks and toned body, 'Mr Handsome'. We're yet to find good fits for Jamal and Assam, Ismail's replacement.

They all have their different roles to play. M&M, Donald, Snaggle and Romeo run the show and make all the decisions. Skids is in charge of the house and the boys. Mr T and Mao are the lieutenants but don't really have that much to do with us. Donkey, Mr Handsome, Jamal and Assam are our guards and bring our food. These last guys are the ones we interact with most often.

We try to communicate with Abdi as best we can, knocking on the walls whenever we think it's safe. They are being kept like animals; they're in the dark all the time and only allowed outside to use the toilet.

Whenever I come back from the bathroom, I use sign language to communicate with Abdi, who can peek out the crack of his partially open door. We check with each other that things are okay, simulating sickness when we're unwell, rubbing fingers together to signal money, and holding fists to ears to suggest talking on the phone. It's extremely risky. If they catch us, Abdi and the drivers will surely take a beating. This communication is short-lived, though, as they are soon moved to the room on the opposite side of the hall, closer to the front door.

Towards the end of the month we get a visit from M&M and Donald. They ask us to join them on the verandah for a talk. They don't reveal much about the negotiations, but we do speak with them about the day we were ambushed: they knew there were four foreign journalists staying at Hotel Shamo, working in two teams. They knew exactly how many vehicles each team was using and our movements. Their intelligence was spot on. I am sure that someone set us up, but exactly who is an unanswerable question. Trying to place blame now seems irrelevant anyway. They had expected to capture the two *National Geographic* men, and were surprised to see a man and a woman.

We ask them what they planned to do with the other two had they captured them. Ahmed says plainly, 'We were going to kill them both.' I have no idea whether it's the truth or not. I think about the *National Geographic* guys; I know Pascal has a newborn baby. It's good to picture him with his family and not dead somewhere on the side of the road. Even so, I can't quite shift the feeling that fate has screwed me over.

One afternoon in late September I am sitting in the courtyard, washing our clothes. I am doing Amanda's too as she doesn't have the strength and isn't feeling well. The boys chide me – as a woman Amanda should be washing *my* clothes.

I tell them, 'You have a lot to learn about the world outside. Why should she have to wash my clothes? I wash her clothes because it is a nice thing to do.' They shake their heads, bewildered at my response.

Donald explains to them that western culture is different; when Somalis emigrate to western countries, the women usually divorce their husbands because they're lazy. I think Donald's on to something. I watch these guys sit around on their arses day after day; the place looks like a pigsty and they seem just to dump waste where they stand.

Thursday, 25 September

Around a month after we were taken Amanda informs me that she hasn't had her period. She thinks she could be pregnant. We had talked about her boyfriend back in Iraq, a Jewish guy who works as a journalist for one of the big American publications. It is a huge concern for both of us, knowing that it is definitely a case of wrong time, wrong place. She needs to take a pregnancy test.

Ahmed arrives in the afternoon, and I leave our room to give Amanda an opportunity to talk to him. I'm sure he'll think that I am the sperm donor.

On returning, I'm happy that he doesn't point the finger at me. His only comment to Amanda is that it's strange that a Jew and Christian could be together. It's an uncomfortable subject; I'm pleased when he finally leaves.

One of the boys brings in a small plastic container to Amanda the following day for a urine sample. It takes two or three days for the result to come back via Donald – both Amanda and I are ecstatic that it's negative.

Kellie
Newcastle
Mid-September

It's clear that the kidnappers' claims that they won't accept money from the families are lies. We're very aware that we might have to get our hands on substantial amounts of cash. Heather and Geoff have an investment property in Brisbane and they've been discussing selling it for some time – it needs a new roof and now they've retired and all the kids have left Brisbane, it's served its purpose. With Nigel's kidnapping, it becomes more urgent to sell Rouen Road. It's an easy option in many ways – everyone else is mortgaged to the hilt and no one has power of attorney for Nigel so his property can't be sold. There goes Heather and Geoff's superfund.

Nicky
Moore Park
Wednesday, 24 September

It's week five and the DFAT and AFP contingents arrive en masse. Both Matt and Kel, and Ham and Amy come up to be present at the big debriefing. We ask to tape the conversation but we're told no. They have someone taking shorthand, but those minutes are never presented to us.

The meeting takes place upstairs around Mum and Dad's dining room table, fully extended. There are twelve of us and six of them.

On 8 September I had talked to DFAT's James, and after lots of to-ing and fro-ing and but not a lot of plain English, I was able to establish that the department had received ministerial approval for the provision of financial assistance to our family if and when we request it. That is, they've agreed to give us a loan to help us pay the ransom. Although no one from DFAT ever uses the 'R word'.

We are not seeking the loan immediately but we do want to know the amount available to us and how much they think we'll need to secure a release. It distresses all of us that resources might be available which the negotiators over in Nairobi have not been authorised to use.

We ask the meeting whether the Canadian is family doing something similar. Are things going to be held up if our respective governments have different approaches to making funds available? What is the government's expectation with respect to reimbursement?

Most of these questions are skimmed over or skirted around using public service jargon. We all scribble notes down madly and look up at them, saying, *Huh? What does that mean?* Only the easy stuff gets answered and it becomes clear that these guys are masters of spin.

Then we ask a question we've put to them numerous times.

'Will DFAT discuss with its Canadian counterpart about providing the Lindhouts with similar payment options so that the onus for Nigel and Amanda's release does not solely rest on Nigel's family?'

James's response is nonsensical.

'The AFP is constantly reviewing the strategy but I don't think things will have changed since I last talked to them so all I can undertake with you is your need for an immediate response, but I just caveat that by saying the minister is overseas.'

How do you go about trying to construct a counter-argument when someone speaks like that? At the end of the meeting Mum, Dad and I ask to speak to James alone and off the record.

We tell him that if we were to sell Mum and Dad's house in Brisbane, we could raise up to US$100K. Prior to the meeting we had offered US$25K by selling off our shares, bringing the amount available to US$50K. Once Rouen Road sells we'll have a total of US$150K that the negotiators can use to bring Nigel home.

As a result of Adan now calling Nairobi more often than Moore Park, the negs get rotated down from twenty-four-hour to shifts from 2 p.m. till 2 a.m.; that is, the time the calls have traditionally come in – daylight hours in Mogadishu.

'What happens if I get a call outside those hours and neither of you are here?' I ask the negs.

'You take and tape the call. Work methodically through the strategy points and get someone else who is in the house to call one of us.' *Christ, how is that for being thrown in the deep end without being told how to swim?*

'But,' I argue, 'didn't the proof-of-life call come in outside those hours?'

'Yes, but since then all other calls to both here and Canada have come within those hours,' comes the response.

Great, I think, *just ignore that the anomaly phone call was the most important one to date.* The negs' phone numbers are put on our mobile phones and on speed dial on the landline. We put in a new line upstairs, seeing as Mum and Dad's phone is now dedicated to taking calls from Somalia. Quite a few friends get a shock when they ring the number and receive a very polite response from me telling them they are being recorded by the AFP. The adrenaline surge I get from these false alarms makes me feel like a brown snake producing shot after shot of venom.

So now I could be taking the calls unassisted. I guess the overtime budget must be looking pretty insane down in Canberra and cuts have to be made somewhere, and that somewhere is Moore Park. *But this is an international kidnapping case*, I can't help thinking.

A call from Adan comes in – outside the shift hours predictably enough – and Mum quickly phones the negs to get their arses down to the house. Meanwhile, I calmly breathe, press the record button, and get on with my role of NOK negotiator – dealing with some slimebag across the world who is holding not only my brother but me and the rest of my family to ransom.

Nigel
The Light House
Tuesday, 30 September

The last morning of the month Jamal comes in with a small plate of dates. He's all smiles and high spirits. He exclaims, 'Eid *whan axin,* Eid *whan axin.*' We ask him what it means and he tells us that Ramadan has finished. Both Amanda and I had thought that Eid was tomorrow. He tells us we have to break our fast before we join the boys in a special prayer in another room.

Everyone seems extremely happy and there is a buoyant feeling in the house. We are even brought sweets and some freshly roasted goat.

They allow us to sit outside in the early afternoon, at which point Amanda tries to get Romeo to pass on an Eid card she has made for Abdi and the drivers. Romeo basically screws it up and puts it in his pocket, again showing us exactly where we stand. We're to have no contact at all with our colleagues.

Eid is meant to be a three-day celebration, with family, friends and feasting but there isn't much for us to celebrate. The thought of entering another month is agonising, but both of us are focusing on the date that Ahmed has promised to release us.

OCTOBER 2008

Team Brennan

Kellie
Newcastle
October

Up at Heather and Geoff's, phone calls from Adan come and go. Nicky is directing all talk of money back to the Nairobi negs. She has been told to tell Adan that a family friend in Nairobi is doing all the negotiations for Nigel and Amanda. There have been a couple of POLs but less and less information is coming through to us. We take this as a good sign – the negotiators in Nairobi seem to have convinced Adan they are the people to speak to. Nic is still training morning and night – I figure by now she is probably better qualified and more experienced than all of the AFP put together.

A pattern has emerged. Each night the Feds in the house come upstairs to update the family about what's going on in Nairobi and what progress – if any – has been made. Then we get a call from Moore Park with the latest. After that, the family writes down loads of questions to be answered by either the AFP or DFAT, which are mostly ignored or glossed over. This goes on and on and on. It seems that whatever the family feels is important – the questions we need answered – the AFP thinks is trivial. For example, I ask for a copy of the AFP information guide to Muslim culture so that the family can understand some of the customs. The logic being that this might be a way of understanding what Nige is experiencing, and if we can plot the holidays and holy days, we'll know to expect less communication during those times. Even though the AFP agrees this is a good idea, the information never comes our way.

Each day Matt and I email our questions for the nightly meeting, but rarely do we get answers. It's either because they just don't know, or they can't confirm the little they do know. We're constantly being told they will get back to us. No one seems to be making any progress – we're all treading water.

Too little information is more damaging than too much. The family takes to the internet with a vengeance and email each other whatever we can find. Sometimes we work ourselves into a frenzy.

Not a day goes by when I'm not reminded of Nigel's kidnapping. When I drop the kids off at school, everyone wants to know the latest titbits. It's consuming my life. Meanwhile, the story has been out of the press for more than a month and already to Joe Public the name 'Nigel Brennan' has been forgotten.

Nicky
Moore Park
Early October

Lorinda, Amanda's mum, has been getting many more phone calls than us for a while, though it takes us a while to realise it. News of a call travels from her home in Red Deer to Ottawa, then from Canberra to Brisbane and then on to us. The content of the calls is vetted at every stage to the point where we get no detail at all. After constantly questioning the AFP about it, I eventually get to the bottom of why this is so. The information isn't being passed on to us because we don't have the right security clearance.

Finally, we break this cycle. After I get a call from Adan, I take to phoning Lorinda to give her a full run-down of the conversation. When we are told that Lorinda has had a call, we ring her for the same thing. We get so much more information this way than through the official channels.

In almost all of his calls to Lorinda, Adan indicates that Nigel is not well. It's almost impossible to manage Mum over this and the only government help I receive comes from Gayle. The AFP and DFAT believe it's a tactic the kidnappers are using to pressure the family. While I understand this, it's not much help when it comes to dealing with an increasingly distressed mother. One of the negs, Kath, is particularly good with Mum; she comes from a big family and actually gets how ours work. I manage to get her rotated back a number of times. Mum makes her a beautiful quilt for her birthday, and then we never see or hear of Kath again. It seems that as soon as any emotional attachment is formed – and we're not playing by the AFP's rules – the neg is pulled forever.

Mum is insisting that if Nigel is sick, we need to get medicine to him. It's a question we put in writing: Can we send over a care package? We finally get a response via the negs during one of our more heated evening family updates.

'Nairobi will endeavour to identify Nigel's illness and get medication to him,' is what Canberra quotes to the negs, who relay it to Mum.

Reading between the lines in the evening updates, there seem to be problems with the Nairobi communications. The information is very sketchy and we have to piece it together. There is no interpreter in Nairobi. Adan is not contacting a new guy called Dave, who is the primary negotiator – he's taken over from Mark. Apparently there was some language trouble that led to a mix up with a $20K amount put to the kidnappers at the end of the first week. This will come back to bite us.

Mum suggests that since Adan is so difficult to understand, surely we would be better off talking to him in his own language via a translator. The AFP and DFAT outright refuse to even consider the idea. Again, it turns out to be a security issue. I'm surprised at this – surely interpreters for the Department of Immigration are professionals who have some neutrality.

The explanation we are given is that if the conversation is in a language the analysts don't understand, they might miss nuances. The calls have to be transcribed, which takes time, and then the AFP needs an interpreter to interpret the interpreter. This is the single most spectacular *Yes, Minister* moment we have had to date.

The government's opinion seems to be 'if we can't do it, no one can'.

Monday, 6 October

Lorinda gets a call from Adan with a ten-day deadline. If we don't pay before then, the HTs will kill Amanda and Nigel. So 16 October is D-day. The AFP is convinced this is a scare tactic. As a result Nairobi is calling their bluff: there will be no communication with Adan until the seventeenth.

Mum is not in a good place about this: what if they're wrong?

She is close to begging the negs downstairs to get in touch before then.

I am warned that if a call comes in to the NOK phone, I should be prepared for increased pressure from Adan. I do a lot of threatening practice-calls, using all the deflective strategies I've been taught.

Friday, 10 October

We get a visit from our new Senior Investigating Officer (SIO), Brian, from the Brisbane MIR. He's the one overseeing what seems to be known as 'Operation Mane'. I only discover this via a bit of paper left sitting on the desk. I have no doubt I've broken some sort of code, but I'm also gleeful and a little bit proud of my sneakiness. Brian is accompanied by Canada's negotiating guru, Gordon.

The meeting starts promisingly. Ham and Amy join us via conference call but the line is shocking, so they hang up and have to rely on my notes to update them later on. I ask about the current situation. Gordon explains that 'at the moment the HTs have all the control and nothing can be accomplished until we reverse the situation. We need to develop a rapport with them. We have to change the dynamics. We have nothing in common with these people culturally, and the lines of communication are dismal; all these things slow the process down'.

Ever practical, Mum asks, 'Okay, how do we continue to build rapport if you keep changing things?' She's referring to the negotiators, both the ones dealing with us and the ones in Nairobi.

'We must move people in and out to keep them at an optimum level,' he replies. 'We have strategies to replace people; experience has shown that optimum performance falls off over time. The hostage takers view this as "our side and the other side". Any change of who he is talking to won't matter to Adan – he just views it as the "other side". They are going to get tired and worn out, and then we can condition the HTs to respond to us.' Adan has to interact with them as they are the only option he has.

Gordon turns to Mum, and I worry that we're about to get a 'let us bow our heads together and pray' moment. He says, 'We sympathise with the family because we are in your personal space, but the experience we have to draw from is great. We have an international group of negotiators working together on this; there is huge international assistance. This has never failed us. Take strength from this, Heather.'

Oh, he's good.

'Okay, if it doesn't matter who is on the phone, can we change the NOK negotiator?' I ask.

Gordon replies that it's better to keep one or two people consistent. 'We need to have the same people on this; this will help Nige and Amanda.' Just enough praise and some guilt to make me stay put. Like I said, this guy's good.

Our old nanny, Julie, who is a journalist and doco maker, has suggested that we look at placing an infomercial on Al Jazeera television, just as the Woods brothers did, to clarify that Nigel was in the country to show the plight of the Somali people to the world, that he is a good person and not an agent of the government. Dad broaches the topic and it gets a reaction from both Gordon and Brian, but not the one I was expecting.

It goes along the lines of 'Al Jazeera is not your ally. These are not our kind of people. Family appeals right now would be contrary to what we're doing. Nigel is not a humanitarian worker; he's a journalist. It could backfire on us. There are lots of people missing in Mogadishu; why would Nigel and Amanda be more important than anyone else? They may not have released all of the [ransom] video, there could be a lot more to it. Al Jazeera is not your friend. We're westerners; they have no use for us.' He is certainly forthright.

I'm trying to digest this information and write it down at the same time, a challenging task. I'm trying to work out if Gordon is implying that Al Jazeera sympathises with the hostage takers and showed the video for that reason. Dad has spoken to the Woods family and didn't get that impression from them. I thought it was a respected Arabic station. While I'm thinking through all this, the conversation has moved on to the actual video.

'. . . the video had a message for the family and a message for the government. They have tried to emulate an al-Qaeda video. There are men with guns in the background. Amanda is in a hijab and Nigel is barefoot; they rehearsed all that. Nigel is bored and, as Lorinda said, the message that Amanda has sent to her is that she is okay – she is sitting upright and staring straight ahead.' This is fantastic information, exactly what we needed from them when the video *first* came out last month.

We all clamour to tell Brian and Gordon what we noticed in the video. Gordon stops us all talking over each other. 'Our cultural expert viewed the video and picked up things like that, and what we did was *not* respond to the video, and this was a deliberate tactic. If we'd reacted, it would have changed everything. These people have a plan and expect a reaction. We have to give them something they don't expect.'

He then has a dig at us calling ourselves 'Team Brennan', and reminds us that everything we're doing is about Nigel and Amanda; it's not about us and how we're coping with it. It's only ever about them.

'We're the people who are trained to bring them home. We

might seem like cold bastards, but we are the experts and you need to trust us. It's not Team Brennan, you should be calling it Team Nigel; that's what they're doing down in Canberra.'

We all look at each other sheepishly.

Then we spend some time discussing how unhappy we have been to date about the communications black hole, and how we get no responses to any of our questions. I am especially burred up about some dick down in Canberra recommending to the negs that 'communication via email cease between family members'. This little comment was accidentally included on one of the evening family talking-points sheets. The sheets are essentially a breakdown of the points the negs plan to discuss with us, updates and so forth. Someone in Canberra apparently objected to us emailing Kel and Matt and Ham and Amy the discussion points and telling them about the latest developments.

Apparently the negs were meant to have amended 'cease' to something more family-friendly, but overlooked it. No matter what the AFP said or how it said it, communication between family members would keep occurring. We were all in this together. The thing really getting up my nose was that both Brian and Gordon were treating the discussion points as some sort of state bloody secret.

'There may be things on the papers that are strategic and could cause problems,' says Gordon.

'That's complete bullshit,' I say. 'Let me get my diary.' I glue all the daily reports in there. I want to prove to Gordon they didn't contain any classified information. This man is held in very high esteem but it's taking all my will power not to swear at him. I mean *really* swear – 'bullshit' doesn't count.

Brian takes the thread. 'The purpose of these notes is strategic development. Some things we want to shield from you. These notes are considerations not final sign-offs . . . this relationship will mature but we need to ask for your trust.'

I glare at Brian. This is the biggest steaming pile of horse shit I have ever heard. It's an arse-covering exercise.

As the increasingly heated discussion goes on, I'm flicking through my diary.

'Ah, here's one. Twenty-nine September: "No contact with Adan in Nairobi. Continuing to wait till he calls; nothing new to report."'

Gordon continues, 'Your emails are on a public server; there's no confidentiality.'

'This is an email to our family; it's not like it's some highly confidential piece of intel,' I spit out. I want to add, *because we don't get told that sort of thing anyway.*

'Nicky,' says Brian, 'the sheets contain information regarding our strategies and what is going on. We can get scrutinised later on regarding our operational security. You're missing the big point: you are the core family.'

'No,' I say to him, just ahead of Mum. 'There are two other family members.'

Gordon continues, 'You have no control over information after you pass it on. We are trusting you, but if you're sending it on a public server, it's not safe.'

'We would much rather you discuss things over a landline phone – not a mobile,' says Brian.

'Well, that's not going to work,' I say. 'Ham's only got a mobile.'

'Well,' says Gordon, 'perhaps you can discuss options for calling him on a public payphone at a certain time.'

What planet are these people from? Ham lives 15 kilometres out of Grafton – 15 kilometres away from the nearest payphone.

The conversation peters out with no conclusion.

Dad then raises the fact that Brian's predecessor had asked the family to supply a figure for how much they could afford to contribute to the release amount. 'I called Amanda's folks to see if they were asked the same thing. I got a generic response: that they were putting all their faith in the RCMP and their government.' We'd actually given Dad a bit of a roasting about the lack of information he was able to extract from Lorinda, accusing him of being a bloody pushover. Ham then rang them back to get a simple yes-or-no answer: do they have anything to contribute? The answer was no. I think they've been told Nige and Amanda can be released without a payment.

Brian responds with, 'There will be things that will happen at different ends at different times. How Lorinda deals with money is her own private business. Let's move this into the future; let's not look into the past.'

'Can I raise an issue?' says Gordon. 'Here is the most important thing about a ransom. Paying the ransom is not always the solution.'

'Do you have more information on ransom amounts that have previously been paid in Somalia?' I ask.

'From zero to in excess of a million dollars.'

'So, why don't we go in with more money?' asks Dad. So far we've only offered US$31K.

'It's a lawless society,' responds Gordon. 'Nigel and Amanda are a commodity. If other people in the country see them as highly valued then we risk them being passed on. Another group may say, "Get what you can for them and then pass them to us and we'll get more and give you some of it." If it were as simple as just paying ransom, it would've been done by now. That's why we're keeping it low.'

'But thirty-one thousand?' responds Mum incredulously.

Gordon replies, 'If we offered them more money, it wouldn't

work. Until they do something good, we can't offer them any more. They may say, "Give us another thirty thousand", and we can say we've got three thousand nine hundred dollars. That shows them we don't have much money. If we came in with, say, forty thousand, they would expect that we're rich Australians who can get two-and-a-half million dollars. We have to get inside their heads and reduce their expectations. If they think they can get more out of you, they will.'

This statement doesn't make much sense to me: I see bugger-all difference between thirty and forty thousand.

'We want to run them down until the only option left is to let them go,' says Gordon.

'There is nothing that you or we can do that will force harm on them. We need you to understand that. If they are harmed, that was in the kidnappers' minds the whole time. It could also be victim-precipitated; they might try to escape or attack them. It would not be the fact that Nic was hostile on the phone or we don't have any money. We have to ask you to understand this. The end game gets tough, especially for the NOK negotiators and that's when you need to trust us and cooperate. We may not have time for family conferences and such.'

The bit I cling to is that nothing *we* do will bring about harm. I've been scared all along of doing something that will get them killed.

I sigh and ask, 'How long do we wait? How long does it take before we get a resolution?'

Brian's answer is along the lines of dealing with averages.

Gordon's is, 'We just don't know when this will end, and we would lose credibility with you if we presumed to tell you.'

We have researched previous kidnappings in Somalia: they have lasted between six and nine weeks. We're up to week seven, and we seem a long way off a good result.

The conversation has pretty much exhausted itself – and us. At the end of the meeting when we have bundled ourselves downstairs to farewell everyone, Gordon places a hand on my dad's shoulder, shakes his hand, pulls him towards him and pats his back with a quick release. A bloke hug.

'I'm telling you now, Geoff, we will bring your boy home.' It's a touching scene and it brings tears to my eyes. Team Nigel needs to believe this is true.

Despite some dead-ends, we are all thankful that someone has finally taken the time to see us and tell us in some detail how this kidnapping gig will pan out. It's not until we sit down and read over our scribbled notes that we start to feel a little bit railroaded; admittedly, it's done with a velvet glove and good intentions.

I reckon if we'd had this guy talk to us from day one we would be like Lorinda – full of faith in the authorities – but we've been left in the dark for a little too long.

Tuesday, 14 October

The deadline of the sixteenth hits the media and we discover it, as usual, via Google alert. No warning from Canberra. They are supposed to be on this twenty-four hours a day, right? I ring Emily at DFAT. Her response is that she didn't know the family would want to be notified of every breaking news story.

Isn't she our media-liaison person? *What does she do?* I think, *Write polite little family statements and that's it?* If so, I want her job: all care and no responsibility. She said she wasn't sure if this would 'add to the stresses of the family'. I reply very tersely that I would rather know from her than log on to the computer and see headlines stating that Nige will be dead in a few days' time.

'Perhaps we need to ascertain and document what everyone's roles are, rather than what we perceive them to be,' Emily says to me. *Oh goody, more bureaucratic paperwork bullshit that just makes people look busy.* I can feel my blood boiling and have to get off the phone before I lose control. Surely someone in the DFAT office is hooked up to Google alert?

That evening the negs pass on from Canberra that it won't happen again. *Yeah, right, inshallah.*

Thursday, 16 October

I wake up on deadline day feeling like I could lose it at any moment. I spend the day eyeing off the NOK phone. I'm grateful it stays silent.

Monday, 20–Sunday, 26 October

By the twenty-first the MIR has moved down to Canberra. It's no longer the MIR (Major Incident Room); it's now called the ICC (Incident Coordination Centre). The move was announced on the seventeenth by the negs ('We need to look at flexibility and review the MIR in Brisbane. It doesn't have ongoing support for twenty-four-hour operation but we do in Canberra'); they were clear there was no room for discussion about it. Brian's no longer on the scene, and we have a new guy running the show – Ben. He called to introduce himself. The negs think pretty highly of him.

It takes a while longer for us to warm to Ben. We are all a little wary of new faces, especially those who come from the upper echelons. But there are indications that he's not a bad sort.

Around the twenty-fourth we hear that a lot of calls are going through to Lorinda from Adan. She has got him to take some new POL questions and has emailed them to him as well. She tells us he was reluctant until she became emotional; then it was like he wanted to placate her. She has also recieved a marriage proposal from the grub. How sleazy is that?

The strategy is now that Lorinda takes all calls because of her strong rapport with Adan. If I get a call, I'm to defer it to Dave in Nairobi.

Both Lorinda and I get a call on the twenty-sixth. It's a shocking line and the content of the call is bugger-all. Adan is talking really fast and he's difficult to understand. He is venting but not aggressively so. He has changed phone lines and is trying to give me the new number.

He says Amanda and Nigel are sick but it is not the same illness as before; last time they were sick in the stomach. I can make out Adan saying, 'I don't know the English word; they have itch. Amanda has eye illness, sore eyes.' Then he suddenly changes tack.

'Your husband, what does he do?'

I freeze. This is a fishing exercise.

'He, ah, he works with his hands on the land, you understand?'

I don't want to say he works on a farm lest Adan thinks the farm is a valuable asset we can sell. It's an asset but a fully mortgaged one, and I have no idea how to explain that to him.

Thumbs up, and 'nice save' mouthed by the neg next to me.

He then asks to marry me.

'Adan,' I say. 'I am very old. I am Nigel's older sister.' *Time to change the subject.*

'Adan, we have put a medical package together for you.'

'Ah, Miss Nicky, the money is finishing on the phone. Call me tomorrow. Call me on this number after 10 a.m. tomorrow.'

There's been a real flurry of activity: ten calls and two emails in the last four days. We are all getting hopeful that this signals the pendulum is finally swinging in our direction. I am not allowed to call back but Lorinda does and under Nairobi's instructions offers him an increased amount – US$35K. Adan then asks if he can marry Amanda. *Double yuck.*

Lorinda gives me a thorough run-down of her calls when I ring her. Adan is acting paranoid, claiming we are working with another group in Egypt. He's constantly saying that both Nigel and Amanda are sick, with some ailments that are the same and some that differ. Amanda's eyes are very bad, and she has no appetite and is 'dismoral' (we assume this means depressed); Nigel has a cough. Adan is pissed off with Mark and Dave in Nairobi, calling them 'liar men'. He calls them 'brokers' and seems to be really upset about being regarded as a broker himself. This is considered some kind of insult.

Lorinda eventually gets Adan's full name so we can send a care package to him. Lorinda asks if there is anything else Nigel and Amanda need, such as clothes. His reply is that they have clothes but she should send eye drops and for entertainment.

It's been about seven weeks since I spoke to Nigel, and we're all getting leery that we've had no POL since the video. Mum's away at the moment and her response to the recent activity is to tell Alli (the neg that's now on) that until she gets a POL she will not be nice. It doesn't matter how many phone calls are coming into Canada or Nairobi, 'I will hound them till I have a POL from my son.' Well, they can't say they haven't been warned. I feel a bit bad putting Alli on the spot like this as she's a good laugh and in the real world (as opposed to our bizarre reality where we are all living in kidnap land) she's the sort of person I would probably be friends with.

The day after this we get a call from Lorinda. Adan has spoken to the group finally. No POL. The group, he tells her, is angry and do not want to answer questions.

Reece has now swapped over with Dave, and is about to move to the Nairobi cell. There's not much love lost there. Reece is the one who whinged about the family emailing the discussion points, and now he's representing us. Dave introduced Reece to Adan and then came back home; his thirty days are up.

It takes a bit of effort for Reece to get onto Adan. When he finally does, he asks if Adan has taken the newest figure – $38 300 – to the group. Adan's response is that he is not prepared to discuss that low an amount. He finishes the conversation with 'if no money, you should find their bodies'. Charming.

So now Nairobi is 'renewing' its strategies. They do not want Lorinda or me to contact Adan during this time. Reece, I'm guessing, has a pretty reasonable idea that we are not happy he's representing us in Nairobi, but it appears he's an astute negotiator. He sends a thank-you note to us via the negs for an idea we had: to include gifts for Adan's children in the care package. We have sent them stuffed toys: a koala, a roo, a moose and a polar bear.

Thursday, 30 October

We have another fly-in, fly-out visit from DFAT and the AFP. It's a pretty ordinary meeting: A big chunk of it is about the health and welfare of the officers up here and in Nairobi. It has become apparent to all that the whole exercise is taking longer than expected and it's getting pretty costly. This is not actually said plainly to us; it's ensconced in phrases such as 'we have to look at where we are at in regards to negotiator strategies with other government agencies'.

They keep banging on about the reasons they moved the MIR from Brisbane to the AFP headquarters in Canberra. The ICC is purpose-built for operations; there, the SIO has instant access to the assistant commissioner and commissioner if required. The SIO can attend meetings with other agencies in person. Many of the personnel are based in Canberra and it's more reasonable for people to work from their home location. I hear the phrase 'availability of resources' more times than I can count. I'm wondering where this is all heading.

I can't believe I'm taking down this crap in my notes. I don't understand a word of it until I hear what I deem to be the death knell.

'There are workplace health and safety issues.'

You hear shit like that and you know something is getting wound down somewhere, and that we will not be getting any benefit from it.

The best information we get from the entire meeting is a break-down of the negotiator strategies in Nairobi. They are trying to find a third-party intermediary, a TPI, in Somalia.

They are looking at 'maximising opportunities for resolution other than Adan', we're told. *Christ, why can't they just say it in English?* They are looking for another spokesperson to talk to the kidnappers 'cause they don't think Adan is up to it.

Ben, the new SIO, is here in person and discusses previous kidnapping cases in Somalia. In the last seventeen years there have been forty-two UN personnel kidnapped. Forty-one of whom were successfully released and returned. One was killed, though this is unconfirmed; it's believed that was as a result of the hostage's relationship with a Somali woman.

'The releases were facilitated through the same avenues we are exploring,' Ben tells us.

Then James says something that makes my ears prick up: it is UN policy not to get involved in any payments. However, they have a long list of people they use to 'advance negotiations'. I think what James is telling us here is that *someone* is paying a ransom for UN hostages but governments and the UN deny it's them. How much must the final amount be if everyone's denying it's even happened? How do we find out?

After the meeting we hear the news that the NOK phone is moving out of Mum and Dad's place down to the Villas, a couple of kilometres down the road. I'm told that because the phone is in the Villas I should get more time at home. This doesn't really gel, as my on-hours are 3 p.m. to 3 a.m. I'm not going to walk anywhere at 3 a.m. so I wouldn't be heading off before about six in the morning.

Mum thinks this means she'll be left out of the loop and be fed less and less information.

The Feds have obviously given Gayle a mandate to convince Mum this is the right thing to do. Gayle is great, but, really, as if that's going to do the trick.

It is, however, cleverly sold to her as being better for the grand-kids. Gayle says there is the issue of the kids going downstairs and seeing the strategies up on the whiteboards.

'I've heard you calling the house "Camp Evans" and that's not good,' says Gayle to me. In all honesty, I thought Ham's nod to the US military base was pretty clever and I still think it's funny.

We are reassured by all that nothing is set in stone; we're told not to be afraid to say so if the situation isn't working. That's bullshit. Once something changes with this lot there is no going back – no matter how much they bang on about 'flexibility'. It's just the first stage of us being cut out altogether. We know it, but are powerless to alter it.

Nigel
The Light House
Sunday, 5 October

Ahmed's promise to release us weighs heavily on our minds – we're pinning all our hopes on it. With only a few days left until we reach that six-week milestone, he comes to visit. He doesn't give us much to go on, saying that they are negotiating with Nairobi but things have ground to a halt.

When Amanda pushes him about his promise, he completely backs down: it's not up to him – there are others who are running the show from behind the scenes. I see a spineless, weak, pathetic creature driven solely by a lust for wealth. I don't think I have ever detested anyone so much in my life.

I start to realise what Ahmed's broken promise means: money is really the only driver here and sooner rather than later they will lean on our families for the cash.

I know the situation Amanda's family is in; it's clear they won't be able to pay. I suspect it'll all land on my family. I'm sure they won't release me without Amanda, and I wouldn't allow that to happen. We've got ourselves into this and we're going to walk out of this shithole together.

Tuesday, 7–Wednesday, 8 October

We are uprooted again with only a few minutes' warning and no explanation. It's as terrifying as the last time, as we wonder whether they are about to execute us. We're bundled into the backseat and I notice the boys are edgy. We weave our way down the road, nearly getting dry-bogged several times. It feels like we've done a massive semicircle when we finally stop outside a row of compounds. I see the stencilled pattern on the wall and realise we're back where we started, at the filthy house, the one we were moved from three weeks earlier. We're ordered from the car into the street before being herded through the small front gate. We're escorted back to our original room.

Now I can see what a disgusting hovel it is. The damp smell of mould is pungent in the air, and our mattresses look grottier than ever.

Both Ahmed and Romeo come to talk with us after our colleagues have been brought to the house with the rest of the boys. They don't explain why we have been moved but reveal they're paranoid about Al-Shabaab trying to capture us. Ahmed says that a number of them live in the house next door and that we should be wary. They leave us, saying they'll be back in a few days. It's clear this is a step backwards.

Again the move disrupts our routine. To counter this I spend the next morning cleaning the bathroom for Amanda. It stops me trying to second-guess what's actually going on.

We've asked for playing cards but been denied them – they're seen as a form of gambling – so I decide to make a backgammon board and teach Amanda to play. I draw the board on the back of a piece of paper, and make the playing pieces from the cut-off ends of cotton buds. Too easy. The dice, however, is a different story.

I painstakingly carve Panadol tablets into cubes using the scissors, then mark numbers on each side with a pen. It doesn't take Amanda long to get the gist of the game and it fills the hours. We play surreptitiously, knowing this too is verboten. We have one very close call when Donkey bursts in unexpectedly to bring us water. I block his view for long enough so Amanda can hide the game under her mattress. He gets a whiff that something's not right and suspiciously looks around the room before leaving.

We don't have much else to entertain us – just the Qur'an and a number of other religious books. Their droney tone and dull text mean the books don't really stand up to repeated readings, although they go a long way in teaching us more about Islam and prayer. Amanda and I talk about anything that takes our minds away from this place. We speak at great length about our families, each other's current and previous partners and life in general. She met Mum and Dad in 2007 so she knows a bit about their situation. I know a bit about her family but have never met them. Lorinda and Jon are long divorced, and Jon has a long-term partner, Perry. All three get along very well. Jon has a terminal illness and his only asset is his house. Her mother has a chequered past and very few assets. As we explain the intricacies of each other's families, I am amazed when she tells me her mother was involved in a cult in Japan and was held hostage herself eleven years ago. My family looks quite dull in comparison.

We play the 'famous faces' game regularly, where the other person nominates you as someone well known and you ask yes-or-no questions to figure out who you are. I always pick sportspeople, much to Amanda's chagrin ('I fucking hate sport'). She talks incessantly about food and even tries to make up a food game, which I'm not so keen on. Our food has become so boring that to talk about chocolate and gourmet fare is torture.

Living in close confines with someone twenty-four hours a day for an extended period means you're faced with the warts-and-all version of the other person. Niceties quickly go out the window. Sometimes this provides comic relief. When one of us farts we giggle like schoolkids. Amanda's always protesting between fits of laughter, 'Spray your cologne! You're going to kill me.' It's a bit like the bond you have with your siblings. One pulls the other up whenever they're having a bad day.

We share everything, even the simplest things, who gets the bigger cup that day, or who gets to use the only plate and spoon. As time goes on, I'm happy for Amanda to have these little privileges, and I eat with my fingers from a plastic container lid. We also make meals for each other, trying to prepare something appetising with the basics they provide us. Papaya and canned tuna salad with onion is our signature dish.

Our colleagues are not faring as well. They've been held in terrible conditions from the very start, concealed in darkness twenty-four hours a day, their only respite being when they're allowed out to wash for prayer or go to the toilet. They are not being fed the same portions as us. I manage to communicate with Abdi in our doorways, and he uses sign language to indicate they need food. They're being held for no reason other than that they were in the car the day we were taken. Their future depends on us.

We think of a way to give them some of our tuna and fruit. First, we ask if we can go outside. I walk out with Amanda following a few metres behind carrying a plastic bag of food. Just as I make it to the front door, I drop my pen to distract the boys. Amanda puts the bag inside Abdi's doorway before quickly catching up with me. Both of us sit in the courtyard, our blood pumping with the risk of it, feeling anxious about how Abdi will conceal the evidence but happy to have been able to do something. It gives me a thrilling sense of power, being able to defy our captors and break the rules.

The time between visits from Ahmed and co. drifts from one or two days to around five. I hear Donald and Romeo's voices, but when I ask to speak to them, I'm told they're not here.

From our bathroom window we can look out into the back of the courtyard. One day I see Donald walk across the courtyard, going to wash his hands, and I bang on the door. Jamal comes in, looking frustrated.

'What do you want?'

'Jamal, I just saw Mohammad in the courtyard and I want to speak to him.'

'Wait,' he replies as he walks away. Minutes later he comes back.

'The Captain refuses them to see you.'

'Why?'

'I don't know; is Captain's orders,' and he leaves. Romeo comes to see us later that morning, asking why we're causing problems. He says they're busy negotiating with people in Nairobi and don't have time to spend with us.

The most difficult thing is not knowing what's going on with the negotiations. It's like being in jail without a sentence. We don't have a date to pin our hopes on, and there's nothing to work towards.

Monday, 20 October

In the late evening Jamal comes in and tells us to gather our things again. We've only been back at this house for around a fortnight.

We're marched into the courtyard, where the boys are all standing about with their weapons in hand. There's no moon tonight and we sit and wait in the pitch-black. Suddenly they order us to stand up; they rip our belongings from us, and push us towards the gate. I can't see a thing, not even the car until they force us into the backseat. It takes a few minutes before my eyes adjust enough to make out Romeo in the front passenger's seat; I'm relieved that it's him and not a complete stranger, but I'm still shitting myself.

Ahmed jumps in the driver's seat; Skids and one of the boys jam in beside us seconds before we lurch forward.

We hit the bitumen road and Ahmed accelerates hard as we swerve around potholes and pedestrians.

Amanda tries to talk to Romeo – 'We haven't seen you for a long time; what's going on? Is everything okay?' – and his silence only fuels our fear. We travel for a few kilometres and I try to get my bearings. It's not until we drive into the courtyard that I recognise it as belonging to the light house and we're pulled from the car and put back into the same room as last time.

Half an hour later we hear Abdi and the other two being escorted to their room. We can hear Ahmed talking with Skids out in the courtyard for a long time before there's the sound of the front gate opening and closing. No explanation from Ahmed tonight then.

Tuesday, 21 October

We're woken by the metallic clang of our flask of tea being dumped on the floor. Tea is the one thing we look forward to, but today neither of us is in a rush to get up. Last night's little jaunt has wiped us out. A short time later our morning meal is delivered but we barely greet Jamal before going back to sleep.

At around 9.30 a.m. we're shaken awake by four of them, carrying guns. Something has changed.

Mao angrily orders us to stand as Donkey, Mr Handsome and Assam look on. I feel exposed, standing just in my jocks, and ask what's going on. Mao brings his finger to his lips. My blood feels like it's pooling in my feet as I realise that whatever is about to happen, it's not going to be good. Assam takes my camera bag and starts rummaging through it, and I'm helpless as I watch these criminals take away every last thing of value, right down to my loose change. Once he's finished, Assam starts on Amanda's bag, taking her bracelets, camera, iPod. Nothing is missed. We try to reason with them but we're curtly told to be silent. I'm actually surprised that this hasn't occurred long before now.

I quickly pull my jeans on while Assam puts our stuff into a plastic bag. Donkey and Mr Handsome move towards me, and I think I'm about to be hit but they brush past, taking my bed and mosquito net with them. We're about to be separated.

Mr Handsome grabs my arm and frogmarches me out the door. I'm not even given the chance to say goodbye to Amanda. I'm moved into the small room between Amanda's and our toilet. I try to ask Mr Handsome what the problem is. He's always been quite accommodating, and seeing that I'm shaken, he says, 'No problem; is okay.' That's all very well but he gives no reason for us being split up.

Donkey then walks in with Mao, and he sums up the situation very succinctly: 'If you try to talk to each other, we will kill you. Your door is to remain closed at all times; you must knock and wait to go to the toilet. Understand?'

Ahmed will have ordered this, once again showing his cowardice by leaving it to someone else to do the dirty work. Knowing that Amanda is now alone fills me with dread.

Mao points towards the wall, referring to Amanda. 'Amina,' I say. He nods then raises his finger to his throat, slicing across it. They're going to kill her. 'Why? She is Muslim,' I say, trying to hold back the tears. He shakes his head, his sinister grin widening as he rubs his fingers together to imply money then in English says, 'No money, no life.' Then he turns on his heel and walks out with Mr Handsome.

Now I'm completely alone. It takes me an hour or two to steady the ship, telling myself that I have to stay in control. I'm determined to stay strong for the both of us. My spirits lift as we begin knocking to each other on our adjoining wall.

A few hours after our split, I hear Amanda knock for the bathroom, and as she moves past my door, she nudges it open and flicks in a note. I scurry across the floor, picking up the note and hiding it in my coin pocket. My heart races. Donkey's threat from hours earlier is still swimming around my head. When I think it's safe, I read her note, with one eye kept on the door.

She tells me that she is okay and we have to stay positive. She tells me to focus on the beautiful things that surround us, explaining that they are there; I just have to look for them. She says we should leave notes for each other at the back of the window ledge in our shared bathroom. She will knock once, then twice, then three times in short succession when she's left a note, telling me to do the same after I have read and destroyed it by flushing it down the toilet.

We communicate two or three times a day, backwards and forwards like we're having a conversation. We change the position of the notes from the windowsill to the vanity, which has a small light at the top with a cover that slides off. There's less chance of the boys finding the notes there. We use the paper from our diaries, tearing pages out carefully so that it's not obvious.

A few days after our separation we get a visit from Donald. He talks with Amanda for a long while before coming to me. He explains that we've been separated because in Islamic culture it is forbidden for a man and a woman to share the same room if they aren't married. I ask him if we are allowed to see each other, and he says it's not up to him; he'll ask Skids – he is in charge of the house. Donald gives me all of five minutes of his time, saying that Canada is causing problems.

I'm guessing that the real reason they've split us is so they can apply pressure to our families.

I tell him about Mao threatening Amanda's life, saying that as a Muslim, this surely can't be allowed.

'They are just boys. I will speak with them and tell them this is forbidden,' he replies.

That conversation with Donald has dire consequences.

Two or three days later, spying out the door, I see Mao and Donkey going into Amanda's room, guns in hand. I expect to hear her scream but instead it's eerily silent. I stand at my door, waiting for them to come out. When I see Donkey leave, I rip open the door and knock. Our eyes meet as I ask for the toilet. He looks like a madman as he flicks his head, motioning for me to go. I then ask him in Arabic, 'Mushkila? Problem?' He slowly shakes his head before walking off.

Later Amanda writes me a note about what happened. They ordered her to lie face down on the bed before putting an AK47 to the back of her head. They played Russian roulette with her as they cocked the gun and pulled the trigger, getting cheap thrills by terrorising her. I can't believe how quickly our circumstances have deteriorated. I feel responsible; I thought telling Donald would give her some protection but it's backfired.

To distract myself I start exercising for two hours every day. I haven't done any form of exercise for the last two months – there didn't seem much need because I had Amanda's company and I didn't think we'd be in here for long. Now that it looks like negotiations have stalled I begin flogging myself doing Bikram yoga, Pilates and push-ups. The rush of endorphins takes my mind off things for a short period and helps me to think clearer. I put my mattress up against the wall so I have space to stretch out, stripping down to my jocks before working myself up into a sweat.

One day Assam and Donkey come in while I'm mid yoga pose, and ask what I'm doing. I explain that it's an ancient Asian exercise, which strengthens the mind and body. They ask if I will teach them how to do it. I'm undecided, having to overcome my hatred for what these people are doing to us, but in the end I see it as an opportunity. I want to show them I am a real person, and there are times when we're together that I see glimpses of humanity in them.

Like all boys trying to impress each other, they show off and over-exert themselves, at times losing their balance and falling into the wall or onto the floor. When this happens we all break into laughter. I end up teaching them for more time than I spend exercising, showing them how to hold each pose and the proper breathing techniques.

As time goes on they relax around me. Assam, the youngest in the group, and I begin to connect. I'm sure Amanda must hear the laughter and wonder what the hell I'm doing. Maybe she thinks I've come over all Patty Hearst.

Assam takes over the role of bringing in my food and often sits and talks afterwards. I enjoy his company – he has a vibrancy about him and compassion for my situation. He willingly tells me things about himself and his family, and I learn that he is the most knowledgeable in the house about Islam. He tells me that his mother was killed by a thief when he was very young, and on hearing this I burst into tears, thinking of my own mother, who I may never see again. This makes Assam incredibly uncomfortable and he asks me not to cry.

'I'm sorry,' I say and tell him I feel for his loss.

Our interaction goes a long way to staving off boredom. Other times I turn to the Qur'an, reading it for hours on end. I ask Assam endless questions about the things I can't understand, using it as a tool to break down the barrier between captor and captive.

A lot of my day is spent standing by my window, as the light allows me to read. On one occasion I notice three small geckos on the window ledge and think of Amanda's advice to focus on the beautiful things. I feed them fruit and watch them chase insects, the electric colours on their heads mesmerising. I even find myself in conversation with them, which makes the time pass even though it almost convinces me I'm going crazy. I try to immerse myself in anything I can so as to not think about my family or what's going to happen to me.

Our existence has changed dramatically since our separation. Skids has revoked many of our privileges, one of the most important being the freedom to go outside. This is now only granted every few weeks so we can wash our clothes. I can no longer see the sun, sky or trees from my window, only my four blank walls. It's a momentous occasion when I am allowed outside. Seeing that the sky is still blue allows my mind to fly high above the compound walls and far from here.

Amanda and I continue to communicate by sending notes of reassurance and support, informing each other as best we can about what's going on.

I panic when my pen begins to run out of ink, asking Amanda

via a scratchy message if she has a spare one she can leave in the bathroom for me. She does, but it too has a limited lifespan. I devise a cunning plan to get a pen from the boys, singling out Assam as the easy target. I have to give him a good reason to get me a pen. I ask him if he will start teaching me Somali and Arabic so I can converse with the boys who don't speak English. I also say I want to learn the pronunciation of certain Arabic sayings and Surahs (chapters) of the Qur'an. Assam is happy to help me, saying it's good that I want to learn.

After telling him my pen is kaput, I ask him if he will buy a new one from the market. He baulks at this, saying he will have to ask Skids first as he doesn't have any money. My heart sinks. I know that Skids already has us on a short leash and I'm sure he won't agree to my request.

I will just keep chipping away at Assam and hope for the best.

NOVEMBER 2008

It's kidnap month in Somalia

Kellie
Newcastle
November

Same old, same old. The NOK cell has been moved to the Villas, and the phone calls are coming less often. Heather has started on a downward spiral. One minute she's good, the next minute she has Nigel in the grave.

Matt, along with every member of the Brennan family, is growing anxious about the decreasing amount of information we are receiving from the AFP and DFAT regarding the case. On one hand, he's incredibly frustrated. On the other, he is a breath of fresh air. Recently, every word that has come out of his mouth is kind and lovely. It's not that he wasn't like this before, but this is an extreme version. My mum and dad ask what has happened to him.

Matt has always had a positive attitude, but this *new* Matt is outstanding. I am wondering how long New Matt will stay. Will this bubble pop and splatter all over the place, leaving me to clean up the mess? To my surprise New Matt seems to be here for the long haul.

November is exhausting. I am catering every weekend, working from our home. The kids are in the way, and I yell at them for being in their own kitchen. I am up to my eyeballs in bridezilla bullshit.

One Saturday night I climb into bed after getting home late from a wedding, and think how wonderful it is to experience the calmness of a sleeping house. I have another big function the next day so I welcome sleep. I am awoken by Matt – it feels like I have only been asleep for five minutes.

'Kel, Kel, look at this!'

I look up to see Matt standing in the doorway, blocking the diffused light coming from Stirling's room down the hallway. Matt is naked and I can see the silhouette of his body and chest hair.

'Look! Look at this!' He starts moving his arms up and down. If he was lying in the snow, he would be making snow angels; giant, hairy, naked snow angels.

Now I sit up in surprise. Matt hasn't been able to lift his arm since being diagnosed with Parsonage–Turner syndrome in July, just before Nige was kidnapped. PTS is an extremely rare nerve condition that stops the use of the shoulder, tricep and bicep muscles. Matt usually can't lift his arm more than 10 centimetres away from his body. He has trouble dressing himself, he can't drive and he can't use a knife or fork. But now he is extending his arm up to just above his shoulder. I am gobsmacked. It's 4 a.m. but Matt doesn't come back to bed – he's off to see if he can lift something heavy.

It's amazing what a positive attitude can do.

Nicky
Moore Park
Monday, 3 November

I'm escaping for a few days. At the start of the year I said I'd go on school camp with the Grade 7s, and I kind of expected this all to be over by the time it came round. There is no way I'm not going – it's Jacinta's year group and they are an awesome tight-knit bunch of kids. It will be sad when they head off to different schools next year and start developing rebellious streaks.

Camp is a jam-packed celebration of finishing primary school: four days of theme parks, swimming, night tours, ice-skating, roller-skating, as well as a trip down to Brisbane and back. They will be shattered by the end of it – I am from just looking at the itinerary.

The evening before I head off I get a call from Adan.

'Nigel is sick, can't get awake, lots of sleep,' he tells me.

'Well, Adan, there is a care package waiting for you. Reece has sent you a package and it's going to Mogadishu. If Nige is sick, it's your responsibility to get the medicine to him. You assured both Lorinda and me that you were looking after them.'

I'm being a bit pushy and the conversation could go either way. But Adan's not aggressive with me, instead he deflects.

'The group is angry and need money for security.'

When I ask if he has seen Nigel and Amanda recently, Adan tells me that he 'is a long way from them now'. After the call I add a new point to my strategy notes: 'How can you protect them for me if you are not with them?' It gets written in my notebook and jotted down on the sheets of butcher's paper that cover the walls. Wallpaper most odd.

AJ has been training up as NOK with me and doing mock calls as well. She'll be on duty while I'm away.

The first day of school camp packs a lot in. We board the bus at 6 a.m. and finish with a night tour of Saint Helena, the old penal colony just offshore from Brisbane. We are back at camp and in bed by midnight. Day two is just as crazy. We've been at Dreamworld all day, keeping tabs on thirty-odd kids. Some try to drag me onto rides to see if they can make me spew. They know I get hopelessly carsick so it becomes a real battle of wills. I am not going on the Claw; I plan on keeping my dignity as well as my lunch. It's madness to think managing this lot is preferable to dealing with Adan. I'm having so much fun.

We all spill into Subway for dinner, and then head off to the ice-skating rink. I haven't been ice-skating since I was eighteen when a boyfriend down in Sydney took me – I got completely saturated and spent the whole time on my arse. In spite of that, I was up for a laugh and wanted to try it again, fully expecting to be even worse now as I'm not as flexible at forty-ish. AJ calls me just as I'm about to don my shoes, and instead of skating, I spend the whole session curled up in the bleachers, freezing, simultaneously trying to watch the kids and talk over the loud disco music that accompanies the ice games.

Nairobi has contacted Canberra, who passed the message on to the negs. Our care parcel has gone into Mogadishu. It's waiting for Adan to pick up and take to the kidnappers. I am delirious with excitement. Maybe the airport has security cameras, or there is a tracking device in the box.

When I finally get off the phone, I'm walking on air. It's ridiculous to get so pumped about a parcel, but I'm overwhelmed by the idea that Nige will be getting our letters and some toothpaste. Books and medicine. This shits all over the letters from home on *Survivor*.

Nigel
The Light House
November

Amanda has two windows with metal shutters in her room. The one that faces west, looking out into the next-door neighbour's yard with the tin shack, has been permanently closed by the boys. They're obviously concerned she will try to communicate with someone. The other window faces the same wall as mine.

Our windows are only metres apart and it isn't long before we realise how good the acoustics are. As our roof crosses over with next door's and the two houses are close together, the noise gets trapped and this makes it easy for us to hear any conversations taking place in the other's room.

We start whispering to each other out our windows, and the new rule about keeping our doors closed works to our advantage. I have become attuned to the sound of bare feet coming down the hallway and to the sight of shadows at the bottom of the doorway, which give me enough warning to stop the conversation. My Qur'an is always in my hand, a prop for if someone walks in unexpectedly.

We knock on the wall near the window to indicate that we want to talk. At the start we'd spend no longer than a minute or two but as time goes on we get bolder and conversations last up to ten minutes. Assam comes in each night to close the windows, and then we knock to each other.

My work on Assam pays off. He comes into my room looking sneaky but pleased, and unrolls the cuff of his jeans to reveal a pen. He's bought it from the market and tells me I should keep it hidden – he didn't ask Skids' permission. It isn't an ordinary pen; it's a big four-colour one like I had in primary school with red, black, blue and green ink. Jackpot!

Assam gets straight down to business, teaching me the basics in Somali: please, thank you, can I have water, can I go to the toilet/shower, can I wash clothes, do you speak English, can I talk with the Captain. This gets me goodwill among the boys, the non-English speakers particularly, and they all laugh at me as I struggle to pronounce each word.

Around this time I get a disturbing message from Amanda: 'I am getting unwanted visitors'. I immediately think of Donkey, the evil little bastard. He's the one who seems to love making her life hell. I talk with Amanda about it via our windows. I don't ask her to state exactly what is happening, part of me doesn't want to know, but she confirms that the culprit is in fact Donkey.

We devise a plan. If I hear anyone in her room, I will bang on my door to attract the attention of the other boys. The problem is that Donkey manages to slip in and out without a sound. I'm sure he must be gagging Amanda as I don't hear so much as a peep. At one point I catch him leaving her room, scurrying down the hallway like a cockroach. I feel helpless and guilty for not being able to prevent what's happening.

Amanda tells Ahmed about the situation on his next visit, and begs him to remove Donkey from the house. But perversely he says she needs four witnesses before he can do anything. She says the same thing to Donald when he next comes, and his response is shocking. He asks Amanda if she enticed Donkey, and if she liked it. These people are complete psychopaths.

I have no idea what I can do to stop it. Out of pure frustration I scrub the bathroom as it's the only place Amanda has privacy. I now stand guard when she showers as I've caught Assam lying on the floor, ogling Amanda through the curtain of our bathroom.

With the bathroom spotless, it becomes apparent we have a little friend: there are fresh rat droppings evident each morning. One evening I hear Amanda knocking for the bathroom, followed by her shrill scream. I'm dying to race out to make sure she is okay but think better of it as I hear a number of the boys run down the hallway.

The following morning she explains what happened. The rat had startled her by running over her foot. Her scream had brought Donkey and Skids, who put a gun to her head. She was told to shut up, that they will kill her if it happens again. The only thing in my power is to check the toilet each morning and night, making sure the rat is nowhere in sight before telling Amanda it is safe for her to go.

We take big risks just to see each other. When Amanda goes to the bathroom, she knocks on the wall to indicate she's on her way back to her room. I creep to my door, opening it quickly so that it doesn't squeak. Then we hold hands and whisper to stay positive, that everything is okay. The pain is there to see on her face. She is also having a lot of trouble with her eyes. They've become infected because she has to clean her contacts in filthy water. Without her contacts, she has difficulty seeing anything. The boys don't give a shit about her health and have ignored her repeated requests for contact-cleaning solution. She's got fungus growths around her nose and top lip. I can feel her embarrassment as she tries to hide them.

Becoming Muslim not only means having to pray five times a day and read the Qur'an. I have to greet other Muslims in the correct Arabic manner, eat and drink with my right hand and wipe my arse with my left. I'm told to cut my hair, shave my moustache and grow a beard. The kinkier side of the religion is that I'm forced to pluck my underarm hair and cut my pubic hair; this is enforced by the younger guys. I'm no longer even able to choose what my own pubes look like.

The one thing I can't tolerate is being clicked at. Whenever I knock to go to the toilet, rather than walking down the corridor the boys now just lean across from their spot near the front door and click their fingers repeatedly. How lazy is that? At times for no reason they shout, 'Wait!', then after a few minutes rapidly click their fingers, signalling for me to go – they love riding their little power trip.

We aren't allowed to go to the toilet after they've locked the front doors so at night I have to piss into a water bottle. It's humiliating. I flout the rules during the day, sneaking back and forth to the bathroom, and giving them the two-fingered salute behind their backs. Jamal catches me in the toilet a few times but I explain that I was desperate and couldn't wait. He wags his finger, but his big smile always tells me he is going to let it slide.

Nicky
Moore Park
November

The parcel has still not been picked up. Reece spoke to Adan, who was seriously pissed off. Adan says he went to pick up the package on the fifth but the courier said he didn't have the correct documentation. Apparently at Mogadishu airport you need more that just a name to pick up a parcel. Go figure. Reece has scanned the list of documents required and emailed it to Adan. Nairobi is not making this easy for Adan; it's no wonder he is suspicious of them.

When Reece next speaks to Adan, on the fourteenth, the parcel has still not been picked up. Reece asks about Abdi, to whom we've also sent a care package. We have asked the AFP on a number of occasions who is paying ransom for him. His wife and father in Somalia have been very vocal about his incarceration, as well as about Nigel and Amanda's. The response has so far been that this is not our problem or responsibility. Our focus needs to be on Nigel and Amanda; Abdi's family will have to look after their own. Dad in particular is dissatisfied with this. It creates conflicting emotions for all of us, considering the fatality rate of Somali journos in these circumstances is high.

Reece asks Adan when he will next see Nigel and Amanda, and Adan's reply is that he 'is not close to them; they are in a nomadic village far from the city'.

On the twentieth we get confirmation that the parcel has left the airport. They can't confirm who picked it up. When Adan rings back on the twenty-eighth, he says his children got the toys but he doesn't mention if he passed on the medicine or our letters. We just have to hope that, if Nige and Amanda really are sick, the kidnappers will give them the medicine – surely drugs would be expensive. I think I'm correct in guessing there are no multinational pharmaceutical companies churning out penicillin in the Dish. Then again, who knows? Their economy is so screwed up: guns are as cheap as chips and they are all imported.

When I get back from the camp, AJ heads down to Brisbane for a bit of a break. The girlfriend and the mother – it's very much *Meet the Fockers* territory. By the time she gets back, she has decided it's time for her to go. My kids love her, as do I, and we are all sad to see her leave. But it's an act of self-preservation, and I understand that. Like the rest of us, she must have lingering doubts about

Nigel meeting up with Amanda; they do, after all, have a history. AJ's relationship with Nigel is relatively new and it just can't sustain his protracted absence. She says she needs to cut ties with us too. My response is to cling together and not break away; it's hard to realise that other people work differently. She's decided she has to move forward and I know it's the right decision for her to make.

Nigel
The Light House
Thursday, 20 November

We get a visit from Donald. As usual, he spends time with Amanda before coming to see me. He finally walks in with a large plastic bag in each hand. After greeting me, he says they have received a care package from our families.

He hands over toiletries, medicine, a crossword and Sudoku puzzle book, three books (Khaled Hosseini's *A Thousand Splendid Suns*, and Hemingway's *The Green Hills of Africa* and *The Snows of Kilimanjaro*), a *Newsweek* magazine, an eraser, sharpener, pencils and pens and two notebooks, a box of digestive biscuits and a five-pack of underpants, one pair of which has already been removed. All of these things might have been touched by someone in my family. I can't control myself and start to cry. Donald chides me for being upset, and I dearly want to tell him where to go. I hold my tongue and put my emotions in check.

I sit on my mattress and spread out everything I've received. I have never felt so unhappy to receive gifts. The sheer quantity scares me – by the looks of it we are going to be here for a long time. But more than that, it's a sign they have begun negotiating directly with our families – none of this makes sense otherwise. This is our families' reward for doing something the gang wanted them to do.

After we hear Donald leaving the house, Amanda and I talk. Her care package is the same except she now has a pair of prescription glasses – a godsend – Nelson Mandela's *Long Walk to Freedom* in two parts, a book on stress release and some sanitary products.

As the day goes on, we begin questioning whether all of this stuff has in fact come from our families. Amanda's drugs are from a Nairobi pharmacy, so maybe the embassies in Kenya had a hand in it. It's a relief to think our governments are still somehow involved and I'm praying they are helping with the negotiations.

My days of obsessively reading the Qur'an come to a halt now I've got better offers. Whereas time had been moving at a glacial pace, the puzzles and books make the hours and days whiz by. I know it's a fool's paradise but I'm enjoying not thinking about the real state of things while it lasts. Amanda is ploughing through her books, reading the first part of Mandela's story in two days.

We begin swapping books, secretly leaving them for each other in the bathroom, and being careful to conceal them in our rooms. We're sure that the boys know exactly what we have each received.

Nicky
Moore Park
November

November, it seems, is kidnap month in Somalia.

We become quite blasé about stories of piracy in Somalia. I'm vaguely interested in the price the boats are released for, but in these cases the crew are incidental; it's all about the cargo. It's only the land-based kidnappings in Somalia where the people are the commodity.

Early on 6 November aid workers with the NGO Action Against Hunger are taken from Dhusa Mareb, 500 kilometres north of Mogadishu. I discover that one of the Kenyan pilots has dual citizenship with Australia. The internet really is an amazing tool. James doesn't appear to be too thrilled that I've found this out.

I suspect that the NGO will have insurance and they will be using a kidnap and ransom company to get them released. K&R companies are risk-management organisations, underwritten by insurance companies, which negotiate the payment of ransoms and the subsequent release of the captives, among other things. I guess the issue for the NGO is that paying a ransom sets a precedent. They are an aid organisation that feeds some of the world's poorest refugees in some truly inhospitable places. If they don't go into a country because they could be kidnapped, who will? I understand their dilemma. We didn't stop discussing the precedent situation for the whole first week: if we pay a ransom, it sets a precedent for every other Australian who gets kidnapped. But what is the price of a life? If money is what it takes to get Nige home, then it's very easy for me to step off the soapbox.

Then on the twenty-sixth an English journo and his cameraman are kidnapped up in Bosaso while doing a story on piracy. They are full time with the *Sunday Telegraph* so I am assuming they have insurance. But I'm sure the experience is just as scary whether you are insured or not.

The day before, Reece confirmed that Adan had delivered the package to Nigel and Amanda. Reece asked for a photo of them with the care package for proof. Adan responded that he has no camera. Reece wanted to speak to Nige and Amanda so he could hear for himself that they'd received the packages, but Adan said their demands would have to be met first.

After that interaction, communication between Adan and Reece seems to drop off. We're getting scant information at the nightly meetings and start to question what is going on. I am not calling Adan as part of the strategy to force Adan to negotiate directly with Reece. The reply we get after much pushing is, 'avenues of enquiry are ongoing in country'.

I get a phone call from Ben indicating that something is in the pipeline and that Reece is getting in contact with a source in Nairobi. This source is, in the near future, going to meet with the hostage takers. All this, yet it's been so long since we've had a POL.

While this is a constant concern for Mum, it is now seriously fucking with Ham's head and he is getting vocal about it. Ben or James just hear him out, offer some platitudes and hang up.

'Alley cat, this whole thing is spinning out of control,' Ham says to me. 'This lot have got no idea what they're doing, and we're the guinea pigs in the cage they're experimenting with.'

I'm not entirely sure he's wrong about this.

Friday, 28 November

When Ben and James fly up to Bundaberg, we finally get some information about the most recent strategy.

There's a third party who the AFP believes has influence; that is, someone who's high up in one of the clans. He wants to assist; he wants to work for the good of the country, and there is no outside motivation (read: money) for him to do the job.

The negotiators decide the best option is to send him in with all the money we have – US$250K.

Ben gets back to us to say that 'the source', who is called TPI 13 (which stands for Third Party Intermediary), met with one hostage taker. There is 'no corroborating evidence' of the meeting, but they have no reason to doubt him.

'The increased offer was met with a refusal and TPI 13 was told to leave Mogadishu. The outcome of which is that to date we have had no feedback from the group or Adan,' we're told by Ben.

'Can he go back in?' I ask. James says he's unsure whether the third party can be used again: 'TPI 13 went in with his son and they were threatened. In fact, there was physical violence involved, so that makes it unlikely that TPI 13 would display a willingness to go back in.' Ben seems uncomfortable that James has given us this information.

James is quick to reassure me, though, that the offer was only made to one of the HTs. There may be a change of opinion when the offer is taken back to the group.

'This is not a short-term strategy. We will have to see how long it takes for the realisation that US$250K is the highest offer they're going to get.'

The new source is offering the lot, everything we have – all of our money. We have jumped from US$35K to US$250K. In fact, it has been done first then discussed with us afterwards. *Hello? Hand waving in the air! Whose money is this?* It's clear that they've done something that Gordon specifically recommended we not do. Gordon had told us our amounts should go up in small increments so that the kidnappers would come to the conclusion that we don't have the full three million dollars.

This is the complete opposite of the government's stance up to this point. The about-face makes me feel very unsettled but I'm not ballsy enough to question it. These guys are the ones with the intel; they know what they are doing, right?

So why the radical change of strategy? James says we have to be aware of other kidnappings. We had to offer the full amount before higher amounts were paid and precedents set.

What's worse is that Ben says that while the team in Nairobi is hoping for a positive outcome, it's doubtful that this offer will secure Nigel and Amanda's release. *What?!* Is it any wonder that when I relay this to Ham, it starts him off on a typical rampage: 'This mob of useless c***s couldn't organise a fuck at a bar with a fist full of fifties.' Obscene, yes. Funny, well, yes for us, less so for the Feds and DFAT.

What the team in Nairobi is hoping this will achieve is that the group will now contact Adan, and he will contact the Nairobi cell, confirming that this is a legitimate offer. If he contacts me, I'm to refer him to Nairobi as per my usual instruction.

Reece is spending time on a strategy that indicates to the HTs that the $250K is not a ransom, it's costs. The idea behind this is that the kidnappers will hopefully see ours as being separate from other cases: we differ from the multinational cases in that we are willing to pay for the HTs' expenses. By rewording 'ransom' as 'expenses' this will help create the impression that this is all the money we have, which it is. *Which boffin came up with this? They are kidnappers*, I want to scream, *they don't give a shit what we call it. They call it what it is: a cash ransom.*

Ben goes on to say that due to the time period that's elapsed, Nairobi believes they are negotiating with 'high-end criminals who are only interested in money'. I rest my case.

I get that. I also get that we have just thrown all our cards on the table and we don't have any money left to take it further. We are going to have to find some more cash from somewhere. Canada's not putting anything up, and we are acutely aware that the Australian parliament goes into its final sitting for the year in three days' time, after which they all head off on their Christmas break and don't reconvene till February. If we want any assistance from politicians, it has to be now. Everyone else gets to live their lives and Nige is stuck in god-only-knows-what conditions over Christmas.

It takes time to get this strategy right in my head; it's bizarre. Reece over in Nairobi is actively not contacting Adan. So we've sent someone in with a new offer that's been rejected and we are not contacting Adan either. Okay, so are we waiting for Adan to challenge me to see if this is a genuine offer? And if this is the case, what am I doing talking about money?

This has never ever come into my strategies; I have, from day dot, referred all matters to Nairobi. Do the negs here trust me enough that I won't do something completely unpredictable and start talking money with Adan?

It's a wild, mad thought; I'd never put it into practice, and I'm far too conformist for that. Surely the psych would have picked that out and stuck it in her report.

By the end of the month the negs have been swapped in Nairobi and Dave is back at the wheel.

Already I am dreading Christmas and it's only November.

There is nothing religious about us, but our Christmases are always spent together. We tend to rotate who hosts, but it's going to be hard enough dealing with Mum and Dad so I ring Matt and Ham: 'I don't care what your arrangements are. This year you are coming up here.' I can't do it by myself; it's going to be too hard and I need the others to take some of the heat.

Nigel
The Light House
Monday, 23 November

Donald comes to us again. He tells me that negotiations are not proving as fruitful as they had hoped. Amanda and I speak at length about my family's financial situation. A few years ago my parents sold their farm for a pretty penny and I know they have a healthy superannuation fund but that it would be difficult to tap into. I also know any action like this would bankrupt them. Amanda asks me repeatedly whether I think my family will also pay for her. It is a no-brainer; I'm sure my family know me well enough that it's clear I wouldn't ever leave without her. Amanda's family don't have access to the sort of cash the gang is looking for, so I guess it will be all or nothing.

DECEMBER 2008

Walking on eggshells

Nigel
The Light House
Monday, 1 December
DAY 100

It is one hundred days since we were kidnapped. That's depressing enough, but now there's Christmas around the corner and the chance of spending it with our families nil to fuck-all.

I get a note from Amanda and sit on the toilet while I read it.

'Congratulations for making it to one hundred days. I can't believe we are still here. We have to remain positive and believe that we will be home soon; remember there is a massive effort and many people on the other side of the world doing everything they can to get us out of here and home safely before Christmas.'

Instead of flushing it, I tuck the note in my pocket and take it back to the room, wanting to keep it as a souvenir. I have begun hoarding, for no other reason than to possess something personal – everything has been taken away except my diary and my hidden notes and drawings. I start to collect plastic bags, empty water bottles, anything that fills my empty room. I'm like a rat nesting.

In the first week of December it almost literally hits home that we're in a war zone. Up until recently, we've only heard distant explosions of mortars and gunfire. Now we're smack-bang in the middle of a massive operation by the occupying forces. At one point what must be a grenade explodes just metres away and dirt sprays the roof. I'd assumed if I was going to die here it would be from a bullet to the back of my head, not a stray mortar screaming through the roof and tearing me to pieces. I cower in the corner of my room.

Amanda tells me out her window, 'You don't have to worry about the mortars you hear; it's the ones you don't that kill you', which doesn't quell my anxiety. After what feels like a long time, the intensity of the battle subsides. I ask Jamal what's going on and he tells me that it's Al-Shabaab and the TFG forces fighting it out. He says they were very close but that there is nothing to worry about now.

Saturday, 13 December

Late at night I hear Assam go into Amanda's room and tell her to get dressed quickly. She asks if she needs to get her things together, and he says to leave everything. I can sense the excitement in her voice. Something major is happening – this may be it, we are about to be released.

I'm expecting him to walk through my door any second. Instead I hear him shepherding her down the hallway, and Amanda asking where I am. Then the sound of car doors slamming and seconds later the car driving off into the distance.

She's gone.

I feel nauseated. I'm sure she's about to be killed, a statement to the Canadians for having stuffed the group around. If either of us was going to be released, I'm guessing I would be first off the block; they know my family has money. The more I think about it, the more I work myself up. I can't bear to imagine how Amanda will meet her end; I just hope that it's not brutal or slow. Tears run down my face and I've never felt more alone.

The house is now deathly silent, and my mind is running totally wild. I sit rigid with fear for what seems like hours before I hear the car pull into the courtyard. *So*, I think, *now it's my turn*. But I hear Amanda; even though she's sobbing uncontrollably I am flooded by sheer relief. I wonder if they told her bad news; perhaps her father has died.

I hear her go into her room and then come to our adjoining wall and slump to the floor. There's the sound of her pawing at the wall, as if she is trying to burrow into my room. She is sobbing hysterically. All I can do is scratch back, letting her know I'm here.

I listen as Donald enters her room; he talks with her for a few minutes, but with my window closed I can't make out any of it. He leaves and I listen to Amanda scratching at the wall until I eventually fall asleep.

The next morning, as soon as our windows are open, she knocks on the wall to let me know she wants to talk. I bolster myself, ready for any bad news. But my guesses as to what happened are not even in the ballpark. She slowly explains what took place last night.

Amanda was put in the car with Romeo, Skids, Donkey, Mao and Ahmed, and they picked up Donald and another man who she had never seen before.

Donald then announced they were going to kill her. They drove her out to the middle of nowhere; she begged for her life the whole way.

My heart is in my mouth and I wonder how she is managing to function let alone talk about this. She says that once the car pulled up, Skids marched her over to a tree and ordered her to kneel. He put a gun to her head. Skids said that because there was no money for her, there was no point keeping her alive. I'm visualising this, trying to imagine the horror she felt.

She pled with Donald not to let Skids kill her and begged them to let her call Lorinda. I can just picture that little prick Donkey at this point, taunting her and laughing in her face, telling her she is about to die. She implored them and eventually they handed her the phone. Amanda was to tell her mother if the gang doesn't get the money in seven days, they will kill her.

Amanda says she spoke to her mum but doesn't go into the detail. She must have been hysterical at that point.

As soon as the call was over, they bundled her back into the car and brought her back to the house.

Nicky
Moore Park
Sunday, 14 December

Lorinda gets a call from Amanda: 'They want one million in one week or they will kill me.'

Lorinda said Amanda was crying on the phone, saying, 'Tonight they brought me out to kill me but they are giving me one more chance. Can you get a million dollars?'

Amanda phones Lorinda again a short time later to say she made a mistake: they want US$2.5 million. We have heard nothing from Nige in a long time. Are they still together? Is he even alive? Are we being asked to fork out cash for just Amanda because Nige is dead and we haven't been told? Or is it another case of 'nothing has been confirmed'?

Tuesday, 16 December

There has been discussion about moving the NOK phone. The Villas are booked out over the two weeks of Christmas.

Si, the kids and I live in a three-bedroom fibro house right on the beach, round the corner from the Villas. Our nursery is on a small cane farm, and we have a tenant in our cottage. We decide to move her out. I feel bad that she has to go but our needs are greater.

In November one of the negs had taken photos of the cottage and sent them down to Canberra, as a potential new NOK cell, and we thought it was all systems go. The house is only a little two-bedroom place, but it's got a phone line and it's close by. What with everyone at Mum and Dad's for Christmas it seemed a pretty good option to us. Up to this point the negs had been looking at moving out to Bargara for two weeks. That was a pretty unattractive choice for me. While everyone was up for Christmas, I'd be at Bargara, forty-five minutes away.

It appears there is an ulterior motive along the lines of 'we are working at building a capability to get the neg cell to Canberra'. By now I am starting to pick up statements that pre-empt a railroading, so I know something's going on – just not quite what.

Ryan, the neg who is with us at the moment, says he is putting together an 'options paper' on what will happen with the phone. Five options are being put forward:

1. Things stay the same, with the NOK phone staying full time at Moore Park.

2. The phone and the NOK (me) move to Canberra.

3. The phone moves down to Canberra and the AFP take over all negotiations.

4. The negs stay in Canberra and the phone is patched to the NOK in Moore Park.

5. One neg stays, the other moves down to Canberra, and the phone gets patched to the NOK at Moore Park.

I am assured the final decision will be made with our consultation. Time will tell.

Nigel
The Light House
Sunday, 14–Sunday, 21 December

I'm sure now that Ahmed and his cronies have finally lost patience with the negotiations. My arse puckers up with the thought that it's crunch time. There's no way Lorinda will be able to magically come up with the money in six days. Amanda is now on death row, her execution date set.

That afternoon Amanda knocks to bring me to the window, and part of me wishes I didn't have to hear what she is about to tell me. She says Donald came into her room under the guise of consoling her. He sat down next to her, and put his arm around her. She believed deep down that he was someone she could trust and rested her head on his shoulder as she cried. Donald patted her head to comfort her.

He said, 'If you want me to help you, you will have to help me', and placed her hand on his lap. Amanda took a few seconds to register that she was touching his cock. She pulled away and backed into a corner, telling him that what he was doing was against Islam. He scampered out of the room.

So Donald is just another snake in the grass. My concern now is that they're not only going to kill her but treat her like their prostitute for the next week.

The following day I take a deep breath and tell Amanda some hard truths. She has to get her things in order; she needs to write a will and a letter to her parents. I tell her if I get out of here alive and she doesn't, the first thing I will do is fly to Canada and meet with her family. She is still in a state of shock, consumed by fear and anxiety, but I think she sees the logic in this.

Two days later I broach the subject again and she snaps.

'We have got to stop this. We are both being completely negative. If we keep thinking like this then they *are* going to kill me and possibly you too. Let's just believe that it's a bluff.' Like a right hook to the head it knocks some sense into me. We have both been so positive up till now, to let go of that would be a form of defeat.

I wake up on the morning of day seven, dread pushing down on my chest. I'm a nervous wreck as the sun sets and it grows dark. Just before our windows are closed I tell Amanda I love her and that everything is going to be okay.

At morning prayer I hear her knock for the toilet; it's the best noise I can imagine.

Nicky
Goondiwindi
Saturday, 20 December

It's a typical stinking-hot western district summer's day. Jacinta and
my friend Simone and I are prepping madly for a marquee wedding
on the banks of the Macintyre River, helping Kel. She's catering for
an old friend's wedding and drove 600 kilometres from Newcastle
yesterday. Matt and the kids will arrive on Sunday and we'll all head
to Mum and Dad's on Monday for Christmas.

Every time I leave Bundy something seems to happen so it's
no surprise when Mum rings. 'Dad and I have just been over to
the Villas for a meeting with Peter and Pamela.' These two are the
worst negotiators we've had to date.

We have had Peter before. He looks like John-Boy Walton and
struggles with our family's argumentative style. I think he'd be a
good negotiator with some dopey meth head holding someone hostage in a domestic situation, but that's not what we're dealing with
here. He expects everyone to automatically respect his authority.
We have driven him mad with questioning the AFP's strategies,
and he's kept his anger in check. Just.

Pamela, however, is a different bundle of sticks. Awful from
go to whoa. Whoever thought she could work with us should be
sent for psychiatric evaluation. We all feel judged by her. She is
not interested in us or Nigel on a personal level. For her, we agree,
it's all about her hours and how she can crawl her way up the AFP
ladder. Simon is the only one who will give her the time of day.

'Dad and I have gone over this a number of ways as to how it
could have been meant, but we were discussing the ransom and
Pamela asked if we could squeeze a little bit more money out.'

'What?'

Mum says it again. I am shocked. Kel can see there is a problem by my tone and my stunned-mullet look. I beckon her out of the catering tent and we wander into the paddock behind it. I fill her in while Mum hangs on the line. Kel sums up the situation succinctly: 'They've waited till the Rottweiler is out of town to do this.' The timing is no coincidence. Get to the oldies when no one else is around.

'That bitch,' I explode.

'Nicole!' Mum admonishes me for the bad language. *Oops, I thought I had my hand over the receiver.* Dad's been talking to his sister Alison about money, and she has offered to chip in on the ransom. We have tossed this proposal around but haven't come to any final decision; we are debating who will pay Alison back. Even if we take the loan, will it be enough? The information we are getting from the two agencies is conflicting. DFAT is saying they won't pay or facilitate a ransom full stop, and here is the AFP's Pamela pushing the olds for more dough when none of us is there to pull the covered wagons into a circle.

Simone suggests I go back to Moore Park straightaway, but I don't want to leave Kel in the lurch. Everything is planned and, after helping with so many events, I've got to know there's always a spanner lurking somewhere, threatening to bring down an occasion. I don't want to be that spanner. The true art of catering for a wedding – and Kel has this ability in spades – is to not let on that there is a crisis. Weddings are stressful enough without hearing some tale of doom and gloom from the caterer. I decide to stick around.

The wedding is a huge success. We manage to hold off the flies, and the caterers' tent, as hot as a greenhouse, keeps the dust at bay. The highlight is watching Simone re-enact Beyonce's bump and grind to 'Single Ladies' after a post-midnight meal of cold, soggy chips at the local servo. I'm so exhausted from the wedding and wired about what has gone down at home that I go into hysterical laughter. I'm crouched over, holding my sides, with tears streaming down my cheeks. I can't speak. I'm trying to tell Simone to stop. It's too funny – I think I'm going to wet myself.

Kellie
Moore Park
Monday, 22 December

This is shaping up to be the worst Christmas ever. Even worse than the first one I had away from my own family. I was twenty-four years old and had never had a Christmas away from home: I cried like a baby. Everything was different – breakfast, lunch, dinner, present giving, what we did, what we drank and ate; it just wasn't the same. But Christmas 2008 will be a new low.

Matt, the kids and I pull up in front of Heather and Geoff's, and I feel awful because I don't want to go in. I don't want to experience the grief this Christmas is going to cause our family, Heather and Geoff especially. The kids are oblivious to the emotionally charged situation and burst through the front door screaming out to Nanny and Poppy. Children are a wonderful icebreaker.

Nic, Si and their kids are there as well. It doesn't take long before talk turns to the 'squeezing a bit more out' conversation. I hear the growing hatred towards government bodies spew from the mouths of my family, and I let the air settle around me before making a comment.

I don't want Christmas to be filled with hate. I will do all I can to make this great for the kids at least. I don't want them to feel uncomfortable about being happy.

Nicky
Moore Park
Tuesday, 23 December

When I get back from Goondiwindi, I make sure Ben is more than aware of how pissed off I am. I try to bypass him and go through the DFAT channels but James's stock-standard response is that the APF is 'the leading investigative agency on this case'. So it's back to Ben. Pamela says Mum and Dad have misinterpreted her but I think there's been a directive from higher up: go fishing to see if there is more money available.

Si and I have numerous arguments about Pamela. 'She's just the messenger,' he says, 'you are shooting the messenger.' He thinks my hate is very ugly and he's right, it is. But nothing is going to make me want to find common ground with this woman. When it's clear my requests to have her removed from our case have fallen on deaf ears, I come to the cold hard realisation that our opinions matter squat.

The Villas have become a war zone. I am resentful of having to spend any time over there. A tense silence falls when I next arrive. There's minimal discussion; I get my book and head upstairs to my room to sulk. As soon as I wake up in the morning, I'm out of there. I can more than match their freeze-out. Si and I have mastered that art in our sixteen years of marriage.

As the Villas' lease crawls to an end, Ben informs Si and me that the cottage is not an option for the NOK phone. It should never have even been considered – there is a conflict of interest because we own the house. Si argues the point that the lease would be done through an agent, keeping everything above board. It's a completely non-negotiable issue. What if rent is not charged? Still a resounding no. We are assured that we will find replacement tenants easily enough as they have asked the local real-estate agents.

Not long after that, Peter and Pamela announce that, because the Villas are booked out and there is nothing else suitable, the decision has been made to take the phone down to Canberra. So much for consultation. Sitting at the table in the living room of the Villas, I feel cold but there is sweat starting to pool at the small of my back.

Back home, I am on to Ben in a flash. He's all very conciliatory but it's clear something is happening here – cost cutting.

I'm almost yelling at Ben. He's on the speakerphone so we can all hear him. 'Don't you dare blow smoke up my arse,' I say to him. God, is there anything I won't say to a police officer? Have I no respect for authority any more? Apparently not, as it turns out. After a little gasp, Ben says, 'No, Nicky, I am not, as you say, blowing smoke up your arse.' His recognising that outrageousness for what it is, is kind of funny. The discussion becomes more civil and there are some genuine concessions made on both sides.

'We believe that building a capability to transfer welfare calls can be achieved. We are working towards implementation on a trial basis. This trial will be progressive and will be designed with the aim of minimal disruption.' I take it to mean the move to Canberra will happen, just not yet.

The next day the negs book into a unit overlooking the ocean at Bargara.

Wednesday, 24 December

It's the day before Christmas. Ben and Gary, the AFP agent in South Africa who was first on the scene in Nairobi when Nige was taken, come to the house. Gary's an older fellow who has been in Africa for two and a half years now. He's back in Australia for a couple of days over Christmas. He describes his role as finding out the identity of the kidnappers, their intentions, and the whereabouts of Nigel and Amanda.

We hear that he met with the last people to be kidnapped over there – Italians. The NGO they worked for was not actually Italian, and so the government couldn't control the payout. Ah ha! So there *was* a payment. This is the first time we've heard this stated explicitly. The Italian government's official policy is 'no ransom and no negotiation'.

Someone from the security industry gave Gary a name and number of a TPI. The TPI put Gary in contact with Adan, thus proving his worth. Gary asked to speak to Nigel and Amanda. Adan put Nigel on the phone. We had no idea someone else had spoken to Nige. I thought the only other person was Mark, as Nige had told me during our conversation in September. Why was this kept from us? Surely they can see in hindsight that us knowing about an Australian representative in Somalia was way more important than their bloody security clearances.

Interestingly, Gary said that Adan appeared to have a genuine interest in Nigel and Amanda. He was regarded as the primary contact, yet now the AFP is telling us they don't think he's the person who's going to make it happen.

We're all grateful that Gary came up to see us. He's only here to spend Christmas with his family and we have taken up some of that time. But we're left with just as many questions as answers.

The negs are going to be located in Bargara till the end of January. Even when the units at the Villas become available, it's clear they won't be coming back to Moore Park.

Bargara is over one and a half hour's return travel for me. I ask if I am supposed to sleep over there. No, when a call comes in, they will pick up and say I'm not available and call me, and I can come over straightaway to call Adan back. I'm not happy with this outcome. I'm no longer ensconced with the negs and the NOK phone. I am out of the loop.

Kellie
Moore Park
Wednesday, 24–Thursday, 25 December

When Ham and Amy arrive with Oscar, Izzy and Mac, the house is buzzing with children. All the cousins are loving each other's company and all the adults are discussing the money and the move from the Villas, again. The talk of Nigel, negotiations and money is making me antsy. I want to get out of the house and experience the season, people milling around the shops and checking out the Christmas lights.

Matt and I are sleeping in Nigel's room and I am having vivid dreams about him being stood up in front of a firing squad. The kidnappers laugh as they pull the triggers. I also see him being led away in shackles with a hessian bag over his head.

Surprisingly, Christmas Day is actually really lovely; everyone manages to have a great time and for a brief moment we forget that Nigel is not here, until we sit down to eat. We make a toast to the black dog, wishing him a merry Christmas and hoping he is getting something decent to eat.

Friday, 26 December

I knew it was too good to be true; things were going along too well.

We are all on the back deck with friends, enjoying some Boxing Day drinks. It's just on dusk and we are making a few jokes about Nige and what he might be doing for Christmas. We're using humour to make the best of it. But Heather has had enough. She yells at us all, saying none of us understands what she's going through. She storms off and disappears.

Unfortunately, the rest of us have had too much to drink and get the giggles at her outburst. Heather has done this before, yelled at us for making jokes at Nigel's expense, so we don't really think much of it.

Our visitors are leaving, looking for Heather to say goodbye. We all assume she is in the bedroom – it is now 10.30 p.m. and she is nowhere to be found. Ham gets on the phone and calls around to see if Heather is there, with no luck. Amy and I decide to walk the beach while Geoff gets in the car and searches the streets. Matt stays with the kids and Ham goes with Geoff. Neither of them should be driving. All of us come back without Heather; we are starting to get concerned. I understand that she needs to get away – I had been feeling the same – but it's late and dark.

Nic keeps ringing from home to see if Heather has come back yet. Ham has picked up the phone to call the police when, just as the clock strikes midnight, she walks into the passage. We all exhale audibly and someone asks where she has been, the same way a parent would chastise a child who's been missing. She glances at all of us, and says she was walking. Heather doesn't look upset; she looks angry. Ham explains that we were all really worried and have been out searching for her. Heather turns and stares him down, saying none of us needed to bother; she was just taking a walk and now she is off to bed. And just like that she is gone.

Heather's mood does not change for the next four days. She's snapping at all of us, including the children. We are walking on eggshells. Matt and I cut short our time in Moore Park as we feel it best to eliminate some of her stress by removing the children; Ham and Amy do the same. As we back out of the driveway, Callaghan asks us why Nanny is so cranky. Our answer is the same as always: 'because of Uncle Nigel'.

I understand that Heather is going through something no mother should have to. Yet I'm not sure she can see that the rest of us are hurting too. I keep thinking that if we share our pain rather than bottle it up till it explodes, some of us might feel better. I stew on this until the kids bring me sharply back to reality, asking when will we be home.

Nigel
The Light House
Monday, 22 December

As Christmas draws closer, we're both thinking that what would normally be a day of celebrating, eating and drinking this year will be far from enjoyable for our families, and most likely dull as dog shit for us. Amanda comes up with the idea of exchanging small gifts. It's a risk but I agree it will boost our spirits.

All women love jewellery, so I set about making Amanda a bracelet. I collect the ring-pulls from the tuna tins. I tear the tasselled edges from the top and bottom of my sarong, and use them to wrap around each ring-pull so that the tassels fall from the sides. I tie each one together carefully, linking them, and finally craft a small clasp to connect the ends. It takes me days to finish but I feel pretty chuffed about my creation.

Using the cardboard insert from my cologne box, I make a small container for the bracelet. The wrapping paper, card and envelope are easy. I tear sheets from my diary and on them draw Christmas trees and candy canes; my four-colour pen provides the festive colours. I go all MacGyver with the stocking, colouring the paper in red and stitching it together with the dental floss from the care package. I use a wet wipe, also part of the care package, tearing off a strip and sewing it to the top as a makeshift lip of wool.

I have to be extremely wary of the boys during the process. Getting caught would mean they'd question our faith. It is pure coincidence that we'd recently asked Jamal and Assam to buy us some chocolates from the market, and over three days they have brought us seven small toffees. I save some to put in Amanda's stocking. The pièce de résistance was getting a gilded ribbon from Amanda, which she had taken off the hem of her abaya. I tie this around the present, the perfect finishing touch.

Wednesday, 24–Wednesday, 31 December

The day before Christmas we sing carols to each other through the window, even though we're both tone deaf. We spend the whole day at the window talking about our families and singing.

The next day we wish each other a Merry Christmas as soon as our windows are open. Our plan is to leave our gifts in the bathroom for the other to collect; I'm going first. But just as I'm ready to knock for the toilet, I notice a shadow pass by my door. I quickly stash everything and then I hear someone rummaging around our bathroom.

Sneaking a look out my door, I see Donkey making his way to the front of the house. Thank god he didn't come five minutes later – of all people who could have caught us. With Donkey gone, we speedily get on with the exchange.

I open my present, and laugh at what Amanda has made. Using a vitamin bottle that Donald had brought us weeks earlier as a body, with a drawn-on face on the lid and a shirt made from one of her socks, Amanda's created a puppet. She has stitched onto the shirt with dental floss the words, 'My little buddy'. In the card she's written, 'This is your little buddy. When you are feeling down, remember that I'm always here and you will always have someone to talk with.' It was hilarious.

I keep the wrapping paper, card and stocking, hiding them under the lino on the floor along with the notes and drawings I have saved. Amanda loves her bracelet.

It's a difficult day, but we get through it.

With the new year only a few days away, Amanda senses a shakedown is coming. She has been spying on the boys through a small pinhole in her door. We have to get rid of all our notes and drawings. I'm desperate to hang on to them but I don't have a choice. The only things I keep are the shirt from my little buddy and the lid with the face on it, burying them at the bottom of my camera bag. The rest I shred and flush down the toilet. A sense of defeat washes over me as I watch them disappear.

The shakedown never comes. I've become my own jailer.

JANUARY 2009

A very dirty business

Kellie
Newcastle
January

The phone has been officially moved back to Canberra. The move, however, comes with a promise that it will be manned twenty-four seven. Any calls will be patched through to Nic at Moore Park. I'm certainly not convinced this is a great option but we have no choice; it's what the Feds have decided and that's that. This deflates all hopes of Nige and Amanda being released any time soon.

I find myself constantly playing the devil's advocate, looking for both sides of the story. The Feds move the phone and I try to rationalise the decision to family members. I really need to put a positive spin on these events; the negativity is overwhelming at the moment, and I am having trouble talking with most of the family.

Being one step removed from Nigel makes me look at things differently, and it also makes me less tolerant of some behaviour.

I'm outside the bubble: I can understand the family's disagreements, but I am also able to see the time wasted discussing things that really aren't important. Of course, I realise that without these discussions no one in the family can move on to the next issue, as each piece of the puzzle needs to be examined and then put on the board before they can get on with next.

January is traditionally a relaxing time, a fresh start to the year. All I want to do is take fifteen steps back from the Brennans, including my husband. Every person I speak to asks about Nigel. All Matt's family ever talk about is Nigel, and I want to think about and do something – anything – that doesn't involve him. I am taking a huge step and opening a café and shopfront for my catering business. What better way to avoid a stressful situation than to bury yourself in a different one?

Matt and I have long discussions about the new business. I'm very grateful that he shares my enthusiasm. And not that he has ever said so, but I think he may be enjoying the distraction too. At the same time I'm feeling incredibly guilty that Nic is still fighting a constant battle with the AFP and DFAT. I have totally copped out: living a fair distance from Moore Park, I don't have to deal with the intense day-to-day running of the show. And now I am totally absorbed in something else and, to make me feel worse, I am actually enjoying it.

I question myself and my loyalty to Matt's family, but I also need to be loyal to my own family. Matt cannot work due to his shoulder injury so I need to take charge and bring in the cash. Why, at thirty-six, do I feel like I am drowning in issues? Is this a pre-midlife crisis? If I am feeling like this, I can't even pretend to imagine what Nigel must be feeling in Somalia, or how Heather and Geoff feel with the everyday reality of a missing son.

Nicky
Moore Park
Sunday, 11–Monday, 12 January

The negs are starting to tell us how it really is. They don't want to be here any more and we all know that as soon as they head to Canberra, we will get bugger-all info. It will become like a missing-persons scenario or a cold-case murder – Nigel will just be a file on someone's desk.

The phone and the negs will be at Bargara for the first two weeks of the new year, and then there will be a mid-month review. We are to consider and discuss where and when the family update meetings occur and whether an agenda should be presented and followed. At this point the negs are getting a 9 p.m. phone update from Canberra. They then pass on the relevant information to the family. They would prefer it to be a weekly family meeting via phone call. Mum is really unhappy about this.

'Heather, you can call us any time of the day,' she's told.

That's the sound of us being palmed off. I'm guessing that where they have us now – as far away from the action as possible – is probably where they wanted us four months ago.

The negs tell us at the family meeting that the strategy is now to put all the money on the table and push. The whole US$250K will be offered directly to Adan.

On 12 January Adan gives confirmation he's received the offer by the Nairobi neg cell.

A journo from Somalia's Shabelle news network has spoken to Nigel and publishes their conversation. The phone to Canberra runs hot: who is he? How do we get in contact with him? And, more importantly, how was he able to contact the HTs so easily when we are having such trouble? Can he be used as a TPI or is he part of the gang? A million questions, none of which gets answered, apart from a response to say they are trying to locate and organise a debriefing with him in Nairobi. It feels like we are just running into one brick wall after another.

Tuesday, 13 January

Adan sends an email to Lorinda. In pretty strangled English he tells us that danger is coming to Nigel and Amanda and that we are not to contact him again until we have US$2.5 million. He signs off with 'have a good day'. All that's missing is the ☺.

This email is good news, so I'm told. Adan has resumed contact with Lorinda. Then we are told by the negs that 'Adan is still around but we are looking at alternatives, eyeing people up to see who is appropriate'. At least they didn't say 'assessing and reassessing'. I hate that phrase. If someone had said that, I think I would have screamed till my veins swelled, distended and burst. The other thing I find out when I ring Lorinda is that she is still ensconced in the NOK cell with negs. Maybe that's the benefit of not making waves – you don't get your privileges taken away.

Wednesday, 14 January

James and Ben are due here today.

Mum is having a really hard time of it and boycotts the meeting; she feels it's just a great big useless talkfest. I see her point but it's also one of our few chances to glean information. I wonder if later on the AFP will use mock-ups of our meetings to help train recruits how to deal with hostile families. These two have become so good at it they don't even look like they are sweating and we are

173

in central Queensland in the middle of January.

James tells us about the number of contacts they've been trying to pin down, but because of the political strife in Somalia most of this work has proved fruitless. The politics of the place is enough to do your head in. It's hard to keep up with who's on top what with the Ethiopian troops and clan in-fighting, but it seems Al-Shabaab, a recognised terrorist group, is on the ascendancy, which is bad news for us, not to mention the Somalis.

The country is in a state of flux, we're told, as everyone battles for control of the state; and the shifting sands make finding allies incredibly difficult.

We find out that the RCMP has identified a new Somali TPI. This information has not been discussed with Lorinda, we're told.

'Why is this?' Dad asks.

'I don't know. Perhaps she hasn't asked. All I know is I am aware that at this stage this new TPI has not been discussed with her,' is the reply.

'You had better let us know when that happens,' says Dad, 'because you know how uncomfortable I am about discrepancies such as this.'

Ben navigates the conversation back to the TPI. 'Engaging him is complex and difficult. As a result we will be limiting the use of other TPIs, possibly including Adan. There is no discussion with Adan in regards to this TPI.

'The current political situation, as we have just discussed, makes negotiations very difficult. The TPI is brokering the deal; that is his purpose.'

I don't understand how Dave in Nairobi can indicate to the HTs that although the AFP is part of the government, the government will not pay a ransom.

Nigel
The Light House
Early January

The new year ticks over but it's just another day in hell, really. There's no sign of change. To deal with the isolation I focus my attention on my daily exercise routine. Assam and Donkey sporadically come in and join me; and although they are my captors, it's hard not to enjoy their company. After two months alone I am craving stimulation, even if it means dancing with the enemy.

Amanda is not as fortunate. While running circuits in her room, she injured her ankle. This has hurt her mentally more than physically. I can tell she is struggling.

At times she comes to the window, asking, 'Nigey, when are we going to get out of here?' It becomes a question I loathe, mostly because I want an answer too. When I reply, 'I don't know, babe,' she berates me for not being more positive, and walks away in a huff. She always comes back to apologise, though. We both have our moments of frustration and depression, moments when we need the other to be compassionate.

Several days later I hear Skids and a few of the boys in Amanda's room. My nerves are rattled by Amanda's shrill scream. Suddenly my door swings open. Jamal stands there, and orders me up.

'Go,' he says indicating Amanda's room. I'm surprised as I enter. They are all standing around her, looking sheepish. It's nice to be in her presence but I can see by her face she's in pain. I'm concerned about what's just taken place, and what's about to take place. I'm on tenterhooks as all eyes are fixed on me.

Jamal asks me to look at Amanda's ankle. It's swollen. When I gently place my hand on it, it feels hard as a rock. Amanda tells me they had her crouching down and jerked the ankle around. Hence the screaming. I give them my medical opinion: they shouldn't touch it; she needs a pressure bandage, ice and to elevate the leg to reduce the swelling. Jamal disagrees, saying, 'In Somalia we do like this.' He then pulls and twists his foot forwards and backwards. 'Then walking is better,' he continues. I shake my head, repeating that it will only get better with rest and ice. Jamal translates this to Skids, who waves me back to my room.

Before I am marched back I ask Jamal to see if Skids will allow Amanda and me to spend some time together. The old guy ponders my request. Jamal translates, saying, 'Okay, in the afternoon you can see each other, now go back.' I'm hiding my pleasure as I'm walked back to my room.

That afternoon, as promised, we get a forty-five minute respite from our rooms. We sit at the back of the courtyard, enjoying the sun. The strain is evident on Amanda's face. Even though we've talked to each other endlessly over the last weeks through our windows I feel like a schoolboy. There's shyness as I try to meet her eyes and I am unable to find the words as she rests a lump of ice on her ankle. Eventually we feel comfortable again and rant on, mocking the boys. It seems that just as we are getting into the swing of it, time is up and we are ordered back to our rooms.

For a moment it was as if we were alone in the world. It's gutting to be ripped apart again, back to staring at those four walls. Worse than not having spent any time with her at all.

It takes nearly a week of agitation before we are allowed this privilege again. This time they give us six hours together, four o'clock is our deadline. I join Amanda in her room, and we share our food, talk and even pray together, which seems so strange after doing it alone for so long. Amanda tells me after we pray that she doesn't bother doing the prostrations any longer; she's surprised I'm still keeping up appearances. I find this extremely concerning. If they were to find out, she'd be royally screwed, but she doesn't seem too worried about it.

At one point I drag my mattress into her room so I can get more comfortable; the concrete floor is too cold and hard on my emaciated body. I then notice Abdi standing in the doorway of their room on the other side of the hall, motioning to get my attention. Our eyes meet.

He shrugs his shoulders and holds his palms up: 'What's going on?' I shake my head side to side: 'Nothing'. We begin our game of charades, passing information to each other, the whole time watching the front door for movement.

Abdi enquires if we have spoken to our families and asked for money. It's clear they won't be going any place either until the group gets cash from somewhere. I gesture that they won't grant us any phone calls. I ask if the three of them are okay. He replies, yes, but that it is taking too much time. No argument from me. Now feeling that we have been pushing our luck, I bid him farewell.

The closer we get to four o'clock, the more my anguish starts to build. Again I wonder whether the pleasure of seeing Amanda is worth the pain of being separated.

Wednesday, 14 January

I hear one of the boys in Abdi's room, then the sound of them shoving things into plastic bags. I begin gathering my possessions, expecting any moment to be hustled into a car and moved. No one comes. I stand at the door, trying to see what's going on but there's only the dark hallway.

Feeling brazen, I creep out of the room and move to the edge of the hall, before kneeling and sticking my head around the corner to look through the balustrades. I see Abdi and the other two being marched out the front door with their belongings. I go back to my room. Something doesn't feel right.

Minutes tick by. I knock to go to the toilet. Assam comes, asking what I want. He motions for me to go to the toilet. On my way back I sneak another look around the corner. Assam is pulling the mattresses out of Abdi's room and throwing them on the verandah, where the boys lie down on them, laughing to each other.

In Somalia when locals are kidnapped with foreigners, chances are they will be killed. I feel sick. As the minutes and hours roll on, I become certain something awful has happened to our colleagues. I try to second-guess what's happening until I fall asleep.

The following morning when Jamal comes in with breakfast I ask, 'Jamal, where are our three Somali friends; what's going on?'

He replies blandly, 'They go,' then leaves the room.

After breakfast I knock to go to the toilet. When Assam comes down I call him into the room, hoping he might be a bit more forthcoming.

He tells me, 'They were released last night; they go back to their families.' I can't believe my ears.

'Are you sure? Why did they let them go?'

'Yes, they have been released. It is too expensive to keep them. Now go to the toilet.'

I'm elated. This is a good sign for us; things are moving forward. I talk to Amanda, and she says she's been told the same, but as the day drags on we begin to question this version of events. If they've been released, why haven't we been moved? Surely Abdi would inform someone of our whereabouts.

In the afternoon Donkey comes in. I ask him about our friends, and he tells me with great pleasure, 'They have been handed over to Al-Shabaab.' He then raises his finger to his throat and mimes slicing across it. The fact they were Muslim means nothing to these people; they will justify it by saying Abdi and the drivers were working with infidels.

We had safety in numbers, but it's now just the two of us. Both Amanda and I are convinced that now we have no other option but to run.

Nicky
Sunshine Coast
Monday, 16 January

I get a 6 a.m. call. 'Alley Cat, wake up.'

'Hhhr, Ham. What is it?' Obviously, I'm awake. His call's just done that.

'Abdi's been released.'

'*What!?*' My red-wine hangover is gone. I've found the miracle cure. Ange had invited us down the coast for the weekend to stay with her dad and his partner so we could get away with the kids for a couple of days. It is, after all, the Chrissy holidays and we haven't gone anywhere or done anything. And last night, as you do with friends, we nudged a couple of reds. I hadn't felt so relaxed in months.

The story is on Google alert. He relays the sketchy details: Abdi and the drivers were released near Bakaara market. Apparently their release was negotiated by a local clan leader. Abdi was separated from Nigel and Amanda after they were captured and doesn't know their whereabouts. He can't identify his captors either.

I'm delighted for Abdi and the drivers but I wish so much that it could have been Nige. I have a bit of a cry, the by-product of self-pity.

Ben rings half an hour or so after Ham. I suspect he's torn about ringing too early and not wanting someone else to pass on the news of Abdi's release. If DFAT has learned nothing else about us, it's that we don't like to be surprised by these sorts of reports.

'Where's Abdi?' I ask him. 'Have you guys heard from him?'

'No,' replies Ben.

'Okay, what about the other two? Or Abdi's wife or father?'

'Nicky, they will be trying to find him. Understand that we don't know his role. If, in fact, he was in on it. If he has gone to ground, his life and that of his family will have been threatened. He may know the identity of the kidnappers and that puts him at great risk.' After the call with Ben I have another cry. Silent tears as I look up at the ceiling, wishing my heart away that it was Nige who was free.

Si and I pack up the kids and head back to Moore Park for a Nippers carnival. I feel emotionally battered. The first thing I hear is the club's president bemoaning one of the teams. 'Of course, our under-twelves is the underperforming team of the club,' says Lee to another parent. Like coming out of a dream, I realise that's *our* team they're talking about: Si is the manager of the under-twelves. I run blindly to the dingy bathrooms behind the clubhouse and grab wads of toilet paper, crush them into my mouth and scream and scream and scream. I sit on the loo, a heaving, sobbing wreck.

I pore over the news articles that come in over the next couple of days, bearing in mind they are unconfirmed 'open source' reports. Abdi has said very little about Nige or Amanda, certainly nothing suggesting their whereabouts. He didn't know where he was taken to and he hadn't seen his colleagues as he was held in a different location to them, and he rarely heard his captors talk about Amanda and Nige. Abdi also said he wouldn't recognise his captors and that he wasn't mistreated.

Speaking to Somali journalists, he says he thought he would never see his family again. I'm guessing that man has been given a good scare. I'm happy he's back with his wife and kids.

Friday, 23 January

A news article attached to our Google alert hits a raw nerve. Some idiot from the Somali-based journalists' rights agency has written that the ransom has been dropped from US$2.5 million to $100K. What a moron; if only it were that low. It's a pretty dodgy bit of reporting. There's some speculation that Abdi was released after his tribal group threatened to attack the kidnappers.

After much correspondence back and forth with Canberra, we get an email stating that there has been confusion in the media about the ransom. This news comes circuitously from another Somali journo who's confirmed that the ransom amount has not been reduced.

Trying to get a hold of this second guy involves too many security issues for the Feds, especially in light of the fact they would be dealing with a journo who, as far as the government is concerned, is a mortal enemy. It all reeks of cutting off your nose to spite your face.

Ham is drafting a fundraising letter and we all discuss who we should target. Hours are spent compiling names. The idea is to trigger people's sympathy and interest in assisting us then to follow up with a phone call for an appointment. We all know that if we have the opportunity to tell someone our story in person, they won't be able to refuse. The tricky bit is getting the face-to-face.

Thursday, 29 January

Dad and I head down to Canberra; we got the invitation back in December. We get a grand tour of the AFP building. We meet everyone, and I mean everyone, almost up to Mick Keelty, the Commissioner, it would seem. We get a tour of the ICC and the negs' base. It's the hub of all incoming intel, the nerve centre. We have lunch with most of the negs who have been up in Moore Park with us.

Another strategy is suggested to us. It's like a missing-person's campaign, targeting people in Somalia empathetic to Nigel and Amanda's plight and trying to generate local interest and concern – and hopefully information. We are given a mock-up poster to pass on to the rest of the family for their views. I immediately see a couple of disadvantages, but choose to keep quiet until everyone else has checked it out.

We're also told there's a new strategy in play but it's too top-secret to discuss in detail. It involves a number of international bodies and possibly the defence force. The prospect of military intervention scares the shit out of both Dad and me. And we are asked to sit tight. Yes, they realise there have been no recent POLs but they have no reason to doubt Nigel is alive – they have intel that suggests he is okay.

Then comes our meeting at DFAT. There are security-tag doors everywhere; the only thing that's missing is the retina scan. After we are ushered in, Dad and I are seated at a table with loads of people I've never met. They are like intern doctors sitting in on a case.

We are told that the Australian and Canadian governments have set a unique mandate, just for this case. They will jointly facilitate a payment of up to US$250K. According to DFAT and the AFP, this is for costs only. Therefore, anything over US$250K sits in the ransom basket, and we all know they don't use the R word.

According to their intel, Nigel is being as well looked after as can be expected. He has a reasonable diet, getting two meals a day, plus pineapple and mangos. Both he and Amanda have been reading the Qur'an. *Well, that's smart*, I think. We were all subjected to religious education at school. Nige will be able to pick bits and pieces out of the Qur'an like we did with the Bible when we wrote essays for RE. It appears they are a part of the village community. They are getting plenty of exercise. In fact, Amanda sprained her ankle while walking. They are teaching the village children English. *Sounds a bit like Club Med, doesn't it?* I think. It's all so fucking polite when this really is a very nasty, very dirty business.

Nigel
The Light House
Monday, 19 January

Amanda and I had discussed the possibility of escape but we'd always end up at the same dead-end: leaving our colleagues behind would spell their deaths. Neither of us was willing to have their blood on our hands. This, however, did not stop us from thinking about escape routes. Now we start considering these plans seriously.

The boys whose job it is to guard us have become lazy. They've fallen into a routine, and over the last few months their monitoring has become patchy at best. They spend their days either sleeping or talking on the verandah.

We have two escape options: up through the manhole in the kitchen and out onto the roof, or through our bathroom window. The roof would be great for hiding in but walking on the corrugated iron would make a hell of a noise. The bathroom window is a better option. The window is about 6 feet off the floor, 3-foot wide and 4-foot high; it's framed by lattice-style besser blocks about 2 inches thick, stacked five high, and five half-inch reinforced-steel bars running horizontally. If I could dig out the mortar of the middle row of blocks and remove two or so bars, there would be enough space for us to squeeze through.

The problem isn't the blocks. It is the reinforced bars that have me scratching my head. Having built houses, I suspect the walls have been core filled, making it impossible to remove the bars without somehow cutting them, obviously not an option.

I decide to take a closer look. Standing on the rim of the toilet, I pull myself up by gripping the bars. Suddenly one slides across into the wall. Slipping it backwards and forwards, I can see one end exposed just in the render of the wall. I hold the bar in the middle and use all my strength to bow it; with my other hand I pull the end of the rod. It comes out of the hole, taking a small chunk of render with it. I'm now able to slide the bar completely out of the other sidewall.

I feel sheer delight at my handiwork. We have the perfect escape route. I replace the bar then try the others. Much to my excitement, all of them move. I will only need to remove the next bar down to give us the room to squeeze out. I manage to take this one out as well, before slipping it back into position. I then race back to my room, banging on the wall to bring Amanda to the window. I tell her the good news. All I have to do is dig out the mortar from between the blocks, which has only been dabbed in there.

'How long do you think it will take you?' she asks.

'Probably two days maximum, but it's going to depend on a lot of things.' Noise and not being caught in the act are the major constraints. Amanda has the perfect solution; she can keep watch via the pinhole in her door.

With my heart in my mouth we try out the plan. After knocking and hearing the click of one of the boys' fingers indicating I could go, I head to the bathroom. Pulling myself up and wedging my thigh under the bottom bar for support, I slowly dig away with a dull pair of scissors and the small file of my nail clippers. I feel like my arse is swinging in the breeze.

I'm terrified the entire time as I laboriously chip away, flushing the remnants of the mortar down the toilet. At one point the corner of one of the besser blocks breaks off, creating a fist-sized hole. All I can do to make it look less obvious is to jam a plastic bag into it.

Wednesday, 21 January

Backwards and forwards I go until finally, after two and a half days, my effort pays off, and I can pull the four top blocks out and put them to the side. Then, after carefully making sure the coast is clear, I stick my head out of the opening, the smell of victory in the air. It's the most magical feeling.

I put the blocks back, wedging the chunks of mortar in the gaps to stabilise them. I knock on the wall once I'm back in my room, telling Amanda that we are good to go.

We discuss at great length our options and decide that it will be better to go after last prayer. The cover of night will give us some protection. My concern is how we will conceal ourselves once we get on the street so we don't stick out like dogs' balls. Amanda has the advantage of her abaya and hijab; being able to cover her face, she will blend in perfectly. It is a different story for me; my jeans and long sleeved shirt will hide my lily-white skin but my hands and face are going to be a problem. We talk about my dressing as a woman but decide against it: if we get caught it will be even worse for us. I decide instead to just wrap my head in my sarong so that only my eyes are visible, and pull my hands inside the cuffs.

The other thing we mull over is what the actual plan will be once we get out the window. We decide to get a few kilometres away and lie low for a while. Amanda, being concealed, would then take the risk of knocking on the door of somewhere friendly-looking and talking to the female of the house.

It is risky and would mean putting our trust in someone. But we both feel that there are good people here who'd be willing to help us. Not everyone is like these bastards – we just have to hope we're lucky in the house we pick.

The other major question is when we are actually going to do this. My thoughts are that we should wait a few days. I haven't slept for the last forty-eight hours, pepped up on fear and anxiety. Amanda is exactly the opposite, wanting to go tonight. She eventually convinces me: if we wait the boys might either notice the window, or worse still move us to another house. So it is decided. We agree to take only the bare minimum: food, water, some personal effects and our religious books, as they may come in handy if something goes awry.

For the remainder of the day I'm on edge, trying to pump myself up, knowing we could very easily be killed tonight. One simple mistake could cause disaster. I run over the plan in my head, trying to second-guess the things that could go wrong.

After five months if feels amazing to again have power, to take control of my destiny and choose the terms by which I live or die. All I can think is, *Fuck them.* I would love to be a fly on the wall when they realise we're gone.

I'm to follow Amanda to the bathroom after 7.30 p.m. prayer, but on the first attempt I baulk. I'm filled with fear; it's like I'm frozen to the spot. Amanda waits for me but I don't materialise. As she walks back to her room, she pushes open my door just enough to see me.

'What happened? Why didn't you come?'

'I'm fucking terrified, Amanda, and it's too risky with Donkey on duty.' The house is now completely silent and I know the slightest noise will send him our way.

'We have to go tonight; we can't wait. This is our chance for freedom, Nige.' I know she's right and she gives me courage. She will wait ten or fifteen minutes before knocking again to go to the toilet. As she walks away I know it's now or never. I suck in air, trying to calm my nerves as the minutes tick by. Then I hear Amanda knock on her door. Adrenaline shoots through every inch of my body when I hear the click of Donkey's fingers.

I stand up, throw my bag over one shoulder and pick up my shoes. *Show time.*

I open my door as quickly as possible to avoid it squeaking. Amanda walks past on her way to the bathroom. Kneeling down, I close my door, jamming a folded piece of paper under it so as to stop it from swinging open. I move silently down the hallway and into the bathroom.

I put down my things in the corner before I stand on the rim of the toilet and begin removing the two reinforced bars. I hand each one to Amanda and she places them near the sink.

Pulling myself up onto the window ledge, I start removing the blocks and placing them on the outside sill. All of this is done in silence as anxiety and excitement press down on me. With a gaping hole now in front of me, I slide onto the floor. My back against the wall under the window, I cup my hands together for a foothold. I boost Amanda over my head and up onto the ledge, spinning around and putting my hands on her bum so she doesn't fall backwards. Thoughts of freedom swim around my head but these soon change to fear and then panic. No matter which way she contorts herself, Amanda can't get through the window. I feel like using all my power to just push her through the hole but I can see that the problem is the two reinforced bars at the bottom of the window. If Amanda can't get through, I don't have a chance.

She finally turns around with a look of defeat.

'I can't fit, you'll have to remove one more bar,' she whispers, barely audible. It feels like every last ounce of oxygen has been sucked from my lungs.

'I can't do it tonight; too much noise. Donkey will hear,' I whisper back. Minutes have elapsed and I know he will start to wonder where Amanda is. I motion for her to get down and we now stand staring at each other.

'You go back to your room. I'll put everything back.'

'Nigey, what about my bag?' Amanda croaks.

'Leave it. I will put it in my room. You can get it at first prayer in the morning.' Waves of nausea push up my throat as I follow Amanda out of the bathroom. I slink back to my room and close the door behind me. I conceal Amanda's bag in the corner under some clothes and slump onto the mattress. I just want to scream. Any minute Donkey will walk down the hallway to find the gaping hole in the bathroom wall.

After a few minutes I stand up and make my way to the door, opening it and knocking. I wait, filled with terror as Donkey walks down the dark hallway. He makes it to the corner, and shines his torch in my face so that I can no longer see him.

'What?' he says.

'My stomach. *Fadlan moscotcha*. Please, bathroom.' I grimace, holding my stomach.

He flicks his head to the left, motioning towards the bathroom then walks back to the front door.

I pull back the curtain on the bathroom door and stare at the gaping hole in the window. Pulling this off is going to be a miracle. Hauling myself back up onto the window ledge, I begin to put the jigsaw puzzle of blocks back together. Sweat drips from my face, my hands are clammy and there's fear in the pit of my stomach. I manage to get all the blocks back in place but they are precariously positioned.

I notice a small wooden stick on the window ledge. Just as I pick it up, my eyes swing back to the window; they must look like dinner plates. The two top bricks are falling in slow motion. By sheer luck, I manage to grab them just before they crash to the ground. I put them back into position. Bile rushes up my windpipe. Minutes have passed and any moment Donkey is going to pull back the curtain. *Fuck, fuck, fuck, how am I going to do this?*

I can feel the bricks wobble like a Jenga tower. I put the stick in my mouth and snap off a piece about a centimetre long. I then split it in half with my teeth. I jam splints down the sides of the bottom block, managing to stabilise it. *Okay, it's going to work, stay calm.* I repeat the process; perspiration runs down my face and is dripping from my chin. Finally I manage to stabilise each block, and put the bars back in place.

I jump onto the ground, and use the bottom of my shirt to wipe the sweat from my face. Noticing the hole where I broke the block the day before, I again stuff the plastic bag into it so it doesn't look so obvious.

I then have a sudden urge to evacuate my bowels. I manage to pull my jeans down and sit just as diarrhoea explodes into the bowl.

I clean myself up and make my way back through the curtain, expecting to see Donkey in the hallway but he is nowhere in sight.

I slip back into my room and close the door behind me. My heart feels like it will jump out of my chest at any moment. I collapse on my bed, in a sense pleased that I managed to fix everything but at the same time furious at myself. I should have just taken out another bar in the first place. I knock on the wall again to let Amanda know I'm back. I'm left with thoughts of what might have been but it's not long before sleep comes; the anxiety and stress of the last few days leaves me exhausted.

Thursday, 22 January

Morning prayer comes and goes. The same routine: wake, wash, pray then straight back to sleep. Assam brings in breakfast some time around eight and opens my windows. He then goes next door and does the same in Amanda's room. Within minutes Amanda knocks on the wall. I drag myself up and slowly walk over to the sill.

'I haven't slept at all,' Amanda says.

'I had the best sleep in days,' I tell her.

Shortly after breakfast, I knock to go to the toilet. I go to work removing the third bar. Within a few minutes, I have managed to take it out and slip it back into position. Walking back to my room, I knock to get Amanda's attention and tell her the good news.

I sit on my bed and think back to the night they threatened to kill Amanda. As they drove, Donald pointed out to her the gangs of armed young men roaming the streets. This fact bounces around my head and begins to frighten me. Maybe there's a safer option than going at night. If I were in trouble in a western country, the first place I would go to is a house of worship. I explain this to Amanda, saying it might be better and safer if we go during the day.

'There is no safer place than a mosque. People will try to help us once they realise we are Muslim,' I say. There's a mosque close by; the call to prayer wails from the minaret five times a day – it can't be more than 500 metres south of the house. I suggest we go just on midday prayer so that there will be lots of people inside. If we leave tomorrow, a Friday, there is certain to be an Imam there.

Amanda is in complete agreement, except she is fixed on going today; she doesn't want to chance waiting longer for fear they will discover our plan. Part of me feels like my hand is being forced. But it is Amanda's life that has been threatened; she knows better than I do what the group is capable of.

We agree that when she goes for her shower just on midday, I will follow, and we'll make our break. My anxiety levels start to spike. I try to occupy my thoughts by reading. My attention is drawn away from the page as I notice a shadow pass by my door. Realising it's not Amanda, I go into a cold sweat. Whoever it is, is now in our bathroom.

My skin shrinks. I expect any second to hear shouting, then it'll only be a matter of time before they come barging through the door, AK47s in hand. I can just see Donkey standing there, his gun in my face, screaming, 'Do you think that we are that stupid?' But there's no noise. The silence is painful.

I stand at the door and peek out the crack. I see Assam walking back from our bathroom, holding the washing detergent. I yank the door open, frightening him as he walks past.

'Assam, what's the time?' I say, the words spilling out too fast. I am trying to gauge his thoughts. *Does he know? Have we been discovered?* He pulls his phone from his pocket, looks at the display. 'It's ten o'clock.'

'Okay, thanks,' I reply, trying not to betray my nerves. I watch as he walks back down the hall.

Amanda is right, today is the day and time is of the essence. I am pulled between excitement and fear. I know deep down we have to do this, but my brain is telling me not to be so fucking stupid.

Before Amanda knocks for the bathroom, we talk one last time, going through the plan.

'Amanda, you realise today we could die? Are you sure you want to do this?' Her reply is a firm 'Yes'.

My body is tight like a spring. Now, ready, I survey the room, hoping it will be the last I see of these dirty walls.

I hear Amanda ask if she can go for a shower and seconds later the slapping of her thongs on the tiled floor as she makes her way to the bathroom. There's no turning back now.

I perform the same routine as last night, slipping along the wall and around the corner to the bathroom. Pulling back the curtain, I see Amanda staring back at me; her face says it all. *This is it.*

'We have to be quiet. I'll pass everything down to you, okay? Pour water into the shower recess so it sounds like you're having a shower,' I whisper. Amanda nods. I get to work up on the ledge.

I hoist Amanda up, and watch anxiously as she manoeuvres her body. She puts one leg through the space then struggles to get her torso out.

It's impossible to tell how noisy we're being. Amanda now has three quarters of her body outside. She grabs the top bar for stability and finally pulls her other leg out. Amanda balances awkwardly on the ledge outside then slowly lowers herself down until she disappears from my sight. I give her a few seconds then throw our bags out followed by my shoes.

Tipping a few cups of water into the recess before moving towards the window, I stand up on the bowl and realise I still have the cup in my hand. I throw it at the bucket; it hits the rim and crashes into the recess. *Fuck, fuck, fuck, that was so loud, Nigel.*

I pull myself up onto the ledge, and get my leg outside, almost crushing my balls in the process, but I can't pull my torso out past the blocks. Frantically, I twist and push, but it's useless.

I have no choice but to go headfirst. Squeezing my torso through, I grab onto next door's roof guttering; it almost gives way before I let go. The thought of a spinal injury at this point doesn't excite me. Grabbing at anything I can, I finally take hold of a solid piece of timber that takes my weight.

Finally I'm through. I slide down the wall and hit terra firma. The feeling of sand between my toes has never felt so good. I can't believe that we are free; the rush is intense.

But short-lived.

'We've been spotted by the boy next door,' Amanda says. It will only take a matter of seconds before the bush telegraph gets going. I reef my shoes on and try to cover my head with my sarong, not that it will make much difference now.

We sprint down the alleyway between the houses, stopping momentarily at the end. Going left isn't an option – that will take us back to our front gate. Directly in front is a mass of thorn bushes. We turn right.

Amanda is out in front with me two paces behind. We make it down the side of the neighbour's house. From the corner of my eye I see someone standing at the neighbour's front gate.

'What are you doing?' I think I hear someone say but I can't be sure as my brain won't compute anything now. My feet move without my thinking, pounding the loose sand. I cry for help. '*I caawin, I caawin, I caawin*' pushes up my throat and projects out my mouth as I race down the street with no direction in mind. My eyes take in the sandy street, thorn bushes, trees, goats and houses, but none of it really registers. It's as if I'm floating. It's like the seconds before an anaesthetic fully kicks in: I'm lucid but completely out of control.

We are both now sprinting down the road, screaming. We come to a woman walking in our direction. Her eyes widen as if she has just seen two ghosts; she runs away in sheer terror.

I am now in front of Amanda as we come to a T-intersection. Glancing right and then left, I see a bitumen road about 200 metres away.

Before I can even think, my legs are off. I have no idea where Amanda is. Hysteria has taken over and my brain feels like it's about to shut down. As I'm sprinting down towards the main road my body suddenly stops and does a U-turn.

Amanda is now just in front of me. Behind her I see a minaret stretching into the vast blue sky. My brain doesn't compute it as quickly as my body; I begin running back in the direction we've just come.

Standing at the T-intersection is the neighbour. He says, 'Do you need help?' I register that he is speaking English so I run to him and grab his arm.

'Please, you have to help us. Where is a mosque? Please, you have to take us to a mosque.' Amanda now has his other arm.

'Please, help us, do you speak English? Can you come with us to the mosque?' she says. Before he even has a chance to reply, Amanda and I have our arms under his, almost like we are carrying him, running. Just as we begin climbing the side steps of the mosque, the sound of an AK47 rings out in the air. Too scared to look behind, we barge through the side entrance and enter a mosque for the first time.

There in front of me are men, some standing, others prostrating, completing their midday prayers. It's seconds before their attention turns to us. '*I caawin, I caawin, waxaan ahay* Muslim; *waxaan nahay* Muslim. Help me. I am Muslim; we are Muslim,' spills out of my mouth. I continue to repeat this, a hysterical chant, before I feel the full force of a fist hit my head.

Spinning around, I see with dread that Jamal is right beside me, AK47 in hand, screaming at me, with fury in his eyes. I feel a kick to my ribs, then to my legs, followed by punches. All I can do is try to protect my head with my arms.

Jamal now has my arm and is trying to drag me out of the mosque. I rip it from his grip, shredding the sleeve of my shirt in the process and scoot away from the door.

I can see Amanda. Donkey is forcing her towards the door. Pandemonium has broken out and we are soon encircled by the men who had been praying. The rush of adrenaline and fear is overpowering: my heart hammers in my chest; my brain feels completely fried.

There's now a short rotund man in front of me.

'*Asalam alaikum,*' I manage to exclaim the traditional Muslim greeting.

'*Walaikum assalam,*' he greets me back.

'*Waxaan nahay* Muslim,' I say. He then speaks to me in English. 'Who are you?'

'I am Nigel Brennan; I'm a photojournalist from Australia; we have been kidnapped for five months. These people are going to kill us if you don't help us; we are both Muslim. Please, you have to help us,' I blurt out, all the while Jamal is yanking me away from the circle of people.

'Calm down. You are Muslim?' he asks with a hint of surprise in his voice.

'Yes, we are both Muslim.' My reply causes consternation within the ever-growing group surrounding us. I start reciting the first verse of the Qur'an in Arabic.

As the words roll off my tongue, there is amazement and belief in the hundreds of eyes staring back at mine. Men now push past and grab Jamal, hustling both him and Donkey away from us, towards the door. Amanda is standing beside me; we hold hands in a white-knuckled grip.

Everyone is talking at once, a mix of Arabic, Somali and English. It's chaos. We are pushed towards the centre of the mosque. I steal a glance over my shoulder to see that our two young guards have been bundled up towards the back wall by a large group of older men.

Everything must be happening quickly but I see it in slow motion. There is the rotund man talking with several other men, including the neighbour. Finally he speaks to both of us.

'If you are Muslim, everything is okay. These people can not kill you; it is against Islam.' I know in my heart that these people are trying to help us, but we're a long way from being safe.

'Please, don't cry, calm down,' he tells us. 'Please, tell me your names and where you come from.'

'I am Nigel Brennan; I am from Australia. I'm a photojournal-ist. She is Amanda Lindhout; she is from Canada. She is also a journalist,' I reply as he jots this all down on a small piece of paper. He then disappears into the crowd to where a small group of men are now standing between us and the boys. It's not long before he breaks back through the crowd.

'There is not an Imam here at present. We have called one and he will be here in fifteen minutes. He will interview both of you to establish that you are Muslim. If you are Muslim, there is noth-ing to fear, you will be safe here.' All I can think is that in fifteen minutes we may already be dead.

'Have you prayed? Do you want to pray?' he asks.

'No, we have not prayed; we need to pray,' I tell him.

'Okay, follow me.' We walk to the middle of the mosque. There is yelling and arguing between the groups of men. One man in par-ticular is jostling us; he sends shivers down my spine. Something tells me that this guy is not on our side. We are finally placed in the pulpit and told to take off our shoes.

People are pouring into the mosque as the whole neighbour-hood must have heard by now what is going on. Older men in the crowd motion with the palms of their hands for us to be calm. An ancient-looking man smiles as I recite Arabic. My eyes lock with his as he says, 'You are Muslim; Islam is good.' I reply, '*Alhamdulil-lah*, all praise to Allah,' and watch his grin widen.

Suddenly, Donkey and Mao are either side of the pulpit, AKs held against their chests as if trying to guard their prize. I can see the perspiration running down Mao's face. He must have run like mad to get here. He looks at me with disgust.

From the corner of my eye, I see a black-veiled woman star-ing at us through the side window of the pulpit. Amanda has also

clocked this dark figure and both of us are not so much terrified by
her presence as by the fact that someone with a gun could easily
shoot us from this vantage point.

One of the men in the crowd closes the metal shutters with a
bang.

Then the crowd that surrounds us dissipates. As the space in front
of us clears, I see masked gunmen pouring into the mosque through
every doorway. None of these men belongs to our group and I am sure
that it's all about to end in a bloodbath as these different gangs go to
war over a prized possession. I'm certain that we are about to die. But
then the crowd form a protective semicircle around us.

An older woman pushes through to where we are seated on
the floor; it is the same woman who was standing at the window
minutes before. She is clothed completely in black and her eyes
peer back at us from behind her niqab; she sits between us and
looks at Amanda. We both greet her in Arabic then Amanda tries
to talk to her in English, but she doesn't understand.

My attention swings between what's happening in front of us
and Amanda. I see Amanda motioning with her hands, using sign
language to show fornication, and then pointing to Donkey.

The old woman now looks at me for confirmation. I can see the
tears well up in her eyes as I nod. She turns back and places her
arms around Amanda and sobs.

I look back at the crowd and see a man, an AK across his chest
and an ammo belt over each shoulder. I have never seen him before.
'You are Muslim?' he asks in English.

'Yes, we are both Muslim, for nearly five months we are Muslim,' I reply completely shit-scared as he holds his gun against
his leg.

'If you are Muslim, you are my brother,' he says using his finger to punctuate the point. He then bends down and kisses me on both cheeks. '*Asalam alaikum*, may peace be with you,' he says softly next to my ear.

'*Walaikum assalam*, and also with you,' I reply. There is something about his presence that calms me but I'm not ready for what happens next.

'The AK47 is the gun of the Muslim. You are Muslim so you can have my gun, brother.' Then he places the gun in my lap. As I pick it up there's a momentary manic thought of just opening fire on anyone in the place carrying a weapon. But I don't have it in me. I know that it would end in a massacre of the innocent people trying to help. I hand back the gun.

'I don't want it. I can't kill anyone; I am Muslim,' I say as he takes hold of the gun with a nod.

'Come with me, you will be safe,' he says.

'No, we need to wait for the Imam,' I tell him.

Then dread fills me as I see Skids pushing through the crowd. What felt like the possibility that we'd actually get out of here comes crashing down. Ahmed and Donald are now also on the scene. Skids walks behind us, waving his pistol like it's some toy. We are pulled to our feet.

I hear Ahmed shout, 'You!' There's rage in his voice as he looks at Amanda. We are then dragged from the pulpit towards the back doors, but I won't give up without a fight. Digging my heels in, I'm trying to wrench my body free.

Donald screams in my face and I manage to glance over to see Amanda. Her hijab has been completely pulled off, there's hair everywhere and she's fighting like a feral cat. She still has the old woman hanging onto her for dear life, trying to protect her as Ahmed and a number of men now pull her closer to the exit.

I continue to fight as men grab at me. I pull away from their grip while still holding my shoes in one hand and the Qur'an and my bag in the other. I look again for Amanda but she is nowhere in sight. Then the crack of an AK punctuates the air. *Oh my god, they have just killed her*, races around my head and *I'm next* quickly follows. There's no way out of this.

Moments later Ahmed is there beside Donald. He begins pistol whipping me across my shoulders and I have no option but to hit the floor and go into the foetal position. Next come kicks and punches then someone grabs my feet and begins dragging me across the carpet.

Then I'm hovering above all this chaos, watching myself, suddenly calm as I come to terms with the fact I am about to die.

Now at the back doors, I'm being dragged down the steps and into the courtyard, the skin on my elbows peeling off on the coarse concrete.

I am pulled to my feet. Ahmed again whacks me with the butt of his pistol before I am picked up by five or six men and carried to the front gate. All the fear and panic has left my body and it's just quietness. *I just wish I could tell Mum and Dad that I love them and I'm so sorry for all the pain I have caused them.*

I haven't got the fight in me to do anything now. Just as we reach the gates, I see a four-wheel drive in the street. I gasp for air as I see Amanda in the backseat still putting up a fight. I can't believe she is alive and the relief is mind-blowing.

I am bundled into the car. I'm next to Amanda and I grab her hand and look at her face; one side has begun to swell from the force of the blows.

People jam in beside us. Donkey and Skids jump into the tray behind and all the doors are slammed closed. I now recognise the man beside me as the one who had jostled us earlier; my gut instinct had been right after all.

Ahmed, Mao, Donald and the other men get into a nearby Subaru and take off. As we pull away from the mosque, I notice a man being restrained on the ground; there are three or four men sitting on him as he struggles. It is the man who had handed me the gun only minutes before.

Our car, now in convoy, speeds through the sandy streets, zigzagging down small laneways until we come out into open bushland. Amanda and I manage to whisper quietly to each other.

'You okay?' she asks.

'Yeah, I'm okay. Fuck, that was intense. Are you all right?'

'Yeah, I'm okay, took a bit of a beating, though,' she says.

'Yeah, I can see that.'

'I'm sorry, Nige, for making you escape.'

'You didn't make me do anything; at least we had a shot, at least we took control finally.' We both manage a smile at this point. 'I thought you were dead when I heard that gunshot.'

'Me too with you. The veil between this life and the next is very thin,' she replies as we squeeze hands. Our vehicle follows the Subaru until we reach a pink two-storey building, a sign on its wall reading 'University of Mogadishu'. The building carries the scars of conflict; it looks as though every calibre of bullet has rained down on it over the years.

As we come around the corner, the axle of the four-wheel drive gives way and we come to a screaming stop. The Subaru finally stops a few hundred metres ahead and reverses.

Ahmed and the others get out and come over to our vehicle. Amanda is pulled out her side and pushed into the Subaru. I am then taken out and frogmarched to another waiting car. Just as

I go to get in Ahmed again raps his pistol across my shoulders for the fun of it. Mao climbs into the backseat beside me. Donkey is beside Amanda, Skids is in the front passenger seat and Donald behind us. We take off again, leaving Ahmed and the others.

Donald begins ranting at us. 'Why did you escape? You have caused big problems. Many people could have been killed at the mosque. This is very stupid.'

'The boys told us that our three Somali friends were killed by Al-Shabaab. We were scared so we ran,' we both say, speaking over the top of each other.

'This is not true; they have not been killed,' he replies angrily.

I try to say something but before the words even pass my lips I feel the force of Mao's fist as he punches me directly in the face. I wince in pain and draw my hands up, not letting him get a second shot. I won't allow myself to show emotion. I think, *You gutless bastard, taking a cheap shot*. My next thought is, *Not my beautiful teeth*, as I push on the back of them with my tongue to make sure they are all still there.

We hit a bitumen road and enter a built-up area; there are many people walking along the street. In a strange way it's beautiful to see them going about their day, a world away from what we are experiencing.

We finally stop in front of a compound. We are driven inside to a large house that looks, by the number of shoes at the front door, to be currently occupied.

Amanda and I are pulled out of the car and marched into a bedroom at the back of the house. In front of us, in all its glory, is a huge queen-sized bed. It's like a mirage. Beside the bed is a dresser with a stack of cassettes at one end and bottles of perfume at the other. We are in someone's home.

My awe doesn't last long as the interrogation begins. We sit on the floor, surrounded by the boys, and Donald lets loose with the questions: 'Why did you escape? Whose idea was it? How did you get out? What did you say to the people in the mosque? Have you been communicating with the neighbour? Amina, did you tell the lady at the mosque that you have been raped?'

Donald translates our responses back to Skids. They are looking for someone to blame and the finger is being pointed directly at Amanda.

The interrogation continues for well over an hour, with Amanda bearing the brunt of it, in particular because of the rape allegation. We both beg for Donald not to leave us, not only because he is the only one who speaks English fluently but because we're sure he will not let them kill us.

He brushes aside our request and leaves. It's the last time we will see him.

Now alone with Skids, Donkey and Mao, the only comfort we have is each other. Assam arrives shortly after Donald's departure, carrying a small plastic bag. He looks at us like we're filth and drops the bag on the floor; there's the *clunk* of metal chains.

I feel my body go cold with fear. Then Skids picks up two small cardboard boxes entangled in the chains. Opening them, he tips out the contents and four padlocks drop to the ground. Confusion at first, then a moment of clarity hits me: *They're not going to torture us with the chains; they're going to shackle us.*

Mao snaps his fingers at me to stand. With him kneeling between my legs, he drags the chain around my ankle and snaps the padlock closed. I wince as the metal bites into my skin.

'It's too tight,' I tell him but he wags his finger at me and gives me a cruel little smile, before tugging on the chain several times.

He does the same with my other leg. And then to Amanda.

I can't spread my legs wider than 20 centimetres. Hobbled, we spend the rest of the day in this same room, guarded constantly. The only time we are allowed to move is to go to the bathroom adjoining the bedroom.

We snatch fractions of conversation and try to steel each other for what lies ahead.

FEBRUARY 2009

Back-pocket strategies

Kellie
Newcastle
Early February

As any family going through a crisis knows, life goes on. Whether it's
a death, a fight against cancer or a divorce, life goes on. Our situation is no different, and actually, I am desperate for life to continue.
I am finding the constant questioning along the lines of, 'Have you
heard from Nigel?' as enjoyable as fingernails down a chalkboard.
It's fine from friends and family but when it comes from people just
sticking their noses in, people who feel like they've had a brush with
celebrity because they know the sister-in-law of the guy who has been
kidnapped, it really gets to me. So I remove myself from everyone
who knows about my situation.

   I have rented a space in the town of Morpeth to use as a full-
time base for my catering business. It is fantastic to have such
an all-consuming distraction. The attention I need to give to the

branding of the store, the design concepts, the daily menu and the direction this little café should take provide Matt and me with an alternative conversation to the one we've been having for the past six months.

I hear rumblings of dissent among the family about how long the negotiation is taking, and while I am still paying attention, having work as an excuse to check out keeps me sane. There is talk of Ham heading to Melbourne see a man who might be able to shed light on Nigel's kidnapping, and Heather, Geoff, Nic and Ham are going to meet the foreign minister, Stephen Smith, about the case. I desperately want these meetings to be successful. I want everything to start moving along – that feeling of treading water we've experienced for so many months is killing morale.

The shop opens without the fanfare I was hoping for. Friends drop in and Mum and Dad come by for the first cup of coffee, but if I were expecting a complete distraction from the rest of my life, I was wrong.

While life does go on, the situation is still there bubbling away. It still needs to be talked about, decisions need to be made, and the brutal reality of Nigel being on the other side of·the world in god knows what condition is still something I think about. All the time.

Nicky
Moore Park
Thursday, 5 February

The foreign minister sends a request via his minions. He would like to see what we have put together in regards to fundraising and how we plan to approach the media. To date, the Australian government and the minister have used their influence 'to prevent adverse media' – they specify 'adverse' but in reality it's any media at all, good or bad – in relation to this matter. The minister wants to understand our thinking. No worries. Our thinking is bloody simple, breathtakingly so: we want Nigel back, and will do whatever it takes to make it happen.

Wednesday, 11 February

We are told that contact with Adan has been shut down and the NOK cell is being permanently transferred to Canberra.

Dave comes to sees us after he's packed up. He and Adrian were our very first AFP negs and they're also our last. He collects my mobile NOK phone. Both of them leave in tears.

If a proof of life comes in, the Feds will look at putting something into place, such as transferring the call. They are doing so well at tying up their loose ends. It's all so neat and tidy.

We know our lifeline to Nige is being cut and we're not being offered an alternative. We are being asked to trust the government, and I'm far from convinced we can.

As per DFAT's request, we distribute the missing-persons' flyer for family members to discuss. We have named it their 'lost-dog-poster strategy'. Ham bags the shit out of it. He's right: it's a stupid idea. Someone has put photos of Nige and Amanda looking happy and smiling on a poster. And whoever did the cut-and-paste has Gladstone-Smalled Nige – he has no neck. It's an absolute shocker and we all swing between being horrified that this is a legitimate strategy and pissing ourselves over the absurdity of it. Wasn't there a B-grade shocker in the seventies about a kid who survives a plane crash with his dog in the African desert, where they letter drop pamphlets telling him to walk east? Didn't they do this sort of thing for propaganda in the Second World War? DFAT's logic fascinates me.

I'm having visions of people sticky-taping the posters to power poles like we did when Zeke, our labrador, went missing. Oh, hang on, there is no one who can safely walk the streets of Mogadishu, certainly not at night. My son Atticus sees the poster and cacks himself over the photo. 'What is Uncle Nigel doing?' he asks. 'He looks like someone has cut his head off and pasted it onto a stick, like one of the characters from *South Park*.' His comment confirms how daft the idea is.

Nigel
The Dark House
Tuesday, 3–Friday, 6 February

Things have degenerated since our escape attempt. We've been moved yet again, and my new room is tiny – 2.5 by 4 metres – with only a small shuttered window on the back wall. Our paper and pens have been taken away. My chains are removed once a day so I can shower. The rest of the time they bite into my ankles and make it almost impossible to sleep. None of the boys is to have more than the bare minimum of contact with me. But worst of all, Amanda and I have been separated completely. I have no way of telling how she's being treated. The only indications she is even alive are her sneezes, coughs and the jangle of her chains as she goes the short distance to her own bathroom.

In this new regime the boys don't move from outside my door. The only advantage is that at one o'clock in the afternoon they tune in

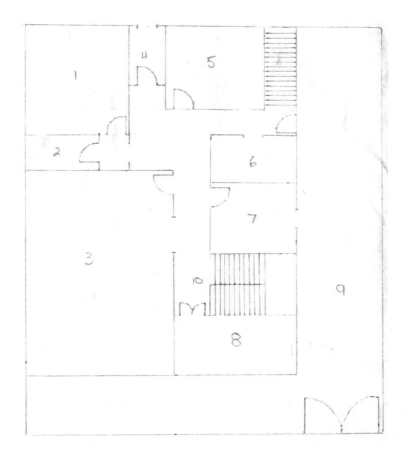

The Dark House

1. Amanda's room
2. Amanda's toilet
3. Boys' room and prayer area, weapons hold
4. Toilet
5. Captain Yahya's room
6. Kitchen
7. Nigel's room
8. Verandah
9. Courtyard
10. Area where the boys sit during the day

to the BBC broadcast. This becomes my window to the world while my life stays stationary. The only downside is that it is in Somali.

I can't believe my ears when I hear Kevin Rudd's voice, and I'm wishing, hoping and praying he is talking about my predicament. It's frustrating as the sound-grab dies and the Somali kicks in. Shortly after, Donkey – Abdullah – walks past. I call him back.

'Are they talking about me on the radio?'

'No, bushfires, over 100 people dead,' he replies. I slump back against the wall. Hearing about Australia is overwhelming enough but this is heartbreaking news. I couldn't feel further from home.

After evening prayer I get mild stomach cramps which quickly intensify, and I have a headache that would kill an elephant. My hands are clammy and I'm nauseated. Then I can feel that my sphincter is about to let go.

I bang furiously on the door, and Mao – Mohammad – appears. He grunts angrily in response and motions towards the toilet.

I dash down the hall on tippy-toes, trying to get to the bathroom before my bowels explode. I barge through the door, barely closing it and just pulling down my jeans before shit sprays everywhere. Like a burst water main, it keeps coming. Finally, I clean myself up, noticing the hem of my jeans has not got away unscathed. I don't really care. Feeling exhausted, all I want is to lie down. Into the early hours of the morning I get no rest, shuffling between the bedroom and the toilet. This is my first experience of dysentery.

With every request for Panadol or antibiotics, I get the same reply: 'Inshallah.' Over the next three days I can only sleep. I barely manage to keep food down and I know I can't afford to lose more weight. At some point a blister pack of Panadol is tossed through the door.

'Allhamdullah,' I reply, trying to sound thankful, but I can't understand why it's taken so long. I'm not much use to them dead.

Nicky
Moore Park
Mid-February

After our unenthusiastic response to the lost-dog-poster idea, we are informed that it is only 'a back-pocket strategy' that would be considered if the current approach fails.

The current approach, which is to have no communication with the HTs, 'would continue until it is certain it will not produce the desired outcome or until another new line of enquiry opens that has the potential to be more beneficial than this one. Should the current line of enquiry fail, there are a number of different options, including the information pamphlets [that is, the poster], which are open to negotiators to proceed with.' This is serious Humphrey territory.

We want to know if there are any other strategies in play now. This no-talking tack with the kidnappers appears totally at odds with what Gordon described to us in September, when he said that communication was the key. It's been months since we've had a proof of life. No one is in contact with the kidnappers, so how can we possibly be building a rapport? This strategy is the polar opposite of what was discussed with us, which was all about gaining empathy and, in turn, some control.

We really want answers. In a conversation I have with Ben via speakerphone, so I don't have to try to explain things to Mum and Dad, he breaks down a possible new strategy for us, one championed by the RCMP.

'We have contact with an extremely influential person in Somalia, who has confirmed he is willing to help us. We believe this person has the power and influence to generate the release of Nigel and Amanda. Unfortunately, this person has been unable to assist until this point in time. There have been a number of reasons, including the civil unrest in the country.' Later Ham will comment that this guy sounds like a coked-up warlord – this moniker sticks and becomes our code name for the strategy.

'This person's connections are with the Canadians, and we are in their hands on this matter. The Canadians have biblical belief in this strategy.' That statement sends a chill up my spine.

In late February Mum gets in contact with Mick F. His name and number come in a roundabout way, from Nigel's old workplace, the *News Mail*. When Mum rings him, he says he has been following the situation closely and shares our frustration that after six months there appears to have been no progress.

Mick tells Mum he was formerly with the Australian Defence Force and has been in the private security sector since 2004. He is now covering the Australian *60 Minutes* team on their story about piracy in Somalia. He tells Mum those in the private sector are not jockeys; they have social responsibilities. Mick believes we won't get any further without having somebody on the ground, and he has contacts in Somalia. He tells Mum that in *all* hostage situations in Africa a ransom is paid; it just comes in different forms.

He offers to negotiate on our behalf, saying it could take another three months. Mick asks if Mum thinks the AFP and DFAT would be prepared to work with him or whether he'd have to work by himself. We're not sure. Mum asks what the cost would be. It would involve airfares and insurance and probably the greasing of a few palms, but he would not charge for his time.

Ham rings *60 Minutes* to establish Mick's credibility and more about his role working with them. Mum discusses the issue with

Ben, and somehow the government interprets this as the Brennan family doing a story with *60 Minutes* to mark Nigel's six-month anniversary. *Eh?* Yeah, we're going to have a party with beers and a band as well.

Ham starts to talk to Mick regularly.

Nigel
The Dark House
Tuesday, 17 February

In the afternoon Captain Yahya brings in my laundry. Just as he is leaving he says, 'Noah, your nickname, *Forebeer debenetchay.*' Shrugging at him, I ask, 'What does that mean?' He tries to explain but I don't understand. He touches his forehead then points at my groin. *Dickhead?* I wonder. He runs outside then brings back Abdullah, who says, '*Forebeer* means wrinkly forehead; *debenetchay* is tight underpants.' They both begin to laugh. From this point on I am no longer called Noah, instead I am 'Forebeer'. I run with it, not wanting to rock the boat. It's funny because since the escape attempt, except in Romeo's case, I've stopped using their nicknames – it's no fun any more.

My illness has settled down and I get a short respite from my room. After three days of my pestering Young Yahya for a haircut, he finally gives in. It's a victory, even though it means breathing in the stench of the toilet for half an hour. I'm surprised by my reaction. The touch of another person is mesmerising. It feels like a betrayal, but I'm not about to deny myself this small opportunity to feel human again.

He moves my head to get the angle right for the razor, and I luxuriate in the contact. All the stress and anxiety I had been holding on to for the last three weeks dissipates for the twenty minutes it takes to shave my head bald. Once it is done, I feel guilt and disgust at my weakness. Amanda is not getting this sort of treatment and has more than likely heard the two of us laughing.

Back in my room I get a visit from each of the boys to see Young Yahya's handiwork. They all respond in a similar way. 'Forebeer, very beautiful. Islam good.' Some kiss their fingers like an Italian would, saying 'Bellissimo.' Others stroke my beard, which makes me feel like I'm in some homoerotic movie. Only minutes before it had felt so nice to be touched by another person, now I feel like a cheap whore and just want them to leave me alone.

In the late evening I hear people talking down Amanda's end of the house. I know Ahmed is here – I can smell his aftershave. It's been nearly a month since we escaped and part of me is desperate for information from him. The other part doesn't want to see him for fear of what he might do.

He finally walks through my door, the half smirk spread across his face, and greets me in the normal way.

'How is your situation?' he says, the pompous, sarcastic arsehole.

Sucking back my anger, I answer him straight.

'My situation is not good, Ahmed. I'm in chains, I'm not allowed outside, I'm sick and have been passing blood. They won't give me the right medicine.'

'The chains are because you cause problem. Why do you run? Do we not give you food, water? Now you cannot run. This is good for you,' he replies, touching my chains.

I change the topic. 'Do you hear anything about our situation? Is there any news?'

'No, there is no news. Nairobi is causing problems; they do not want to finish this. What should we do?' he replies nonchalantly.

Unsure if this is a rhetorical question, I sit staring. It's been nearly seven months and it feels like the wheels are just spinning with no traction.

'Maybe you will be here for a very long time,' he says, taking the wind even further out of my sails.

'Ahmed, the Australian government does not pay ransoms; they have signed a treaty,' I say for the thousandth time.

'If the government doesn't pay, your family will,' he replies.

There it is, clear as crystal for the first time, the cold honest truth.

'Ahmed, you promised you would not take money from our families,' my voice rises slightly as I struggle to control my fury.

'We can take money from your family because they are Christian,' he fires back at me, almost mockingly. I just want him out of my sight; I'm afraid what might come out my mouth. I sit there passive-aggressively, waiting out the time till he leaves.

That night I toss and turn for hours, replaying the conversation over and over in my head.

MARCH 2009

What if?

Kellie
Newcastle
March

When Nigel was first taken, many people came out of the woodwork to offer assistance. Someone knew someone else who was involved with other kidnap cases, and so and so had an uncle who had spent time in Somalia and has connections. A lot of these people made themselves known to the AFP as well. The family followed up all the leads. However, on the advice of the AFP and DFAT, we didn't pursue them.

That is, up until we encountered the no-talking strategy, and things ground to a halt.

Heather has been given the name of a gentleman who looks after media crews in Somalia – Mick F.

Ham and Mick have many discussions about who's who in Somalia, how long our government has taken in this process and how Mick thinks they should have handled it. Those two definitely have a good connection, and Ham is adamant that Mick can get Nigel out. The rest of us are unsure as Mick has never been involved in a rescue before.

It's March, and Heather and Geoff are visiting for Callaghan's sixth birthday. Ham informs us that Mick lives nearby. So on a Tuesday morning, Heather, Geoff, Matt and I meet Mick F and his wife.

Mick is in his late thirties and works out a lot by the look of him. He sits opposite us at a large table in the coffee shop. He has many Somali contacts, and is due back in the country shortly. He seems very capable, and his ideas for getting Nigel out sound plausible, but you need to trust your instinct and mine is not jumping up and down, wanting to put this man to the task. He has a young family and a stunning wife, and if anything were to happen to him, I couldn't live with the guilt. Mick isn't going to charge us for Nigel's rescue, only for the costs incurred – around $30K – and money for dealing with certain elders. He believes we'll need to give the group around US$500 000.

Mick and Ham talk about paying for Nigel first and then raising more money to get Amanda out. Most of the family know this is not going to be an option – none of us believes Nigel will leave Amanda behind.

The Lindhouts are furious about Mick's involvement. They feel it will jeopardise the strategies we've got in place. But we're so unhappy with the AFP's current approach that any communication with Nige and Amanda, regardless of where it comes from, would be good news.

Ham and Lorinda have a huge argument. Lorinda says that Ham will have Amanda's blood on his hands if anything happens to her, and Ham accuses Lorinda of leaving her daughter there to die by doing nothing at all. The Canadians definitely feel threatened – all the money we've got for Nige and Amanda's release is ours.

Nigel
The Dark House
Early March

At the start of March I hear Romeo's distinctive voice in the house. The last time I saw him was at Eid, well before the escape. It's a relief in some respects: he speaks English and has some pull over the younger guards. I welcome any change, no matter how tiny.

'*Asalam alaikum*,' he says, a ridiculous false smile spread across his face as he comes bounding through my door. I greet him in the traditional Arabic way then hug him, immediately feeling that I've betrayed myself.

'Noah, what is this?' he says, feigning surprise as he touches my chains.

'We tried to escape,' I reply dully; his buddy Ahmed will have already filled him in on our misadventure.

'Ah, yes, I hear you cause big problem at the mosque . . . How is your Islam?'

The lie rolls off my tongue. 'My Islam is good.'

'You are very beautiful Muslim now, like Osama,' he laughs, rubbing the end of my long beard. *I am not some goat-rooting madman, thank you very much*, I think, my skin crawling.

'What do you read about Islam?' he asks next. I explain that the boys have taken away all of my religious material, which Romeo seems displeased about.

'*Inshallah*, you must have these books,' he says. I then press him about my Qur'an, which Donald has. He assures me he will collect it the next time he goes to Mogadishu. He asks me if there is anything else.

Apprehensively, I ask, 'Is Amina okay? I am worried about her.'

'She is fine. I will go to her now,' he replies before walking out the door.

Later in the day Romeo delivers some of my religious books and a pencil. I'm not overly excited about the books, but the pencil is a win.

He asks me if I need anything else. I ask for a macawiis, the Somali sarong. My jeans have become uncomfortable and are extremely difficult to go to the toilet in. Romeo comes back five minutes later, with the macawiis he was just wearing, saying, 'You can have this; it is mine. I will buy another at the market.' I'm reluctant at first, not really keen on anything that's been in contact with his balls, but I'm in no position to be picky.

'Thank you, can I put it on now?' I ask.

'Yes, of course.' He calls one of the boys to bring the keys to my chains. After they've unlocked me, I take off my jeans, feeling exposed as all the boys crowd into my room to watch. Romeo shows me how to put on the macawiis and I stand there like part of a freakshow. All the boys laugh and say, 'You Somali now.'

'Is good?' Romeo asks. I nod. My qualms about wearing his clothing quickly vanish without the feeling of rotting denim clinging to my legs.

The boys slowly file out, leaving me to my first night's sleep in a long time where I don't have to lie in a pool of sweat.

Friday, 6 March

Several days later Young Yahya comes into my room. I am disturbed by what he has to say. 'Amina, no Muslim,' he growls, shaking his finger.

'Amina is a Muslim; she is our sister,' I reply, trying to sound forthright.

'Not real Muslim,' he retorts. 'We watch praying, like this, like this, no good.' He moves his head from side to side, as if looking around for something.

'Nobody has taught her how to pray properly,' I say.

'Amina says Muslim but not real Muslim. Forebeer Muslim,' he says. I can feel him trying to gauge my reaction.

'We are both Muslim, Yahya,' I say, the conversation making me increasingly nervous.

There is an uncomfortable silence before he says, 'Forebeer, you have this?' He begins drawing with his finger on the ground.

'What is that?' I ask, thinking it's maybe a star or a flower.

'Here,' he says, touching his forearm then drawing it again.

'Tattoo? No, I don't have one,' I say, smiling at him.

'Tattoo,' he repeats. 'Amina, tattoo; Muslim, no tattoo.' Amanda has a small tattoo on her ankle.

'Her mother did this when Amanda was fourteen,' I try to explain but Yahya doesn't understand. Neither do I, come to think of it. What sort of mother tattoos a fourteen-year-old? I don't like where the conversation is going so I say nothing more and he eventually leaves. In a bit of a panic, with no way of communicating with Amanda, I want to tell her, *Just play the game. If you're going to try to bluff someone, don't do it half-arsed.*

Over the past seven months the boys have done little more than eat, sleep, pray and read their Qur'ans. Their only task now is to guard us and make sure we don't embarrass them by escaping again – a virtually impossible feat now we are chained and monitored by them around the clock.

Since our escape attempt Assam has kept his distance; he only comes in when he's forced to and his manner's cold. My guess is he copped some flak for teaching me Somali and Arabic. I need a friend on the inside, someone who I can ask for things or push for information. I need to win back his trust. So, when he comes into the room while Romeo is talking with me, I leap at the chance.

'Assam, you do not speak to me for a long time. I know you are angry at me because we tried to escape. I am sorry if I have caused problems for you; you are my brother. In the Qur'an it says we must forgive one another; I am asking for your forgiveness.'

He breaks into a big broad smile as he replies, 'Okay, I forgive you.'

Walking over, I embrace him. I can't help but feel like the older brother who has just pulled the wool over the eyes of his credulous sibling.

Saturday, 7–Monday, 9 March

From the corner of my eye, I see Amanda coming out of her room. She is bent over and looks weak as she hobbles to her toilet. Abdullah, who's shepherding me, flies into a complete rage. He lunges towards her, arm raised ready to strike. 'Go back! Go back!' he screams at her.

I continue on, so happy to have seen her for just a second but heartbroken at how she's being treated.

It's especially painful to see as I'm winning a few small privileges Amanda is obviously not afforded. Having a pencil legally means I can do my crosswords and sudoku puzzles, which they've given back to me. I have also restarted my diary. On a blank pages torn from the front of a novel I start jotting down our movements, the comings and goings in the house, when phone calls occur and when I speak to the guys in charge. I hide this with the other contraband items down the side of my mattress. It stops me from losing time. Just knowing which day of the week and month it is helps my mental state.

The following evening I get a visit from Ahmed.

'Noah, how is your situation? Everything is okay?' his voice is shrill.

'Everything is okay. Do you hear any news?' I reply morbidly.

'I think,' he starts off before pausing, a smile at the corner of his mouth, 'maybe in two days is finished, you go back to your family.'

Trying to hide my excitement, I give the flattest response I'm able to: 'Really?'

'*Inshallah*, in two days – finished; you will go to your family.' He looks pleased as punch. Part of me doesn't want to believe it, doesn't want to be tricked. I won't have the energy to pull myself up again if it's not true.

'How is it finished?' I ask him.

'Nairobi says they will pay. *Inshallah*, it is finished.' I can't hold it back any longer, and the rush of adrenaline charges my entire body. I can't help smiling and laughing. I could burst into tears at any moment, but I stop myself as I know Ahmed dislikes it and sees it as a weakness.

'Is good,' he proclaims as he pats me on the shoulder.

'*Alhamdulillah*,' I repeat over and over. *We're going home*. After he leaves I lie there, like a kid on Christmas Eve, the anticipation travelling through my body like electricity.

The next morning, with a spring in my step, I replay the previous night's conversation in my head. Assam and Abdullah come into my room, and Abdullah asks me what Ahmed said the previous night.

'He said in two days I will go home.' Doubt creeps in as the words come out. *Surely they would know what's going on?* They both smile sheepishly then Abdullah says, 'If Allah says, you will go.' This does not put me at ease. I try to reassure myself that the boys are as ill informed as I am, or perhaps they are just playing mind games with me.

Around sunset I sense something is imminent.

The boys have begun putting their things together; I watch as they go back and forth past my door. I'm sure we are about to be transported. Hastily, I gather my belongings. Jamal walks into the room.

'Quickly, take everything; in five minutes we go.'

I throw the last of my things together. I sit, waiting, looking at the bags, amazed at how much crap I have accumulated. Twenty minutes tick by painfully slowly. Then I hear the sound of chains coming down the hall. I get a split-second glimpse of Amanda as she walks past, shepherded by two guards.

Shortly after, Mohammad comes in; gun in hand and ammo belt slung over his shoulder, he barks at me, '*Bax, bax.* Go, go.'

I jump up, grab my bags and shuffle to the courtyard. All the boys are anxiously milling about. Joseph stands there, holding a massive machine-gun. I'm pushed towards the car and ordered to get in next to Amanda. Seated beside her, I grab her hand, our fingers interlocking. I tell her everything is okay.

We take off through the gates at breakneck speed and soon turn right onto a bitumen road. If my sense of direction is correct, we're heading towards Mogadishu. I'm doing all I can to suppress the excitement bubbling away. Amanda tries to say something to me but Young Yahya, who is behind us, pushes her head away violently. 'No talk.'

All I can think is, *Please, please, please, let this be it. Please, let us go home; I just want to go home.* We continue driving for what feels like ten or fifteen minutes before peeling off again to the right. We come to a stop about 300 metres later.

My excitement turns to dread. *This is not part of the plan.* Captain Yahya gets out of the car to unlock the gates. The car drives in. Amanda is taken first, out of the car and to the front door and then she disappears into the dark hallway. They come back for me, pushing me through the front door and into the first room on the right. Taking my torch from my bag, I survey the room.

I'm surprised by its size; it's maybe 4 by 9 metres. I'm even more shocked to see a sofa and two matching chairs. I drop into one of the lounge chairs; after months of sitting on the floor, the rubber foam feels like silk against my skin.

Mohammad walks in and, looking furious, gestures for me to get off the lounge. 'Sorry,' I say timidly as I move onto the floor; he then leaves. Minutes later, Abdullah throws my mattress through the door along with my other bag. I set up my bed on the back wall between two windows.

We're not going anywhere. I'm so angry at myself for stupidly believing Ahmed.

I bash on the wall to get Abdullah to take me to the toilet. On the return trip I see a dull glow coming from the door diagonally opposite mine. As I walk past, I spy Amanda lying on her mattress. It's a comfort to know she is just across the hall.

Nicky
Moore Park
March

Have a cup of tea and tell someone your problem – up here, it's usually crippling debt as a result of the drought – and the other person, as well as everyone else in the district, feels it with you. But the government line is: if you talk to an outsider, you lose control.

Through the country grapevine I've been able to contact Colin Freeman, the British *Sunday Telegraph* journalist, who was released after being held for forty days in Puntland, in northeastern Somalia. I'm sure it drives DFAT crazy that we have the ability to do things without their help – they don't have a clue how our network out here works. It doesn't have monetary value and can only be acquired after many hard years on the land, where friends and neighbours have to rely on each other and, heaven forbid, even trust each other.

DFAT is sceptical of Colin; after all, he is part of the media – the enemy. As it turns out, he is a godsend. By the end of our conversation I'm wishing I'd been put in touch with Colin, or in fact any other kidnap victim, earlier. Colin says that he and José Cendón, the photographer he was captured with, had discussed Nige and Amanda and often wondered how they were faring, having been held for so long.

Colin and I don't discuss strategy. All I want to know is how they coped. How often they got POLs. How they were treated – *really* treated, not the airbrushed version. What sort of a rapport, if any, they established with their kidnappers. How he is now.

I am elated to hear his responses. Here is someone who has been through the same experience as Nige, and who is far from being messed up. There is every chance that Nige is going to come out of this okay. I haven't felt so good about his chances in months.

But both Colin and I know not to compare the cases too closely. Different gangs, different parts of the country. And as corrupt as it is, Puntland has some semblance of government. The south, however, has zip.

There are a couple of things I am interested in that Colin has no idea about so he puts me in touch with his titular head, Adrian. Not to be confused with Adrian from the AFP.

'I love how you Brits use language,' I say to Adrian. 'You couldn't be called "tit" anything here without piss-taking.'

Adrian, as it turns out, is just as delightful to talk to as Colin, and incredibly informative. All the don't-discuss-anything-with-the-media warnings are unwarranted. There is no way these guys would do anything to jeopardise Nigel and Amanda's safety; they have just got their own people out of a hostage situation.

I ask him so many questions that Adrian gives me the number of the security agency that facilitated Colin's release.

I am thrumming with excitement. I phone David, the *Sunday Telegraph*'s K&R guy, and he certainly seems to know his stuff. David's view is that we cannot move forward till we set up our own crisis management team with Amanda's family and remove any other players – that is, the government – and preferably run the negotiation process in Nairobi.

David passes on some alarming news: he has heard that Nigel and Amanda have attempted to escape, going to a mosque for sanctuary. I am chilled by the thought. What would be happening to him now? Unsuccessful escape attempts historically have been a pretty good way of getting the shit beaten out of you, if not killed.

David also tells us there are unconfirmed rumours that Amanda is pregnant. This sends us into a tailspin. Amanda's unmarried: won't she get stoned? What if she and Nige were madly shagging and it's his baby? Or if it's her boyfriend's, what's his say in all of this?

The worst case scenario is if this is a product of rape by the kidnappers. I feel sick. This 'what if' is a place I don't want to go. It's too gut-wrenchingly scary, and all too possible; they are in a war zone and men in wartime can do the most hideous things.

We ask DFAT if Lorinda and Jon have been told. It appears not. Ham is now at the point of 'verbals are for gerbils' and is writing and emailing everything so we have a paper trail. In the subject line of his latest email to DFAT, Ham writes, as only he can, 'one toasted shit sandwich coming up'. Ham gives DFAT a day to have this discussion with Jon and Lorinda or we will have it for them.

DFAT's response is surprisingly prompt, a twenty-four-hour turn around. *It's amazing what a threat will do.* The reply is that the Mounties have talked to Lorinda about the unconfirmed reports.

Good, I think, that was not a phone call I wanted to make. It made me feel like a real Mrs Jessop, but I couldn't let the rumour go unspoken, none of us could. If it's true, this would not be a case of ignorance being bliss. But DFAT has thrown some extra info into the email for fun.

'As has been discussed with members of your family, negotiators have agreed not to limit efforts to a single line of enquiry and other strategies are currently being considered, including direct contact with the kidnappers.' *I can't tell where this is going.*

'As you would be aware, we have made various efforts to convey to the kidnappers the offer of a family payment of US$250 000. On 12 January negotiators contacted the spokesman for the kidnappers to make the offer. The offer was rejected and the demand for US$2.5 million was reiterated. Third-party intermediaries have also relayed the offer to the kidnappers.'

The letter continued, 'While a decision to proceed with a fundraising campaign is entirely the family's to make, I would reiterate that any publicity of the case would likely raise the kidnappers' expectations that the full ransom demand will be met. Separately, I would also reiterate that the activities of third-party contractors have the potential to undercut or derail Australian and Canadian Government efforts.'

The weird thing is that Ham didn't mention fundraising in his email, but it is something that we had been discussing a lot with DFAT recently.

Ham's response is just as prompt; it's become a game of email tag. I'm glad he's running this.

'Re. your concerns about fundraising and the activities of third-party contractors, both points are noted; however, the family must consider all options and we'll agree to disagree on some of your comments. After six-plus months it feels we have really made very little progress. Thanks and apologies for being a pain in the arse, but we have to do what we have to do.'

That's Ham: subtle as a sledgehammer.

Wednesday, 4 March

We have a big meeting in Canberra. This time it's Mum, Dad, Ham and I. Once again we are off to see the AFP and DFAT, and after months of requesting it and in the last six weeks being downright belligerent, we finally have a meeting with the Minister of Foreign Affairs, Stephen Smith.

Our meeting with DFAT once again has a cast of thousands. We revisit old strategies and ask about the state of Somalia's politics. The abbreviated answer to which is still 'shit', just varying depths of.

There's been a change of government and the Ethiopian troops have moved out, but neither action has significantly improved the situation. Al-Shabaab, the splinter group of the Union of Islamic Courts, is still throwing its weight around. There are still disaffected, disenfranchised youths who it would seem are willing to risk all for an idea of a heaven filled with virgins. The formation of the new government is encouraging to a point, but the situation is still fragile. It is a government in name only. There is a lot of militia fighting going on for control of the state.

The new government is working out of Djibouti, a country to the north of Somalia. The new government is under constant attack, and as a result President Sharif Ahmed is struggling, and governance is difficult. Violence in Mogadishu has intensified as Al-Shabaab has targeted African Union Mission in Somalia (AMISOM) forces. Twenty thousand people each month are fleeing the city. AMISOM's role is protecting Mogadishu International Airport (MIA), and they are suffering heavy losses. Al-Shabaab's objective is to institute Sharia law. Not all the population want this.

The Australian government still sees value in engaging with the new government, we're told. The president has spoken out about the kidnapping of Nigel and Amanda, but he's not thought to have much influence in Mogadishu.

DFAT discusses its TPI option, the coked-up warlord, which it views as our best hope. The source has his own militia and is in the process of trying to get the hostage takers to release Nigel and Amanda for costs. But at this point in time he is not in a position to access them as they are in an area outside his control.

Once again we are told that bringing the issue to the attention of the media will be counterproductive. The HTs are frustrated with the lack of publicity the kidnapping is getting. Australia has a large Somali community and information gets back to the country.

Abdi, we are told, has finally been debriefed in Nairobi, two months later – could the wheels have turned any slower? They could get nothing from him other than what was in his earlier media releases.

We also spend some time with the AFP. They all agree that the lost-dog-poster strategy was flawed. In fact, they don't argue any of its merits (if there were any).

We tell them how unhappy we are with the no-talking strategy. The Australian government can understand our frustration, but the Canadians have absolute faith in this approach, and the two are united. They confirm there has been a POL from a TPI. It appears Amanda and Nigel are unwell but have received medicine. They have received books and writing material. They are getting two meals a day and are allowed to wash their clothes weekly.

We are assured there are other strategies, if for some reason the current strategy doesn't work out. How could it not? Everyone has such faith in it and the governments' abilities to get Nige and Amanda home.

In the car on our way to see the minister, we run over the document we spent days compiling, indicating what we think our fundraising options are. We'd forwarded this to the minister, as requested, so he could review it before our meeting. It's a completely honest and open account of what we think we can achieve. We even ask DFAT if it has a preferred publicist.

TOP: Brennan family holiday at Diggers Camp, NSW, in the late '70s. Left to right: Nicky, Heather, Nigel, Ham, Matt and Geoff.
BOTTOM: The kids at Marlow in front of the old peppercorn tree with Nigel's dog, Gopher. Left to right: Nigel, Matt, Nicky and Ham.

TOP: Nigel and Amanda, exploring Queensland, during her visit to Australia.
BOTTOM: Moore Park, 2006. This photo was taken on Nigel's return from Ethiopia, after he first met Amanda. Back row, left to right: Kellie, Heather, Simon, Amy, Geoff. Front row, left to right: Matt, Nicky, Ham, Nigel.
OPPOSITE TOP: Mogadishu, a beautiful coastal city devastated by decades of war.
OPPOSITE BOTTOM: Somalia's ongoing conflict has created a food shortage and a humanitarian crisis. Nigel took these photos only days before the kidnapping.

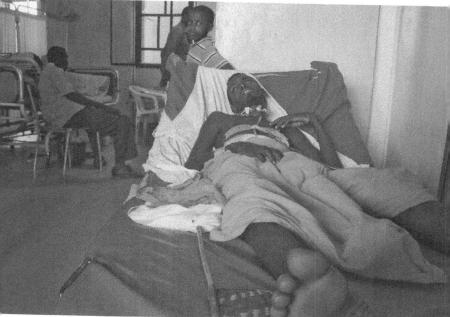

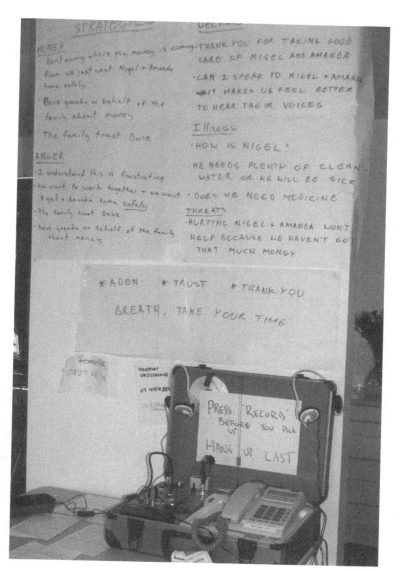

TOP: Next of kin phone with instructions for Nic when talking with Adan. This photo was taken downstairs at the Moore Park house while the AFP was still there.

OPPOSITE TOP AND BOTTOM: The streets and faces of Mogadishu.

NIGEL and AMANDA are still held hostage!

On the 23rd of August 2008, our son Nigel and our daughter Amanda were kidnapped just outside Mogadishu. They are still held hostage. We are very worried about them. Nigel and Amanda were uninsured freelance journalists reporting on the troubles of Somalis. The Brennan and Lindhout families are not rich. The Australian and Canadian Governments do not pay ransoms.

We the families, love Nigel and Amanda dearly and are desperate for their safe return home. We are appealing for YOUR help.

From the parents of
Nigel Brennan and Amanda Lindhout.

Nigel reporting in Mogadishu

Amanda with children at a food kitchen

OPPOSITE TOP: DFAT's proposed 'lost-dog' poster. Atticus, Nicky's son, on seeing it exclaimed, 'What is Uncle Nigel doing? He looks like someone has cut off his head and pasted it onto a stick.'

OPPOSITE BOTTOM: Moore Park Beach 2008 – the Christmas from hell. Back row, left to right: Simon, Jacinta, Izzy, Nicky, Kellie, Stirling, Matt, Amy, Hamilton. Front row, left to right: Gigi, Atticus, Monty, Mac, Oscar. Missing: Callaghan, he was playing on the computer. Oh, and of course Nigel.

TOP: Enjoying dinner at Gas town, Vancouver. All of us except Aunty Alison would make up the Crisis Management Team, working with John Chase. Clockwise from left: Kellie, Lorinda, Jon, Amanda's best friend, Kelly, Aunty Alison and Nicky.
BOTTOM: Kellie and Nicky in Vancouver.

Geoff and Heather in Nairobi. Visiting tourist attractions was the only way to make the time pass while waiting for Nige and Amanda to be released.

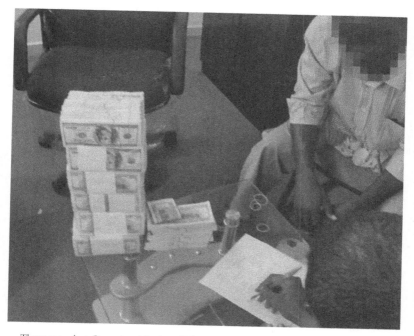

The money shot. On seeing this photo Kel exclaimed, 'Is that it?' This money was counted by hand three times, just to make sure it was all there.

TOP: Freedom! The smile says it all. Nigel on the plane to Nairobi.

OPPOSITE: Amanda, Nigel and the extraction team, getting the hell out of Mogadishu.

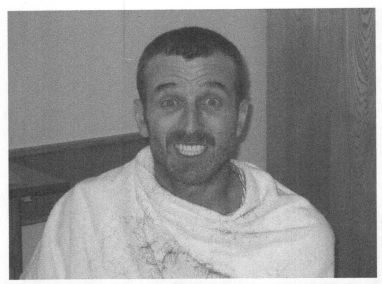

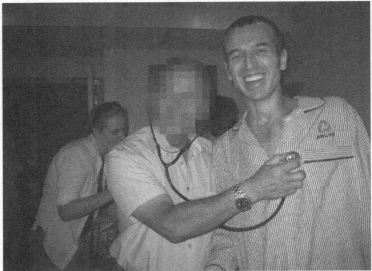

TOP: Fifteen months of hair growth, gone. Nigel in hospital in Nairobi.
BOTTOM: Joking around with a member of the extraction team at the Aga Khan University Hospital a day after being released.

TOP: Nigel and Amanda back in Nairobi with Nicky, John Chase, Lorinda and Kelly.

Nigel and Amanda enjoying time together out of captivity at the Canadian High Commissioner's residence in Nairobi.

TOP LEFT: Reunited. Matt and Nigel embrace at Sydney Airport.
TOP RIGHT: Kellie, Dick Smith, Nicky and Nigel. This was the day Nigel first met Dick to thank him for his help.
BOTTOM: Nigel and James Hardcastle, Nigel's best mate, catching up post Somalia and emptying a few cold beers at Moore Park.

ABOVE: Christmas, 2009.

NIGEL: 'Out of a horrific experience have come many good things. I am more compassionate towards others, and infinitely more patient. I have a greater understanding of myself and the world around me. I have been given a second chance at life and I don't intend to waste it.'

In the meeting it's clear Stephen Smith has barely even looked at it. Under no circumstances can the government condone fund-raising or put their name to anything. There's nothing else. No support. No suggestions. Zip. One of Smith's offsiders warns us we will be opening up a can of worms if we embroil ourselves with the media. The media will approach our family and intrude on our privacy and that of our children. (*Ah, good one, go the guilty-parent play.*) We need to bear in mind there may be critics of Nigel and of the family. It's a veiled warning: do we want to end up like the Corbys? *That can go both ways,* I think. The AFP hasn't exactly come up smelling of roses over either the Haneef or the Lapthorn case.

We ask a hypothetical question: if we raise more than US$250K, will the government use it to facilitate the release of Amanda and Nigel? That is, will they help us move the cash if the kidnappers and another agency, such as Mick F's, come to an agreed price over that amount? No matter how many ways or angles we go at it, we can't get an answer.

I watch Ham go in guns blazing and by the end of the meeting he's muttering under his breath, 'This was a fucking waste of time.'

It is completely exhausting listening to this crap. Everyone talks in riddles. I'm glad Canberra is so climatically inhospitable; these people deserve punishment for being so bloody obtuse.

Moore Park
Tuesday, 17 March

Lorinda has had a call from Amanda; the tone of the conversation is ominous: 'You have to tell me how much money you have; there is a gun to my head.' Lorinda tells her they are doing everything they can and to please trust her.

Amanda says, 'These people aren't joking. They will kill me.'

Amanda goes on to say that the gang is aware that the Canadians have less money than the Australians. She says that Mick is a problem, that he is making the HTs really angry and nervous.

I quickly jot the notes down as Lorinda relays the conversation to me; it looks so innocuous on paper. Lots of 'Amanda said' and 'Lorinda replied'. I know the call would have been harrowing.

I'm on the phone in a nanosecond, trying to find out what's going down. Have Ham and Mum sent in Mick F in without our knowledge? Mick hasn't acted but he has established an in to the gang if we want it. But half the Brennan family think Mick is too inexperienced, and Amanda's family believe their government's line that this can be done with minimal amounts of money. So to date the family has made no effort to raise any.

Mick is pushing for a deal whereby we hand over our money to get Nige released and he then does whatever's necessary to get Amanda out. Ham and Mum like the idea. I think it's too dangerous. I've just finished reading Brian Keenan's book in which he had to make that decision as well, to leave John McCarthy behind. It makes me wonder when that would change: how long Nige would have to be held before he'd make a similar choice.

Nigel
The Couch House
Thursday, 16 March

I can hear Romeo across the hall talking to Amanda. My ears prick up but I can't hear any detail. They seem to talk for hours. It's been an ongoing theme of the last seven months that whenever the higher ranking guys come, they spend hours with Amanda and then give me five minutes of their time. There seems to be a lot of commotion in the hallway, with boys walking back and forth.

Then the sickening feeling, like that of touching an electric fence, from hearing the sound of an impending conference call, the sound of birds and whistling blasts from the speakerphone as it's walked down the hall and into Amanda's room.

Now completely alert and sitting up, I strain to hear the conversation and try to block out the background noise from the boys. The phone connects.

'Mum, I need to speak to you, call me back,' Amanda says. A short time later another phone call comes in.

'Mum, we only have three minutes. Someone called Mick has told these guys he is only here for Nigel.' There is a short break then surprise in Amanda's voice, 'They don't want to speak to Mick.'

'Mum, they don't want to speak with Mick,' she repeats. Silence, then Amanda's voice again; she's speaking to Romeo.

'She says that Mick is working on his own; he is not working for the families.' I'm confused as to who Mick is. I thought they were dealing with Mark in Nairobi.

Again silence, then I hear Lorinda's voice now on loudspeaker.

'They should not speak to Mick or anyone working for Mick; he does not speak for our family or for the Brennans. They have to call the number that I have given you for Nairobi because they have all the money. Is Nigel okay? Are you together?'

'We have been separated, but I know he is okay,' Amanda replies, then silence. The phone call seems to be over as I can now hear Amanda talking to whoever is in the room with her, but I can't work out what is being said.

Frustration consumes me. Who the hell is Mick? And what's he got to do with whatever is going on?

Saturday, 21 March

In the morning I'm confronted by Captain Yahya, Romeo and a few of the other boys. I'm handed the phone. I'm surprised to hear a strange man's voice on the other end. He asks me to identify myself and explain my condition. I am no sooner finished than the phone is ripped from my grasp and they all walk out, leaving me more confused than ever.

Nicky
Moore Park
Saturday, 21 March

Lorinda gets a number of new messages on her mobile from Amanda: 'If my life depends on Mick, then my life is over.'

Lorinda is not allowed to answer the call and another message comes in from Amanda: 'I need to speak to you. Call me back.'

The AFP is pissed off beyond measure that we have done something behind their backs, which is not entirely true. They were well aware that we had entered into discussions with Mick. It appears that the RCMP has given DFAT an absolute bollocking as they feel the AFP has no control over the family, and, yeah, that would be correct.

It's ridiculous for the RCMP to think that they are not going to have to pay a ransom or costs or whatever the hell they want to call the handing over of money. I just don't believe that anyone, even 'a person of great influence' is going to get Amanda and Nigel out for $30K. I can't believe that, and therein lies the problem: we are no longer believers.

Every other person who has been involved in a kidnap situation has said it's all about the money and from what we can gather with the recent releases, the final amount is always a shitload more than thirty thou.

Lorinda is livid. She rings Ham and absolutely shreds him. Amy watches him go grey as Lorinda verbally flails the flesh from his bones. How dare he endanger Amanda's life? Ham doesn't like Amanda but he doesn't wish her harm. None of us was comfortable with Amanda when she came over to Australia a couple of years ago. She was the younger, shinier version for which Nige had traded in his wife, Janie. We were all pretty fond of the original model.

Mum's staying with Ham at the moment. She gets on the phone and gives it right back to Lorinda. What is *she* doing in order to get her daughter out, as it's obvious the governments are failing. Lorinda might be satisfied that Amanda is alive but we've had no proof of life for Nigel since early September . . . It was a nightmare, Amy tells me later, like watching dogs fight in a ring, both of them prepared to tear out the other's throat. Mum refuses to discuss anything more with 'that woman'.

Lorinda tells me the RCMP suggested she apologise, which she does graciously. I think they must have been well aware of how much is at stake.

Saturday, 28 March

We get an email from Lorinda and Jon. Both families are working on bridge building. I have been on the phone to her, voicing our disatisfaction about the lack of progess.

Lorinda's reply is very sincere but naive. She and Jon don't seem to be asking their government any questions; they just believe they are going to look after things. They certainly don't want to engage a private K&R company.

Ham has almost reached fever pitch about getting someone else in and Mum isn't far behind.

I can't see how we can reconcile these opposing stances on either side of the world.

Nigel
The Couch House
Thursday, 26–Friday, 27 March

I hear Ahmed in the house; eventually he comes to see me. The same smug smile is spread across his face as he asks me how I am, like I'm at some fucking holiday retreat.

'Ahmed, the last time I saw you, you said that it was finished. Two weeks have passed.'

He looks at me blankly. 'Nairobi does not want to finish. They cause many problem. Now they say if you want, you can kill them.' Hearing the word 'kill' isn't pleasant. I wonder at any negotiator throwing around that sort of language.

'Mick said this?' I ask him.

'No, we don't speak with Mick any more. It is a woman in Nairobi. She offers US$250 000 and says if we don't accept, we should just kill you. The people in Nairobi treat us like we are stupid, like boys. They think they can wear us down,' he says, irritation in his voice.

'Ahmed, please don't kill us,' I say. It's hard not to sound like I'm begging.

Sounding annoyed, he exclaims, 'You are Muslim; we cannot kill you.' But I can't trust a word he says. I'm sick of the lies and bullshit, I don't want to hear it any more and withdraw from the conversation. He eventually gets up, leaving me to ponder our fate.

The next morning I wake up in a foul mood. Two weeks earlier believed we were on our way home: to have it ripped from my grasp completely screws with my head. I realise I have to let it go or risk falling in a big black hole. I have absolutely no control over circumstances outside the house and there is no point in wasting energy or time trying to change them.

Things are made a little easier over the coming days. The boys have started coming into my room to sit on the couches while they read their religious books. This gives me a chance to talk with them. I will do anything to stem the mind-numbing boredom. I show them how to do one-armed push-ups, and laugh at them as they try to do the same.

I challenge Young Yahya to an arm wrestle. Lying there on the tiles, our hands clasped tightly together, I convincingly beat him. He laughs before meeting my eyes.

'Forebeer very strong, but I have AK47.'

APRIL 2009

Stuck in Groundhog Day

Nigel
The Couch House
Sunday, 5 April

The morning starts like any other. I have to say that I'm pretty happy with how I've managed to connect with the guys over the last week. The tension seems to have dissipated.

Abdullah brings the food that morning. He informs me that Romeo is going to the market soon to get an exercise book I'd asked for. *Well, that's another win; it's going to be a good day*, I think. '*Inshallah*,' I say to him.

I'm lying like a lizard in the afternoon sun, reading a book, when Abdullah and Mohammad barge through my door. Just the looks on their faces tell me things have gone to shit.

'What's wrong?' I ask.

'No talking,' Abdullah barks. At the same time Mohammad wags his finger and puts it to his lips. He then snaps his fingers and motions for me to sit on my mattress. Full of fear, I sit down, grabbing my shirt and pulling it on. They each walk to a window and close the wooden shutters. The darkness is instant and my eyes struggle to adjust. Abdullah walks over to me. Recoiling, I expect to be hit.

'Pencil,' he orders.

I fumble around on the floor to find it, then I pass it to him. He snatches it from me, and they turn and leave. I sit there in the dark. The only light comes through the door and two small vented windows near the top of the ceiling. I can barely see my hand in front of my face.

This must be Captain Yahya flexing his muscles. I can only guess that Romeo didn't ask his permission about the book, and the old guy's cracked the shits. Any ground I make they quickly rescind, just wanting to show me who's boss. It's certainly effective; with each fall it's harder to pull myself up. The darkness almost swallows me and with it comes fear. I thought I was slightly better positioned than Amanda, but this just shows me that we are both in deep trouble.

The intensity of the surveillance is once again ramped up and the concessions I'd won are stripped away. It's a sombre dinner under the ever-fading torchlight, but as I try to sleep I hear rain falling on the roof. It's been months since the last storm. The smell and the sound take me away. I remember peeling off my clothes and running around in a downpour as a child back on the farm, and the sound of rain on the tin soothes me to sleep.

Tuesday, 7–Thursday, 9 April

Things slide further still. This time, though, Amanda takes the heat of it. A ruckus is coming from her room; Mohammad is grunting

239

furiously, then there's a meaty thud, followed by Amanda's scream. My heart sinks.

A few minutes later, the shadow of a figure blocks the doorway. I lie there under my mosquito net too afraid to look. Feet come pounding towards me, and I feel utter fear at what is about to happen.

The net is ripped from around me, tossed to the side. Mohammad is there, standing over me with murder in his eyes. I try to sit up as he grunts at me. Before I can get to my haunches, he storms off. My heart is hammering; it's like the day we escaped. I don't know how much more of this I can take.

The next day the regime becomes even tougher; the boys seem determined to break me. Just before I go to shower Jamal stops me.

'Captain says four minutes.'

It's almost impossible to undress, evacuate my bowels, wash my body and put my clothes and chains back on in four minutes, but I'm not going to tempt fate as Jamal stands outside with a watch in hand.

I squat over the hole, pushing excrement out, and then furiously dump water over myself in the shower recess. I run out and Jamal says, 'Three and half minutes.' I'm wet rather than clean as I walk back down the hall and into the darkness of my room.

The following morning I'm marched to the bathroom by Abdullah. I idly look out into the courtyard.

He screams at me. 'What you see?'

'Nothing,' I reply, eyes on the floor.

'No looking. Four minutes. Go,' he barks, holding up four fingers. It's like looking at Hitler reborn.

I feverishly wash myself. He starts banging on the door. Still dripping wet, I throw my clothes on and walk out. He's right in my face, spit flying from his mouth as he screams, 'Ten minutes!'

Unable to back away I say, 'Not ten minutes, not possible,' noticing that he doesn't have a watch or a mobile phone.

'No talking,' he retorts, pushing me up against the wall. 'Go!' he snaps as he slams me through the doors and into the hallway. I try to walk quickly while he continually shoves me in the back, causing my chains to bite in and almost making me face plant.

Around midday I hear someone banging on the front gate, then the sound of a woman's voice. Romeo comes into my room and frantically tells me, 'Quickly, take everything.'

I start jamming things into my bag. I hold it and my shoes against my chest as he pushes me out the door. I turn left expecting to go into the courtyard, but he grabs me and ushers me across into Amanda's room. He orders me to sit in the corner diagonally across from Amanda. Joseph follows him in and closes the door. Romeo takes up position next to the door while Joseph guards the window, opening it and peering out.

I look over at Amanda, trying to give her an inconspicuous smile. I'm shocked at how frail she is; she's too terrified to return my gaze. She looks broken. I can only imagine what she has been through these last months. I just wish I could give her a hug and tell her to stay strong.

People are now walking in the hallway and I can hear a woman's voice; Romeo and Joseph are extremely edgy. I sit there biting down on the urge to scream out and make our whereabouts known. Huddled in the corner, I can't bring myself to do it, knowing the ramifications would be severe not only for us but for the strangers in the house.

The minutes tick by slowly. It's frustrating being this close to Amanda and not able to communicate. Then someone raps on the door. My heart jumps. Romeo says something in Somali. One of the boys replies on the other side. Joseph closes the window and then orders me out. As I leave, I glance towards Amanda, again giving her a thin smile, not sure when I will see her again.

On entering my room, I can see that everything has been sanitised. The things I hadn't gathered up are all stuffed under the chairs. Minutes later, I hear the clunk of the front gate shutting.

In the afternoon Romeo comes into my room. I ask him what had transpired earlier. Still noticeably anxious, he says, 'No problem, the woman comes to collect some belongs from the house.' Feeling more at ease, I ask him, 'Why do the guards close my windows? What have I done wrong?' He looks sheepish.

'This is not my decision. It is the Captain and the boys. I tell them what they are doing is wrong, but they will not listen to me.' He is a born liar.

Kellie
Boomerang Beach
Friday, 10–Tuesday, 14 April

It's the Easter long weekend and the shop is closed. Matt and I head off to Mum and Dad's beach house so the kids can spend some time with their grandparents.

I haven't had a break since Christmas and I really can't wait to just relax and do nothing. Matt has been doing the stay-at-home Dad thing with fantastic results, but he is really looking forward to spending some time reading. He has also been going back and forth to Moore Park to help out where he can, giving Nic a break from their folks or helping out Si on the farm.

We haven't heard from Nigel since September or October, I'm not exactly sure of the date. All I know is that it has been a long time and everyone is getting very anxious about it. Lorinda has asked Amanda about Nigel and she's said that Nigel is fine. This is passed on to us but it doesn't bring much relief.

Easter at Boomerang Beach is always lots of fun. Mum organises an Easter egg hunt in the backyard for all the kids. I have been going to Boomerang for as long as I can remember and we have always had Easter egg hunts.

I love that my family don't ask about Nigel; they know that if anything happens we'll tell them. Mum asks me quietly if Matt and I are okay and if we need any help. To know that we can turn to them at any time is comforting, for me at least.

Matt's positive attitude is still getting him through. Not a day goes by when he thinks we've hit a dead-end. His resolve is so solid; he has absolute faith that Nige and Amanda will get out safely, and that's separate to the issue of who gets them out or how it happens.

It's Sunday and the Easter bunny has well and truly been. I'm a chocolate freak, but after the first two eggs the novelty has worn off and I need to eat something real.

The hunt is starting at 10 a.m. so we have a bit of time to get the kids sorted and the eggs hidden. It is a grey day; the ground is moist from a light smattering of rain that came in the early hours of the morning, and there is a slight hint of autumn coolness in the air.

The kids are already on sugar overload. Matt and I rely on our chocolate-management strategy: we let the kids eat as much as they want on Easter morning, because once it's gone, it's gone. We've learned that if you regulate the chocolate intake, the sugar high can last for days. If you let them go for it with no restrictions, they tend to gorge themselves, and the sugar rush only lasts a few hours before it's over for another year.

It's Tuesday. The shop opens again tomorrow so Matt, the kids and I are preparing to head home. I've enjoyed my break and am looking forward to going back to work.

My mobile phone goes off as I'm packing the car. It's Heather and Geoff's number.

I take a deep breath, as I am not sure what mood Heather will be in when I answer. Lately I've been bracing myself whenever I answer a phone call from her. It feels like I am donning a suit of armour each time I do it, and after I've hung up, I notice that I exhale and my armour disappears. Sometimes, though, it seems like I don't exhale for three or four days; it just depends on the situation. Actually, the more I think about it, it's not like a knight's armour but more like a coating of mercury that covers my entire body and protects me from negativity. It reminds me of that man in one of the *Terminator* movies. Silly as it sounds, it's a little bit of self-preservation that I have no trouble indulging in.

I answer the phone and imagine myself in a slick of mercury all shiny and silver. It's Geoff. He is talking so quickly I can hardly understand what he is saying.

'Nigel phoned on Saturday night. No one was there to take the call; he left a message pleading with us to call him back. The AFP office was closed and the phone was left unmanned.'

Oh god, if I am understanding this correctly, Nigel phoned thinking he was calling home, but got an answering service. The shit is going to hit the fan. The only reason the family said yes to moving the phone to Canberra was because we believed it would be manned twenty-four seven and all calls would be patched through to Nic. I explain to Geoff that we are at Boomerang but are just about to leave, and that we will call as soon as we get home.

I hang up the phone and turn to Matt.

'Nigel's alive. He has called and left a message to call him back. The phone was unmanned, the long weekend, I guess, but he's alive. It's a good proof of life, and that is what your mum has been wanting.' I can tell just from looking at my husband that he is both elated and angry. We decide to leave straightaway. We say goodbye to Mum and Dad and pile the kids into the car. Matt and I drive home in silence. I know Matt is thinking, *Six months with no contact and he gets an answering machine. What must be going through Nigel's head?*

Every time Nigel phones or we get some new piece of information, the sense to do something urgently is tremendous. But we can't phone him back now; it'd be the middle of the night in Somalia. Even if we wanted to call him now, the Feds would disagree and explain to us in their police talk that a strategy needs to be worked out before anyone can call.

The entire family is disheartened by the Feds and DFAT's lack of progress; yet when they say not to call, we all listen. We all obey whatever they tell us, even if we don't like it. All of us except Hamilton.

Nicky
Moore Park
Sunday, 12–Monday, 13 April

It's Easter Sunday. Si, the kids and I are over at some friends' place, doing the Easter thing, catching up and having a few drinks – trying for a normal life. I've deliberately left the mobile at home so I know something serious is up when Dad arrives flustered at Richard and Fern's place. Not that Dad uses the phone; he was never a convert to letting your fingers do the walking. He would have driven to our place and all over the farm trying to find us. Then he would have started driving around town, looking for our car. There's a chorus of 'Hi Geoff's but I can see in his eyes he's in a real state, almost at the crazy-as-a-shithouse-rat stage.

He searches me out in the crowd.

'There's been a call,' he says to me.

I've gone into question mode: Where? When? Who? After he's gathered himself, Dad explains that Ben has called. He's on holidays but work has rung him to say that we should expect a call from Nigel.

With that established, I'm gone. People have become quite used to this behaviour. I get home and check the messages on the home phone. Nothing. Likewise nothing on my mobile. I check Si's mobile. Zip. I ring Mum; nothing on hers either.

'So what was Ben's message?' I ask her.

'He just said that a call had come in.' I ring Ham and Amy and Matt and Kel. Nothing. I wonder about the phone in Canberra and discuss it with everyone else as we play phone tag for the rest of the day. Well, if something came through there, they would have answered it. That's its purpose, right? I don't have a direct line to the ICC and I don't want to ring Ben while he's away so I try the Canberra main office: no answer, Okay, it's Easter, leave a message.

I wonder how I can get a call in to whoever is manning the phone. I don't doubt for a second that there's someone there. Maybe Ben meant there was a call coming in tonight. I don't leave the house for the rest of the day, just in case. *The calls almost always come through at night so that's when it will happen,* I reassure myself.

Next morning, still no call. Ben phones Mum to let her know there has been a call on the NOK phone. It went through to the ICC and was recorded on the answering machine.

What!?

Mum gets the number of the policeman who was on duty and goes absolutely berserk. I'm not privy to this call, but I could easily envisage Mum in full attack mode and the poor unsuspecting cop on the other end. No doubt he had a preconceived idea of how to pacify an older country mother. How wrong was he?

Mum initially gets some excuse that it's Easter and everyone is away on holiday. She establishes that no one was manning the NOK phone, as we had been assured would be done all day, every day, but that it is checked 'every day or so'.

'Why the hell wasn't it checked earlier? Ben had specifically called us to tell us there was a call,' Mum wanted to know.

'Well, I'm the only one here and I was very busy,' was the reply. It is all one monumental cock-up for which no one in the AFP wants to take responsibility.

We eventually get to hear the message. 'Mum and Dad' – no 'Hi', I note. Nigel must have had the phone just shoved at him. There's a pleading tone in his voice – 'If you are there, you really need to pick up now. If not, you've got to ring me back. It's urgent.' The pleading tone has peaked and his voice is quivery. 'There's no food or water. These guys are telling me Nairobi is saying they don't want to solve this problem. You have to do something. You have to get the money to these people.' Resignation starts to creep into his voice. 'I don't know who you are talking to in Nairobi, but if you want to see me again, you have to talk to them and get it sorted out.'

And with that the call's over. No goodbyes, no I love yous.

I guess once he'd said what he was supposed to the phone was snatched from him.

Christ, how disturbing must it have been for Nige to finally get to talk to one of us only to get the answering machine. He must think we've all moved on and are busy living our lives. That thought couldn't be further from the truth: we are stuck in our own personal Groundhog Day until he gets out.

Nigel
The Couch House
Friday, 10–Sunday, 12 April

Having been cooped up in the dark for five days with little ventilation, I wake up disgusted at my own stench. The room has a layered smell: sweat, sleep, unwashed clothes, over-ripe mango and food scraps. It hits me every time I walk back into the room from the bathroom – it's so thick and textured you can almost taste it. The boys aren't happy about it either; they snort and hold their noses when they walk in.

Mohammad comes in shortly after midday and hands me a bottle of aftershave. He motions for me to spray my bedding and myself. The sweet-scented musk is overpowering and floods my nostrils. I prefer the smell of my filth over this crap. It would make more sense just to open a window but I'm not flagging that idea with Mohammad; it's just something I will have to grow accustomed to.

The following day Captain Yahya, Mohammad, Abdullah and Romeo confront me. They close the doors and it's like a prelude to the OK Corral as Yahya sits down on the lounge seat, his pistol resting on his knee. Fidgeting like mad, I move over and sit on the floor.

'You have to call your family and tell them to pay whatever they have and we will release you,' Romeo says.

'You will release both of us?'

'No, only you,' he says.

'They will not do this; they will not just pay for me. They want both of us because if they pay just for me, you will kill Amina,' I reply.

'We will not kill Amina. Your family does not know Amina; why would they think we would kill her?' he says.

'They think you are terrorists. They do not know we are Muslim, so of course they are going to think you will kill her if they give money for me.' I try not to sound like I'm lecturing him.

He turns to the others and starts to translate; I butt in. 'They won't do it, I'm telling you. I know my family and they will not just pay for me.'

There's an awkward pause as they digest this, then Yahya turns and talks directly at me in Somali, waving his pistol just inches from my head. I have the sickening realisation that I was too forceful. I'm now watching his finger tapping the trigger guard of the pistol.

Romeo looks straight at me. 'The Captain says this is your last chance. If your family does not pay the money, they will kill you in a few days,' he translates, his expression deadpan.

They're not pissing about. A glance at the four faces now staring at me and I can see their patience has vanished. Trying to suck in air, my head spinning, I say to Romeo, 'Pass me the phone, I will speak to them.' It's not the time to be brave.

Yahya takes his phone and calls someone; as he speaks in a rough tone, I sit there in complete panic, unsure of how to explain this to whoever picks up the phone.

I desperately want to hear the voice of someone in my family but at the same time feel like smashing the phone against the wall. Yahya hands me the phone; it begins to ring.

Swallowing hard as it finally connects I hear Nic's voice, the recording on Mum and Dad's phone. *C'mon, guys, now is not the time to be out*, I think to myself as the message plays through.

Hearing the beep, I say, 'Mum and Dad; it's Nige. Um, if you're home, I really need you to pick up. If you're not, can you please ring back; it's urgent. Um, there is absolutely no food and water here any more. They're telling me that Nairobi is saying they don't want to solve this problem. You guys have to do something if you want to see me again. You, please, have to do something, get money to these people somehow. I don't know, talk to whoever you are dealing with in Nairobi and get them to sort this out if you want to see me again.'

As I hand the phone back, Romeo translates what I've said. They seem satisfied and file out. I lie down, a sense of abandonment filling me, which quickly turns to guilt and shame for what I'm doing to my family. I don't move for the remainder of the day, except to wash for prayer.

It's a strange feeling to have a time limit put on your life. I think of the things I wanted to achieve. The grandiose plans don't matter any more; I think of spending time with family and friends, falling madly in love again, having children, and it all seems to be slipping away.

The next morning I'm a complete wreck. I jump each time someone comes in. I'm trying to ready myself for what's coming but how do you prepare for death? This is my darkest day since we were taken, and there are times when I just wish that they would finish it. As the day drags on, I fight with myself to take control. I take strength from an old Maori proverb I'd heard years before, 'Turn your face to the sun and the shadows will fall behind you', and by the evening I've managed to pull myself out of the hole.

Saturday, 18 April

I wake up with a slight headache that quickly turns into a full-blown migraine. It is crippling; with the slightest movement it feels like my head is going to pop. I have to shield my eyes as the variation in light causes incredible pain. As the day continues, my body feels like it is at war with itself. There are aches and pains in every joint as a fever takes hold. I beg the boys for Panadol, telling them I think I have malaria. They seem unconcerned, shrugging their shoulders and exclaiming, 'Inshallah.'

I lie there in a pool of sweat, shaking uncontrollably, alternately feeling on fire and freezing cold. I can't eat anything. Captain Yahya comes in to check on me, holding his hand to my forehead. He allows me to shower several times, which lowers my core temperature, but whatever I have has taken hold, and my immune system feels like it's losing the battle.

Being bedridden is not good for my headspace. I'm struggling with what has taken place in the past few days. I can't help but think that I'm actually going to die here. If not from a bullet then from my body shutting down.

Sunday, 19 April

By the morning the migraine has eased but fever continues. I ask the boys again for medicine. Assam at least shows some concern.

Touching me he exclaims, 'Very hot!' *No shit, Sherlock*. Going in and out of consciousness, I find it hard to tell dream from reality until later that day when Young Yahya charges in, yelling at me.

'Quickly, quickly, go, go.'

I go into autopilot. I struggle to stand as my vision turns white; stars circling my head, I stumble towards the door. 'Bag, bag,' I hear him command.

Turning back around, my vision clearing, I pick up what belongings I can. He takes my arm and leads me into Amanda's room. I take up the position in the corner, happy to sit down as he closes the door.

Looking over at Amanda, I can see compassion in her face. We steal glances at each other. I just want to lie down in her lap and hear her say everything is going to be all right. Yahya suspiciously watches us, his foot jammed up against the door. Seeing the fear in Amanda's eyes is almost like reading her mind. Yahya catches on and orders Amanda to face the wall.

I drop my head onto my knees and listen as things are being moved around in the next room. There's the sound of unfamiliar voices, but I'm too weak to really care what they're saying. Finally I hear the front gates close, then a knock on the door: the coast is clear.

Yahya orders me out of the room; as I leave I try to give Amanda a smile.

Whatever's just taken place has put the boys on edge and they continue to carry their guns for the rest of the day. It makes me think that they've been spooked and a move is imminent.

Later that evening, Jamal throws a blister pack of Panadol on the floor. It's incredible how such a simple thing can lift my spirits: I pop four tablets at once, praying that they will have some effect.

Nicky
Moore Park
Tuesday, 21 April

Another message is left on the NOK phone answering machine.
We hear about this one almost immediately. The message starts
with 'Hey Nic.' Oh god, that cuts me to my core. This message
is for me. I feel bitterly disappointed that I wasn't there for Nige.

'It's crunch time,' he says. 'We have no clean water and we are
running out of food. They are saying they want the money.' Nige
is uncharacteristically economical with his words and he sounds
exhausted.

Then he's pleading, 'Can you call me back? Please, call me back.'

Ben plays both messages to us. Nigel's morale must be at an
all-time low. The only two calls he's made since our POL in September last year and he gets the answering machine both times.
I desperately want the AFP to be accountable for how he's feeling;
in fact I want them to be accountable for how shit we are all feeling. I should have been allowed to answer that call. Nige should
have heard one of our voices, to make sure he knows we haven't
forgotten about him.

I want to call him back. The response I get from the AFP is
that 'it is not in the strategy' and I am point-blank not allowed to.
I don't have access to the number that Nigel rang in on and the
AFP will not give it to me.

I point out that Lorinda has not had to adhere to this strategy
as she has been able to call Amanda back. Yes, well, that was the
RCMP taking matters into their own hands, I'm told. The negs
with her were aware of the no-communication strategy but chose
to disregard it as Lorinda was so distraught.

Something's got to give. It's just not working. Ham and Amy and the kids are up for a few days and we decide we have to put the extra money on the table that Aunt Alison has offered Dad. She has said to Dad that it's a gift. This is something that sits badly with us. Since my grandparents' deaths many of Dad's family have become estranged. I know it's not uncommon with wills and probates but I'm sure, as with every family, when it happened it was still a shock: *How did it all come to this?* Dad's family arguments are ugly and not something I want any part in.

I'm already up to my eyeballs in debt. We've had to sell the house on the beach, so we are now in the cottage. The cottage is far too small for us and it's hard to swallow the loss of everything we've worked for over the years. The kids have mixed feelings about the move. There's every chance we will lose the farm as well. If we can't get Nigel back, the blow will be too crushing. I discuss it with Ham and Matt; there is no way I can pay back Alison's money, whether she wants us to or not.

We are all pretty financially taxed and the issue is raised: if it's getting both of them out and if this money is getting paid back, the Canadians will have to wear half. There has to be a point at which they take financial responsibility for Amanda.

With this in mind, Ham and I sit down to compose an email, very politely broaching the issue of Jon and Lorinda helping us to pay back Alison's US$250K, or pursuing fundraising options. We send it off.

All hell breaks loose. The only description that comes close is 'shitstorm'. Ben rings, absolutely furious: 'What sort of threats are you making to the Canadian family?'

'Threats?' I reply, 'I know we can seem pushy but we didn't threaten them.'

It appears that rather than answering the email, Jon and Lorinda have taken it straight to the RCMP. Meanwhile, the AFP has the shits with us big time because we've been communicating with the Canadian family without their knowledge. In sharp contrast, the RCMP has full confidence that their family will pass along everything they are told. I'm pretty sure the RCMP has pointed out to the AFP how ordinary they are in being able to achieve the same sort of order with our family. We've made the AFP look bad in the eyes of their Canadian counterparts. *Tough titties*, is our collective response.

The upside is that everyone now knows we have double the amount of money on the table. How's that for efficiency?

Nigel
The Couch House
Friday, 24 April

In the evening we're transported again. Just before I am taken to the courtyard, Jamal says sternly, 'No talking to Amina. Okay?' I nod. In the car, Amanda is beside me, our interlinked hands concealed by our bags.

We drive into rough bushland, following a dirt track. At times I've been my own worst enemy as I've hung onto hope, but that seems to have evaporated and now I'm just living with fear.

We finally pull up and it's not until we drive into the compound that I realise we are back at the dark house.

Exhausted and mentally fried, I'm marched back into my shoebox-sized room and left to kick the dead cockroaches into a corner.

Lying there under the net, with the concrete floor hard and cold underneath me, I realise that I now have Amanda's mattress, which isn't as compressed as mine. Then the sudden thought that I no longer have my pencil. To lose it feels crushing, but my fear that

Amanda will get caught with it is much more concerning. Unable to do anything about it, I try to look on the bright side; she may find it gives her a way to communicate with me.

The boys have been able to strip me of my initiative and power, the things that give me my individuality.

But the human spirit is an amazing thing, and whenever I think I am completely empty, spent, I somehow manage to find a spark, something that steels my determination to go on, not to be broken but to fight to see the end of each day.

MAY 2009

All pitch in

Nigel
The Dark House
Tuesday, 5 May

With each new month it's harder to stay buoyant, all the more considering I'll likely spend my thirty-seventh birthday in captivity. My hopes are slightly raised when Ahmed comes to the house. I hear his voice in the courtyard as he speaks with the boys. I wait my turn; it's been many weeks since he last spoke to me.

Time ticks by, and then I hear the front gate open and close. The only person I can rely on for information and he's left without even bothering to see us.

I have a small victory, though: Romeo brings me a pencil. Then Abdullah comes into the room carrying a plastic bag, while several of the boys loiter near the door. He hands it to me, and I can feel it's a book. It's my Qur'an. I say '*Alhamdulillah*' over and over, and kiss it. I'm hamming it up but I'm also genuinely grateful that I'll now have something to do. The guards all look very pleased with this reaction. Abdullah asks with a big smile, 'You are happy now?'

'I am very happy. Thank you, thank you,' I reply. I will use it to show them what they are doing to us is completely against Islam. My plan now is to pore over every page, every word, to become a scholar of this book. I'll find a way to convince them that what they are doing is for the love of money and against Allah.

Nicky
Bundaberg
Thursday, 7 May

Amanda rings and leaves a message on Lorinda's mobile phone. The message is, 'Mum, I'm really, really sick. Some woman in Nairobi keeps saying, just take the money or kill us.'

We get our arses dragged over the coals because Mick has supposedly put Amanda in danger, yet here is an AFP negotiator telling the kidnappers they should kill them. When I ring Ben and go off my brain again, he denies this version of events. Patiently, he explains to me it's the kidnappers' tactic to get more money out of us. Now I'm aware that Pamela is the lead neg in Nairobi, I'm not sure I can take his word for it.

Nigel
The Dark House
Saturday, 9–Sunday, 10 May

In the early afternoon the boys start packing up the house. Then Jamal brings me a plate of food. Having not received a meal during the day for well over six months, I know that something's up. As soon as I finish, Jamal walks back in and tells me to get everything together. We have never been moved during the day before.

I'm ordered from the room and out to the courtyard, where all the boys stand, looking ready for battle with their ammunition belts, hand grenades and guns. I'm shoved into the boot of a four-wheel drive.

Amanda climbs in next to me. The boys argue over who has to sit in the back with us. Finally Romeo clambers in awkwardly and the tailgate is slammed closed. He takes up half the room as we are jammed up against a 50-litre drum of diesel. Three boys and Captain Yahya jump in the backseat; Joseph, with his massive machine-gun, struggles into the front seat, and I don't recognise the driver. I'm worried what it means that Ahmed isn't joining us for the ride.

We drive through the rabbit-warren streets until we come to a busy market area, where we pull up on the side of the road. We're sitting ducks, with hundreds of people milling around, our only protection the tinted windows.

There's a four-wheel drive pick-up beside us with Ahmed in the front. He jumps into our vehicle and we take off again down a side road. Looking over my shoulder, I notice an escort vehicle, a four-wheel drive with a massive machine-gun anchored on the back and eight guards, their faces covered, all toting AK47s. We turn right onto the main road, and my heart sinks. *Mogadishu is the other way.*

The sun sets over the African bush and we slow down as we enter a small village. There are dozens of masked gunmen on the sides of the road, and we stop at a checkpoint swarming with militia. Ahmed leaves the car. As the minutes tick by, I torture myself with possible scenarios. We edge towards the boom gate, and I wonder how they are going to explain the two gringos in the back of the car.

The gate lifts, and we're waved through. We turn onto a gravel road; it looks more like the moon's surface than a national highway. We are now heading south. We pass through many checkpoints; at each one I notice a black flag with white writing scrawled across it; this is Al-Shabaab country. Passing each one unchallenged, we continue ghosting the two red tail-lights up in front, dust peeling from the road as we speed headlong into the darkness.

An hour before dawn we enter a town; three- and four-storey buildings line the road. We pass the occasional palm tree and there's the smell of salt water in the air. The only living creatures I can see are gangs of feral dogs. We eventually pull up at a non-descript apartment complex and we're shoved out of the car and up a staircase. I'm pushed into the living room, Amanda into an adjoining bedroom.

Completely exhausted by the twelve-hour journey, I no longer give a fuck what's happening or where we are and collapse.

I wake feeling strung out but the journey isn't over. Several days later we're taken to yet another compound. Once we arrive, I take in my surrounds. The new room is 4 by 5 metres, and there are two small windows with closed wooden shutters. It's already sweltering in here.

Ahmed walks in and ignores my request to open the shutters; he's only come to make sure the windows are secured. There's no light in here at all. I lie back down in the dark and listen to the sound of a nearby diesel generator's *thump-thump-thump*.

Moving from one house to another always means a period of adjustment but this time it's different. While we were near Moga-dishu it seemed things could happen quickly if the negotiations got back on track. Now we're twelve hours from anywhere, in a town whose name I don't even know.

Nicky
Moore Park
Friday, 15 May

James rings to ask Mum and Dad to send an official letter to the minister stating we have an extra US$250K for the ransom. Everyone has known about it since we sent the email to Jon and Lorinda. At least now we'll find out how the Australian government plans on using it.

Nigel's birthday is looming. I've rung Gayle, Ben and James, voicing my concern over how I think Mum is going to cope – that is, not well. While she says she's still feeling optimistic, I see her moments of despair more often. While the Canberra lot sympathise, the overall attitude is 'suck it up'.

Ben points out that Amanda had her birthday in December and Lorinda didn't make a song and dance of it. The implication is how much better behaved Lorinda is than Mum; she doesn't carry on about her child's birthday during this ordeal. I'm not sure that Amanda's birthday is in December but I let it go. As it turns out, her birthday is after Nigel's. When Lorinda does make something of it, Ben's response will be, 'Oops, we didn't realise . . . You know how it is in North America; they have the day and the month swapped around.'

Gayle's doing her best, but it's awkward. Even though we haven't been told anything, it's clear to us that her role is being wound down. The irony is the longer the situation goes on, the more we need her help.

Nigel
The Beach House, Kismayo
Saturday, 16 May

I overhear a conversation of Abdullah's in which he mentions 'Kismayo' a number of times. I recognise the name as a southern coastal town run by Al-Shabaab. Our new home.

In the late afternoon Assam and Mohammad arrive at the house, and the boys all sound happy now their little crew is back together. Assam comes in to see me; he looks rejuvenated and tells me he has spent time with his family. Bully for him.

Every night, just on evening prayer, the generator splutters to life and four fluorescent lights flicker on across the road. After eight months without it, electricity seems novel and exciting, though I can barely see to the far wall of my room. But it's enough for me to work on reading the Qur'an and writing down verses I can take to my captors.

Nicky
Brisbane
Monday, 18 May

On Nigel's birthday Mum, Dad and I are summoned to Brisbane for a meeting with Ben and Tim. Oh, I geddit: this is them doing something to mark the occasion. We meet in a generic donga on the Brisbane airport grounds. No one else is in the office – it's just us and the hum of the air-conditioner.

First, we go through the standard diplomatic update.

With a flourish we are presented with a letter from the Somali prime minister expressing his solidarity with our family. We have a letter from the head of the country that Nigel has been kidnapped

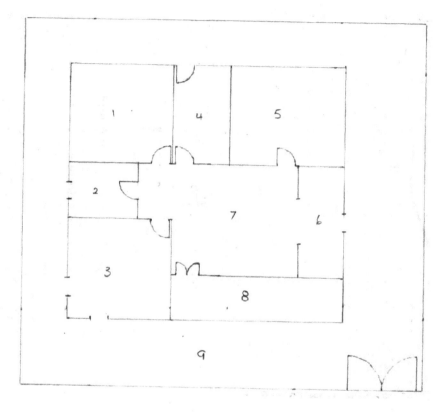

The Beach House

1. Amanda's room
2. Toilet
3. Nigel's room
4. Kitchen
5. Boys' room and weapons hold

6. Captain Yahya's room
7. Prayer area
8. Verandah
9. Courtyard

in and not a thing from our own PM.

Finally, we get down to the business at hand. 'There is a new TPI who has approached us', an older Australian gentleman. 'I met him while I was over in Nairobi and he's very credible,' says Ben. 'The Canadians have talked to him and got on board straightaway.' TPI 14 is an Anglo guy who works for an NGO. He's not in-country but has representatives on the ground who he believes can get in contact with the gang holding Nigel and Amanda.

Then a big stick is waved at us: if we do anything outside this strategy, we may fatally undermine the credibility of TPI 14's source. These constant digs at us for trying to find out what is happening on the ground really irk me. We are sick of leaps of faith. Every time we are asked to make one, we fall into a fucking crevasse.

Over the next week we get some really good feedback from TPI 14 and his source via the Feds. There are reports that Nigel and Amanda have been seen, Amanda in a box-like dress and Nigel wearing a sarong. There are six main hostage takers. There are reports they're considering a drop in ransom to US$750K, and the source is pushing to get it down to US$500K. Their aim is to get the ransom down to below US$200K. I don't care if it's US$500K; we could get that amount. Just get them out, I tell the AFP.

TPI 14's source will at some stage have to get a POL. He has asked for the names of Nigel and Amanda's grandparents, but this strikes me as being pretty easy. That is, it could have been inter-rogated out of them months ago.

There is lots of conflicting information. On one hand we hear how techno-savvy these kidnappers are and how they have the ability to Google us, and it was even implied to us early on that they may be clever enough to hack into our computers. Then we are told they are a bunch of inexperienced kids, the equivalent of

Papuan rascals, which sounds endearing but isn't.

A little bit of information can be a dangerous thing. We all go into research mode and through a process of elimination try to work out who TPI 14 might be.

Nigel
The Beach House
Wednesday, 20 May

I feel ready to face Romeo. He knows more about Islam, but I am better educated. It's time to take down this twenty-four-year-old petty tyrant.

With him now sitting in front of me, I show him Ayats to support my argument. I know I have to walk a fine line, not seeming to question his faith but also not letting him get away with anything spurious. I throw verse after verse at him, mainly about how one Muslim cannot take the property of another, but he's always got a quote to trump mine. Then I ask him flat-out about Ahmed's promise that he wouldn't take money from our families.

He blatantly lies to me. 'I didn't hear Ahmed say this, but they can take money from your family because they are Christians.' I think of quoting an Ayat I found about the evils of hypocrisy but resist.

Instead I say, 'If you take money from my family, I will have to repay them. Can't you see that you are then taking my property and it clearly states in the Qur'an that this is against Islam.'

He sits there shaking his head. 'You don't have to repay this money to your family because they are disbelievers.'

'But the Qur'an says we must be dutiful to our parents even if they are not Muslim.'

Taking the Qur'an, he flips to a page and then points to an Ayat about Ibrahim dissociating from his heretical father.

'You see, when you go back to your country, you can have nothing to do with your family because they are not Muslim,' he says bluntly. I try another angle, badgering him about the wickedness of greed.

I can see his annoyance; I've overstepped the mark.

'This money will be used for Jihad; the soldiers will not get any of this money,' he says. I feel like telling him to stop bullshitting me. I know they'll all get a share of the war booty. They've spent too much time and presumably a bucketload of cash holding us so there's no way they are going to give up now.

I realised months ago that money was their only motivation; it didn't matter what I said or did now, I wasn't going to be able to change that ugly fact. It was worth a try but I now back-pedal, sensing that I have seriously pissed off Romeo.

Softening my voice, I explain, 'I only ask these questions because although I've been a Muslim for nine months, I know nothing about my religion. I just want this to be finished. I want to find a solution so that you can go back to your family. I want to go to mosque and talk to an Imam and learn. I'm sorry; it's frustrating for all of us to be here.' He seems to relax at this.

'*Inshallah*, you will learn the Qur'an; you must be patient. Allah will find a solution, soon it will be finished.'

It's pointless to fight any more; with no options left, I resign myself to towing the line.

Kellie
Newcastle
Wednesday, 27–Sunday, 31 May

The world according to the Brennan family is officially crap. Ham and Heather are hell-bent on using Mick F but the rest of the family isn't on board.

May is the biggest month of the year for my business. For the last three years we've held the catering contract for the Dungog Film Festival (DFF). This is always great fun but takes me months to plan and coordinate. And this year is obviously more stressful than usual.

Funny things happen to a family in crisis. Sometimes you splinter in different directions but if you're lucky you stick together, more than you have ever done in the past. Nic and Amy always come to help out at Dungog; but this year Ham and Matt are joining us too. Ham is running the bar, and I am running the kitchen. We've never done this before.

It hasn't stopped raining for days and the ground is very soggy. I arrive in Dungog on Wednesday morning to set up the kitchen in the marquee being built on the pony-camp ground. The ground has been churned up by the large earth-moving equipment they've used to construct the marquee. There are trucks arriving with alcohol, cool rooms, ovens, tables and chairs, and none of them can get through as they will definitely get bogged. I have a huge trailer on the back of my car and I'm waiting patiently for my turn to unload. I get a phone call from Ham and Amy, who can't get out of Grafton due to flooding. They are making plans to get to Dungog another way. It seems in every task I undertake there is some obstacle.

Ever since Matt and I left the farm in 2005 the things we've set out to do have always become complicated. The day we decided to leave the farm was the day I found out I was pregnant. When beautiful Stirling was born in December, I was hit with a bad dose of postnatal depression. Then I landed a job with a clothing company that involved lots of upfront costs; the company turned out to be dodgy and I lost all of our savings. The following August I found out I was pregnant again, only to be told that our baby had severe deformities and we had to terminate.

So I guess you could say we have had a string of bad luck, but Matt and I just try to get on with it and do what we need to. I believe these obstacles are here to test my resolve and strengthen my character. One day things will turn around, I'm sure.

Ham and Amy finally arrive and we are all at home having dinner. Heather calls with what she believes is a brilliant idea. Since news of Nigel's kidnapping first broke, *Australian Story* has been asking if we'd be interested in participating. Heather had put them off, until now. She's phoned Kristine Taylor from the show and told her that Nigel's siblings are together for the weekend in Dungog. Heather informs us that the crew will be arriving on Sunday to start filming. *Hmmm, we will still all be working on Sunday night; this will be interesting*, I think.

Thursday night is opening night and we are preparing to feed 500 guests a three-course seated meal. Ham has the bar sorted and the kitchen is ready to rock and roll. It is still pouring with rain.

I have thirty staff members and they pull off dinner with the precision of an army passing-out parade. With all hands on deck, we rearrange the kitchen to resemble an army mess washing-up station: we have 1500 plates, 500 wine glasses, water glasses, champagne glasses, knives, forks, and spoons to clean. All the while the rain keeps flogging down and we trudge through mud and slop. Our feet are soaked and our shoes ruined and this is only the first night.

It is 4 a.m. by the time my head hits the pillow and I am absolutely exhausted. Thank god tomorrow is only prep for Saturday night.

The next day Nic gets a phone call from Ben; he explains they

need her to talk to Nigel. The AFP is confident things are progress-
ing with the kidnappers and tell her she needs to come to Canberra
ASAP. This sets the family buzzing; it will be the first time anyone
in the family has spoken to Nigel for eight months.

Before this phone call, we were laughing and joking and enjoying ourselves. I hadn't seen Nic like this for a while; she was back
to normal. After the call, she goes back into 'Nigel mode'. She
starts pacing, vagues out, and starts unconsciously tapping at her
sternum. When Nic is like this, nothing else in the world exists
except Nigel and getting him out of Somalia.

The rest of the evening's conversation revolves around what
plan the AFP might have in place. Nic reads up on some notes she
has brought with her. Matt will drop her off at the airport in the
morning so she can fly to Canberra, talk to Nigel and move this
situation up a gear.

The rain has continued all night and as we arrive at the show-
ground in Dungog, it's clear there is no way I am going to be able
to get the van anywhere near the marquee. The big tractors have
been moving out the equipment from Thursday night's dinner,
and moving in equipment for tonight's cocktail party. Down a set
of hands with Nic in Canberra, we do our best to get the equipment into the tent with enough time left to start prep. Tonight's
function is for the NSW Minerals Council. They are the major
sponsor of the festival and my biggest client. This event needs
to run like clockwork; my reputation is on the line. I am expecting sixteen bar-staff volunteers to help Ham's team of six. We are
catering for over 800 guests tonight and while it is important that
everyone gets enough to eat, it's even more important that no one is
left standing around waiting for a drink, and that the room doesn't
look like a dodgy nightclub, with glasses left all over the place for

tiddly patrons to smash.

In the back of my mind I can't stop thinking about Nic and Nigel. *Has the call come in? Has Nigel made contact? Is Nic going to talk with Nige or a TPI?* All these questions keep banging around my head as I lug boxes of beer from the cool room to the bar.

We are getting close to kick-off and my volunteers haven't turned up. I have twenty-five staff of my own tonight, but they are distributed throughout the kitchen, bar and waiting services.

I rally the troops, all of those with a Responsible Serving of Alcohol certificate need to move to the bar, and all those without need to stay in the kitchen. I tell Nat, my apprentice, that she will be running tonight's kitchen. I have absolute faith in her, she has been with me for four years, and knows what I expect.

'Will you be right?' I ask.

'Yep,' she replies with confidence.

I walk out the door, wish her good luck, and head straight to the bar.

Twenty-five staff for 881 was never going to be enough. I needed those extra volunteers. I feel I have failed my clients, and I am disappointed with myself and the film festival for the volunteers' failure to turn up. My staff were wonderful and did all they could to cope with the hordes of people clamouring for food and drinks.

I phone Kerry from the NSW Minerals Council, who I now consider a friend, and apologise. Don't get me wrong: the event was great and all those who attended had a wonderful time, but we as staff struggled to keep up with the rubbish control, bar queues and food distribution, and as the owner of the business the buck stops with me.

One thing I have learned in business is that if you are honest and upfront, explain the situation calmly and take responsibility for your actions, most people will understand. That's partly why I can't comprehend why DFAT and the AFP have never done that with our family. I am not one to cause conflict. I can sound very scary in my head, but it always tends to come out of my mouth in a much more diplomatic tone. Some family members say I'm too quick to compromise on some of the situations we have been in to date, but the truth is I feel the fight is unwinnable.

All this talk of whether the government has done the wrong thing by us is completely irrelevant as it doesn't help to get Nigel out. What we need to be doing is looking at K&R specialist organisations. Mick F doesn't work for one of these but he makes me look at our case in a different light. He makes me question what is possible.

What we are facing is a lack of government capability; we need more money to get Nigel out and it's not clear the government will work with us if the ransom goes above a certain amount. What has become clear is that this whole kidnap thing is about money and money only.

It is Sunday and Matt, Ham, Amy, Simone and I are heading to Dungog again for the final night's function. Tonight we are only doing the bar, thank god, as the local Lions Club is doing a barbecue. My mobile starts ringing; I don't recognise the number.

'Hello, Kellie speaking.'

'Hi, Kellie. It's Kristine Taylor from *Australian Story*. Are you inside the big tent?'

'Oh, hi. Yes, we are. Come on in; I will meet you at the front.'
Bugger, I had forgotten they were coming.

Kristine walks in the entrance of the marquee with Mark, the sound tech, and Anthony, the cameraman. They have come down from Brisbane and will be spending two days with us. Kristine is petite with shoulder-length brown hair and a pretty face. Mark is tall and burly, but has a non-threatening vibe about him. Anthony is extremely good-looking, and as I learn in the days to come, all three of them are amazingly kind people.

I introduce Ham, Matt and Amy to the crew and we sit down to explain the latest goings-on to them. I'd spoken with Kristine briefly on the phone before there was any indication of Nic going to Canberra. I can see her journalist's mind ticking over; this means she will get vision of the family meeting up after this call. *Television gold*.

Anthony films us working in the mud, lugging boxes of booze into the tent to set up the bar. He can't believe we are actually working in these conditions without complaint. I hadn't really thought about it. The job needs to be done so you just get in and do it.

Finally, the weekend comes to a close. Dungog is done and dusted for another year. I am so thankful to all my staff and family for helping me get through it. On the way home in the car I joke that Nigel will be doing his stint in Dungog next year all on his own. We still haven't heard from Nic, so god only knows what is going on in Somalia, let alone Canberra.

It's Monday night and I am cooking a slow-roasted lamb shoulder, a family favourite. Matt has gone to the airport to get Nic and the *Australian Story* crew have been filming us all day, packing up our equipment, getting dinner ready, interacting with the kids and also listening to recorded calls from Nige. Tonight they are joining us for dinner so that they can film us all together and get the blow-out from the phone call.

They are filming as Nic walks through the front door. She looks shattered: the phone call never came. She holds it together very well, but one of us laughs at the awkwardness of being filmed. The crew takes a break and Nic introduces herself to Kristine and

Mark. When she meets Andrew, Nic immediately turns to Amy and me: 'Cute!' It's good to see our Nic hasn't totally checked out.

Nicky
Dungog–Canberra
Friday, 29–Sunday, 31 May

It's the start of the Dungog Film Festival. It's Kellie's biggest weekend of the year. All of Nigel's siblings are here as well as Amy; it's the typical 'all pitch in' Brennan family event. The next morning Ben confirms that a POL is coming in and someone has to go down to Canberra.

'This is Kellie's busiest event; can't the phone line be moved across to a mobile?' I ask. It's far less hassle for us, but far more hassle for the AFP. The answer's no.

I fly from Newcastle to Brisbane to catch a flight to Canberra. I am absolutely fuming that the whole day is spent travelling. It would have been faster to have caught a bloody cab.

Ben meets me after I arrive and we grab a cup of coffee. He's got what looks like camping stuff in the back of the car. They haven't had time to move the phone line anywhere with accommodation so I will be bunking down in the AFP building while I wait for the call. If Ben hadn't provided me with a sleeping bag and pillows, I would be without bedding. I would've been better off with my own swag. We've all got one from our B&S days and that skinny old rum-smelling bit of foam would have been a damn sight more comfy than what was waiting for me.

The room we set up in is not the major incident room I saw last January, all bright lights, technical and shiny. This room is very basic; we are in a big communal workspace, with lots of desk workstations.

Jason is on first shift. He has been up to Bundy in the NOK cell a couple of times, so I'm pretty comfortable with him. He is absolutely straight down the line. We call him Ned, as in Flanders. I acquaint myself with the strategies, which are essentially getting a POL and confirming the TPI's credibility. Jason and I do a couple of mock calls to familiarise ourselves with the phone and our respective techniques. And then we settle in and wait.

As the clock ticks on, I look around for something to bunk down on. The floor is carpet over concrete, cold and hard. There is a little two-seater couch in the waiting area of the office. I can only remove the seat cushions, the backs are fixed. When I put them on the floor and curl myself into a question-mark shape I can fit the length of my body, which is a grand total of 5 feet 4 inches, onto the two bits of synthetic-covered foam. These shoot out from under me every time I turn to roll over. I get bugger-all sleep. No call comes through.

On Sunday I walk the streets of Canberra to get some air before I go into lockdown for the call that will hopefully come in that night. I walk in and realise the new neg on duty is Pamela. Of all the people. She tries to make polite conversation.

I pick up my two pathetic cushions off the visitors' lounge and move to the furthest point of the office behind a row of desks, and bury my head in a book. I hope the call comes in early in the morning when she has been rostered off.

In the early hours I hear the neg change over but feign sleep. Later on I get up and discover it's Ben (a different one) who's been rostered on. I'm fine about taking a call with Ben. He's a giant – you could use his thongs for skis – and sweet, very quiet and a bit of an intellectual. I wouldn't blame him if he felt the same way about me as I feel about Pamela. The poor bugger spent the end of December in Bundaberg Hospital with appendicitis, so his Christmas must have been as crap as ours. But I guess he's put his hand up for this gig.

The call doesn't come in on Sunday night either. By 8 a.m. Monday when the other Ben from the AFP arrives, I can hardly function I am so tired. My brain is cotton wool, my mouth birdcage dry. What joy, all the symptoms of a hangover without any of the benefits of alcohol. Ben sits next to me on the couch and cups his hand over my knee in a conciliatory gesture. 'It's all fucked.'

Huh? I swing my head towards him. Everything is in slow motion, something is very wrong. Ben doesn't swear; I'm the one who can make sailors (and I suspect the odd cop) blush with my language. Ben never curses, not in front of me anyway.

He bounces off the couch again. 'The strategy has fallen over.'

'What?' I ask, trying to push through the fog in my head. I'm not sounding like much of an intellectual giant here.

'C'mon, let's go and have a coffee and talk this through.'

I'm pretty keen to get some answers now but we do a quick bolt across the cold Canberra wind-tunnel street and settle down in a coffee shop.

'Okay, Ben. What's the story?'

The kidnappers didn't give TPI 14's source a proof of life. He was the intermediary who thought he could get to someone in the group. The fact that he didn't get a POL indicates to the Feds that he can't get access to the kidnappers, so he loses his credibility. *Obviously, the same rules don't apply to the Feds*, I think, *they have been unable to get a POL for quite some time now*, but I bite my tongue.

The strategy was a one-off; if it didn't work, it wasn't going to be repeated. Ben gives me the reason he thinks it failed. We, the Australian family, have made too much 'noise': the kidnappers aren't prepared to negotiate for a smaller amount of money, as they think there are others out there willing to pay more for Nigel and Amanda. This doesn't sound believable to me but it's still a blow.

Later on Ben and James will elaborate. TPI 14's source required a POL to be seen as credible. The POL didn't come through and he lost face (such a bizarre concept to me as someone who's grown up in Australia). It seems that the loss of face was so great that he couldn't go back in to make contact with the HTs.

I head back to Newcastle the same way I came. This time I'm too weary to fume. I am so, so tired. I nap in the airports and on the planes. I don't move from the boarding gates for fear of falling asleep and missing my flight.

Matt picks me up from Newcastle airport.

'Okay, Nic, so *Australian Story* are going to be there when we arrive – we have to call them before we get to the house so they can film you arriving back from Canberra.'

Great, this is the last thing I need. I'm tired – no, exhausted – and on an emotional tightrope as it is. I'm apprehensive about the whole *Australian Story* thing. Ham and Mum are pushing hard for it; Ham thinks it's the best way to make a public plea. I've got the Feds, and DFAT's warning about media coverage ringing in my ears, but they have not offered a reasonable alternative. All of us are *Australian Story* watchers; we like their approach. I'm rooted to the spot with indecision. I have to face my family some time so it might as well be with the cameras rolling – it'll stop me from losing it.

Ham gives me a big hug as I walk into the kitchen, 'G'day, Alley cat.' So like him to get that on national telly. I want to cry: Kel has cooked for us and the TV crew. They are really concerned about how we are coping. It's pretty easy to see I'm a mess and that something has gone terribly wrong, but it is no biggie having them here. We grew up with large numbers of people around the dining table, especially at harvest time. If we weren't so bloody Irish, we would make great Italians; we're all about big clanny families and comfort food.

I just can't do an interview today, though; it's all too close to the bone. I'll just unravel, and if I fall apart in front of everyone, I'm not sure I will be able to get myself together again.

My brother really, really may never come home. Is this the future for our family gatherings? Nige never physically here but his presence always felt? I scuttle around the house, hoping desperately I won't be the first one singled out. We do a couple of group shots, watching footage of Nige, and of Stephen Smith being interviewed about the case.

Ham is up first. He settles into a chair. Kel and I sneak down the hallway to watch. Kris is sitting opposite him. There's a big furry mike that looks like a dead brushtail possum being held over his head, out of the line of the camera.

'So, tell me about your brother Nigel,' says Kris. With that, Ham opens his mouth and dissolves into tears. It's as shocking as seeing Bruce Willis cry. He gets shot up, falls out of buildings and loses the girl, but he doesn't cry. *Thank god, I'm not doing my interview till next week.*

Nigel
The Beach House
Sunday, 31 May

With the move south it seems we have lost our cook. It is Jamal who's stepped up to prepare food for everyone. Portions have become smaller, fruit has disappeared from the menu and the monotony of the meals destroys my appetite. It's always a small bowl of dull dishwater-like broth and three small cubes of camel or goat meat with bread or rice.

But on the last day of May the smell of cooked meat wafts through the house; the boys seem to be cooking up a feast. I sit there salivating, knowing it's unlikely I will get a taste of what's on their menu. Shortly after midday Jamal whips into my room to grab my plate. I'm sure it's for them to use but I'm astounded when Young Yahya comes back not long after and slides the plate across the floor.

There in front of me is a plate of grilled goat meat, the fat glistening and the smell overpowering. I vacuum up every skerrick and it's mouth-wateringly tasty. Sitting back and sucking every last morsel from the bones and my fingers, I feel uncomfortable for having eaten so quickly, but satisfied for the first time in months.

JUNE 2009

Limbo

Kellie
Newcastle
Early June

The *Australian Story* journalists are like flies on shit. Kristine is calling me every week with updates about what they are doing and who they are interviewing. I have done my interview. I looked terrible – it was filmed straight after the film festival and I hadn't slept properly for four days. Kristine kept asking if my mascara had run because of the dark shadows under my eyes.

I discover why gorgeous Anthony is here. You're forced to look at the camera because he is standing right behind it. Kristine and I build a good rapport. I really like her and I suspect she thinks our family is a bit of fun, despite the venom we sometimes spit out about dealing with bureaucracy.

I am gobsmacked at how disparaging the government is about the media. To date we really haven't had anything but positive experiences with them. Take Glenda Kwek, for example. She spoke freely to Heather and me about Nigel on the day he was taken; she had a huge story about how she, not DFAT, informed the family, yet she chose not to run it. Glenda and I speak on occasion; she calls to see if there are any developments and I am comfortable that if I ask her not to print something, she won't.

Kristine is cut from the same cloth. She's researching who insures the ABC journos in the event of a kidnapping, as she thinks it could help us.

We are currently at a standstill with the government. The AFP and DFAT have spoken sternly to Nic and Ham about how danger- ous it would be to task Mick F. And according to the security guy who helped rescue Colin Freeman, the *Sunday Telegraph* journalist, Mogadishu is too dangerous to even enter.

So where do we stand? I know where we are: we are in limbo. We are in such uncharted territory that none of us knows what to do next.

Nigel
The Beach House
Saturday, 6 June

Romeo spends hours in Amanda's room. I can make out the sound of an Arabic voice playing on a mobile phone, stopping and starting, and then Romeo verbally annotating. I'm slightly jealous that the more senior guards spend more time explaining things to Amanda.

It isn't long though till I find out exactly what the topic of con- versation is. Romeo walks in with his exercise book and explains that he's written down a message that Osama bin Laden has sent to the Somali Mujaheddin, the Islamic guerrillas. Bin Laden says it is a Muslim's duty to perform Jihad and that we must rid the world of infidels. Romeo then asks, 'Forebeer, will you fight Jihad?'

I mutter something vague, hoping to appease him. To kill someone because they do not share your beliefs sounds more like some twisted cult than a religion to me. Reading the words on the page just makes me realise how indoctrinated these guys are.

When Romeo finally goes, he leaves the exercise book, telling me to read Osama's message many times. Instead I take the chance to steal a few sheets of paper.

Thursday, 18 June

Romeo bursts into the room, mobile phone in hand, screaming 'Allah *akbar*' (Allah is the greater) and pumping his fist in the air. Before I get the chance to ask what's going on, the other boys swamp the room, all of them chanting, 'Allah *akbar*', while hugging and high-fiving each other.

Finally I get Ahmed's attention to ask him, 'Is it finished? Have they paid the money?' He shakes his head.

'The security minister in the government has just been assassinated, along with several of his guards, who were Ethiopian.' I have never witnessed such celebration here – and it's at the death of other human beings. It is the ugliest thing I have seen yet.

As they file out, I ask Ahmed, 'Is this not against Islam to kill another Muslim?' A smile spreads across his face.

'This man kills many Somalis; he uses Christians to protect him and doesn't follow the true religion of Islam, like many in the government, including Sheikh Sharif.'

'But Sharif is part of the Mujaheddin, no?' I retort.

'He used to be but now he and his government work with America, so we wait and soon we will kill him too,' he replies, running his finger across his throat.

As time has gone on, especially since we moved to Kismayo, I have been able to watch the instruction of the younger boys. Now every morning for what seems like an hour and a half they listen to propaganda inciting violence and hatred. The boys are isolated from their families for months at a time, and any sign of individuality is stamped out. Poverty and a lack of education are the tools used to manipulate their minds. They are in prison just like us, only their prison has more people.

Nicky
Bundaberg
June

We are in limbo, seeking out the floating log that is bobbing in the ever-rising flood waters. But what is the future of the unwilling travellers on their precarious raft? Our government has no life rafts for us so we widen the search for other forms of help.

Simon has resumed communication with David, the K&R guy for the *Sunday Telegraph*. Dad is trying to get assistance from the Jordanians. We had been given the name of a private company in the UK by a friend of Nigel's, which appears to be very corporate-orientated and dauntingly expensive (they were estimating a starting price of $1.5 million! We might as well have gone with the kidnappers' first offer) and Ham is still pushing for Mick.

Time is passing, the government is doing nothing: we can't negotiate separately from Jon and Lorinda, and they don't want to move away from their government. It's as if Nige is being left to rot. I wake every morning and fall asleep every night keenly aware of the procrastination and the numbing effect it has on everything else in my life.

Friday, 19 June

Ham and Mick F instigate a meeting in Brisbane with DFAT and the AFP. Mick is attending to try to get the Australian government to assist us and him in getting Nigel and Amanda out. Lorinda and Jon are on the line to hear the entire thing.

It's a meeting the government doesn't want to have. They've already made up their minds about outside assistance and I'm sure they're lamenting the fact they can't seem to get this through our thick skulls.

Hamilton and Ben face off, two pitbulls straining at their leashes to tear each other to pieces. Ben's face shows poorly concealed distaste for Hamilton. Hamilton doesn't even attempt to hide his contempt. The government has made its stance clear and no amount of coercion, bullying or questioning will alter it; and they don't have to justify their actions. After all, they are the ones running the show.

Unless, of course, we want to bust out on our own. In which case Ben and James state, they can continue monitoring proceedings and offering consular support. Which is, as far as Ham is concerned, a great big spoonful of fuck-all.

What the government *can't* do is negotiate with – or support anyone who is negotiating with – a sum greater than $250 000. This is really interesting news to me. For the first time we have a straight-out acknowledgment of this restriction.

Regardless of DFAT and the AFP's response to Mick, we know the Canadian family will not go for him, and this is a signal we should look for more palatable options. We need to persuade them that it's up to us to get Nigel and Amanda home.

As we can see the door to Mick being closed, Simon calls David. The aim is to get a little advice from him and suss out if he would work for us. Si and I have always been keen on employing this guy. He has runs on the board.

Si asks David what he thinks about fundraising, as we would have to find extra money to employ him on top of the ransom, whatever that ends up costing. Si tells him that, throughout this entire saga, the Australian government has maintained that going public with our cause would raise the kidnappers' expectations of us paying the ransom.

David's response to Si differs considerably from the government's stance. He thinks fundraising activities are appropriate and in no way raise expectations, as they are for the most part invisible to the kidnappers. And, as for expectations being raised, the mere fact that the Australian and Canadian governments are involved has done that already. His belief is if it had only been the families in contact with the kidnappers, expectations would have been low from the outset.

David indicates the situation in Mogadishu currently is such that, even with both families in agreement, he wouldn't take us on. His visit earlier this month to Mogadishu showed him the situation on the ground is the worst it's been in the past four years. He would very much like to assist under the right circumstances, but those do not currently exist, either in-country or among the parties involved.

At least he's able to give us an estimate of costs. David's opinion is that the ransom for Amanda and Nigel will settle between US$500 and US$700K, perhaps a bit less. The average ransom runs between US$250K and US$400K per person, with the upper

284

range being the expectation when governments are involved. This explains the HTs' outright rejection of US$250K. If nothing else, we finally have a figure to work towards.

David's suggestion is that we continue to raise funds and attempt to 'educate' Amanda's family on the realities of Somalia.

Not getting him on board is a blow. And the body hits keep on coming.

Mid-June

We finally have something in writing from Minister Smith and it's an absolute pearler. He states that 'the strategies implemented by negotiators in Nairobi have primarily been based on wearing down the kidnappers. It is of course clear that our efforts have not been successful to date.'

If it had been explicitly stated to us that this was their main strategy, we would have pulled the plug on DFAT months ago. The emotions of family members range from despair to fury. It's soul-destroying for Dad; he has always been political by nature and believed in the process. He's been completely let down by the government and its inability to help Nigel. It's the hardest thing to watch, seeing a person lose their faith.

The letter is initially cloying and conciliatory – our family has been courageous and determined in dealing with this extremely difficult and stressful situation. *No shit, Sherlock.*

Minister Smith realises that the decision to look for help out-side the government to offer a ransom payment is one the family has made after much deliberation – *at the risk of repeating myself, Watson* – but he has grave concerns about our particular choice.

The AFP and DFAT made it clear they don't think Mick has the depth of knowledge or expertise needed in a hostage situation. But ultimately, James admitted they will not consider the use of contractors full stop, 'as they may be considered mercenaries'. Carrying a weapon even for protective purposes may be categorised as mercenary behaviour. It appears the government is concerned about charges arising from retrospective cases, not even ones related to us or our country. We are playing by the rules when Somalia burnt the rule book on a pyre sixteen-odd years ago.

After reading Stephen Smith's letter, Ham moves into full-on research mode, trying to find other options. He gets in touch with Reporters Without Borders (RWB). This lot have reasonable contact with NUSOJ, the National Union of Somali Journalists.

RWB then puts Ham in touch with someone who used to live in Mogadishu and lectured at one of the universities there. He now lives in Nairobi and has had some involvement in piracy cases in Somalia. Hamilton gets in touch with the Professor and explains what has happened to date. Ham's view of events at this stage is very dark and he finds an ally in this man.

The Professor is able to get an 'in' with the kidnappers; one of his past students has found a spokesperson, and it turns out to be Adan.

June, as it turns out, is the expectant month, the pregnant pause. I know we can't continue this way, we all know that. It's all got to change and we need an alternative plan. But how do we convince the Canadian family to leave behind their cosseted faith and move into the expensive expanse of the unknown?

JULY 2009

Blink and you'll miss Vancouver

Nigel
The Beach House
Wednesday, 8 July

Captain Yahya tightens the reins even further. Before now, to get the boys' attention when I needed the toilet or water I would stand up and knock on the door. The simple freedom of being able to stretch my legs is now gone. I'm ordered to bang a cup on the floor when I need something. It's Abdullah's duty to inform me of the new rule.

'It is not my decision; the Captain says.'

These small indignities are the things I struggle with the most — I have come to terms with the chains and the isolation, but now having to bang a cup on the ground like a leper, strips me of all self-respect. I'm feeling more like an animal than a human being.

I hear Amanda sobbing for what seems like hours on end. The cracks are finally starting to show. She's been strong for so long.

I just wish I could reach out and tell her everything will be okay.

I manage to see her in the doorway; we have become brazen in trying to communicate, using the times when we wash for prayer to get a glimpse of each other. She's standing there gesturing to her groin, using sign language and I suddenly realise what she's implying. Having not had her period since we were taken, Amanda is menstruating, and judging by how distraught she is, they haven't provided her with any sanitary products. I'm sure for the gang it comes down to money and them not wanting to spend it, especially on a woman. Maybe they treat their own wives like this, who knows? I can do nothing more than blow her a kiss and mouth 'I love you' before she disappears.

Saturday, 11 July

After dinner Jamal and Abdullah tell me I will soon take a call from a man in Australia. This man is going to give me my brother's number and I am not to answer any questions.

Joseph walks in, handing me the phone. I recognise Adan's voice on the other end. 'Nigel.'

'Hello, Adan,' I reply, the static over the line making it hard to hear.

'Yes, yes, Mr Nigel, it is Mr Adan. Um, hear you well, Mr William?' he asks.

'Yes, I am here,' comes another voice. The accent is clearly not Australian; it sounds more German.

'Hello, Nigel Brennan,' I reply, unsure who I'm actually talking to.

'Ah, yes, ah, okay, ah, Nigel, good evening. How can you hear me?' he asks, the German accent now very strong as he stumbles over his words.

'I can hear you okay,' I reply.

He continues, 'Can you, can you take down a telephone number, uh, so that you can talk, ah, to your bro directly?

'Yah, and, ah, also one, one important question was, ah, what do you think is the best way forward?' *Yeah, I wish I knew, mate.* Even if I did, it is too risky to convey it with the boys sitting around me and Adan on the line. Instead I repeat his question back to him.

'Um, what is the best way forward?'

'Yah, I mean, ah, um —' before he gets the chance to finish Adan cuts in over the top saying, 'The line cut, the line cut.' There is irritation in his voice.

'No, it's okay; I'll, ah, give you the number,' Mr William says, sounding defeated. Then, painfully slowly, he gives me the digits of Ham's phone number. After that, the line goes dead. I'm annoyed that Adan has cut the call but I feel certain that I've got the number right. Once I've handed the phone back, the boys are eager to know what was said. I rack my brain about exactly what is going on. The unanswered questions bounce around my head: who was I speaking with? How did he get my brother's number? But most importantly, will I actually get the chance to talk to Ham?

Nicky
Moore Park
Saturday, 11 July

Ham's newest contact, the Professor, gets a direct line in to the kidnappers using an alias and asks to speak with Nigel. He passes on Hamilton's phone number and advises Nigel to call 'his bro'. All this is going on without the rest of the family being aware of it.

Adan calls Ham a couple of times, possibly to check the

Professor's bona fides. All the while, Ham is juggling work – supervising the building of a bridge – and taping calls to pass on to us.

Ham asks the AFP for negotiator assistance and the request is denied. Hardly a surprise as the relationship between Ham and the government is pretty sour. It's dangerous ground to be on: I feel like the little help we have at the moment could be pulled because of these personality differences. Ham doesn't care that we are over a barrel; to him assistance is just K-Y Jelly. He's of the opinion we are going to be buggerised by the government regardless, all that's missing is the gimp mask and billiard ball.

The government's stance is that it will not provide assistance for a strategy they have not implemented. If we have tasked someone else to negotiate the release of Nigel and Amanda, they must step back.

We haven't tasked anyone. All we are after is a proof of life and this professor guy is saying to Ham he can get one. I go over all my strategy notes with Ham and give him a crash course; I recommend he tells them loud and clear that we've sold everything, we're not holding out, and this is it. He should use the 'selling off' line to explain the extra money we now have. Ultimately, though, he'll have to fend for himself.

Tuesday, 14 July

Kristine from *Australian Story* has done a pretty remarkable thing. She knows we are on the hunt for credible private crisis-response companies and has done a bit of research into who trains the ABC journos when they go into inhospitable places.

She passes on the name of an English company called AKE – Andrew Kane Enterprises, Kane being Maggie Thatcher's right-hand security detail while she was the Iron Maiden. AKE insures journalists from the ABC, CBC and NBC. As well, she's tracked down the number of their director – John Chase. At the risk of losing him as a major part of her story, Kristine is on the phone to me straightaway.

'There are days when I need to put my job aside and be a human being, and today is one of those days. You need to phone John Chase.'

I count back the hours to UK time. It's 4 a.m. over there. Should I hold off for a couple of hours?

Bugger it. I'll leave a message.

'Hi, this is John Chase, leave a message and I will get back to you.' Oh, he sounds very English. I'm a sucker for an accent.

Deep breath. 'Hi, John. My name is Nicky Bonney; I'm calling from Australia. My brother is the photojournalist who has been kidnapped in Somalia. I was wondering if I could talk to you in regards to this.'

By the time John calls back, AKE has been solidly Googled. Si and I chuckle over one of its principles: 'The Indispensable Virtues of Humour and Humility'. They're so going to need that when dealing with our lot. I silently hope it's not humour of the *Benny Hill* variety.

The first thing John states is that we have to negotiate for both Amanda and Nigel. We have to get the two families working together. I explain to him that this is a major stumbling block, that Jon and Lorinda have unshakeable faith in the RCMP.

'Look, I have worked with the RCMP,' says John. 'I've just had a kidnapping case of a Canadian citizen in Afghanistan.'

Bingo! I think. *This is the guy.*

'I'm going to be in Vancouver in late July. Maybe I can talk to Amanda's family when I'm there?'

'Oh, Kel, he sounds great,' I say when I report back to the rest of the family.

'What's he going to cost?' is Ham's response.

'Hammy, I don't know. We didn't get into that.'

'Yeah, well, Mick's only going to charge for expenses.'

'Ham, Lorinda is so pissed off with you both, she will never agree to Mick getting Amanda out. She thinks you're both the devil's spawn. I don't think it was a great relationship but this guy's worked with the RCMP. That's the point we need to push with Lorinda.'

'The chances of talking her around are pretty fucking slim.'

I don't disagree with him. But in my gut I know John Chase is our best chance yet of convincing Lorinda to go with a private company. This has to be a softly, softly approach, but I'm sure it means more indigestion for me. *Bet I'm getting an ulcer.*

Nigel
The Beach House
Wednesday, 22 July

Almost eleven months after I last spoke to my family, Romeo informs me that my brother will call later that night. I have to prepare a statement.

Ham is three years older than me and we are incredibly close. I saw him as a hero figure while I was growing up. That said, I'm a bit worried that he has been put in charge of the negotiations, knowing that he is way too emotional and aggressive to act coolly in this sort of situation.

I draft the statement while Romeo constantly asks what I will say, adding his two bob's worth. For the rest of the day I psych myself up. As darkness approaches, my anxiety levels jump. I'm nervous that I won't be able to pull myself together once I hear Ham's voice. Romeo comes in after dinner. The call is only minutes away. He is soon accompanied by Jamal and Abdullah.

I sit there as Romeo goes over the rules of engagement.

'Do not answer any questions, read the statement only and do not talk about Amanda, understand?' There's a hard edge to his voice. Suddenly I hear the conference call being made from the other room, then Captain Yahya walks in, phone in one hand, pistol in the other. I'm holding the phone to my ear, and dread pushes down on my chest. I hear Adan's voice, then Ham's.

'Ham, Ham, it's Nige.' I try to maintain my composure but the tears roll down my cheeks. At last my family will know for certain that I'm still alive.

I struggle to get the words of my statement out as my throat clamps up; my chest tightens with each gasping breath.

'Mate, I'm hearing you, Nige,' Ham replies. I know it's just as hard for him to hear this as it is for me to say.

'Ask Mum and Dad and the family to pay, to pay for my release —,' there's desperation in my voice, and I feel disgust at myself as these words pass my lips.

'I want to come home,' I bawl, my self-control lost. I'm no longer able to hold it back.

Romeo is in front of me, tapping the paper, gesturing for me to stick to the script. Trying to steel myself, I say, 'Ham, they are saying you must pay this money or else they will kill me. I know it's a lot of money, I know you are doing everything you can. I'm so sorry for the hurt and pain I've caused all of you —' Ham cuts me off.

'Mate, don't stress about that, don't stress about that. You haven't done this on purpose so don't stress about that. We all love you, mate, you know that? So just hang tough, all right?' Romeo, anger etched across his face, snaps his fingers then points to the paper, instructing me to continue.

I'm certain the call will end at any moment. Under pressure to get the words out I say, 'You've got to listen, you have to talk with these people, you have to try to pay this money as soon as possible. Please, please, please, this is my life, Ham.' Now I'm a complete wreck, sobbing uncontrollably and hating myself as I beg for my life.

There is a softness in his voice. 'I understand, mate, I know, I know what you are saying.' Then the phone goes dead.

Sitting there, my face wet, snot running from my nose, I'm sick with guilt. I try to regain my composure but there's no time as Romeo starts firing questions at me.

'What does your brother say to you? How much money do they have? Why do they not pay?'

I relay what has been said during the conversation, saying it loudly, hoping that Amanda will be able to hear. As always, they leave me once I have satisfied them.

I'm left alone in the dark and I bury my head under the pillow and completely lose it.

Nicky
Moore Park
Wednesday, 22 July

The call from Nige comes through. Afterwards, Ham plays the call to us over Skype. Nige sounds scripted, similar to Amanda's calls. Ham tries to make it as familiar as he can.

'G'day, black dog, howyagoin mate?'

Nige's response is automatic. 'Yeah, all right.'

This is owed to years of Mum drumming into us when we were

kids that unless you're carrying your head under your arm, there's nothing wrong with you. Then he realises what he has said and corrects himself, 'Aah, not really that great.'

He sounds really upset. He's sick and passing blood then goes through a textbook of ailments he has had. If it weren't so serious, it would be the perfect opportunity to take the piss out of him. In the past, if Nige was sick and didn't get sympathy from us, he'd take himself off to the doctor to a chorus of deserved ridicule.

Nige goes on to say that he's chained up in a dark room and has been isolated. Does he mean from Amanda? I assume so. That is not good to hear – we Brennans are gregarious by nature. Being isolated is going to be really tough on him. There's no clean water and very little food. All his thoughts are 'very dark at the moment, I don't know how much more I can take'.

I don't like the way he has phrased that at all, it sends a chill through me. Nige pauses in conversation – it sounds like he's fortifying himself or gathering his thoughts.

Ham talks over him, telling Nige about what we've done at this end.

'We've sold houses, mate, we have, we have sold houses. Rouen Road has been sold, I've sold Cairns, we've sold houses, but these guys don't understand the government doesn't give a fuck. They're never going to give us one dollar, the government; the Australian government and Canadian government will never give us one dollar, so we have sold houses, we've sold cars, we've done everything we can but these guys still think we can raise a million dollars.' There's frustration in Ham's voice.

Ham starts laying into the Nairobi cell, heartily criticising them. He compares the difficultly in raising money to how hard it would be for Adan if we stole his kids or wife.

Ham then tries to calm Nige. 'It's okay, mate, I know you didn't do this on purpose. Shit happens.'

It is so amazing to finally hear his voice after so long. The relief is liberating. I am crying and laughing at Ham, especially at the end of the call. The 'Ah, fuck me dead' said and recorded by Ham after Adan had hung up captures the full gamut of emotions, the sadness and the frustration. I see the humour in it – how else do you end a call from a kidnapper?

The call confirms Nige is alive. That's what matters. Ham, I decide, is a legend. He got what the government couldn't, a proof of life.

Kellie
Newcastle
Mid-July

A lot has happened this week.

Heather and Aunt Alison, who has lived in British Columbia for the last thirty years, had a doozy of an argument over the phone. Alison is convinced that the Canadian government can use her US$250K, plus the money we already have, to get Nige and Amanda out. A young chap in the RCMP has told her so. There's no convincing Alison otherwise.

Jon and Lorinda are still on board with their government too. They have 'biblical faith' that the RCMP and DFAIT, the Canadian version of DFAT, are going to get Nige and Amanda out.

The family is in turmoil. Ham and Heather still want us to task Mick F. Geoff and Heather are fighting because of her argument with Alison. Nic and Si are madly investigating third parties. All of us are going back over DFAT and the AFP's strategies to find somewhere to start on our own. And this is all completely futile if the Canadian family wants to stick with the RCMP. Fissures are starting to open up within the family. A thought keeps nagging: *This situation is going to claim a marriage and I need to make sure it's not mine.*

I head off to bed after another exhausting day of where-to-next thoughts going over and over in my head.

I wake early the next morning and Matt and I have another 5 a.m. discussion about what to do next.

Matt, in a moment of clarity, says, 'We have no choice but to go this alone, and we have to get the Canadians on board. We have to go to Canada.'

I get out of bed and head to the shower. I do my best thinking there – for some reason it helps me to see my path clearly. I call out to Matt.

'I'm going to ring Nic and suggest that she and I go to Canada, and if she can't afford it then we will pay for her ticket. Is that okay?'

'Kel, it's the only way forward.'

'All right. Let's do it.'

I get on the phone to Nic. We talk it through. She thinks it's a brilliant idea but is concerned about the cost.

My phone rings on the way to the shop. It's Matt with the news that Heather and Alison are going to foot the bill for the trip. John Chase is in Canada at the moment as well, and it'll give us an opportunity to talk to him.

I hang up and the immensity of what's about to happen starts to roll in on me like a king tide.

All right then, I think to myself, *I'm going to Canada.*

Nicky
Mid-July

Kellie calls with an unexpected proposition.

'Hey, Nic. How would you like to go to Canada?'

I focus hard on the St Andrew's Cross spider web stretching from roof to verandah rail, something to fix on so I don't cry. We don't have any money, our loans have been called in, the house has gone, and we are only borderline keeping the farm. I feel panic rising; I can't even come close to buying a plane ticket to Canberra, let alone Canada.

Then Mum calls with an offer to pay for the tickets. This is one big roll of the dice and we are dipping into the ransom coffers. If this doesn't work, we won't be recouping those funds.

While we are flying to Canada, Kevin Rudd arrives in Bundaberg. A friend of Nige's has called Mum and Dad to tell them that he is there to open a new museum, the Hinkler Hall of Aviation. Dad has the flu and in typical Oz-male style is dying on the couch, but he thinks it's a good idea for Mum to go in to ask him exactly what he is (or is not) doing about Nige.

Kel has nominated a code word that Matt can send us via text to signal an emergency at his end. The code word is 'Hadyn'. It was always a bad-news word when we were growing up. All our parents' fights revolved around this brother of Dad's. When we turn our phones back on in the Los Angeles terminal, messages pour in. Kel's message bank has a sparrow-tweet ring tone. There is a flock of sparrows going off. Matt's first message is 'Oh Hadyn, Mum has kidnapped the PM.'

We can't get into the transfer lounge quickly enough to open Kel's laptop to see what is going on.

Kel and I watch a video of the interview. Kevin Rudd doesn't even know Nigel's name; he keeps saying 'this Australian'. How bad must his advisors be? Bundaberg is a marginal seat and they should have informed Ruddy that it's a prominent local issue. There is an article about Nigel every day in the local rag. 'Inept' barely covers it. *Schmucks*. Yes, I like that more. I like the way saliva sprays out on the *sch* sound if you yell it loud enough. Be warned, if you do this, people will, and do, look at you sideways.

Kellie
Vancouver
Friday, 24–Sunday, 26 July

We land in Vancouver on Friday morning and are driven by bus from the airport to the hotel. Our accommodation, along with Jon and Lorinda's, has generously been organised by Aunt Alison. I'm hoping, though, that this isn't part of a plot to get Jon and Lorinda to side with her. Alison is convinced that the Canadian government can get Nige and Amanda out with her extra money added to the pile. Nic and I know that there is no way this is possible; the Australian government has told us this on quite a few occasions, we even have it in writing, but Alison is determined to prove us wrong. We're hopeful we can change her mind: after a few rounds in the ring with DFAT and the AFP, Nic and I have learned a thing or two about persuasion.

We meet up with Alison on Friday afternoon and have an in-depth discussion with her regarding what we would like to hear from the Canadian government. We also ask Alison if she'll pull her money if we go with a private negotiator. This is a delicate issue. She assures us the money will remain regardless of who we go with, but she would like the RCMP to explain its stance and state how they can help us before we make any decisions. Nic and I both agree, knowing full well the Canadian government is as hamstrung as its Australian counterpart.

There is no way in hell this meeting will sway us, so Nic and I decide that when we meet Jon and Lorinda, we need to let them know that we've got the okay to go private and Ally's money will still be available for us to use. If John Chase is any good at what he does, he should be able to convince Aunty Alison to go private as well.

Vancouver is a beautiful city. It's right on the water, with giant mountains behind it. It has beautiful Stanley Park that goes from one side of the city to the other, bordering the bustling harbour. It's a shame we are here for such a short time as I would love the chance to explore. I'll have to come back here with the family. This time, though, it's a case of blink and you'll miss it.

Jon and Lorinda arrive on Saturday and we all get along really well. Not that I didn't think we would. They are very nice people and we have a lot in common. We head out for dinner to get a chance to know each other properly, away from the Nigel–Amanda connection. Jon loves Vancouver and keeps Nic and me informed at each street corner about the history of this part of the city or the significance of that building. It's nice to talk about something other than what's bubbling under the surface.

It's Sunday and time for Alison, the Canadian family and us to meet with the RCMP. The night before, after dinner, Nic and I went through all the questions we needed answered. At the top of our list was: are you, the RCMP, able to get Nige and Amanda out with the extra money on the table? Nic and I already know the answer to this. Now we just need to hear it from them.

On the wall in the foyer of the RCMP building is a giant bison's head. Really huge. This makes me giggle and I take a photo of it.

We are ushered into a large conference room with us, the families, on one side and them, the RCMP, on the other. We are informed that DFAIT is a no-show. I find this hard to comprehend as we will be discussing a Canadian citizen's fate.

I also find it difficult not to slap the table and shout 'I told you so' when the RCMP disclose to the Canadian family that they can no longer help them, or us. What stops me is the look of shock on Jon and Lorinda's faces. Their biblical faith has been shattered. I feel sorry for them but this is what we've been trying to tell them was coming for months. Something stirs inside me; I don't know what it is called, but it sets me plotting. I can see the vulnerability of Jon and Lorinda and I know if I'm clever about it, I can talk them into going private without being heavy handed. I will be using the susceptibility of two parents, who want nothing more than to get their daughter back, to do things the way we want. Yes, I guess you could say I was about to railroad my first set of Canadians, but that's what I am here for.

Nic and I have two more days to convince the Canadian family that one, we all need to start actively raising money for Nige and Amanda's release; two, we need to go private; and three, that John Chase is the man to help us do it.

Tuesday, 28 July

I am pleased that Alison isn't with us for today's meeting with John Chase. I don't want money to be the deciding factor. If it's going to happen, it has to be on his merits. Truth be told, I'd already pinned my hopes on him before I arrived in Canada, but today will be the real test.

I have heard a lot about John through Nic. I Googled him before I left home, but even in a world where everything feels tracked he only came up as an author of a paper on security, and he didn't feature in any recent news. I couldn't find a photo of him online either, and so I'm taken aback when I walk into the room.

He stands to greet us. John is about 5 foot 10; he has an English mother and a Chinese father, and he's very handsome. He is not what I was expecting, but I'm not sure what I was expecting. If I wanted James Bond, then he isn't far from the mark; he has that same air of sophistication and comes across as quite suave – and did I mention he was handsome? – but a buffed, ripped SAS soldier-type he is not.

John welcomes us and says how sorry he is that we have found ourselves in this position. He then tells us he has seen many families in this same situation and reassures us that there is always a happy ending.

My eyes start to water, and I try to hide my face just as John slides a box of tissues towards me. I am thankful that I am not the only person who needs them. This man is the light at the end of the tunnel; he is the knight in shining armour we have all been waiting for. He continues to tell us about cases he has been involved with and how the process is done.

John starts to explain to us how we – meaning Jon, Lorinda, Nic and I – would go about getting Nigel and Amanda out. We'd need to set up a Crisis Management Team, known as a CMT. John asks if we'd all be comfortable as members. I turn to Nic and tell her that she doesn't need to include me on this; if she wants someone else by her side, like Simon, Ham or even Ange, I'd be completely okay with that. I don't want her to say yes just because I am here with her.

'No, I want you. You are more level-headed and you don't have a temper, and the Canadians would never work with Ham.' John agrees with Nic. Ham is too much of a hot head for this to work. She can't work with Simon as it would be too difficult on their kids if both parents were involved. So I am the logical choice.

Okay, I think, selfishness starting to kick in, *how the hell am I going to do this?* I have a business to run. I am the only breadwinner. I have three children to look after. How am I going to find the time and energy to do this as well? *Snap out of it, Kellie. Nicky needs you, Nigel needs you, and Matt, your wonderful husband, who is at home taking care of our three children is unable to help his brother and sister so you need to suck it up, girlfriend, and do this.*

The idea of working side by side with Nic takes a while to get my head around. Nic devotes every day to getting Nigel out. I only think about it every day and do what Nic asks of me. I was actually comfortable living away from Bundaberg away from the action as it allowed a bit of normal life to seep into the house, but now I am on the frontline, and it's freaking me out a little. The role is both empowering and nerve-racking.

Each day the CMT would meet via Skype and take guidance from John as to how to take the next step. It feels very DIY, very simple. We ask John about intel and how we would get it. He then says something that floors me: intel about where Amanda and Nigel are, which clan the HTs are part of and all the crap we have been going over endlessly with the AFP and DFAT is bullshit, and we don't need it. All we need is a point of contact, someone who can provide a POL for Nigel and Amanda, and to start a dialogue with them. Intel is only important at the end when we are about to exchange the money for the hostages.

John walks us through a document that describes the mechanics of a kidnapping. All security companies use this chart. He explains that kidnapping is all about money and as long as we look at it as a business transaction, everything will be fine. It all makes perfect sense, yet I am still mystified why his method is so different to the AFP's.

Nicky
Vancouver
Tuesday, 28 July

Despite our differences, and there are many, we get on well with Jon and Lorinda. I know they want Amanda home as much as we do Nigel. As savvy as they tell me Amanda is, I keep coming back to the fact she is in a radicalised Muslim country so she is persona non grata. It makes me feel both relieved and guilty that Nige might be better off simply because he has a dick.

The meeting with John Chase blows us all away. He is straight-forward and clear in a way that the government never was.

He suggests we set up a Crisis Management Team. This team will decide how we progress at every stage. If we choose to use his services, John will tutor us but he won't make any phone calls, and all decisions will have to be made jointly by the CMT. The question of who should be on the team comes up. Normally family members are not on the CMT as John regards them as being too emotionally involved for what is essentially a cut-and-dried business transaction. But in this instance, John is convinced we can do it.

I've got history with Adan, and Kel is my perfect back-up as she's got great skills when it comes to getting people to see things from another perspective; after all, she specialises in managing bridezillas.

Lorinda wants to bring in someone else as a sounding board, Kelly, a girlfriend of Amanda's. Now we've got two Kellies and two Johns, so one becomes Kel and the other Kelly B, along with Jon and JC. *Oh man, we'll give him a messiah complex.*

'Under normal circumstances we have found that the average land-based kidnapping in Somalia is ninety days,' JC tells us.

'No fucking way!' I exclaim. My language, already bad, has completely crawled into the gutter and remained there since the start of this ordeal. I hope this lot can cope with it. 'This has been going on for eleven months.'

'This may take a bit longer as we don't know who has offered what and I can't imagine either government will forward on any of their case-study notes.' JC explains to us that even when someone is disgruntled with one company and chooses to go elsewhere, the first company is obliged to pass on all the information pertaining to that case. The government's preoccupation with security clearances will put the kibosh on this.

So it's going to be like starting from scratch. The day we decide to formally engage AKE will effectively be day one.

The next big-ticket item we discuss is who has helped us to get a proof of life. As far as both Lorinda and I know, it has only been Adan.

'In 99 per cent of cases the first person to make contact in a kidnapping is the person in charge,' JC says.

'But the governments have written Adan off. That's why our phone was pulled. They said he had no influence,' I say.

'Seeing as Adan is the only person who has supplied a POL and he was first contact for both Nigel and Amanda, statistics indicate he is the guy to get back in contact with.' I'm convinced.

JC then does the cleverest thing. He brings in the parents of Mellissa Fung, who was kidnapped in Afghanistan, to meet us all. They are softly spoken Hong Kong-Canadians, yet this ordeal has given them such strength. I'm pretty sure JC gets a Christmas card from these good folks. They tell us John gave them a time line of how kidnapping cases usually play out, and events unfolded exactly as he had predicted. They are scathing about how their government treated them and the RCMP doesn't get off scot-free.

The biggest thing for all of us is being able to ask how their daughter coped. Talking to someone who has gone through the same ordeal makes me so much more confident. Nige and Amanda are going to get out, and we are going to have our families back together again.

Later on Kel spends a fair bit of time chatting with Kelly. She tries to get some answers in regards to one of the questions we've asked ourselves since this happened. Did Nige meet up with Amanda to get his leg over? After all, they have a history and there is the lingering thought that this may have been the case. If so, I hope that shag was worth it 'cause it's been nothing but trouble for the rest of us. Kelly tells Kel that Amanda sent her an email saying there was nothing going on – she hadn't even shaved her legs.

Tuesday, 28 July
Day # 340

We catch up with JC before Kel and I leave to come home. We discuss the matter of costs. It's pretty formidable. Thirty-five grand a fortnight. We have to be really careful; we can't afford to eat into our ransom money. JC can massage the figures for a little bit while he is not on location, but as soon as he is working exclusively on this, it's going to be expensive. We are clearly going to need more money.

This is the last day we recognise the Australian government as being in control of this case. Nigel has been incarcerated now for 340 days.

Wednesday, 29 July
Case Day 340+1

We have officially taken the reins. Kel and I restrain ourselves from high-fiving each other till we get to the airport. Then we let rip. *We did it!*

This is what we call Day One. Now we add the days that we are with AKE to the 340 days the government was involved. It makes it so much easier for our case-day chart.

It's a blessing to have case-day and communication charts. We'll be able to follow the progress and not be completely in the dark as we were with the government. Not wanting to sound like a patchouli-wearing, crystal-worshiping age of Aquarius child, I don't voice it, but this DIY thing is definitely empowering.

Vancouver is beautiful, I think as we are flying out. It's very like Sydney and we have been lucky with the weather. We're in a heatwave apparently – it's 34 degrees (hardly the same as a summer's day at Marlow). Kel and I consider Jon's health. The heat really knocked him for six. He looked like he was going to pass out whenever we were outside. Lorinda told us that it was his morphine intake. He uses it for the pain and it's one of the reasons they have some communication difficulties and why she wanted Kelly on board. The family politics at play here are interesting to say the least and make me feel quite okay about our craziness at home.

I reckon I've reached a new personal best while I've been here: eating my body weight in raspberries at Granville Island. Mum is so jealous when I call to tell her. It's very mean of me to do so – fresh raspberries just don't exist in Bundy. One day, when we have money again, I'm bringing the kids here. I refused to go to the zoo as they have otters there, and they are Atti's favourite animal. It would have been just too unfair to see them without him.

Thursday, 30 July

As we walk through the doors into the arrivals lounge, Kel's three kids burst through the international barrier, screaming 'Mummy!' at the top of their lungs and jump all over us. It's *so* good to see them.

We hit the ground running. No time for jet lag. We're old hands at running on empty – harvest, the Dungog Film Festival – so we just keep going till the job's finished. We spend the day prepping for a catering gig of Kel's in Newcastle, and hang about for a few hours there till it's well under way. Then Matt, Kel and I drive up to Grafton for Ham's fortieth birthday party the next day.

There is already a house full of people when we get there at midnight. Everyone's warming up for the main event the next evening. Oh, boy, it's going to be a long piss-fuelled couple of days.

AUGUST 2009

Keep calm and carry on

Nicky
Grafton
Saturday, 1 August

Ham's party is huge and gets wilder as day moves into night. The *Australian Story* crew is here for the kick-off but luckily leave before it all gets too debauched. They do a couple of stints filming Kel and me out in the paddock while we swat away flies and talk about the Canada trip. It pre-empts our family discussion about AKE but it's a measure of how comfortable we feel with Kris and the boys.

Ham has declared his party a 'Blackie-free zone', but Nigel's absence is massive – it's the elephant in the room. This is meant to be Ham's day, but we are surrounded by people who love Nige and miss him, and so invariably talk gravitates towards that topic.

It's cold, and we all stand around a massive bonfire made from building off-cuts. Throughout this saga, Ham and Amy have also been building their house. We are out the front of Ham's property, overlooking the butter-smooth Clarence River, the big sky above us salted with stars. The scene is quintessentially Oz, bordering on B&S – we've had about thirty-seven drinks each.

DFAT and the AFP have drummed into us that we're to tell no one what's going on, to trust no one, as information could get back to the kidnappers. It's so hard not to ease our friends' minds and it's unreasonable of us not to. *Stuff it*, I think, *these are Nigel's friends*. So when people ask me how bad it is, I let them know.

'What can we do to help?'

I tell everyone we need money to pay for AKE. On top of the ransom amount it's going to cost us seventy grand a month – paid in fortnightly increments. It's a lot of money but I have faith in John Chase. When I tally up how much money we suspect the Australian government has sunk into this with no result – negotiators in Moore Park, the Major Incident Room in Brisbane and another in Canberra, along with an entirely separate post in Nairobi – John Chase actually looks pretty cost-effective. They must have thrown hundreds of thousands of taxpayers' dollars at this, all in an attempt to 'wear the kidnappers down'. And an unsuccessful attempt at that.

Nigel and Ham's friends brainstorm fundraising ideas that night. The T-shirt concept resurfaces. We eventually decide that we'll print 'BLACK DOG' on the front. Below it will be 'N.B.' and a stencil outline of a little chihuahua, which we love because it'd so offend Nige's sensibilities; he'd be expecting a blue heeler. On the back we settle on: 'HE OWES ME MONEY FOR THIS'. Underneath that will be a blank space in which each person can write the amount Nige owes them. I didn't think 'a house' could be bettered till someone suggests 'a BJ'. Someone else thinks we should go with stubbie holders: 'I knew the black dog before he was famous'. It should probably read 'infamous'.

Sunday, 2 August

Resplendent with hangovers and bugger-all sleep, the entire family gets together for a debrief on the Canada trip.

Kel and I are feeling pretty pleased with ourselves. We went to see once and for all if the RCMP could do anything more than the Australian government with the increased amount of money we have on the table. Kel and I established that its hands were as tied as the AFP's – no surprise to us, and at least now we had an answer. We were finally able to get the Canadian family to come to the party: they'd agreed to forming a joint CMT using a private company to facilitate the rescue. So it is a complete shock to me when Mum falls to pieces in front of us.

I am broadsided, bewildered, and I don't know how to handle the situation. I go for the ride-out-the-storm option. Mum is sobbing into her hands; Dad is unable to console her. They are united on getting Nigel home, but their relationship is anything but at the moment. Mum wants immediate responses from me to a raft of questions.

'When will this happen by?

'When will we get Nigel home?

'When will the Lindhouts pay for some of this? Why are they not paying for Amanda? How dare they think that this is Nigel's family's responsibility to have to get their daughter out?

'How long do we have to pay John Chase?'

While Mum is over-emotional, these are all valid questions – ones for which I don't have reasonable answers. I am knocked down a few pegs. Here I was thinking we had done so well.

Kel and I go over the replies as best we can.

'The reality is that Jon and Lorinda have no money. Jon and his partner, Perry, are sick and are both on medical benefits, unable to work, and have to focus pretty hard on keeping themselves well.

'Lorinda really didn't think they would have to pay a ransom – slightly naive of her, of course. All our research had led us to the conclusion that this was nonsense long ago but they just heard what they wanted to hear. We had to show hard evidence in order to convince her she was mistaken, and that is what we did in Canada.

'They have said they will start trying to raise ransom money. What more can we do?'

We show the family the kidnapping chart describing the typical nine-week time line and tell them how the Fungs' case followed it exactly. I realise it all looks a bit slick and boardroom-ish.

'We don't have the money to pay for that nine weeks; we'll start eating into the ransom money. That will reduce it by $150K straight up,' says Mum, sharp as a tack even when distressed. God, that is so like her.

'I know, Mum. We're just going to have to somehow put together the money; it'll mean public fundraising.'

As things are cooling down and the family debrief is coming to an end, Ange rings me. She and Dennis have been looking after the kids this weekend so both Si and I could go to Ham's party. Ange tells me Atticus has broken his arm at Rep Soccer at Gympie. *Terrific*.

Later on in the day Kel and I have our first CMT meeting via Skype. Ham's place is in a telecommunications hole and we keep falling in. Our hefty phone bills, a result of ringing Canberra, and family members to keep them in the loop, are already hurting. The Skype call is essentially free. I shudder at the thought of how much daily conference calls to Canada would have cost.

We track down Adan as per JC's suggestion. He actually proves very easy to contact: Lorinda still has his phone number and email address, and she simply sends him a text message. JC's view is that we should communicate via email rather than phone. That way, the threats won't feel as personal or direct. It's a good idea – we think it will also stop Adan going off on tangents and rants, as has happened in the past. Hopefully it will stop the marriage proposals too. Most importantly, it puts us in control: we'll be deciding when we communicate. I will never let him have my number; I'll contact him when I want, not the other way round. It's a little concession but none the less it feels good, and this scrawny little terrorist has put my family through enough. I don't want him disrupting our household at 3 a.m. He's already done enough damage to my kids' psyches. Adan will just have to trundle off to the internet café. It's all about power plays, this kidnapping gig.

We send our first serious money email, offering Adan US$280K. The last offer we know of was US$250K in April. We let the HTs think that since then we've scraped together more cash. We have a formulaic budget to work to – we have US$500K in the kitty and this has to include the payment to AKE. There are whispers of a consular loan coming through from the Canadian government of perhaps a hundred grand, but we won't count it until it's in the bank.

Monday, 3 August
In the previous night's email to Adan we were at pains to say that Nigel and Amanda's families are working together on this, and that the government is not involved in any way. We deliberately stoke

Adan's paranoia by telling him the government is reading his emails; we want him to set up a hush-mail account, an encrypted system, so the government can't monitor our emails.

The response back is pretty quick and – surprise, surprise – negative. We're told the amount is US$2 million and that Ramadan is only twenty days away: 'this time is the time of killing'. I'm glad we have gone for the email option; it would have been hard to hear that on the phone. Yet, Adan writes to Lorinda, 'Really, I love you because you respect me every time.' Totally Monty Python. If it wasn't so bloody serious, I'd be laughing my arse off.

Lorinda gets a tape from a Canadian journalist, and confirms the voice on it is Amanda's. Most of the call is the standard scripted stuff: they are not well; the governments must pay. I've started to feel immune to it, but I'm still concerned about their health. Lorinda tells us Amanda has a broken tooth. The fact that it is abscessed and Amanda is in pain racks up the pressure for Lorinda. This is exactly the sort of stress the kidnappers want.

We discuss the call in detail at our daily CMT Skype – 11 a.m. for us, night-time for the Canadians. I find Lorinda a bit emotionally driven at the moment. I know she's seriously worried about Amanda, but her head seems clouded. Because Lorinda is being so vocal, JC suggests a change in tactic. Maybe an offer above the US$300K mark might move them? Normally, we would avoid this path: 'We try not to raise the offer until the kidnappers give us something.'

Even so, I'm going to run with it: I trust that JC knows what he's doing.

We discuss sending another care package with medicine. I don't know if the last package got to them. Surely most of the contents will be sold on the black market, but some of it might get through. It's something we rehash for quite a long time. I ring my doctor cousin to get him to write me prescriptions to be filled in Nairobi. This time we opt not to send letters and only a limited number of clothes. New undies and pads for Amanda are a must. I'm sure Nige will be in need of some deodorant; he'd be a pretty stinky Pete by now.

Saturday, 8 August

We up our offer to US$319K and ask for a POL. Our question is piss-easy: What were the names of our dairy cows when we were kids? Answer: Daisy and Mabel. Adan has completely ignored our POL questions in the past and will probably do so again.

We also ask if we can send medicine to Nige and Amanda. Adan just wants money for keeping Amanda safe: 'Where is my $3000 you promise me?' That was never in the deal. This guy is a monumental pain in our arses – anything he says (or writes), he believes, regardless of our response or lack of it. I assume this is why the Feds pulled away from him. JC assures me we are on track; we just have to re-educate him.

There are lots of mixed-up emails going back and forth. Adan can't seem to come to grips with the encrypted emails and so is sending stuff via his Yahoo address. We have to establish first that the emails have come from him and then write back through Yahoo while now having to alleviate his paranoia that we are doing something to his hush mail. We can't possibly say that he's just a dumb fuck who blames everything going awry on everyone else. Tempting as that is, it will just have to wait until we have Nige and Amanda back.

Tuesday, 11 August

We are getting mixed signals about the Professor. Reporters Without Borders is the channel Ham used to contact the kidnappers. RWB put him on to the Professor, who put Ham in contact with Adan. This has only proved that all paths lead to Adan, and that he is the one with whom we should be negotiating.

This hasn't stopped the Professor sticking his oar in. Annoyingly, he has indicated he plans to keep communicating with the HTs, and he won't tell us any of the kidnappers' names or who else apart from Adan he is dealing with. Adan keeps trying to negotiate with him rather than us.

The Professor has said he won't stop till Amanda's parents contact him, but they don't want to talk to him. We are all starting to think he may actually be in on the kidnapping. Why else would he be trying to make himself so integral to the case? We also can't understand RWB's involvement and why they are being so forceful. They do all their own negotiations with any kidnappers so why are they recommending the Professor? It's all too much subterfuge for me.

In the end Ham establishes that Amanda has contacted the Professor and, according to him, asked him to negotiate her release. Jon sends him an email asking him to pull out. Whether he will or not, we will just have to wait and see.

Kellie
Newcastle
August

I haven't been part of this CMT too long but I am starting to find out how important it is to document phone calls, and not to get too excited or shocked by the content.

JC is amazing. He is so cool, calm and collected whenever we phone him in a flap about a news report or a Google alert we have seen. He knows exactly what to say to make you relax: keep calm and carry on. Hey, they should put that on a tea towel.

The number of random people who contact Nic, Ham or me to help in the case is incredible, so I am not at all shocked when Ham phones one night to give me news that he has just spoken with Katherine Borlongan from Reporters Without Borders.

Ham is in a state about Katherine's phone call. He is going on about RWB having proof that Amanda has had a baby and that I need to phone Katherine straightaway. RWB are planning to get Amanda and Nigel out.

Right now I am very thankful for JC's guidance in how to handle a panicked relative. Ham is in overdrive; I can hear it in his voice. He can't get the information out quickly enough. Ring her now, he keeps saying, she is waiting for your call. After the CMT formed, Nic and I decided not to disclose anything to the family that would cause unnecessary emotional strain, as it is very difficult to deal with and extremely draining. Nic and I need all of our energy to manage the daily goings-on of the CMT.

'Ham, you need to calm down. These people cannot get Nige and Amanda out unless they get approval from the family, and as far as I know, no family member has spoken to RWB since the CMT was formed.

'I will call Katherine now and find out everything I can. Please keep this to yourself until I find out what's happened.'

I look at the number Ham has given me and call Katherine via Skype. She answers the phone and starts talking immediately, saying the information she is giving me is in the strictest of confidence. *Right*, I think to myself, *all information that comes to us 'in the strictest of confidence' has turned out to be a crock, but maybe this will be different.* Confidential or not, I tell Katherine, I will have to disclose our conversation to family members and our person of interest (JC).

Katherine tells me that a source close to RWB saw Amanda being taken to hospital, and was told that she has had a baby boy, Osama.

'Okay, so did your source tell you when this happened?'

'She was taken to hospital yesterday.'

'Is she still there?'

'I don't know.'

'Well, did your source see her come out?'

'No, our source hasn't seen Amanda since she went in.'

'So has your source or any of your RWB colleagues asked a doctor or a nurse in the hospital to confirm if it was in fact Amanda Lindhout and that she did in fact give birth?'

'No.'

'Right. So you are telling me that no one has any confirmation on this at all.'

'Ah, yes.'

'Any journalist worth their salt would be in that hospital, trying to find a doctor or a nurse who delivered this so-called baby. We are not talking North Shore Private here. I'm sure anyone with info who works at that hospital would supply it for a couple of bucks. Now, if you have nothing else for me, I would appreciate it if you'd stop wasting my time and let me get on with the real task at hand, and that is getting Nigel and Amanda out.'

'But we are only trying to help.'

'Well, Katherine, if you want to help me, give me your boss's phone number so I can speak with them directly about what RWB wants to do exactly, because as far as I am concerned you are not helping, you are starting rumours that appear in the press and heighten emotions within the family. So, I ask you: who put you up to this?'

'Oh, it's not like that at all. This information came to us from one of our contacts on the ground.'

'Well, your contact sounds like he or she is helping the kidnappers. Now, please, leave us alone.'

This was my first real confrontation with anyone on the other side and it felt good to know what I was talking about, and to have just a small amount of control over the situation. Okay, one battle down; bring on the next.

So the DFAT contingent is coming, flying up from Canberra in a tiny Brindabella Airlines plane, then they will drive a hire car to my house from Newcastle Airport.

They arrive on time and spill out of the car. They'd been packed in like sardines and their suit coats and pants are crushed – not the look they were going for, I believe – and they are fidgety and uncomfortable. Even the hire car looks ominous. It's the same grey as the bitumen. The car and the road blend together. If you unfocus your eyes like you are looking at one of those 3D images that were huge in the nineties, the grey suits and the car seem to just disappear.

We'd offered to pick them up from the airport but this was knocked back; so is the morning tea spread I've prepared. Maybe they think I am going to poison them with tea cake, but not one of them eats or drinks a thing the whole time they're here. I would like to put it down to nerves. The idea of telling our family that the government can no longer help us in any way to get Nigel back would terrify me. Especially after it has taken them close to a year to reach this conclusion.

We know that's why they're here. Nic joins us on Skype – she's got sick kids, no money and she's really over it – so it is Heather, Geoff, Matt, me and the suits. This is to be the final handover meeting. Nic and I came back from Canada with a list of questions we wanted answered by them, but once we'd told them we had put AKE to task, they wanted info from us.

The meeting starts with the usual government garbage led by James. He goes on to discuss a letter from Minister Smith then confirms that the Australian government will provide full financial support for Nigel's extraction from Nairobi. He confirms there will be extra officers in Nairobi for family support.

Ben from the AFP goes through the strategies that they've implemented throughout the last year and he names everyone Minister Smith has contacted, from the high commissioner to the Somali ambassador, the current Somali prime minister and deputy prime minister. None of which worked and none of whom could help.

Nic via Skype asks if we can get some information from the AFP and DFAT to help us now we are on our own. She asks if she can contact any TPIs. James and Ben's response is a definite 'no'. The TPIs have asked that the government protect their identities and not disclose them to the family. This is a very easy way for the government to get out of giving us anything useful to go on.

Nic asks, 'Is Adan the correct person to speak to?'

Ben and James both answer 'yes'.

I shake my head as I remember when all lines of communication were cut with Adan as the AFP didn't believe he was the man to deal with.

Talk now starts about the ransom payment and the legal

consequences involved in facilitating large sums of money. I really need to get this clear in my head.

In Australia it is illegal to engage with a group that has terrorist links, and the assets of anyone found doing so will be frozen. And at this stage no one can confirm whether the group is associated with Al-Shabaab – a known terrorist organisation. So, if I'm involved in giving money to the kidnappers, I could end up in jail.

Well, I am stunned. I try to tease out more info, looking for yes-or-no answers, but I should know by now that these won't come. Ben asks Nic and me to divulge everything we are now doing with John Chase.

Over my dead body.

After this meeting I feel like I will need to find a shit-hot lawyer to bail me out of jail if I am prosecuted for paying money to free my brother-in-law. *Nigel, you owe me.*

Nicky
Moore Park
Sunday, 16 August

Our consular loan is set in place. The Australian government has indicated to us we can use this money however we see fit. Needless to say it's going straight into the ransom kitty for both Nigel and Amanda. We let them know that's exactly how we are going to spend the money. At this stage Dad has to pay it back as Nige can't sign the contract, what with him sojourning in Somalia.

Adan says there is fighting in Mogadishu, and he can't get to the internet café regularly. He seems to have a litany of excuses so we decide to get Lorinda to call him. She is getting really impatient with the length of time everything is taking; it takes him days to return our emails. Never again will we tolerate the wait-and-see approach.

Over the phone Lorinda offers Adan a new amount, US$320K, and Adan is not happy with it. Same old, same old. He doesn't even seem to take it to the HTs. Instead he goes on about how he's already reduced it from five million down to two million dollars. The good news is Lorinda gets him to agree to provide a POL.

Wednesday, 19 August

Lorinda talks to Amanda. Amanda doesn't pass on any new information; it's as scripted as her earlier calls, but this confirms that Adan still has a connection to the kidnappers. While it's undoubtedly shit that the conditions they are being held in are terrible, it feels like we've taken a giant leap in the right direction. Now if we can just get Adan to come down in price.

Adan is trying to bargain for Amanda and Nigel separately. To underline that we are negotiating for them together, Lorinda asks for a proof of life for Nigel, indicating to Adan that afterwards, we will increase the offer.

Sunday, 23 August
Day 365 – one-year anniversary

We are told that the Canadian government will not offer a consular loan. They are, it would seem, more than happy for Nigel's family to take out a loan with the Australian government, half of which is to pay for the release of one of their citizens.

There is not a lot we can do. Dad makes a formal protest to our government, which James passes up the line to no effect. It's now up to the Canadian family to pursue it at their end.

Alison spends time talking the decision through with her local member and DFAIT, implying threats of bad publicity. She writes us a long letter about what happened, how different their system is to ours, and how she thinks she can get them to recognise this and supply the loan. It's all very admirable of her and Alison is displaying typical Brennan sheer bloody-mindedness but I suspect it will be to no avail. She has far more faith in her ability to change her government representatives' decisions than we do ours. We've already swallowed that bitter pill many times; the metallic tang is still in my mouth.

Lorinda puts a hole in our balloon by telling us that she has never heard mention of a consular loan, even though Stephen Smith had expressly told us otherwise in our meeting with him in March.

'Where the hell did you think the extra hundred grand we talked about was coming from?' we ask Lorinda during one of our phone calls.

'The RCMP told us not to worry about the money. We assumed it was a gift. There was no mention of a consular loan and certainly no mention of paying it back.'

Jesus, the blind faith shocks me. I am not a fan of the ignorance-as-a-defence disclaimer.

The twelve-month mark is a dark cloud that hangs over all of us. I can't believe Nigel has been gone for so long.

We decide to send out a blanket statement so we won't be inundated with interview requests. We want to use the media as a tool but be clever about it. The dog that bites the hand that feeds it is a genuine threat. We have to be careful not to appear to be bashing the government's role as much as we would like to.

What we say in the statement becomes a battle of wills. At one point in time the word 'prayers' appears. Kel and I are horrified. The Brennans are the biggest bunch of atheists around. Anyone who read a statement from us that made reference to 'God' or 'prayer' would not-so-politely cough 'bullshit' into their clenched fist. Luckily we win that argument.

It's a pretty bleak day, and I don't want to face it or the world. I plan on getting shitfaced with Ange.

Friday, 28 August

The twenty-eighth is a big day for me. It's my turn; I get to speak to Nigel. I ring Adan two hours before my prearranged call to make sure it's still going to happen, and then I try to get some shut-eye. Amazingly, I sleep. I ring Adan back via Skype.

Adan spins me some tale about Nige and Amanda being separated. He doesn't even sound like he's got his story right; it's as if he's just making stuff up on the run. I am filled with conflicting emotions, seemingly unrelated but all strong and disorientating. I've got to keep it together. I so desperately want to talk to Nige so he can hear my voice. I know the morale boost will be enormous for me and can only, perhaps naively, assume it will be the same for him.

Eventually Adan puts me through after the standard bells and whistles, literally. Then it's Nige.

'Hello, Nic.'

It's euphoria and panic rolled up in one. It's been almost a year since I last spoke to him. There's so much I want to say. There is so much I can't say. The most important thing is that I don't let myself cry. But I can feel a lump in my throat. I lift my head and look at the ceiling to force the tears back into my eyes. I can feel them running down my throat over the boulder that's now lodged there. I really should be looking at my scripted notes Blu-tacked to the wall but they would just be a blur.

Don't cry, don't cry. If that happens I will never regain composure. I can't let that happen. There's too much here to get done.

We are talking over the top of each other, both of us trying to get across as much information as we can, both spoken and implied. I tell Nige how much Mum and Dad love him, how much we all do. I know that is enough to convey we will be here forever for him. I tell him that we are in this with Jon and Lorinda and that we have offered $US320K.

Adan butts in and tells me I shouldn't talk about the money.

Huh? That throws me. Is he going to let me talk to Nige again? I'm going to have to suck up big time. Surprisingly, Adan lets me back on the line but Nige launches into a scripted spiel. He says he's sick, and I have no doubt he is, but his voice sounds okay. So he's not dying, that's a plus, but I know Mum's not going to be happy about the passing blood stuff.

When Nige says he's sorry that he's got us all into this, his voice starts to quaver.

I tell Nige not to cry, becoming the bossy older sister. Even hearing my own voice it's not convincing; I'm perilously close to dissolving.

Then: 'I'm so sorry, I love you all, I miss you all a lot.' He's gone. The call is done.

I download the call and send it to the family as well as the CMT to be transcribed, but mostly so everyone can hear his voice and listen for the tiniest of inflections.

Meanwhile Adan can't get on the phone to Lorinda fast enough for the new offer. He is no longer using his email so it looks like we're back to the phone calls. We discuss bringing in a translator. JC says they use them a lot and that he will get in touch with a couple to see if they are suitable for this case.

When Lorinda gives Adan the new offer, she tells him that I have sold my house. It's not untrue though none of the money has gone to the ransom; it's all for the bank. We haven't been able to finance my acting as NOK and something had to give. So now the offer is up to US$434K. Adan doesn't dismiss this outright. This is a really good sign. Adan says he must go off to pray. We all assume he is going to tell the HTs the figure and so wait for his call back. So much wasted time is spent waiting.

Nigel
The Beach House
Friday, 28 August

At the end of the first week of Ramadan, Jamal and Abdullah come in to inform me I am to take a phone call from my sister. I'm relieved that it will be Nicky and not Ham on the other end. The two of them tell me to script something. I rehearse in front of them several times until they are satisfied. Joseph enters with the phone, squats down on his haunches between the two boys, and resting his gun on his knee, hands me the phone.

Finally it connects.

'Hello, Nicky and Nigel,' Adan says.

'Hello,' Nic's voice comes through.

'Hello, Nic,' I manage, trying to keep a hold on my emotions. She tells me Mum and Dad and the rest of the family love me and it just about destroys me. Abdullah motions that I should continue reading my statement as I hear Nic say, 'We're talking with Jon and Lorinda every day. We're doing everything we can to bring you home, mate – both of you, okay? We've offered —' Nicky's voice suddenly cuts out. There's the sound of background interference from Adan then her voice again, '— and three hundred and twenty thousand, Nige, and you know that's a lot because it's American dollars not Oz.'

I'm confused and certain I have just missed a vital piece of information. All I can manage is, 'I know.' I want to ask Nic to repeat what she just said but I can't get a word in edge-wise.

'You know we're trying to talk to the kidnappers. We need for you and Amanda to help us get across to them that they have to be realistic because we will never have the two million that they are asking for. It's insane, um, the governments have dropped us like hot pies, mate —'

'No, uh, Nicky, Nicky,' Adan's voice cuts in over the top as I struggle to hear her.

'Yes,' she replies with some annoyance. Adan continues, his accent thick and difficult to follow, 'Don't enter, enter affairs, we want you to ask . . . not political affairs about kidnap. What we want is two million but you cannot talk about any money.'

Nic seems determined to get her point across. She's calm as she talks over the top of Adan.

'Okay, so I can't. Okay, that's okay, but can I talk to Nigel?' The boys are now impatiently demanding that I read the statement.

I tell her things have degenerated: the conditions are bad; my arse is bleeding and my mental health is poor. With softness in her voice she says, 'Nige, we will never give up. You know that, don't you?'

'Tell Mum and Dad that I love them and I know that you are doing everything you can, please, please, please, please, try and talk with Adan, try and talk and negotiate with him. I don't know how much longer I can last here, I'm begging, I'm begging, I'm begging —'

Nic cuts in. 'Nige, I know, I know it's hideous . . . we are trying extremely hard to work with Adan to get this sorted, mate.'

'I know, I know, I know you are, I'm so sorry, I love you all, I miss you all,' I just manage to say before the phone goes dead. I bawl like a child.

I can barely hand the phone back to the boys. They're clamouring, wanting to know what Nicky said.

I pull myself together. 'I think she says that they have offered 1.3 million dollars but I'm not sure, it was difficult to hear and Adan was talking over the top so I can't be certain. Adan was listening; he will know if this is correct. You will have to ask him.'

In the morning Abdullah comes in.

'You are a hundred per cent sure she offers 1.3 million?' I start doubting myself – it's a huge amount of money. I tell him I think that was what she said but I'm not sure. He needs to speak to Adan.

Last night's conversation has caused excitement within the house. During the day, Jamal comes in and announces, 'The Captain is talking with the commanders.' I try to reassure myself by doing sums, adding up what everyone's houses are worth. I keep telling them: Adan will know exactly what has been put on the table. It would just take one phone call to clear up all the confusion and it seems stupid to keep asking me for confirmation.

Monday, 31 August

The younger guys come to me on the last day of month.

Jamal says, 'They have agreed to deal if your family has 1.3 million.'

'Jamal, has Adan confirmed this with Captain Yahya?'

'*Inshallah*, tonight you talk to your sister, you ask her how much money,' he replies.

I tell him that if the 1.3-million-dollar amount is correct, then it's both families' money. That they'll have to release both Amanda and me. It's impossible to get a straight response from Jamal about this. He seems to have gone off half-cocked with the thought of all that money. I'm not convinced they've confirmed the amount with Adan, and they seem to think the money's only from my family, but on the other hand there is a tiny bit of hope.

That evening and every night for the next week I ask about the call. I'm fed the same lines: 'Your sister does not answer, your sister doesn't return calls, the phone always engaged, Adan is absent.'

They are stalling and something isn't right. I know deep down that I must have misheard Nic. The disappointment is desperately hard to take. I just hope my faux pas doesn't have serious consequences with the boys, whose expectations have been raised and patience worn razor-thin.

I think I might have just fucked everything up.

SEPTEMBER 2009

Big squabbling families

Kellie
Newcastle
Early September

Bob Brown has become concerned about the family's plight and offered $100 000 of his own money, for which he has taken out a loan. This man is generous beyond words. He doesn't know us from Job, but is moved by what we are going through and set his politics to one side to help us. He also contacted Dick Smith and told him about our situation. Dick gave us a donation straight off and then suggests we meet in early October at his office in Sydney.

Nicky
Moore Park
Early September

The third AKE bill has come in. Mum and Dad paid the first one outside the kitty, pulling the money from their super. We sorted out the second one with Dick Smith's generous donation. There appears to be an expectation on the part of the Canadian family that we'll also look after the third. There's a silent battle of wills being played out as to which country can hold off longest without paying; the implication is that because we have money in our ransom fund, we can afford it.

Mum refuses to pay the third bill; she will not allow any money to be pulled from the kitty. Good thing too, as we are getting perilously close to going over our budget.

Kel and I are well aware of what a blow-out could mean – we've both got struggling businesses, and we're staring down insolvency and crippling debt like the great gaping, carrion-smelling maw of the Kraken.

'I understand Heather's frustration but we don't have the money,' Lorinda tells us. She then shuts me up by saying that Canada has a major fundraiser coming up and the organisers they have on board are raising substantial amounts. Their target is three million dollars. I hope they can pull this off but I am by no means convinced.

Thursday, 3 September

Lorinda gets a call from Adan. We log it as 'TC 15' – telephone call number 15 – AKE's preferred method of recording the calls. It creates a massive amount of excitement for Kel and me as we read the transcript at the CMT meeting that night – it says Adan's accepted the offer. We're just about to start whooping it up when Lorinda cuts in.

'No, no, don't get your hopes up like I did. Adan said to me the gang accepts the offer to keep Nigel and Amanda together.'

Argh. Instant deflation. JC believes that it's a divide-and-conquer ploy – a standard threat. We dissect the rest of the call. Adan is so hard to understand. He always sounds like he has his mouth pressed up against the mouthpiece, then he coughs and to my constant horror – I can never get past it, it's just too gross – he spits. I suspect that it's probably from the khat, a mild narcotic popular in parts of Africa and the Middle East, but I silently wish him a solid and fatal dose of TB.

After trawling through the transcript, we are not even sure that Adan has given the HTs the newest price of US$434K. He says, 'I will tell the group but I do not think they will accept this amount of money.' Bloody hell, he's had this offer since 29 August.

It all feels like one step forward and two steps back.

Saturday, 5 September
Lorinda has a very long-winded call in which she confirms that Adan has not taken the most recent offer to the gang. Lorinda puts him on the back foot by demanding to know why. Adan gets really peeved with Lorinda and starts raving. His rant culminates in 'maybe they don't want to come home after all'. Then he changes tack once again, saying he might set up a call so Lorinda can ask them herself.

When Lorinda calls back later, Adan is as nice as pie. He confirms during this call that the group has agreed we can talk to Amanda. Lorinda asks if she can speak to Nigel as well, but Adan wants a family member to speak to him. When we discuss this conversation with JC, he says it is very curious behaviour for a kidnapper to be upset and angry at a victim's mother and yet to be so conciliatory on the next call, *very* odd.

While I would love to speak to Nige, I put it out there that perhaps we should get Lorinda to speak to him. It's a big sacrifice but the intel benefits are huge. We could establish if they are together and push that we are negotiating for both of them – that is, we won't entertain separate deals. Lorinda suspects that Adan won't let her speak to him. On confirming this is the case, she tells Adan that I'll speak to Nigel.

Kellie
Newcastle
Tuesday, 8 September

The CMT is working well even though there have been disagreements. But the day of TC 21 we realise we're all in this together. Lorinda and Nic are on a high: they're going to be able to talk to Nige and Amanda. Lorinda is to go first, then Nic will call Nige.

These calls are scheduled for before our morning CMT, so we'll all get to hear new recordings of both Nige and Amanda. I am so excited about the prospect, I get up early to shower so that if the CMT call goes longer than normal, I can stay online and go straight to work afterwards.

I am sitting in front of my computer, waiting; the calls with Nige and Amanda must be going for a long time. *Wow, this is great*, I think. Then the call pops up on the computer screen. It's JC saying they've had a horror call and that Lorinda and Jon won't be joining us today. I get Nic online and we discuss TC 21.

Nic plays the call over Skype. Amanda is being tortured. She is screaming out to her mother, crying – no, sobbing and howling – and yelling, 'Mummy, Mummy, Mummy,' over and over. Lorinda is doing the most amazing job of remaining calm and sticking to the lines she's been coached to say. JC wisely advises Nic not to make the call to Nigel. The likelihood is that it would be a similar situation with him.

This phone call rocks me to the core, and my admiration for Nic and Lorinda shifts up a few notches. I know that it is nerve-racking for them to talk to Adan, with the threat of a bad call coming in always present, but hearing a real one changes things. It's horrific. I play the call to Matt, and we're both in tears. No one would wish this treatment on anyone, let alone a young woman. It really makes me wonder what else they're doing to her.

After this call, JC decides that we need to get things moving faster and brings in Alto, a Somali man who lives in the UK and works at a university. He will act as a translator for us. JC has used him before and he introduces us to him in our next CMT call. From now on Alto will discuss our case with Adan directly and the calls will be interpreted.

Nigel
The Beach House
Saturday, 5 September

At the start of September I go down again with a bout of dysentery – after three debilitating days of diarrhoea I'm feeling like the worst has passed, but that is nothing compared to what takes place on the night of the fifth. Amanda's screams penetrate the bricks and mortar. The volume of her screams increases as her door opens and closes. There is no begging or pleading, just screams of terror.

A ghostly outline of a figure passes by the archway leading back to my room. Any thoughts of bravery are quickly reduced to ashes when Mohammad appears in my doorway. His AK47 is held across his chest, his eyes are burning; it's as though he can read my thoughts. A maniacal grin spreads across his face, which in a split second turns to a look of hatred as he brings his finger to his mouth motioning for me to be silent. Shaking with fear, I try to prepare myself for their arrival.

Sunday, 6 September

At morning prayer it's utter relief to hear Amanda knocking for the toilet. Fatigue and stress have left me drained and I fall back asleep but it's not long before I'm jolted awake by the sounds of screaming. At first it seems like a dream, then reality slaps me in the face, and I hear the groans and grunts of Amanda being gagged. Unable to listen any longer, I squeeze my hands over my ears and bury my head under the pillow, trying to force my mind to go to another place, far away from here, from this horror. I'm almost hoping they will move on to me so that Amanda will have some relief and I can share her burden. For over an hour this continues, and I'm in shock that one human being could do this to another.

Monday, 7 September

In the evening they again go to work on Amanda, and this time it seems even more brutal. What starts off as loud talking soon turns into muffled screaming. I hear the sound of a metal plate skipping across the concrete floor, followed by the hollow sound of a glass as it topples over. I picture Amanda desperately trying to get away but there's nowhere to run. The screams for help seem to last for hours, and there's constant movement of the boys going in and out of Amanda's room. Each time the door opens her screams sound as though she is right next to me, begging me to help, begging for mercy.

Finally there is silence. Maybe she has passed out. Then I hear the sound of the conference call, knowing that any second she will be connected to her mother.

Her gag is removed so she can speak. The words coming out of her mouth are almost indistinguishable. She's hysterical, trying to talk but bawling uncontrollably. 'Mum . . . Mummy, please, listen, okay, please,' she wails. 'Okay, things have changed here, Mum, you need to pay the money now, you need to pay the million dollars now because they have started to torture me. Mummy, today they have me tied up, please, please . . . My arms are tied to my legs behind my back and I can't handle it, they are going to do it and I'm going to be in pain . . . Mummy . . .' Her sobbing is like that of a young child. I hear something solid hitting flesh, and Amanda's gasp makes me sit upright in bed. I hear something skittling across the floor.

The telephone call finished, she's crying and pleading with the boys. Then there's deafening silence, except for my pulse pounding like a drum in my ears. The sound of the conference call somewhere in the distance brings me back to my senses, and Amanda is again put on the phone. 'They have started to torture me, okay? I cannot handle this, you have to pay them money now, it cannot wait because they are going to do this to me every day and I can't, I can't handle it. Mum, you have to pay the money now, where is the money?'

I can only imagine what Lorinda is going through for the second time. 'You have half a million,' she manages before again breaking down and weeping. 'We need one million, we need it now because I can't handle what they are doing to me, Mum, I can't handle it even one more day, it hurts.' She's crying for mercy. 'It's one year, Mumma, it's one year,' she pleads desperately. 'Mum, do you understand what they are doing to me?' Amanda's words lose sense as she becomes completely hysterical.

For hours afterwards, I lie there, empty, too terrified to sleep.

Nicky
Moore Park
Tuesday, 8 September

As recommended by JC, we refuse to speak to Adan. We won't reward him for such abhorrent behaviour.

Alto the interpreter is now part of the team. He will not be involved in the decision-making process. His role is that of a communicator only; he will not answer anything outside the script. Alto is a perfect candidate because he's been out of the country for thirty years and has no close family there. He has no clan affiliation and the origin of his accent can't be pinpointed. JC will brief him prior to any calls, and Adan cannot contact him directly.

JC sends him the communication charts and he comes to grips with the whole case pretty quickly.

Sunday, 13 September

Six long days after the hideous TC 21, Lorinda introduces Alto to Adan. TC 22 is a really, really long phone call. It is weird listening to Nigel's life being discussed in a language completely strange to the ear – there is nothing similar, and no anglicised words used. Alto is obviously charming – he gets Adan chuckling a couple of times – and masks his true feelings well.

He gives us a brief run-down of the conversation. Adan tried to get some idea of Alto's background but Alto didn't bite. He says Adan is fearful of the gang. They have fired him in the past but have since asked him back to be their spokesperson because they didn't get anywhere without him. Adan says he spent four months talking to five Australian spies (okay, that's Gary, Dave, Mark, Reece – who is the fifth one?) and that these people made the situation worse. And the result of these negotiations is that they don't believe what Lorinda is saying.

Thursday, 17 September

The next call of note to Adan is TC 24. Adan talks himself up to Alto and mentions a 'mockery of period of silence when people in Nairobi thought Nigel and Amanda would be released by force or without payment'. So much for the 'elder of much influence', or the coked-up warlord as we know him. I'm pretty sure our complete lack of respect for this strategy upset everyone who wore a maple leaf. Adan also says, 'The boys guarding tried to kill Amanda on a couple of occasions during this time.'

Adan also makes a disturbing reference to a 'loss of faith' that soured things earlier on. That is, the first time I got to speak with Nige, way back on day ten. He implies that the original US$25K offer was meant to be the payment for supplying proof of life and they were seriously put offside by our reneging on the deal. I am in complete disorder about this. I don't trust Adan as he tends to rewrite history. But I have a nasty sensation burning away in my gut that this could be a colossal cock-up due to the fact that the government was so steadfast in refusing to get a translator from the word go. It seems that Adan has misunderstood the Feds and thought that it really was payment for POL. Because it hasn't been paid, he has lost face in front of the gang and we are still dealing with that a year later. It is a disquiet I can't shake. I know I will never know the truth, but we have got pretty good at filling in the gaps.

Sunday, 20 September

It's Eid, the breaking of Ramadan. That seemed to go so much faster this year than last. I offer up silent prayer – well, hopes, any-way – that they are getting something decent to eat and are being looked after in this time of celebration. I've read somewhere that watermelon is often eaten. If Nige gets to eat some, his memories of hot, baking summers, sitting in tractor tyre tubes in the creek, scoffing down cold watermelon and pelting the pith-sucked skins at each other will no doubt come flooding back.

Nigel
The Beach House
Sunday, 20 September

Ramadan comes to an end. I'm happy I no longer have to fast. I've seen a goat tethered to a tree just outside the bathroom window. Assam explains that the goat will be killed as part of the feast to celebrate Eid and tells me he will be the one given the task, as he is the most learned. I ask if it's possible to watch, not expecting my request to be granted, so I'm surprised when he says, 'Inshallah, I will come and get you just before I kill it.'

I'm not sure what my motives are: whether they're born of mor-bid fascination, or a chance to reconnect with something from my youth. As a boy, I butchered sheep on our farm. I sit at the back

THE PRICE OF LIFE

door while Assam goes about his bloody business, hacking away with a knife that's as blunt as a spoon.

It's not long before the smell of roasting meat floats in the air. My empty stomach growls. Late in the morning, after the special prayer of Eid, they bring me a plate of the goat's kidney, liver and heart. I try not to think about it and I devour everything in a matter of minutes. I'm surprised how delicious the offal tastes.

The boys seem to be in a festive mood, each one coming in and exclaiming, 'Eid *wan axin*' before hugging me. The day turns out to be a goat fest, as plate after plate of meat is brought in. I demolish the meat before the fat turns cold. I sit there, my stomach distended, feeling content for the first time in months. Even though Eid lasts for three days, the next morning things revert to normal.

Nicky
Moore Park
Monday, 21 September

TC 25. Adan claims he heard a figure of 1.3 million from me and that Mark said we had three million available early on. Adan also says that Amanda has been working for the government and that she has been captured before. *WTF?* Lorinda explains to us after the call that Amanda had been 'captured' once before, in Iraq, but she had given them all her cash and talked her way out of it. She also suspects that Amanda thought she would be able to talk her way out of this as well. No such luck. The only thing that talks here is money. If we keep procrastinating, the price for them, Adan claims, will not go down. In fact, it will go up.

Adan reckons there is a gentleman in Nairobi offering

US$2.5 million for their release. Adan pulled this stunt earlier with Ham who told him, 'Go crazy, mate. Take it, 'cause we are never going to be able to match that amount.'

We all wonder why he is trying this strategy again and decide to call his bluff. If he can get that, he should take it, Alto tells him. Typical Adan; he just changes the subject. He cuts to examples of piracy and how much money is being paid for boats. Alto is already on it, breaking down the price for the vessel, underlining the fact that the price for the captives onboard is minimal.

During the following CMT, we finally organise getting medicine into the country. My cousin has researched the medicines they might need, but he can't write prescriptions that would be filled in Nairobi. We don't want to jeopardise the safety of an NGO and we don't want to ask the government – we're not sure if they would help us anyway. JC tracks down someone in Nairobi who he thinks can get their hands on the meds and send them to Mogadishu airport.

If they really are as unwell as Adan says, we have to get Adan to take it.

Wednesday, 23 September

TC 26. Lorinda, Alto and I call Adan. We take it in turns to talk to Adan then Alto translates just in case Adan hasn't heard us correctly. We explain that I do not have $1.3 million but that we are gathering more money. Adan asks me why I didn't call Nige. As if I would. I make it really clear to him that what happened with Amanda was not okay, and that I held him responsible. Adan is clearly getting pissed off with me. He says that he was offered three million dollars in the beginning. 'Well, you sure missed your opportunity then,' is my tart reply.

Our next offer will take us over our initial budget. We discuss how we are going to put the new offer to Adan. It's a considerable jump. With the donations we've been able to adjust our budget to US$610K. Every time I think about money or our lack thereof, I get that nasty, queasy feeling like I've lost my stomach on a show ride. Kel and I don't know how much Canada has raised. Lorinda sounds supremely confident: 'We don't have it but we will have.'

I know we don't have enough to pay the next AKE bill; we haven't even paid the last one. I find consolation in the fact that Kel is as apprehensive about this as I am. We've got a fundraiser on Saturday night and we're both hoping this will help plug some of the holes.

Friday, 25 September

Adan sends a text saying that Nigel is crying for his sister. Yeah, right.

When Alto and I next speak to Adan, we say a new offer is on the table but we want a POL. Adan wants me to speak to Nige. He can jam that request up his arse. A quick burst of adrenaline shoots through me: I don't want to hear Nige being tortured. I want and insist on the answers being texted to Lorinda's phone. For Lorinda, the POL is 'What is Dad's [Jon's] favourite colour?' And Nigel's is, 'What is Jumbo's wife's name?' Jumbo is a mate of Nige's, who he has known since he was about six.

Adan tries to get some leverage with Alto by asking him which clan he is from. Alto has been palming this off for a while but tells Adan that he is from the Midgaan clan.

'Yes, yes,' says Adan impatiently, 'we all belong to the Somali lower-caste Midgaan.'

Alto chuckles when he relays this to us. He's been gone so long he has no affiliations, and he thinks himself quite crafty. Alto's laugh is wonderfully infectious.

Kellie
North Star
Saturday, 26 September

It's true that your friends come through at times like this and my friends from North Star, near Goondiwindi in New South Wales, Mick and Kate Owen, are lifesavers. Kate and her friend Belinda, who also happens to be Amy's sister-in-law, have arranged a fund-raiser for Nigel in their town. Ham has organised a day of rugby with the teams wearing the 'Bring Blackie Back' T-shirts, and Mick and Kate will host an auction and dinner at their home that evening.

All of us, except Nic, head to North Star for the fundraiser. This is our old stamping ground – it's close to where the farm was. Heather and Geoff's friends are here, along with my friends and those of Matt, Ham, Nic and Nigel. It's a great gathering of sixty or so people. I need to play the emotion card if this is going to be a success so I've put together a montage of Nigel's life to show everyone at this event. I don't feel bad about this – the whole thing has been a roller-coaster but it's become so easy for us to just present the anger and frustration, not the sadness.

I'm surprised when Ham gets choked up making a small speech about Nigel, but I shouldn't be. I always thought Ham would be the strongest one, but as it turns out even the strongest crumble. We play the video montage of Nigel and even though I have seen it over and over, it still makes me cry, especially at the end when the screen goes black and the words 'Nigel Brennan: kidnapped 424 days' then the phone call with Nic and Nige kicks in. This brings the house down, the pleading in his voice, how sorry he his, and him telling everyone he loves them. There is not a dry eye. The auction raises $35 000 and lifts all our hopes that we may just have enough money to get him out without having to pay too much back at the end.

Nigel
The Beach House
Saturday, 26 September

Assam brings me my Qur'an, which I'm now sharing with Amanda. When I open the front cover, I'm surprised to see she has written a series of page numbers below those I had marked when I was trying to show Romeo the error of his ways. Amanda must have tried the same tactic.

I flip to the first page she's numbered and slowly scan the text. I come to a dead stop when I see a few words underlined in pencil. I turn to the next page number in her sequence, noticing several more words underlined. It's a message for me.

The first thing she says is 'I love U'.

After midday prayer Ahmed casually enters my room and sits down. We make small talk before he finally comes to the point.

'Noah, today I speak with Adan. He has a question from your family. They want to know what the name of Jumbo's wife is.'

I immediately give him the answer: 'Sonya'.

'Do you understand the question?' he asks.

'Yes, it's simple, the answer is Sonya. Jumbo – James – is one of my best friends, and his wife's name is Sonya.' I get a momentary flashback to times of indulgence with James before snapping back to reality.

'I want you to think about this question. We believe your family is trying to communicate with you without us understanding,' he says. I have to stop myself from laughing at this; they must think this is some James Bond movie.

'It's not possible,' I say. 'The answer is Sonya. The only thing they will understand from this is that I am still alive.'

Still not satisfied he says, 'You must think about the answer and ways that your family may be trying to communicate with you. I will come back in a few hours; you must have a solution.' Then he stands up and leaves.

For the rest of the afternoon I rack my brain, but no matter which way I twist it in my head I come to the same conclusion: it is nothing more than a proof of life. When Ahmed returns a few hours later, I talk about our history together, about James's religious background, his wedding and the fact that Sonya had the same last name as mine before she got married. I tell him it's inconceivable that my family could possibly take anything more from this than simply knowing I am alive. Ahmed doesn't seem convinced.

The Bush House
Monday, 28 September

We've been moved again. I wake fatigued after another hellish car trip. This new room is very dark; I'm barely able to see my hand in front of my face.

When Jamal comes in with breakfast, I ask him to open the window just a centimetre. He ignores me and slides the plate across the floor. The bathroom is also a downgrade: there isn't even a running tap, just a hole in the corner where I'm supposed to crap.

It doesn't feel like we are staying long: the boys are camped out in the hallway and the food is being brought in from the market. I don't bother unpacking my few belongings; it all seems pointless.

Nicky
Moore Park
Wednesday, 30 September

TC 28. Alto and I call Adan as he has still not sent a text. He doesn't answer the POL but has clearly discussed it with Nige; he's in a bit of turmoil. Nigel, Adan says, will not answer the question. *If my brother wants to get out of that rat hole, he will have to answer the question,* I think. Amanda's POL question is what is Dad's (Jon's) favourite colour?

'Okay, Adan, then ask Nigel another question for me: ask him what a "happy Jack" is?' I have to get Adan to repeat it to me. I am so chuffed with myself; no one who has lived anywhere but out west would know that they are stocky grey squawking gregarious birds that flock together in large families, earning them their other name of 'apostle bird'. Country folk either love them or hate them. I'm firmly in the first camp. Big squabbling families – what's not to love?

We give him a deadline. He's got twenty-four hours to get the answer or he doesn't get a new offer.

OCTOBER 2009

Trust

Nigel
The Bush House
Early October

After being holed up for three days in virtual darkness and with the start of a new month, I'm battling to keep it together. I'm living in a tomb. I have no idea where we are, and I can't even glimpse Amanda any more. The months of my manipulating the boys have come to nothing. I feel like I'm an invalid, unable to make my own decisions, no longer even able to fill up my own water bottle, having to comply with the guards' every demand. My thoughts are the only thing they can't influence, but it's hard not to let depression and frustration get the better of me. I desperately miss the last house and its small privileges. There I could see out the windows. I miss the blue sky, the tops of green trees, but, most of all, I miss seeing the sun.

The days drag on endlessly, and trying to fill them becomes that much harder as each one passes. I begin making up memory games. Inspired by what Nelson Mandela did at Robben Island, I commit my diary to memory. What begins as a game turns into a fixation. I am terrified about them finding my scraps of paper, detailing my records, and I know deep down that if we ever get out of here, they aren't going to let me walk out with them. In my crossword and prayer books I also begin making duplicates and triplicates of relevant dates, using very basic shorthand to prompt my memory. This means I look like I am reading while I'm memorising every-thing. Three to four times a day I go through this process until I can recite everything I've written verbatim.

Having not seen Ahmed since the move, I'm actually excited when he visits me on the morning of the first.

'Has Adan spoken with my family?' I ask, hoping that the answer to the question about Jumbo from days earlier will have resulted in something. His vacant look isn't encouraging. He finally replies.

'Yes, Adan speaks with your sister last night. He does not give the answer from the last question. We think it's a trick. Adan asks your sister for a new question: they want to know what is a "happy jack?"'

I don't know how the answer to this is going to convince these idiots that my family aren't still trying to do the same thing. Push-ing these thoughts aside, I repeat the question.

'What is a happy jack?'

'Yes,' he replies, his eyes now squarely fixed on me. I draw a complete blank. I'm sure that it is the type of bird we used to get on the farm; they would congregate on the lawn when Mum put the sprinklers on. As a kid I had only known them as 'crazy jacks' because of the commotion they used to make. It all seems so far away and I'm struggling to properly picture them. It seems like a lifetime ago and I'm desperate not to get the answer wrong.

'I don't know what a happy jack is, but I think it's the same as crazy jack; it's an Australian bird, their common name is apostle bird.' He seems perturbed by my answer.

'You think your family is trying to communicate with you?' he asks.

'This is only something I would know, from my childhood. Maybe my sister calls them happy jacks but I know them as crazy jacks. The only thing my family can take from this answer is that I am alive,' I explain. We go round and round in circles until he finally tells me to write the answer down. Then he leaves.

In the late afternoon, after my months of agitating Romeo, he finally caves in to my pestering and begins teaching me Surahs of the Qur'an in Arabic. A few days later he begins doing the same with Amanda. This means we can pass the Qur'an – and our messages – between us more often.

Nicky
Moore Park
Early October

It's an auspicious start to the month. Adan sends two texts to Lorinda. The first one says: 'hunter green'. We were expecting 'green' but to give the exact shade indicates that Amanda has gone to some lengths to answer the question.

The second one says 'Apostle bird'. It's the correct answer too.

Now I need to do my thing, even though we're right up against our budget. This is a reward system after all.

Over the next couple of CMT meetings we decide the next jump is going to be up to $548K. A few months earlier, one of our great aunts, Dulce, died. She was a great old bird. She had nursed her husband, Albert, who was an absolute favourite of the kids, through stroke and cancer twenty-five years ago. She went blind, but lived unassisted well into her nineties. Mum told me she had said something along the lines of, 'It will be wonderful to see Ab again. I do miss him so,' as she settled into her Smoky Dawson recliner a few days before she died.

As with all the strategies, everything we tell Adan is based on truth so we can't be caught out. It was probably the first thing I learned when I did the negotiator 101 course with the Feds all those long months ago. You can simply not answer a question or deflect, but you cannot lie.

After much discussion at the CMT, we decide to tell Adan that the increased offer is a result of Dulce's estate being settled. I script the conversation and pin it to the wall. I go over the possible ways our talk could go, then I make the call.

'Our sad loss is your gain,' I say to Adan. And then I lose it totally. *That wasn't in the script.* Si is rubbing and patting me between my shoulder blades. Dulce had a great long and happy life, and I know that if Adan tells Nigel that Dulce has died, it will be no surprise. But I'm terribly saddened at the thought that Adan could, and probably will, be gleeful at Nigel's grief. Alto saves me by launching into conversation with Adan.

It's really rattled Adan that Lorinda and I are refusing to talk to Nigel or Amanda. He has a whinge to Alto that he is misunderstood and has done his best to look after the pair, and they will confirm this 'after they are released'. We're all cheered up at this. It's positive talk.

Adan then says he will accept one million dollars. This is a big deal too. Alto doesn't think that Adan will take our new offer but it feels like we are starting to get near the ballpark. Things start to move fast from this point on. Adan also discusses for the first time an exchange rather than a money drop. This would mean using the hawala system.

JC has used the hawala money-exchange a number of times, as it's much safer than lugging wads of cash around. Hawala is the middle-eastern and African money-transfer system. Muslim countires don't really believe in banks. They're usually privately owned, and in the case of Somalia, owned by a bunch of MPs. He explains to us that essentially what would happen is that a hawala dealer, say in another Muslim country such as Saudi Arabia (we're likely to move the money from there as it is a big banking state), will have a counterpart in Mogadishu. The hawala dealer would physically handle and count our money. He would then ring his Somali counterpart, who'd then release the money to Adan. We will have to pay a handling fee of 2 to 5 per cent. Adan's unlikely to split that with us so we will have to tell him it'll come out of the ransom amount.

We'll need to impose a couple of caveats: the money will not be released till Nigel and Amanda are at some agreed exchange point. I can remember hearing that at a recent kidnapping, there was a time delay of four hours between the money being delivered and the arrival of the kidnap victims. I'm struck by the thought of how completely mind-numbingly terrifying those four hours must have been. Plenty of time to get captured by another group.

AKE's on-the-ground logistics guy, Sam, starts looking at on-the-ground logistics. He's an advocate of the 6 Ps: perfect planning prevents piss-poor performance.

Possible exchange points are the secure aid agencies'

compounds – probably the AMISOM compounds.

JC suggests we speak to the authorities about getting Nigel and Amanda's passports released. It gives us some control over their extraction. The passports are being held at the High Commissions in Nairobi. I am really apprehensive about them being forthcoming and doubt they will release them.

We have been given a list by DFAT of their possessions. The HC had their things collected from the hotel room – we all speculate by whom – after they were taken. Going through the itemised list was horrible; it felt like reading through a deceased estate. I was crying hard over a list of clothes, the likes of a T-shirt, green, red writing, 'more trees less bush'. T-shirt, 'Ramones logo'. Underpants, green, Bonds brand. One pair tube socks red trim. Reading through the contents of the list, I let my guard down. Somewhere tucked away is a pain not to be probed at, like a torn-off nail you accidentally bump and try so hard not to touch again. If you do, the pain is too intense.

It is one of the times it really hits home that my brother may not ever come back.

What if he dies? What if we've worked this hard and he doesn't come home? We will never be able to survive it as a family. I can't start to think about the dysfunction it will create. Nigel's life has been reduced to this: the love of his family, a list of his T-shirts in a embassy on the other side of the world. We will never have a body to mourn. I can't have this happen to Mum and Dad. The weight of it falls to me and it is such a heavy, heavy load. Tears sheet down my cheeks, dripping off my chin. *Shit, the keyboard is wet.* I can't have another computer crash on me.

JC can organise for a counterpart in Nairobi to pick their gear up.

The RCMP has said to Jon that the government has multilevel plans in play for Amanda's extraction but won't disclose them to Jon. Statements like that freeze my blood. They also won't disclose them to JC. What we would really like is some assistance from the government in the form of medical care. In an ideal situation, if we were not stretched financially (read: if we were insured), the family members would stay at AKE secure accommodation in Nairobi (the closest capital city to Mogadishu). The families and AKE would take over a wing and seal it up. Nigel and Amanda would have adjoining rooms for ease of contact with each other. Private medical staff would be made available for both and all would stay for up to a couple of weeks until they'd acclimatised. The time can vary greatly as some people want to ease back into society slowly and others want absolute freedom as they have been locked away for so long. We know an awful lot about what happens to people on release – we've done our homework.

Jon and Lorinda tell us they have been constantly discouraged from going to Nairobi to retrieve Amanda. Both governments have told us that as soon as Nigel and Amanda are physically well enough to travel they will be repatriated to Australian and Canadian soil respectively.

Alarmingly, the Canadian government has implied to Jon that Amanda's mental health is 'less of an issue' than her physical health, and as soon as her body is okay to fly she would be sent home. When DFAT came to dinner, Kel had asked James about the mental health services available for Nigel: 'DFAT doesn't have psychiatric support agencies available for Nigel in Australia. There are other agencies such as Centrelink that we can approach.' Looks like we will be starting from scratch when he gets home then. JC is adamant there should be a family member with both Nige and

Amanda when they get out so someone is there to keep the respective embassy and police forces in line. The authorities will want to debrief them as soon as possible, and often that's not good for the victim. The family members need a Rottweiler to tell them to back off and reassure Nigel and Amanda that they don't have to do anything until they're ready.

Friday, 9 October

We don't hear back from Adan for ages, so Alto and I call him. The call coincides with Canada's fundraising night and JC is over there for it, so I'm going over points with him while he's in a stairwell in his dinner suit. Lorinda says he looks very James Bond. JC is saying everyone is confusing him with the Chinese waiter and if we can't find him, it will be because he's in the kitchen washing dishes.

Adan says to Alto that he went to the gang and they will only accept 1.3, so it looks like we've gone back up again. We're told the gang is split into two parts: the good guys and the bad guys. Alto implores Adan to convince the good guys that there is no more money. He tells Adan that he knows the families don't have this sort of money and that Adan has to convince the good guys to get this message across to the bad guys.

Adan does, however, go on to discuss exchange matters with Alto. Adan has heard of and is happy to use the Dahabshiil agency, an international hawala funds-transfer company. So Alto has arranged for our next call to be early Monday morning. This is good as I will be down in Sydney with Kel, and she can keep me company when I take the call; it's much nicer having someone there with me.

Saturday, 10 October

I fly to Newcastle. Jacinta calls and leaves a panicked message, which I get when I stop over at Brisbane. One of the neighbours has been welding; everything is bone-dry and an easterly is blowing. Sparks got away, and our farm is on fire. I scramble to call back. It's pretty much under control; the kids are all accounted for and the house and sheds are still standing, but the fire has burnt the cane from one end of the farm to the other. Si has a huge battle on his hands to get it cut before the sugar content disappears.

I later hear that he hasn't had enough help on the ground to do it. The crop has turned to mush. We really needed that income.

Kellie
Sydney
Sunday, 11 October

Nicky and I have an appointment arranged with Dick in his office at Terrey Hills, a suburb of northern Sydney. We drive down from Newcastle, and the *Australian Story* Sydney crew are meeting us there. I'm starting to get a little frustrated with them following us around. I really don't want them filming me asking Dick Smith for a million dollars.

Nic and I are both struggling with the idea that Canada has no money and as yet has not contributed to either the kitty or the AKE payments. On the phone Dick asked Nic how much money Canada had, and we've been trying to get something out of them since then.

It's 7 a.m. We're halfway to Sydney and still on the highway when we have to pull over to take our CMT call. What I need from the Canadians is to know exactly how much they have to contribute so

I can tell Dick Smith at our meeting in three hours' time.

Lorinda says they have mortgaged Jon's house and have US$100 000. I don't think I have ever been so excited. Not only can I tell Dick that the Canadians have money to add to the pile, but it will also get Ham and Heather off our backs.

Dick refuses to be filmed by *Australian Story*, to my relief, and then welcomes us into his office. It's full of books, photographs, maps and beautiful Australian wood carvings. His desk is a giant polished piece of raw-cut tree trunk. Almost straight after greeting us he says, 'Don't worry about money; I'll take care of all costs.'

My eyes start to well up, and Nic and I both say that no, we can't accept that. He tells us he has spoken with JC at length and wants this case done like an insurance job, that is, like we have unlimited funds. Nic and I tell Dick exactly how much money we have so far, and about our plan to pay all the AKE costs, with the Canadians' help. Dick says he will fund the shortfall once all bills are in. So if we need a hundred thousand, then it will be a hundred thousand, but if we need a million dollars, he will give us a million.

Nic and I fairly glide out of this meeting, unaware of anything apart from feelings of overwhelming gratitude to this wonderful man.

We even forget that the *Australian Story* people are at the top of the driveway waiting for us. We do a quick interview through our car window then head into the city. Once we've checked into our hotel, we head to our next meeting, with AFP and DFAT.

Our meeting is very interesting. James revisits the legal implications of the family paying a ransom, and again I ask James if he will send me to jail and freeze the assets of the family if we pay the money. I get the same response as last time: we cannot confirm that the gang holding Nigel is in any way related to Al-Shabaab; we believe that they are criminals seeking money, not political gain. Decrypting this statement, which we've heard a few times now, I start to think this is the clause that will get me off a charge, or at least will mean that any charge will be hard to make stick. I really need to discuss this with Clayton Utz tomorrow. If I can take control of the money situation that is so vitally important to the whole case, it is one less thing for Nic to worry about. If Nic is the lead negotiator, I am now the money launderer.

The rest of the meeting is a fishing exercise: DFAT and the AFP are after information from us. Nic and I have the upper hand this time, and we don't give much away. What we want from this meeting are further details about how the government would repatriate Nigel from Nairobi to Australia. DFAT goes over it: as soon as Nigel lands in Nairobi from Somalia, he will be passed into the hands of the Australian government. They will arrange his medical checks and flight home.

The government has also agreed to fly two family members to Nairobi to be there when Nigel gets out. James asks if Nicky will be one of those family members. I see him turn pale when Nic tells him Heather and Geoff will be going. I think James is scared of Heather and secretly wants Nic there as a buffer. Nic picks up on this and asks for a third ticket for her. James says that 'a third ticket has not been accounted for', but I have a feeling he will change his mind.

JC is pretty happy with a lot of this and thinks we can pick out some pretty important and cost-saving extras. Jon and Lorinda arm themselves with this information to take to their government to ask for the same consular assistance.

At the beginning of September, I'd met up with an old uni friend. Helen has had a lot to do with the Jane McGrath Foundation and gave me some fantastic tips on how to set up a tax-deductible foundation to which our supporters could donate money. She gave me the names of some law firms she thought could help us with pro bono advice. I called Clayton Utz, which not only agreed to help us with pro bono advice on the foundation but offered free legal advice on some of the rules we were breaking regarding the payment of ransoms. They also have an international contact who has said they will advise the Canadians pro bono as well.

I feel I have kicked a huge goal. Neither we nor the Canadians will need to pay for valuable legal advice, so we can keep as much money as possible in the ransom kitty. Nic and I will meet with Clayton Utz tomorrow.

Nigel
The Bush House
Sunday, 11 October

In the evening the boys go back and forth from Amanda's room. It's not long before I hear her voice as she takes a phone call.

'Mummy,' she says, causing my skin to prickle as the memory of the last conversation to her mother comes flooding back. 'Okay, listen, listen, last month when I talked to you, you said you had half a million, right?' I'm surprised at how calm and coherent she sounds. 'Can you hear me? Okay, so you had half a million, now listen, if, if that money is for me and, like, for me only and you're ready to pay it, then they will accept that, that half a million for me and release me.' I'm hit with giddiness as anger and terror mushroom in my stomach at the thought that they will sell her – only her.

She continues. 'Listen, Mum, Mum, listen. Any, any agreement or promises that you have with Nigel's family, right now, ah, like we all love Nigel, but they have to be broken, because Nigel and I have been separated for nine months already, so it doesn't make sense any more to negotiate together. Like, this is the only chance that we have, they will take half a million for me now, but this is like the only chance that we have, Mum.'

I don't think that I have ever felt so lonely and cheated in my life. She is going to leave me here. We all have a built-in survival mechanism but I can barely contain my anger. Maybe she's got a gun to her head. I can't hear what Lorinda is saying to her; she'll jump at the chance to free her child, especially after their last conversation, won't she? I'm trying to get clues from what Amanda is saying.

'Our family, us, you and me, we have a chance for me, for me only to be released, but for me only, Mum, so you have to break any kind of commitment that you have with Nigel's family, because I know that Nigel's family have said they have more than a million dollars.'

I feel like I've just been struck between the eyes with a cricket bat. She's not following any script; no one's forcing her to say this. I feel like a complete fool. What has she told them about my family's financial situation? Has she been angling for this for a while? I sit there and listen, trying to make sense of it all.

'Nigel's family have said to these people that they have more money than that, so, just a second, just a sec, if you can agree to pay five hundred for me, for me only, I will be released tomorrow. If you could pay that money for me, today, I would be released today.'

I could be alone here tomorrow.

'Mum, can you call me right back? Can you try calling me back on this number, okay?' she says. The silence is now deafening. Then I hear Romeo's voice. I'm desperate to hear what he is now saying to her but it's useless as their voices are hushed and muffled. The phone rings. Amanda answers.

'Hi, Mum, Mum . . . Mum . . . Mum, if you —' but then she suddenly stops. Has the phone been disconnected again?

I'm jolted back as I hear her say, 'Is there anybody, what . . . ?', then a short pause before she continues. 'Yeah, I'm with, I'm with a few people here. I am with one man who is the reason that we have this chance; he has been the only person here who has been kind to me and I trust him and he has persuaded the other command- ers to give this chance for us, for our family, to pay five hundred for me . . . one chance, Mum.' It's horrible to listen to this, to hear her say it so easily, as if I mean nothing to her.

Something in my gut, though, tells me that things have seriously gone awry; for so long she has been their target, to now suddenly change doesn't fit.

'What,' she says sounding flat, obviously listening to her mother before continuing, 'Mum, but Mum.' She's trying to reason with her.

Amanda then says, 'He is one of a few people who are in charge, Mum, this is what, this is what you have to understand, okay? Nigel and I are not together. Nigel and I have been separated for quite, quite a while. I don't know what's going on with Nigel and me, but you guys are working together, but that sort, that sort of commitment to work together, now has, has to finish. This money, Mum, Nigel's, Nigel's family has said that they have more money than that, they have more than, I've heard 1.3 million dollars.'

I told her this via our code in the Qur'an after I'd spoken with Nicky. This is both our families' money. I'm furious with myself for trusting her.

She's now desperately trying to talk her mother around. 'Wait, but Mum, Mum, Mumma, Mumma, this can only be, this money can only be, this one chance we have, we have one chance, okay, for, for you to pay half a million dollars for me and what they're telling me is if you don't take this chance, if you don't agree to that, then the money for me which they have been asking for, which is one million, it's going to go back to that and even beyond that. It could be more than one million if you don't accept that.'

It's like listening to a broken record. I sense her frustration as her mother doesn't bite. She continues pleading, sounding like a spoilt child who's about to have a tantrum.

I can understand her wanting to get away from these people but I can't believe she's doing this after all we have been through. We have been stuck together all this time; we made a pact not to leave our three Somali colleagues and now it's just us. Something's changed her mind obviously. My bitterness starts to eat away at me.

'What you're saying to me is that there is no more money than that, that there's no 1.3 million dollars or one million dollars, there's nothing. You're saying that there is only five hundred and that is for both of us,' she states, making it clear to the boys in her room what the circumstances are. As though not believing what she is being told, she again asks for clarification: 'And you're saying that Nigel's family has not said that, because everyone here is under the impression that there's far more money than that.'

I know this is my fault. I must have got things confused when I spoke to Nicky. Amanda's arsenal is empty, her powers of persuasion useless. She says, 'Okay, Mum, then I have to get off the phone. You can try and call me back tomorrow at the same time if you have any more information.'

Lying there, I feel like the skipper on a mutinous ship, although I'm relieved beyond words that Lorinda has refused to deal and the boys haven't got what they wanted. It's another sleepless night as Amanda's words play over and over in my head. I waver between disgust and pity for what she has done. My insecurity gets the better of me as I try to second-guess where things will go from here. The chattering monkeys in my head are unrelenting; it's like I can't hold any thought for more than a few seconds.

One of the boys parks himself outside my door. He's taped the conversation and now sadistically replays it just for me. To again hear Amanda sounding coherent and composed, telling her mother to pay just for her is soul-destroying.

But I know she must be desperate as she has suffered far more than I have. My compassionate side is telling me to forgive her as she is only doing what human instinct tells us to – survive.

Nicky
Sydney
Monday, 12 October

Kel and I are in Sydney for an epic meeting fest with lawyers, DFAT and a PR company. But it's preceded by some news. Lorinda has spoken to Amanda and it's a shocking phone call.

All of this went down while we were asleep, so JC gives Kel and me a summary of the night's proceedings. Amanda has been given an out: if Lorinda can pay half a million dollars to the HTs, they'll release her. Fragments of the conversation clang inside my head.

Lorinda is saying over and over again, 'Amanda, this money has been raised by both our families.' How much does Lorinda wish she had been fundraising from the word go and that the money was in her account? Amanda says to Lorinda, 'I am talking to you frankly now; no one is forcing me to say this. Nigel and I have been separated nine months ago. Now our family – us, you and me – have a chance for me only to be released. You have to break any kind of commitment that you have with Nigel's family because I know that Nigel's family has more.'

It's got to be horrific for Amanda. She desperate, I understand that. I recognise the pleading in her voice, but all I can hear is the what-about-me attitude.

'Amanda,' says Lorinda, 'there is no separate amount from Canada and from Australia. It has been raised together for both of you by both families.' If I were Lorinda, there would be a part of me that wanted to take the money and run. I feel relieved all the ransom money is still in a bank account here in Australia. Logical brain tells me this is exactly the kind of ploy that kidnappers use to divide and conquer. Emotional brain is finding it all pretty tough going.

I can't get the conversation out of my head while I'm trying to talk to Adan. It turns out to be very uneventful in comparison. There are now apparently four factions with two particularly nasty characters who want a cut each on top of the ransom money. Adan thinks if he can split a fraction of the payment between these two gang members they might agree to a deal. He's not terribly clear on the detail, and it's all pretty confusing.

Kel and I set up for a call with Adan, Lorinda, Amanda and me to sort this money-from-two-different-sources situation out hopefully, finally.

Adan puts Amanda on pretty quickly and we are able to get through to her that the US$548K offer is from both the families for both of them. There is no other amount – certainly not 1.3 mill. Amanda says she thinks she can get this point across to the HTs then she's cut off. Adan goes on to say he thinks he can get the gang to agree to US$548K but we'll need an extra US$300K on top of that – US$150K each to the difficult gang members. It must be done quickly and he is the only one who can do this deal. We thank him for this but explain that we don't have any more money; we can't raise this extra money quickly, if at all.

What this means for us is that the new offer comes to US$848K, and if the gang has agreed to this, they will surely be putting pressure on Adan to get it sorted. Even though there are probably divisions within the gang, we are pretty sure some if not all of this extra money is going to line Adan's pockets. We consider the option of offering a little bit on top with the promise of sending more when we have raised it after they are out. Adan may come at this due to the time constraints that the gang are surely putting him under.

There's not even time to dwell on any of this as we have to meet the Clayton Utz people.

Kellie
Sydney
Monday, 12–Tuesday, 13 October

Nic and I head to the offices of Clayton Utz, the lawyers, again with *Australian Story* in tow. They don't really get in the way; it's just having to walk down the same street five times that gets a bit tedious. Today we are getting legal advice about the ransom payment. I find out the jail term for paying the ransom amount is twenty-five years to life, and that I will be breaking both commonwealth and international laws regarding terrorist activities.

I inhale and hold my breath. *Is it really worth it?* I am unconsciously shaking my head as I think this, over and over. I exhale quite loudly and exclaim, 'Bloody Nigel!'

More good advice has come from my gorgeous friend Helen – we're going to need help with the public relations and media side of things. First, none of us wants a media circus at the end of all of this like we had at the start. Second, we need to go public to raise more money, so having a PR group to manage this would be handy. Third, because Nigel is going to owe bucketloads of money, if he wants to make anything from his story, everything needs to be managed properly. Back in September I started contacting PR firms to arrange some meetings.

We meet with people from one company, Kreab Gavin Anderson, on the same day as the lawyers. They're located in an old wool store in Pyrmont. I grab hold of the door handle, a big brass ram's horn. In the foyer is an old wool press and a statue of sheep going down the shoot. I have a really good feeling before I've even met anyone – I like the agricultural feel here.

Brian Tyson, the managing director, introduces himself. I tell him Nigel's story and what I am hoping to achieve by having a PR group manage things. I also explain that we have to factor in the family in Canada: we would need pro bono work from the KGA Canadian office as well. It's a big ask but I put everything on the table; I have nothing to lose. What's the worst they can say? No?

Brian listens intently. He explains to me that they do a lot of work with the government and can't help us if we bash the government in public. I completely understand and reassure him that I can keep the family under control. I have my fingers crossed under the table. Brian tells me that if I can stop the family from talking to the press, stop them from publicly discussing their unhappiness with the government, then he can definitely take us on pro bono. This is such great news that I feel I don't need to see the other company I've approached, but the decision about who to go with is not mine alone. I need to put all the options available to the family on the table. I can tell them which one I like better, or feel we should go with, but the final decision needs to be majority rule.

I head over to North Sydney for my next meeting and I can tell instantly that this group is much bigger and more media orientated than KGA. The meeting is completely different. I plead my case and again the company says yes, they will help pro bono, but this time there is a lot more talk of magazine deals, news reports, getting the story into the media to raise its profile so Nige can make more money when he gets out. I don't feel as comfortable with this group as I did with KGA – this one feels very commercial, and very experienced, but I sense the family would not feel as good about being subjected to so much media coverage when some of them are still struggling with the idea of *Australian Story*.

I head home loaded up with all this information, while secretly wanting to task KGA straightaway. But I do the right thing and put all points together in an email and send it off for the rest of the family to discuss and decide. It's been an exhausting day, and I am happy to put my head on the pillow as I need to be up at six for our CMT meeting. I will give Jon and Lorinda the good news that both companies are able to provide pro bono support for them as well.

In our morning CMT I explain all this, only to be told that Lorinda already has someone taking care of them. I'm sure my gasp is audible; so are Nic's and Jon Lindhout's. There is something going on over there in Canada that I am totally unaware of. For the last week in our CMT meetings I have been talking about doing all of this for both sides, not just us, but now Lorinda tells me she already has someone handling the PR. What the hell is going on?

Nic and I Skype after our CMT and ask 'what the?'; she is as confused as I am. Jon Lindhout then Skypes and explains to us that he had no idea that Lorinda had asked someone else to do their PR; like us, he thought we were doing this together. He is very concerned that Lorinda is making decisions without consulting him. After Jon hangs up, Nic and I discuss this – it's what we suspected but were a little afraid to say. It feels like Canada is working only for Amanda, whereas our side are rock solid on working as a team.

What a clever family I have – they all decide that KGA is the way to go. I phone Brian immediately and tell him we would love them to look after us. I arrange another meeting with them to plan how the next few months might play out. We need to discuss the media, Nigel's return and his future. This looks like the start of a beautiful relationship with a fantastic group of people.

Even though Dick Smith has agreed to meet the shortfall, I totally agree with his suggestion that we continue to fundraise. I have shifted in my hesitation about asking people for money, I no longer have any issue with it. I need money to get Nigel out, and people can simply say no. I figure there is no harm in asking.

Wednesday 13–Thursday, 14 October

Now that the family has access to enough money, we face the problem of how to get it into Somalia. This is the million-dollar question. There are a number of options but we have to decide which is (a) the safest, and (b) the one least likely to land me in jail.

The CMT has already discussed the hawala banking system as our preferred method of transfer, but now we have to look at it in much more detail. JC has mentioned that this method is widely used throughout African countries and has been used successfully in the past to move ransom money.

I look up 'Dahabshiil' on the internet and discover there are some local branches around Sydney.

International money transfer of large amounts is a major bell ringer to all governments, including our own, especially since September 11. No bank will enter into discussions about the money transfers, as we need the government's permission to shift that amount of cash. We've been told *not* to ask the minister for permission because the act we are about to commit is illegal and carries a hefty jail sentence.

I become a signatory on Heather and Geoff's account as they will both be in Nairobi when the money needs to be moved, so I will be the only member of the CMT left to do it.

The next part is to Google Earth the Dahabshiil branches to find out which one has a back lane where we can park while we move the cash. This might sound crazy but there is no way I am carrying a rucksack of hundreds of thousands of dollars through the streets of any suburb, let alone one I know nothing about.

One branch looks promising. It is in a building that looks like a mall; it has staff parking out the back and you can enter the building from the front or the rear. I do a drive-by to check out the location and the back entrance, and it's clear this branch ticks all the boxes. I phone JC to let him know, and now all I need to do is persuade the manager to get on board.

I've done all of this work – days' worth of organising and planning – and the blokes in the London AKE office have organised a driver and security detail ('knuckle draggers' as we affectionately call them) to look after me while I do the transfer, but if the Dahabshiil manager says no, it'll be back to square one, and I'm not sure where that is any more.

JC gives me strict instructions that under no circumstances am I to tell the Dahabshiil manager what we're doing. My cover story is that we're purchasing some goods in Somalia and that my client has requested payment by Dahabshiil. The silver-tongued devil is going to have to give me a little direction on this; it's a story I know no one is going to believe. I mean, who buys goods in Somalia worth US$800 000 just because?

I phone the Manager to make an appointment. I tell him I need a large sum of money moved to Somalia and ask if he is able to help me. He tells me that he is, so we arrange to meet the next day at 11 a.m.

On Thursday I drive out west for the second time. Every single woman on the street is wearing a hijab; all the men are sitting outside the coffee shops smoking and playing some sort of game – I'm not sure if it's cards. When I step out of the car, I am the only Caucasian person in the main street. All eyes fall on me.

I am wearing long pants and a long-sleeved top, and it is hot. I leave the comfort of the car's air-conditioning and head into stifling heat; there's a strong smell in the air of cooking spices and body odour.

I walk into the Dahabshiil office; it's a tiny room with a huge map of Somalia on the wall, and there's a high counter with bars on it.

The room is long and narrow, and behind the counter are two gentlemen. One is the Manager.

We shake hands and he escorts me out of the building and onto the street. We walk a little way, making small talk until we reach a coffee shop. He leads me inside, all the way to the very back corner where no one can hear or see us. He nods to the girl on the front counter and she takes our coffee order.

The Manager sits opposite me. He is incredibly handsome with the most amazing skin. It is such a beautiful colour, smooth and blemish free. His eyes are like pieces of black coal, you can't tell where the pupil and the iris meet, they appear one. The whites of his eyes are a rich cream colour with a smattering of bloodshot. Those amazing eyes are boring into me. He sits upright with his arms folded; he isn't tall and slender as I imagined him to be, nor is he bulky. He is average, yet he cuts a very imposing figure sitting opposite me, waiting for my explanation as to why I want to move nearly US$800 000 through his agency. It turns out he thought I'd said 'one hundred thousand dollars' when I asked about moving 'hundreds of thousands of dollars'.

His English is broken but I can comprehend everything he says. He asks me to explain very clearly what I want so he can understand. I start with the spiel JC has given me, going on about buying something in Somalia and needing to use Dahabshiil. He asks me what I am purchasing that costs that much money.

I keep telling him we want something very special and that only he can help me. He starts shaking his head and tells me that I need to be honest with him otherwise our meeting will be cut short – he thinks I am wasting his time.

Oh crap, he isn't going to allow this to happen; I have to tell him the truth. I don't know this man but all my hopes are pinned on him helping our family get Nige back.

Tears start stinging my eyes. I don't want to cry but every time I tell someone our story for the first time, I feel the tears well up.

I come clean and tell him the truth: that Nigel Brennan, my brother-in-law, was kidnapped in Somalia and I am paying the ransom money to get him out.

He sits there in shock, and then his eyes start to water. He apologises for the actions of his countrymen, and tells me how Australia has been so good to him and his family. He asks me if Nige is the one taken with the Canadian girl.

I confirm this and tell him a little more than I probably should, especially how much I need his help to move the money. He has only just met me and I could land him in a lot of trouble.

The Manager finally nods and says he will help me.

I have to stop myself from jumping over the table to hug him. At last we're really making some progress – we have the money and now we have a way of getting the money to Somalia.

We sit there for quite a while, talking about what Nige and Amanda were doing in Somalia. He is really saddened that this is happening to us.

The rules of Dahabshiil are very clear: no money must be moved for illegal activities, and guess what? Kidnap and ransom payments are illegal. The Manager is bound by the rules of his bank unless he gets permission from the head of his organisation.

No more than AUS$10 000 can be moved at any one time out of the country without it being flagged. Once it is flagged, it must be explained what the money is for, and if we want to move money to a country like Somalia, it is stated by law that we must have the approval of the foreign affairs minister.

I convince the Manager that the government isn't going to stop him; his business isn't going to be investigated and he isn't going to be prosecuted. He has to trust me that this will all be okay, without any piece of legal documentation to confirm this.

We say our goodbyes and I tell him I will be in touch with further details once the deal is ready to go ahead, which will be in a few days.

Adrenaline is surging through my body; I feel light and floaty. I phone JC immediately with the news that the Dahabshiil is a goer. He is ecstatic – it means that we can let the hostage takers know that we can move the money.

Oh, we are getting so close, I can feel it, but I need to keep a level head as this has happened too many times before. You get excited then *smack*, disappointment. I just have to stay positive.

Nicky
Moore Park
Monday, 18 October

Alto and I talk to Adan, and it seems the heat is on. He has dropped the add-on amount by US$100K, making the current demand US$748K. Adan is definitely under pressure to settle. I tell him we are still selling things and I can report back on Wednesday. Meanwhile JC lets us know how Sam is panning out. He has found a charter plane and pilot. Who, as it turns out, is an old SAS guy and they kind of know each other. He's got heaps of back-up plans for random landing spots. I'm not feeling entirely comforted by that option as Australia's last kidnap victim was taken captive on an airfield back in '96.

There are a couple of Dahabshiil problems. JC has been talking to someone pretty high up at the UK Dahabshiil. They have been, as is the case with most hawala operators, under serious pressure since the Bush administration, and, as with almost everything Islamic, under constant scrutiny. They have to report all transactions, especially those over $10K. Their only duty is to report but authorities can take action if they so wish.

This is not such a big deal for us, as we are okay with the movement of the money being traceable. Dahabshiil can't verify who the money goes to; it's released to whoever the agreed recipient is. They don't know what that cash is going to be used for in the future. If something goes wrong, the Dahabshiil office gets frozen. Dahabshiil UK said if it were them doing the transaction they would like written authorisation saying that they will not be prosecuted for the transaction.

A precedent has been set: in the past the US has closed down a hawala transaction when money was moved in a piracy case. After the deal was done the government froze the company's assets and the company worldwide went down. I can understand them being so leery about wanting to assist us if that's a possible outcome.

If worst comes to worst, Sam the madman has said he will do the bagful-of-money run. This is almost prophetic.

Wednesday, 21 October

When I next call Adan, he sounds like he has been asleep or more probably chewing khat. He sounds a bit upset when I give him the new offer of US$460K. He says he won't accept it and that he told us we had a deal if we could pay an extra US$200K to the bad guys. Both Lorinda and I state to him we don't have that much; we can try to raise it but it will take more time.

The weird thing is, he doesn't sound mad with us, just upset. It's dawning on him he's not going to get the extra money for himself. Lorinda says to him, 'Well, Adan, what happens if the gang puts Amanda on the phone and wants to know the full amount? I'm not going to lie to her.' He gets really worked up and the line goes dead. *Did he just hang up on us?*

We leave it for a couple of days till we call him again but the conversation is pretty much the same. Just some vague threats that he has been approached by others in Nairobi and Zimbabwe and he may start discussions with them, or he may resign altogether. Then where would we be without him?

We hold off for another couple of days to see what pressure the gang will put on him.

The Australian government wants to have a chat to JC before they release Nigel's passport. The Canadian consular staff will do the same thing a couple of days later. Ever the smoothie, JC makes all the right noises. He thanks James and expresses how grateful he is on the families' behalf for the government's assistance, for facilitating aircraft, medical assistance, customs and immigration. Like I said, he's smooth.

The outcome is that Nige's documentation is being released.

James rings me shortly after and offers more assistance. After Nigel and Amanda are released from hospital they can be set up in a wing at the Tribe Hotel. If Lorinda and Jon have no accommodation provided for them, as long as they tick it off with the Australian government, they would accommodate them as well. There is no longer a set deadline for when Nige will be brought home; it will depend on his health.

It is pretty piss-poor form that Jon and Lorinda still haven't heard from DFAIT. So I make an official request of James, asking him to contact his Canadian counterpart to establish what consular support they would be providing to Amanda and her family. Humphrey would be proud of me.

Two days later Lorinda and Jon inform us that the Canadian government will match the Australian support. They specify they want their own Canadian psychologist and actually trump the Australians by snagging meals for the family.

Friday, 30 October

We have an agreed offer! US$680K. It's finally happened. We've come to expect the inevitable and encounter another hiccup. Sure enough, we don't have all the funds together. We ring Dick and ask him to cover us till we can pay him back, when Bob and Alison's and the rest of our fundraising money comes in. No questions; it's in the bank by midday the next day.

JC wants this done. His ninety days are up, he jokes. We are going to ring Adan every day till we have the transaction and exchange sorted and we get them out.

Nigel
The Bush House
Late October

Several days after Amanda's call I receive a message from her. She starts off by asking for my forgiveness and explaining that she was forced to say what she did. It's hard for me to swallow, but I realise she is only human and is living in constant fear. I can't continue to hold this against her. Forgiveness is far easier to grant than to grasp onto the hatred and bitterness that I felt from days earlier. She goes on to explain that Romeo has caused her a lot of pain. I'm not really sure what she means by this.

As always, I make myself read the message twice before erasing the evidence, taking great care in case someone walks. Then begins the whole process of sending my reply, which takes days to organise.

I spend the next few days putting my message together for Amanda, starting by telling her that I forgive her. I truly mean it. Ahmed is again with us. It's not just his cologne that gives him away these days but his unforgettable ring tone. I'm feeling marginally better after the last few days, and he makes me wait until early afternoon before gracing me with his presence. As it's the last day of the month I'm desperate for him to give me some good news; with Christmas just around the corner my thoughts are heavily slanted towards my family.

He gets directly down to business, singling Lorinda out as the problem as to why negotiations continue to stall. 'I think she is a Jew, she is trying to cheat us out of money,' he explains sternly.

I try to reason with him. 'Ahmed, she is Christian. I know because Amina tells me this, just like Amina is Christian before she becomes Muslim.'

He expresses his disapproval saying, 'No, she is Jew. She behaves like a Jew, she tries to keep her money, she offers one amount but now she tries to reduce, this is like Jew.' I can't help think that all religions are the same, blaming others for their own shortcomings.

I'm conscious of the fact that Adan could have cleared up this rigmarole months ago but has chosen to allow the group to believe otherwise. Instead of Adan taking the blame, it's squarely directed at Lorinda, and by proxy Amanda has borne the brunt of their frustration. It's useless even trying to argue the point. Ahmed is so pigheaded he leaves me no option but to shrug my shoulders and exclaim, 'I don't know; I've never met her.'

I know the only reason he is with us is to give Captain Yahya a break, allowing him to go back to see his family; it's become routine every four or five weeks. Ahmed continues to ramble on, airing his grievances that they are being treated like idiots, and I can't help but think that the truth hurts.

NOVEMBER 2009

Sometimes you just have to take a chance

Nigel
The Bush House
Early November

Ahmed is back in the mix, the only real benefit of his return being the dramatic improvement in the quality of the food. The bland repetitiveness of bread and meat is quickly replaced with what seems like a smorgasbord of smell, taste, colour and texture. I can't believe my eyes when a plate of salad is slid across the floor to me. It seems like months since I last saw a green vegetable – my body is craving vitamins and minerals, and the remnants of fever from days earlier still plagues me. I can't think about how much more my body can take if this drags on into another year. I'm sure that my liver and kidney function will start to shut down.

I ask Romeo for my Qur'an, desperate after a week to hear from Amanda. My stomach knots up as I make out what she is telling me: 'They are planning to sell us to Al-Shabaab.'

I don't want to believe it. If this happens, our chances of survival will dramatically reduce. I think of having my head cut off – I'd much prefer to take a bullet than to go out like that. The boys have taunted me enough over the months so that I know Al-Shabaab means business. Feeling sick, I make myself read on. 'This is not going to happen in weeks but possibly days.' She says Romeo has given her this on good authority.

For the next few hours I can't stop my mind racing; I'm feeding my own anxiety, and wishing that Amanda hadn't dropped this bombshell. I begin replying to her but I'm interrupted by Ahmed's appearance in the afternoon. He confirms that they are, in fact, toying with the idea of on-selling us and that Al-Shabaab is the only buyer. Ahmed says they are sick of being treated like fools.

'Your families have offered $560 000. Al-Shabaab have said they will give us half a million for you now; they will then keep you until they receive two million dollars,' he explains. He is getting great satisfaction from relaying this to me, watching me squirm as he draws it out.

'When they get the two million dollars, they will give us another half a million. What do you think about this?' *What do I think?* I want to scream at him that he is fucking insane and nothing but a liar and a thief, but all I can manage is, 'Please don't sell us to another group; they will kill us.'

He laughs straight in my face as though I've just told him a great joke, shaking his head again.

'They will not kill you, you are Muslim, no one can kill you, understand? Now is already one year; we can no longer afford to keep you, but Al-Shabaab they will be able to keep you for years until they get what they want, they have a network that they can pass you around, is easy for them.'

I'm too angry to even look at this punk. The only positive spin I can put on it is that they seem to have dropped the asking price by a million.

'Ahmed, please, you are my brother. I can't stay here for years; I will die,' I say, snivelling like a child. 'You have to help us, please.'

'No, I want this finished. Everyone wants this finished. I cannot do anything if the commanders decide this,' he replies.

It's a sleepless night.

Shortly after breakfast, Ahmed reappears, telling me there might be a solution that the commanders will accept if we agree to five conditions. I'm hooked already – any solution is better than being sold to an extremist group – but I won't agree to anything unless Amada is with me.

'The commanders want one million dollars for your release —'

I jump in. 'One million *each*?'

'No, one million together. Currently your families have offered US$560 000. If we accept this, you have to agree to pay the remaining amount to make up the one million dollars after you have been released.'

It has to be a trick. They can't seriously think I will hand over money once I'm out of this shithole, can they? But I run with it.

'There are four others that you have to promise to keep also,' Ahmed says. The second is that we are never to speak about the treatment or conditions we have been held in. Third, we must promise to never leave the religion of Islam. Fourth, we have to promise to learn the Qur'an, to speak Arabic and invite people to the religion of Islam. *No problem.* I assure him that my mother will become Muslim as soon as she reads the Qur'an. The last condition is that we must promise to pray five times a day, each time saying a prayer from Ahmed to Allah.

I can't help thinking how self-indulgent this arsehole is – the only thing I'll be praying for is that he gets hit by a truck. He has his stupid smile spread across his face, like that of a vanquisher after defeating its enemy. I can see that he is pleased with himself. '*Inshallah*, if you can promise all this, then I might be able to convince the commanders to let you go.'

It's a massive relief when I'm finally alone, exhaling as though I've been holding my breath the whole time. Ahmed has almost certainly walked next door to offer Amanda the same deal.

Later that afternoon Ahmed comes to cut my hair, accompanied by Jamal, Young Yahya and Donkey. They all seem to be in high spirits as they take turns with the scissors. The boys explain to Ahmed my nickname for Captain Yahya, that being Captain Muufo. The simple rationale behind this name is that *muufo* – bread – is all he seems to eat, so unfortunately that's all we get too. They laugh.

Ahmed explains that because he is from the bush that is his staple diet. I reply, '*Muufo*, *muufo*, every day *muufo*, I'm starting to look like *muufo*.' The boys piss themselves, as does Ahmed. It seems both weird and wonderful to be laughing with them, and I realise just how deprived of laughter I have been for well over a year.

Before Ahmed leaves the room, he asks if I'd design a house for him, telling me about the block of land he owns in Mogadishu and giving me its dimensions. I'm happy to keep myself occupied even though I know that construction will be funded by my family.

I spend the next day on a number of designs for Ahmed. In the afternoon he pays me a visit, looking cheerful.

'How is your situation?' he asks. I have grown to detest this remark. 'I have very good news. Adan has spoken to your family and has agreed to accept the money they have offered. I think in one or two days you will go to your country.'

I try desperately to hold back tears – I know how pissed off Ahmed gets when I cry – but I can't stop myself.

'How will this happen?' I ask. I want details.

'It will be a handover. We get the money then we release you.'

This scenario doesn't sit well with me – they could get the money then kill us, just as Ahmed said they would in back in the first week. If it's true, why haven't I spoken to Nicky? Things don't seem to add up.

'Soon you go to your country. *Inshallah*, it is finished,' Ahmed says. His attention now turns to the house that I have drawn.

'Is very good, quickly you must finish before you go, also one last thing you must write these promises down on a piece of paper and sign it as proof, then give it to me.' He walks out the door.

I want the promise of release to be true, more than I've ever wanted anything in my life.

Abdullah and a few of the boys come to me throughout the day. They're in high spirits as they explain that it will soon be finished.

I am starting to believe that I will get my freedom back.

Nicky
Moore Park
Sunday, 1 November

Finally we have a deal. Adan has wrangled a massive amount for himself, completely screwing over the kidnappers but none of us cares. All we care about is getting the deal.

We can barely keep up with the phone calls.

Adan says, 'The gang, they are agreeing to US$548 000.' However, Adan wants US$135 000 for himself. It's actually *more* than we have and I feel financially overexposed. JC assures us that this manipulation and squeezing out just a little bit more is how kidnapping and ransom always happens. Regardless of his assurances, I still feel anxious. But it's so close now, so very close. The thought that makes me sweat and my skin prickle with nerves is, what happens if the kidnappers get wind of the fact that Adan is asking such a large amount for himself?

The way I see it, we are relying on Adan's greed to get Nige and Amanda out, and if the gang finds out we have done this deal surely Nigel's life will be forfeited. This extra cash is making Adan wary. He doesn't want us to say anything to the rest of the gang. He has to trust us to a degree and we have absolutely no trust in him. It's an awkward existence – nerve-racking and more than a little bit mad. I make it quite clear that no money will change hands till we get a proof of life from Nige and Amanda.

It's a crazy rush here in Australia to get our flights booked. We send passports down to Canberra to get visas for Nairobi. Mum and Dad go into the bank to organise Kel to be a signatory so the money can be transferred to Dahabshiil while they're away. Their biggest but unspoken concern is, I believe, if the bank moves the money to Dahabshiil and the government confiscates it for any reason before it leaves the country, where does that leave the bank?

It crosses my mind more than once that the Canadians are really not taking a stand. Why are we the ones who keep stepping up to the plate? It would have been so easy for us to throw our hands in the air and cry, 'It's against the law! I could go to jail!' But that would get us nowhere. I guess it's just lucky for Amanda that we are so determined to get Nige back at any cost and she is part of that package.

Kellie
Sydney
Monday, 2 November

There is nothing I hate more than money. It is a parasite, attaching itself to people, and once we have it we cannot live without it. The host wants more and more of this parasite, sometimes going to extreme lengths to get it. Now I'm a money launderer, the money parasite has well and truly taken hold and it's showing as desperation, obsession and gratitude. I am desperate for more, as I know the ransom is not the only cost involved in Nigel and Amanda's release. I am obsessed with how much I have in my control and how I have to get it to the other side of the world. And I am constantly grateful to Dick Smith, Bob Brown, Aunty Alison, and all of the friends, family and strangers who have donated money to our cause.

It is my job to move the money from Australia to Somalia via any means JC and I can find. I am the one who has a tally on all the comings and goings of every cent. I know who has given what and how much needs to be paid back, and exactly how much money – right down to the last cent – is ransom, the Dahabshiil commission, and Adan's cream on the top. Never have I been so in tune with currency, its origin, its destination and its value on any particular day.

All the money is here in Australia, in Heather and Geoff's bank account, so really the only option is to move it from Australia in whatever way I can.

Once Adan agrees to a price, there's a chain reaction, and everyone's energy levels lift. However, as great excitement starts to stir within the CMT, I am feeling waves of panic because my role is about to come to the fore.

Today the money is to be moved from Dahabshiil Australia to Mogadishu. As I'm driving to Sydney, Nic, Heather and Geoff are getting ready to board their flight to Nairobi. We've been waiting months for this. Nic and I knew this time would eventually come, but we still don't know exactly *how* it'll play out. JC is giving us instructions on a daily basis; it's crazy to try to plan ahead. The plans change all the time, depending on the mood of the kidnappers.

All week JC and I have been trying to organise insurance for the ransom money through an underwriter who used to work with AKE. No company will touch us, though, because we're not insured with a K&R group. So on Monday, 2 November 2009, I will be moving around AUS$800 000, the majority of which is someone else's money, to a third-world country to pay kidnappers. Without insurance. Whenever Dick Smith asks me if the money is insured, I reply, 'Yes, Dick', with my fingers crossed behind my back. Sometimes you just have to take a chance.

I go to the Dahabshiil office and I am even more self-conscious than last time. Today the street is busy: there are prams, young children, women dressed in western clothing. I don't stand out like before. It's 9.05 a.m. and the little community is abuzz.

I make my way to the Manager's small shop and am greeted by four men, all Somali. *Why are all these men here?* I sit in the patched-up vinyl chair and look up at the Manager.

'This is a good day, yes?' he asks.

'Yes, today is a very good day,' I reply, nodding.

Then from the back corner of the room one of the Somali men

steps forward and takes my hand and apologises for the actions of his compatriots. Then the next one does the same, then the next.

The Manager sits next to me and explains that in the beginning, he was not going to help me.

'I help you because your country has been very kind to my family, and now my countrymen have not been kind to your family. I am very sorry that my countrymen have done this. I love Australia and I am very happy and lucky to be here, and I am very sad for you.'

'Thank you, thank you so much. With your help my family can get our brother and son back.'

The Manager puts a sheaf of paperwork in front of me. I need to provide exact details of how much money will be transferred along with who will pick it up on the other side. The 'other side' details haven't been set in concrete yet – everything will lock into place this evening – so I put down John Chase's name and passport number and a security password JC has set.

I sign my name on the document that could land me in jail. However, this is also the biggest piece of the pie, the money, the bit that will seal the deal and get Nige and Amanda out.

I can't believe this is happening. The first part is done. *Un-fucking-real*. Now I need to go to the Bank of Queensland to transfer the money from Heather and Geoff's account to the Manager's Dahabshiil.

The big problem we have is the ransom money amount is in US dollars not Australian. To move this money into Somalia it has to be in US currency and nowhere in Australia can you exchange AUS$800 000 into US dollars. So we have no choice but to move it in Australian dollars and convert it through Dahabshiil, which costs more. And once it's converted, you can't get it back.

The bank manager knows I am coming, and he knows why. He has a broad and gentle-looking face. He speaks to the girls behind the counter and they both move into action. I'm not sure what he says but it is probably a polite version of 'this is the woman moving shitloads of someone else's money to a group of kidnappers without insurance. What a wacko!' Or maybe that's my conscience talking.

I sign the documentation: the transfer will take approximately one hour. As soon as the Dahabshiil Manager receives the money and converts it to American dollars he will notify me, and once that is all done I will tell JC. Then he can arrange a drop-off point for Nige and Amanda and a pick-up location for the money. If all goes to plan, Nigel will be out by Thursday.

As I sign the paperwork I start crying. These are tears of happiness. I'm happy that this nightmare is nearly over, happy that this pile of money the family has been working so hard for is finally going towards getting Nige back. The manager offers me tissues and comforts me. 'It's okay,' I keep saying, 'this is good, it's all good.'

He escorts me out of the bank and up the ramp and onto the street. I am now in broad daylight, crying like a child. I am on the street and walking away from the manager, saying goodbye and thank you at the same time, heading towards the city. Then I stop. I have forgotten something. Oh, the getaway car is in the car park.

Last night I booked a stay in the city as JC told me I can't leave Sydney until the money hits Mogadishu. If it's stopped at any stage, I will have to ask Dick for a really, really big favour – to fly me and my backpacks full of his cash into Nairobi to give it to JC.

My secret lair is the Hilton. *Not bad*, I think to myself, *I suppose if I have to spend a few stressful days in Sydney waiting for this to happen, then it may as well be somewhere nice.*

I walk into the elevator and for the first time in ages I look at myself in the mirror. What I see is not the Kellie of sixteen months ago. The one I see now has sadness in her eyes, furrows between her brow and dull skin. Her face is fatter from bad eating habits acquired over the last five months. She just doesn't look like me.

I push the heavy hotel door open, drop my handbag and collapse on the bed from exhaustion. I must have nodded off immediately, as the luggage boy is suddenly standing in my room placing my bag on the luggage rack. He apologises for disturbing me and quickly leaves. I drift off again, while waiting for the phone to ring.

The Manager calls me to let me know he has the money and it has been converted to American dollars. It is ready to go.

'I will call the Mogadishu branch this evening when they open and confirm they will accept the money.'

'What did you say?' Suddenly I'm wide awake.

'Mogadishu, I will call them when they open to confirm they accept.'

'I thought you had already confirmed with the Mogadishu manager that the money could go there.'

'Yes, I said I would help you get money to Mogadishu.'

Oh, crap. Another communication problem. *JC is going to kill me for not having this sorted.*

'Okay. You let me know.'

I look in the mirror and I see that I also have grey hair. As soon as I get that little shit of a brother-in-law back into the country he is paying for a lifetime's supply of botox and hair appointments.

I phone JC and drop the Manager's bombshell on him. He is remarkably calm. 'That's fine,' he says, 'as long as we get it here.

We're not quite sure where we want it yet anyway.'

I breathe a sigh of relief. I'm pleased I don't have his job. I am so tired I can hardly keep my eyes open, so I don't.

Some time later I am woken by my mobile ringing. It's the Manager.

'Ah, hello, Kellie. Yes, they will take the money at Mogadishu branch.'

I punch the air and dance around the room. I haven't felt much euphoria over the last few months so I happily let this feeling wash over me. This is all going to be okay.

Now all I need to do is record our CMT call tonight since I'm the only team member left to do it. Nic, Jon, Lorinda and Kelly are all in transit to Nairobi and JC will be heading off as soon as our CMT call tonight is finished. Once tonight's phone call is done, the location for drop off and pick up will all be confirmed.

I am suddenly starving. I can't remember the last time I ate. I know I have drunk a lot of coffee, but I feel that if I don't eat something soon, I might just pass out. Not eating for long periods has become the norm during the last four months. I get too busy and caught up with work, kids or Nigel stuff that I forget to eat and then I usually crave sugar and I eat something incredibly unhealthy, hence my horrendous weight gain. I have also discovered I am a comfort eater. When things go bad I eat. I don't gorge myself, I just eat really bad food like chocolate or chips or something I can get my hands on quickly. This has done terrible things to my metabolism. I order room service.

Around 11 p.m. I get Skype ready to make the call that will seal the deal.

I call in Alto first and then we connect to JC. My Skype account is full of credit and I am ready to dial in Adan when given the go ahead.

JC runs Alto through the way he wants tonight's conversation to go. Alto needs to confirm with Adan his full name for the money pick up and the exact location the exchange will take place on Wednesday.

After JC gives Alto the instructions, he leaves us to it. Adan and Alto chat in Somali for thirteen minutes, then Adan hangs up.

'How was it?' I ask.

'Not good; he is very suspicious. Let's get John back on the phone.'

Adan has called off the deal. Alto says he thinks we are trying to trick him into being caught at exchange.

I am about to fall apart. I have the family on the way to Nairobi to pick up Nigel, and the deal has just fallen over. I can't get the family back, all the Canadians are in transit so I can't stop them either. And the money, oh god, the money! The money has been changed and is in cyberspace somewhere. And did I mention that it's not insured, and that I lied to Dick Smith and said it was?

John and Alto have a big discussion about what to do next as JC is due to leave London on the next plane and fly to Nairobi. We need to sort this *now*. I am pacing the hotel room, waiting to get the next lot of instructions. JC calls to tell me we have another call with Adan in an hour. He will be in a cab so it'll be just Alto and me. Okay, I reply, thinking one hour to go and we do it all again. I need to relax so I head to the bathroom.

I let the water in the shower beat down on my head. My body is aching. I've been so tense every muscle in my body is clenched and now the hot water is starting to make some of them relax. I keep looking at my watch, needing to be mindful of the time. I have a ten-minute shower, such a luxury as I live in a house with tank water.

Once I'm out of the shower, I spot the flash of my mobile. Four missed calls from JC.

I call him back: he's in a cab on the way to the airport.

'We changed our plan. We called Adan early. It has all fallen through. We've arranged for Nic to call him when she arrives.' JC sounds different, frustrated. I think he needs some thinking time about what to do next. As for me, it's 3 a.m. and I need to sleep.

Tuesday, 3 November

My mobile goes at 6.45 a.m. It's the Manager.

'Yes, Kellie, I have spoken to Dahabshiil manager and they will not take the money.'

I sit bolt upright in bed.

'Sorry, what did you say?'

'I spoke to Dahabshiil manager and he will not let the Mogadishu branch accept the money. He does not want to put his business in danger and does not trust that a good person will pick up the money. I have been trying all night to get hold of the big boss, but I cannot contact him. I will keep trying tonight and call you again. I am sorry, Kellie.'

I start to cry. The Manager does his level best to console me.

I breathe and tell myself it will all be okay as soon as we get the head Dahabshiil guy on the phone. I have everything crossed.

Now I discover that not only am I an emotional eater but I am also an emotional shopper, and shopping on the afternoon of Melbourne Cup Day is too easy. There is no one around. I buy clothes, shoes, Christmas presents, trying to make myself feel better, but it makes me feel worse because I've spent all my money doing it.

By night time, the Hilton is full of partygoers, celebrating – some winners and some losers. I get back to my room and it's all over the news: Shocking has won the Melbourne Cup. I order room service for dinner and wait to hear from the Manager.

I stay awake long enough to hook up Alto and Adan. They talk in Somali for seven minutes, then Alto tells me. 'Adan is very suspicious, but I told him the family will be arriving in Nairobi today and we are serious and we have to get this deal sorted. I also told him there is money waiting for him in Mogadishu and we really need to get a plan together so he can get his money.'

Alto says he will let JC know what was said, and we sign off.

My mobile starts to vibrate across the table. It's the Manager.

This is the call I have been waiting for, this is it. After this call I will know if Dahabshiil has said yes or no to the money drop.

'Ah, hello Kellie.' His voice sounds tired and a little stressed. Even though I don't know this man very well I have started to pick up meaning in his voice, and right now I am not hopeful.

'They will not accept the money.'

'Why?'

'Because it is too much money and head of Dahabshiil does not have permission from your government that he will not be prosecuted. The money is going to bad people and Dahabshiil does not want that for their bank or their country.'

What do we do now?

'Can you get permission from your government, Kellie?'

Now I'm angry that the Manager said he could do this but didn't look into it properly. But I need to keep a clear head.

'Leave it with me. All the DFAT staff are in Nairobi. I will try and get hold of James and I will get back to you.'

I hang up the phone and cry, and cry and cry and cry. All this emotion just spills out – I have totally fucked up my end. The only piece of the puzzle I'm responsible for and it doesn't fit. When JC and Nic sort the issue with Adan, he will be expecting the money. Without the money, there is no exchange.

I call Nic and leave a hysterical message.

Then I call Matt and sob down the phone, explaining to him what is happening. Tomorrow is Wednesday and the rest of the family is expecting to get Nigel out. Now I have to explain to them that this isn't going to happen. I'm not looking forward to calling Ham. I am a little too fragile and I think that would push me over the edge so I ask Matt to let Ham and Amy know there has been a delay. He needs to pretend it's nothing huge.

Before I go to bed, I phone James and get his voice mail. I leave a message asking him to call me. I need to get James to okay this transfer.

Nicky
Nairobi
Tuesday, 3 November

The upside to a middle-of-the-night flight is there are lots of empty seats to sleep in. The flight is uneventful, and then we hit Nairobi. I've got a voice mail from Kel.

'It's fallen over. I've fucked it all up. I'm so, so, sorry.'

I'm alarmed that Kel is being so hard on herself. She's probably awake but I don't want to ring her – it's the middle of the night in Oz. If it's all gone to shit, she is going to need all the recuperative value she can get from sleeping. That's what I'm telling myself, but I'm not very convincing. When I ring her back, I'm faking calm.

My big concern is hiding from Mum and Dad what looks like a major stuff-up. I especially don't want to send Dad into a tailspin.

Visa arrangements in Nairobi are a nightmare. We were warned to have our palm-greasing US dollars at the ready. We encounter for the first of many times in Nairobi a lack of speed and efficiency. Finally we are processed.

'Why are you visiting Africa?'

To get my dumb-arse brother out of Somalia springs to mind but I hold back and say in a more circumspect manner, 'To collect and repatriate a family member.' All that DFAT poli-speak has rubbed off on me. Passport stamped, we're through at last. We eventually find our bags in the care of two airport officials, who lead us out. We can see James outside and make our way over. We step out into the humid, pleasantly Brisbane-like, Nairobi night.

We check in at the Tribe and go to the bar, where I meet Jack and Sam, the mad men who will be doing the run into Mogadishu to retrieve Nigel and Amanda. Sam looks as harmless as a teddy bear. Jack looks like, and brilliantly imitates, one of the huge marabou storks that invade the acacias in Nairobi, leaving the ground in a whitewash of guano.

Kellie
Sydney
Wednesday, 4 November

My mobile goes. It's 10 a.m! Shit, I've slept in – then I remember last night's events and can't think of one reason why I would want to get out of bed today.

It's Mum and she's on her way to Sydney with Di, a very special family friend whose husband, Chud, is dying of brain cancer. Chud and Di have been a very big part of my life and it tears me apart to have someone so close to our family slipping away, and there is nothing anyone can do. I'm cross with myself for wallowing in self-pity when there are people like Di and her beautiful family who will inevitably lose their loved one. I need to do everything in my power to get one of ours back.

Mum and Di are shopping in the city. I have a lot to do today but nothing really until Nairobi and Somalia open for business so I agree to meet them for lunch – the distraction will be good, then I can come back to the hotel and get ready for my calls with JC, Nic, the Manager and James.

Mum cannot get over how terrible I look. She thinks I shouldn't be doing this alone and wants to stay with me. I love my mum to death, I really do, but I'm not sure I want her to see me at my wit's end, struggling to make a shitty situation right. I would hate to see my children go through this and not be able to help them.

I give in and agree to her staying, and she puts Di on the train home.

Around dinnertime, Mum and I are driving out of the Hilton car park to meet an old friend of mine, Elissa, for dinner when the phone starts ringing. It is the head of DFAT operations in Canberra, Greg Moriarty, saying he's received an email from James.

I pull over into a side street and pull my notebook out of my bag. I need to get Greg to give permission to get this money through. We exchange brief pleasantries.

'Greg, look we have a bit of a problem. The head of the Dahab-shiil bank wants reassurance from the Australian government that this transfer is all okay.'

Then something happens that I will never forget. Greg Moriarty laughs at me.

He says, 'Kellie, the government is unable to facilitate a payment of over $250 000 and the family decided to go on their own. We cannot help you.'

'Hang on, I'm not asking you to move it, I'm asking you to make a phone call and tell them you know it's happening.'

'I will say again, the family has decided to go on its own with AKE. The government is no longer tasked by the family, and the government is not able to facilitate a payment of over $250 000.'

'So, you are telling me that you can't do anything.'

Again, he laughs.

'Kellie, this is your problem and we are not able to help. We won't stop the money going through but we can't help you get it there.'

I am now furious.

'I am so pleased you find this funny, this is not fucking funny. Do you know what you are doing? You are killing them, KILLING THEM! It's a simple fucking phone call. The government has done *fuck-all* and now you're laughing that we can't get the money through. What do you suggest I do now? The kidnappers are waiting for this money. Goodbye, Greg, and thanks for nothing.'

I sit in the front seat of the car with my head in my hands. I understand everything he has said, and I know that if he phones Dahabshiil, then the government is facilitating our payment. But all I need is him to make one little phone call and everything will be okay.

Mum is sitting next to me in shock that I have just spoken to a government official in that way. I don't think she has ever heard me speak to anyone like that. Actually, I don't think I ever have.

We are late for dinner. I sit down at the table and order something to eat. I'm not hungry: all I want to do is go back to the hotel and sort this out. My phone goes again and this time it's JC. He must have listened to my fifteen messages about the crumbling situation. I excuse myself and walk outside.

'JC, I am so sorry I messed this up so badly. You are all there and my one job as fallen into a pile of shit and I'm having trouble fixing it.'

'Kel, Kel, calm down. You haven't stuffed up anything. These things happen; it's all just part of the process. Now explain what has happened.'

I rattle off my catalogue of problems. JC is clear headed and calm.

'Okay, can you call your guy and convince him that we are sorting out the Mog end. Give him Adan's details as the pick up and we will go from there. Don't worry, Kel, everything will be fine.'

I am on the footpath outside the restaurant, pacing and crying. People nearby are staring at me like I am a crazy person, and right now I think I am. All this talk of moving money – the people on the street probably think my divorce settlement has gone bad.

I call the Manager. 'Okay, John Chase is organising the Mogadishu pick up now, so I am going to give you the name of the man who will pick it up in Mogadishu. The government is not going to stop the payment, and JC is in Nairobi for the head of Dahabshiil to talk to if there is any problem. Is all that clear?'

'Yes, Kellie, I will phone the Mogadishu branch and call you back.'

My meal has arrived when I walk back into the restaurant, and Mum has poured me a glass of wine, but I ask the waiter for some water. Now is not the time for alcohol, but god, I wish I could drink the bottle.

I manage to eat a little of my dinner and make small talk while all the action is taking place on the other side of the world.

The first call to come back is from the Manager, so again I excuse myself from the table.

'Kellie, Mogadishu will not accept this money. They say they know the man who's going to pick it up and he is very bad,' the Manager tells me.

'What do I have to do?'

'You need John Chase to pick up the money. They will give it to him.'

I call JC and fill him in. Back inside the restaurant I manage to eat the rest of my meal, which is now cold, without any phone calls. But I am quite anxious to get back to the hotel in case there are more dramas.

As we are leaving the restaurant, JC calls me with news he has spoken with the Manager and a new pick-up destination and person will be arranged in the next few days.

'Kellie, I have told the Manager to hold onto the money and take direction from you, as you and I are in contact and I can't call him every time. He was happy with that. Now we need to concentrate on this end to get that sorted and get Adan back on track, so everything is fine. Okay?'

'Oh, great, okay. So do you think I can go home tomorrow, or do I need to stay in case it falls though?'

'No, I think you're safe to go home.'

I apologise to Elissa for being bad company and Mum and I head back to the hotel. I need to get ready for our CMT call tonight and then I can sleep. Mum looks really tired so I let her have a shower first and hop into bed, and I sit up and answer some emails and call Matt and tell him what is going on.

Our CMT discusses the plan from here on in. The CMT is now working on two fronts: we need to clear the money transfer and we also need to get Adan back on board. JC, Nic and Lorinda will work on Adan, and JC and I will work on Dahabshiil. Hopefully by the end of the week at least one of the issues will be resolved.

Nicky
Nairobi
Friday, 6 November

Mum, Dad and I get the run-down from Tony at the Australian consulate on how unsafe Nairobi is. He goes through a massive list of what we can't do and where we can't go. I'm thinking, *Nige didn't get into trouble till he got to Somalia, and he certainly wasn't staying in a secure (read: flash) hotel like this one.*

The government representation is ridiculous – there is a cast of thousands. We count at least ten Australian consulate, AFP and defence personnel, and they're just the ones we can see.

We meet the Australian defence psych, who'll look after Nige once he's out. He's fantastic and a straight-up kind of guy – a perfect fit for Nige. He and the Canadian psych are acting in conjunction and, unlike other Australian–Canadian working relationships, they're actually at ease with each other.

The Canadian family arrived twelve hours before us. The CMT settles in JC's room and tries to nut out what's gone wrong and how to fix it. Adan now knows Lorinda and I are in Nairobi.

Abdul, the Mogadishu Dahabshiil branch manager, is telling our Manager that Adan is not a 'respectful business man' and refuses to deal with him. Adan claims that if Abdul calls him, he 'will know him and understand who he is'. This lot honestly couldn't organise a piss-up in a brewery, even though that's a bad analogy to use in a Muslim country. Lorinda tells Adan that he's meant to be running this show; if he wants his money, he has to get it organised.

JC's room is pretty standard, and we are all piled up on his bed while he sits next to Lorinda, Skyping Adan on the laptop. It's a very odd sensation to have everyone around when we are making a call to Adan. It's been such a solitary experience for me up till now, getting up in the dark to have a chat to JC. This is much better. There is a big mirror behind the laptop so we can all make eye contact with each other. When Adan is talking, different people pick up different nuances. The sound of pencils on paper and the crinkling of notes as we pass them to JC reminds me of trying to dodge the teacher's attention at school.

When Kel calls JC to report in, she says the Manager is feeling pretty damn uncomfortable with Abdul. Is he trying to protect us? Does he think we are going to get rolled? JC has got hold of someone pretty high up in Dahabshiil and has an assurance that the money can stay in the system till we organise someone respectable to pick it up. This is quite a big deal as the transactions usually have to be completed within twenty-four to forty-eight hours.

The dithering goes on for a day or so – it's Chinese whispers on coke. Adan is constantly texting and ringing to see which Dahabshiil office the money is being sent to. The pickle he has got himself into is that there are two transfers: the money for the kidnappers and the cosy little deal he has made for himself. Mogadishu is a sieve. If there are two transactions, everyone will know about it. On top of this, the information we are getting is that Abdul is dodgy as well, so we don't know if he has a connection with the kidnappers. Perhaps Adan has to do an extra deal with him so he doesn't get double-crossed? Lorinda and I are steadfast on getting a POL from Nige and Amanda:

the money can be in the Dahabshiil office for Adan, but it cannot be picked up until we have Nige and Amanda safe and sound. No matter how many times Adan tries to get around this we will not budge.

Lorinda and I are constantly on edge, waiting for the next call or text to come in. The respective embassy staff are pretty much relegated to spectators at this stage, their main job being to entertain Mum, Dad and Jon and Amanda's friend Kelly.

Kellie
Newcastle
Thursday, 5–Saturday, 7 November

Mum and I drive home from Sydney in silence; I have way too much on my mind to talk. This is the end and I should be elated but 'the end' could take another month. I now need to slide back into being a wife, mother and a businesswoman and not let anything from the past four days have too much of an impact on 'normal' life.

The next few days are frustrating. Everything is working on African time, which means not much gets done in a hurry. JC calls me with a list of instructions and I carry them out. Meanwhile, I am busy with the boys from KGA, preparing the statement we will release to the press when Nigel is finally out. I undergo a few hours of media training so that I am not too bamboozled by the press. The boys tell me I am doing a great job, but anything could happen on the day.

JC calls me to explain we have a few issues on the African side and that I have to go back to the Sydney Dahabshiil. *WTF?!*

'We need to move the money into someone else's name so that we can pick it up. Jack has volunteered to go and get the money. You need to put the money in his name. Also, we need you to change the Dahabshiil branch in Mogadishu and transfer more money.'

Here we go again.

I call the Manager and update him on the goings-on in Nairobi – how we need to change the recipient, the branch and send more money. JC sends me all of Jack's details and I fax them, and a blown-up image of Jack's passport, to the Manager, along with a transfer confirmation from the BOQ for the extra amount. The Manager faxes back the paperwork; I sign it and send it back. So civilised, anyone would think this was a regular occurrence. The new branch is just on the border of the 'safe zone'. Jack will go there, accept the money and collect the receipt. Nige and Amanda will then be brought to the airport and the receipt will be handed over in exchange for them. Simple.

Now we just have to wait. Matt paces the house, mows the lawn, swims in the pool; we watch trashy pay TV to numb our minds, and keep us from looking at the ever-ticking clock.

I am thankful that Matt gave up drinking many years ago as I wouldn't need much encouragement at the moment. A drunken stupor would suit me down to the ground, but I need to be there for him, the kids and Nicky, if she phones. I'll also have to face the almighty roar of the media when the news finally breaks.

Nicky
Nairobi
Saturday, 7 November

Last night we finally got confirmation from Adan that we can speak to Nigel and Amanda.

We get a long list of things we can say; he's shitting himself that we will spill to the rest of the group that he's got extra money for himself. So he should, the greasy little slime.

We call and get through. Our last POL. I get to tell Nige that we are here and that hopefully we will have someone to collect them in the next day or so.

I get pretty upset talking to him. JC's patting me on the shoulder in an 'it's fine, you've done good' kind of way but I realise too late that I've given Nige too much information. Stupidly, I've raised his hopes when the gang could bring them crashing down again.

Oh, so close, so close. Adan can't get the money from Dahabshiil so we have to start looking at alternative drop-off points. Adan wants us to take the money to him at Bakaara market. He's completely insane.

We have a plane chartered so maybe we can fly the cash in and do a swap out of town, but it turns out there are too many warring factions and he and the rest of the kidnappers would not be able to pass through those areas as they do not have alliances with them. It's becoming increasingly clear that this place really is a shithole.

Adan starts threatening Nigel and Amanda's lives, saying it's our fault and that we should have organised it better. *You're right, sorry, Adan, I should be up to speed on the working methods of incompetent but dangerous Somali kidnappers.* Because we can't get the money to him in a way that is satisfactory to both of us, Adan gets sulky and things go quiet.

Nigel
The Bush House
Saturday, 7 November

I'm aware that something's going on in Amanda's room. I hear her say 'Mum' and realise she is on the phone. There's jubilation in her voice but I can't make out what she's saying. A minute later Ahmed marches through the door and hands the phone to me, telling me it's my sister. Just to hear Nic's voice is pure joy, then she tells me, 'We're in Nairobi, and if everything goes to plan then we should have you out by tomorrow, okay?' I can't believe what I'm hearing but before I get a chance to reply, Ahmed snatches the phone from my grasp then leaves the room. I'm confused. Why won't he let me talk with Nicky? My body feels electrified yet it's hard to fathom that it could be all over tomorrow.

As the sun begins to set, Jamal enters the room and says, 'Quickly, take everything, we go in five minutes.' There's a flurry of activity as the boys prepare for our departure. Stuffing my worldly belongings into two bags, I have to pinch myself to make sure it's not a dream. I'm anxious as the minutes tick by. Assam comes in and drags my mattress out of the room. I walk over to the window to watch the last of the evening light in the apocalyptic landscape, and I feel the breeze against my skin – exquisite. Watching the horizon slowly fade to black, I can almost taste freedom – it's so close, but butterflies swirl in my stomach because I know any number of things can go wrong once we're on the road.

I pace the room and it feels like an hour has passed even though it's only minutes since Jamal came in. Then Assam appears, throwing my mattress back on the floor.

'Assam, what's going on, is there are problem?' I ask with a quiver in my voice.

'Ahmed will come to speak with you,' he replies, before dashing back out the door.

Fuck, fuck, fuck, fuck. I slump to the floor – something has gone wrong again. Ahmed makes me wait well over half an hour before

403

coming to see me, and he gives nothing away.

'Your families break their promise.'

'What do you mean? you said everything had been agreed, that it was finished.' My hysteria is building but his reply is blunt.

'They tell Adan they would call by a certain time and they don't do this, he tries to call them but they don't answer, so we don't go, we wait, tonight we stay here.' I unpack my bedding, reluctant to admit defeat.

I know Ahmed's lying: I'm sure our families would be in constant communication and monitoring every call from Adan. Whichever way I twist or turn it, nothing makes sense.

Sunday, 8 November

It's heartbreaking to wake up in the morning, feeling that it was just a brief flirtation with the idea that we'd get the fuck out of here. Shortly after breakfast Ahmed explains that they still haven't heard anything and that we now just have to wait. Instead of dwelling on the circumstances, I spend the day putting a message together for Amanda. I tell her that Ahmed has confirmed my worst fears of being on-sold. I finish by telling her to stay strong, that we are together and that we will be with our families soon.

Nicky
Nairobi
Sunday, 8 November

JC gets a text and its scary heart-in-mouth stuff. Someone representing a man by the name of Musla wants to get this sorted; he is getting tired of Adan. He knows we are in Nairobi and even has Lorinda's correct room number at our hotel. In a mad rush we swap her room and decide to contact him.

We all bundle into JC's room and call Musla, who has very little English. He also has a really high voice so we wonder if he is really a woman. The whole conversation has the feel of the stoning sketch in *The Life of Brian*. It's insane, I'm on the edge of maniacal laughter with all this intrigue, danger and espionage going on around us, while feeling sick about how confusing it all is.

Musla has an interpreter on the line who is translating for us. Musla wants to know the agreed figure. What to say? Does he mean the agreed amount with the kidnappers or the total? We hedge our bets and tell Musla and his translator the amount that has been offered to the kidnappers, guessing that Adan has not passed on that he has his own substantial sweetener. But it's okay – US$548K seems to be the amount that Musla has heard. *Phew*. We ask Musla and his interpreter if we can speak to Nigel and Amanda. He assures us that we can talk to them the next day.

We immediately call Alto in the UK and play back the conversation so he can interpret. We gather that the interpreter had reported pretty accurately what was relayed to us. Poor Alto – he was all excited and thought we were calling him to say we had them. He's as disappointed as we are.

Monday, 9 November

Adan is constantly trying to call but we're not responding. I'm in favour of telling him to go jump but JC warns me not to burn bridges. Bummer, I'm in a torching frame of mind. We try to organise with Musla a drop-off point for the cash. He tells us that he is still convincing the kidnappers to go with the amount. We

THE PRICE OF LIFE

are guessing that they're holding out for a little bit more.

Musla confirms they may have to get a government official to pick up the cash from Dahabshiil. I don't really care who picks up what as long as we get an exchange. It's all so dragged out and trying to organise these people is incredibly frustrating. Musla explains to Alto that the person acting as his interpreter is a go-between who also knows Adan. Finally, they get down to discussing some possible drop-off points.

The boys become very motivated about finding neutral ground – expanses that are open and safe-ish drop-off points for Nigel and Amanda, somewhere that is neutral to both the AMISOM troops and Al-Shabaab. It all sounds extremely scary to me. I have visions of Nigel and Amanda being pushed out of a moving vehicle in some shot-up bit of parkland. Jack and Sam have a two-year-old map (*the most recent available!*) and pinpoint all the possibilities.

Tuesday, 10 November

We get Alto on the line. Musla is suggesting bribing government troops to do the swap at the hotel they were originally taken from. We explain that there is no more cash. If he wants to do this, it has to come out of the kidnappers' piece of the pie. Musla tells Alto that there is a higher boss than him, but he is away fighting. When we all establish with Musla that no extra money is forthcoming, he goes back to the idea of a neutral drop-off point. After the phone call Alto tells us that he thinks this guy is pretty high up in Al-Shabaab and controls most of the northern part of the city. Great, so now we are dealing with the terrorists, and they are the guys who are helping us get Nigel and Amanda.

Musla's interpreter, Nur, starts to contact us directly. He is in

Nairobi and would like to meet with Lorinda and me. He confirms that he is a friend to both Adan and Musla. He wants to finalise a couple of things to get this sorted. Once again we get Alto on the line. The poor man is up to his eyeballs with his uni work, the other head of his department is on sabbatical and he's gained his workload, and now on top of all that, he's translating more and more calls and sending the transcripts back to us.

Nur tells that he has government connections and that we should talk face to face, so we organise a meeting at the tapas bar in the village next to the Tribe.

JC, Sam, Lorinda and I head up there, and Jack is on another table, lurking as back-up. It's like a scene out of a spy movie. *Do not make eye contact with Jack.* How can I not? He's sitting there like a spare dick at an orgy. We all order juice. We people watch trying to guess which one is Nur.

We finally spot him; he comes in wearing a brown leather jacket. 'What does he think he is, a French spy?' JC exclaims. Nur is slight and looks like Morgan Freeman. Once we've done all the introductions, Jack slinks off and does a recon to see if anyone else is around. Nur is all smiles and condolences for what has happened to our families. He gives us his history. He was a fighter pilot, he tells us, with the Egyptian air force. I only just pull myself up in time from eye-rolling the others. I look down and focus on the skin on the back of my hands so they can't see me smirk. *Get it together*, I admonish myself. I'm going to need to remember this stuff. Nur is now a Somali MP, an honour that was thrust on him, rather than one he actively pursued. However, he is assisting us with the SNSA director, and the deputy PM.

Nur says he will require AMISOM assistance by way of security, and that we would use the K4 Dahabshiil near the border for cash-transfer. K4 is so-called because it's about 4 kilometres from the airport. This is a bit too open-ended for my liking.

Nur tells us he has experience – he has already got one French soldier intel guy out. Interesting sales pitch. We wait with bated breath at the end of the meeting to be hit up for travel expenses such as taxi fares. We know this is standard practice but surprisingly he doesn't want anything. For now.

Nur then starts negotiations with Adan and Musla, as their go-between. Musla is looking for a respectable businessman to pick up the cash. It's screamingly obvious that Nur wants to be that person but we have to go through the motions and dither back and forth for days before this happens. JC likens dealing with Somalis to 'herding cats' and he's not far wrong.

Wednesday, 11 November

Nur suggests that Sam sign the Dahabshiil papers at MIA which sounds good to us, or at least safer, because then it's Nur who has to make sure the cash is not stolen. Needless to say we will be stung for more hawala fees for this. Nur is unclear as to who is in charge, security-wise. Is it AMISOM, SNSA or the TFG (Transitional Federal Government)? Sam pushes for answers from all angles but it's still about as clear as mud. We come to the conclusion, out of Nur's hearing range, that security will be dictated by the colour green. At this stage Nur is going to fly into the Dish with a commercial flight from Djibouti, while Sam and Jack charter a flight with a pilot from Kenya.

If the commercial flight doesn't happen, Nur will fly in with the boys. He claims to be in contact with Musla who is busy fighting while keeping Adan in line. Because Musla and AMISOM are on opposite sides, everyone needs to know what the other is doing. Needless to say, there is a problem and Nur calls back later in the day. Musla's boss (*Jesus, who is that if Musla is Al-Shabaab?*) is in Mogadishu on Thursday so that is not a good day for an exchange. Friday is out as it is prayer day. It looks like Saturday is going to be the day. He also organises for Sam and Jack to stay at MIA – the Dahabshiil branch manager will go there to sign for the cash.

Thursday, 12 November

Nur is going with the boys after all, but still hits us up for expenses. It had to happen. He plans to fly out of Nairobi on a commercial flight. He has stuff to do in Somalia.

He calls later that day asking us to contact the Manager in Australia about the transfer. *WTF?* It would appear that even though Abdul is in charge of Dahabshiil in Somalia, he has some issue with the cash coming from K4. The man is really difficult to deal with, and I suspect he's on the take. But who isn't in Somalia?

Nigel
The Bush House
Thursday, 12 November

Late in the afternoon the boys seem on edge and I'm positive we are about to be moved. I have grave concerns as Ahmed isn't with us – he's gone back to Mogadishu. Each time we've been transported he's been there. My fear is that the group has now split and that they are abducting us for their own gain, that Captain Yahya is now going to sell us to anyone willing to make an offer. I'm sure now that tonight we will be in Al-Shabaab's hands.

Just after dinner Jamal marches in. 'Quickly, take everything, we go, five minutes. No talking, quickly,' he orders. Fifteen minutes later, outside, I can see the boys are all geared up, ammo belts, grenades and guns hanging from them. I'm pushed around the side of the car and into the backseat, Abdullah ordering me into the middle. I hear Amanda's chains as she is brought out and forced into the back of the land cruiser with Jamal. It takes about fifteen minutes before they all clamber in, Abdullah and Captain Yahya on either side of me, Assam squashed next to Mohammad with the machine-gun in the front passenger's seat.

About five hundred metres up the dirt road we're stopped, and surrounded by four gunmen guarding a checkpoint. Abdullah pushes my head down between my legs as the front passenger window is cracked. I'm certain there will be a bloodbath if these guys get a sniff of us. Finally Abdullah pulls me back up. It's not a good start; I'm jittery as fuck.

It doesn't take long before the constant swerving and accelerating turns my stomach. Amanda, travelling backwards, isn't coping and I hear her retching, and she eventually vomits in her lap. The smell makes me swallow that much harder so as to not do the same.

We seem to drive for hours, jostled around like we're in a washing machine – I no longer care where we're going, I'm just desperate to get out of the car.

We come to a large town and I begin recognising the IDP camps we had passed months earlier on our way to Kismayo. Now I'm sure we're heading back into Mogadishu. I tell myself that this is a positive thing and that we may in fact be going home, all the time trying to get my bearings.

Up ahead I can see Ahmed's Subaru – the same vehicle that was used to transport us after the escape attempt – and we pull up next to it. I'm happy to see both Ahmed and Romeo get out of the car, even with their AK47s. There's a quick reshuffle of people, and Young Yahya and the other man move to the Subaru before we set off again. I'm half expecting to end up in one of the houses that we've already been held in, but when we come to a halt we're in a compound facing a house that is much fancier than the others. I notice there is actual glass in the windows, but I don't get long to contemplate this before I'm ripped from the car. I'm pushed down the hallway, ending up in large room in the back right-hand corner of the house. I can hear Amanda being marched in the same direction and placed in the room opposite me.

Fishing out my torch, I survey my new cell. It's surprisingly big, with two large windows, and relatively clean. I set up my bed and mozzie net before collapsing, exhausted, after the marathon five-hour trip. I fall asleep, slightly reassured to be back in Mogadishu. Things may actually be moving in the right direction.

The Flash House
Friday, 13 November

I get the shock of my life the next morning when I go to the bathroom. I've only had a small shard of mirror to look at myself since we were taken, and I'm astonished at the face now staring back at me in the mirror.

I almost don't recognise the pale, gaunt, hollow-eyed and bearded features. It's a face that shows the strain of the last fifteen months.

It makes me realise just how much pain and anguish we have endured at the hands of these people. It's not just my face that tells a thousand words, my body also bears the scars: my ribs are clearly visible and there's not an ounce of fat on me after the starvation diet they've had us on.

Nicky
Nairobi
Friday, 13 November

This is it. The boys are flying out to pick them up. The air is alive with tension and tightly-held hope. It really is happening. We have to hurry Nur up to get to Wilson Airport so they can fly and stay overnight at Wadjir, a frontier town on the Kenyan border. For the hundredth time, we insist that we must get a POL from both Amanda and Nigel before there can be a trade.

I am really distressed when Jack and Sam leave. I'm very scared for them. Even though Sam has pulled me aside to tell me that this is his job and he is very good at it, and yes, it involves high risk, but essentially he gets off on that, I'd still feel completely responsible if something went wrong in the Dish. I know they have families and now having lived and worked with them, I'm attached to them, so I'm crying pretty hard when they leave. I feel emotionally drained, all the spiking of adrenaline is taking its toll. I Skype everyone at home to fill them in and would like to get rolling drunk but I'll have to leave that till later. I need my wits about me.

Kellie
Newcastle
Saturday, 14 November

This is supposed to be the first exchange day. I'm catering for a wedding at a location without good phone reception, so I take two phones to check which one has better coverage.

The exchange is to take place at 8 p.m. Daylight Saving Time or 10 a.m. local Mog time. It is 7.30 p.m. here, just before dinner service. I check my phone and notice I have a message.

Why didn't it go off? I received calls earlier that day so I can't understand why it hasn't rung this time. It's the Manager, asking me to call him as soon as possible because there is a problem.

My heart jumps straight into my throat. *A problem.* Shit, what sort of problem, what's going on now? I can hear the message but my phone will not connect, then I notice the wind has changed direction. I have no choice but to run to the top of the hill where I know I'll get reception, but if I do that, dinner will be late and the bride will be waiting . . . Thankfully, my wonderful staff are used to these emergency phone calls by now and they do what needs to be done.

I phone the Manager; he's very stressed and angry. He keeps saying, 'You told me K4. Mr Jack now wants money to the airport, Abdul is very angry; we had a deal for K4, they have changed the deal, you are my client, you have lied to me.'

Oh my god, have I really stuffed this up? Or has the Manager misunderstood again? Is he on the take with Abdul? All these things are racing through my head as he yells at me over the phone, on the hill, under the stars on a beautiful balmy November evening. A bride's perfect day is slowly becoming my worst nightmare.

I try not to panic. I call JC and explain the Manager's carry-on and ask what he wants me to do. The call to Nairobi keeps breaking up, so I keep telling JC about the Manager calling me a liar and yelling at me about the pick-up change.

It seems JC smoothes things over with the Manager and gets everything back on track. In the end, the money is picked up in

Nairobi by Jack and transferred to another money exchange and then carried into Mogodishu in backpacks. The money is so heavy it breaks one of the backpack straps.

Nigel
The Flash House
Saturday, 14 November

In the evening I'm caught by surprise. Abdullah walks in and tells me, 'Quickly, we move in five minutes.' We've never be moved so soon after arriving at a new house. Maybe the group has splintered and the boys and Captain Yahya have other plans for us. I can't hear Ahmed, which confirms these suspicions. It's not long before I'm pushed into the backseat of the car where Amanda is already waiting.

There seems to be great urgency to get moving. We roar out of the gates and start weaving through the streets. The boys all seem incredibly jumpy. Abdullah continually looks over his shoulder, making sure we are not being followed. We drive for no more than five minutes before pulling up outside a new compound. Captain Yahya races to open the gates, then they slam behind us.

Amanda and I are dragged from the car and marched into a ramshackle house. We're marched into our respective rooms. We share an adjoining wall but it now feels as though the Atlantic Ocean separates us. I can't even get a glimpse of her when I go to the toilet and I can't hear anything coming from her room.

The place looks more like a rat hole than a house; it's by far the nastiest little hovel they've concealed us in. White ant trails run halfway up the walls, there are cockroach carcasses everywhere and the floor is covered in dirt and crap. The heat from the roof makes the room stifling; it feels like I'm in a pressure cooker. I set up my bed behind the back of the door, trying to give myself privacy from the boys' prying eyes, but they come in regularly during the night, shining their torches in my face.

The Rat Hole
Monday, 16 November

In the morning I get a better perspective of the shithole they have me in. The bathroom is just a hole in the floor to defecate in and worse still, the door doesn't close properly. As I leave the bathroom, from the corner of my eye, I can see down the small hallway into Amanda's room. It's practically pitch-black and I know she will be doing it tough. The boys laze around in the verandah area, like a bunch of sloths, scratching themselves.

Late in the morning Captain Yahya comes in, handing me the phone. He's joined by Abdullah, who plonks himself down right next to me, getting a good position to listen in on the conversation I'm about to have. Pressing the receiver to my ear I say, 'Hello, Nigel speaking', and I hear a voice say, 'Hi, it's Sam. Mate, just want you to know we're here to get you.'

'Okay', I reply, dumbfounded, with no idea who I'm talking to, but it's such a relief to hear his words. Finally some proof that things are nearing the end. He says, 'We are trying to do the deal, but we need you and Amanda to talk with the people in charge there and push them to finish this.' *That's impossible; they're all grunts and the people that are running the show are elsewhere,* is what I'm thinking but I say, 'Okay I will try.'

Sam asks, 'Are you okay? Is Amanda with you?'

'Yeah, I'm okay. Amanda's here but she is being held in another room.' He asks to speak to her. I tell Abdullah this, and he grabs the phone from my hand before they both leave the room. Moments later I can vaguely hear Amanda becoming excited as she talks with Sam. I won't allow myself the room for belief that we are getting out of here soon – I learned my lesson ten days earlier after talking to Nicky.

Fifteen minutes later Abdullah comes in with Joseph, wanting to know exactly what was said. They high-five each other and exclaim, '*Alhamdulillah*, it is finished', grins spread across their faces. It's a phrase I'm getting sick of hearing – every time they bandy it around things seem to turn to shit. I just want to be left alone. Later that afternoon, the sounds of war ripple through the air as motars fly then explode somewhere in the distance. It would only take one stray shell on the flimsy metal roof to cause disaster.

For the next two days it's as though time stands still, the heat and boredom all-consuming. *What the fuck is going on and why is it taking so long* runs on a loop through my head.

Nicky
Nairobi
Sunday, 15 November

We start the day by sending out feelers to everyone: Musla, Nur and Adan. It would appear that the Somali people are not early risers unless it's to pray or eat, so Sam and Jack have a late start. They have no idea where Nur stayed or who he has been in contact with overnight. They suspect he's had a big night on the khat. He meets them at the general's house and they all head back to MIA. After considerable faffing around, the money is counted in front of everyone. The boys load it up and move it to a different hawala operator – Qaran – at the port office. Adan's share has been left with the general to go through the Bakaal hawala so he can get his cut without the rest of the gang knowing.

According to the boys, the run through town was pretty crazy. At this point their presence in the Dish is quite obvious and they are starting to look and feel like easy targets for an ambush. Adan is notified of the deal and, in theory, Nige and Amanda should be getting dropped off at Dabka junction, which the boys have checked out the day before.

Then Adan and Nur have a massive argument where Adan demands the cash to be moved to Qaran hawala at Bakaara markets. Even though I suspect the boys secretly consider this option, the CMT vehemently opposes it. As far as I'm concerned, the chances of things turning to shit are far too high. We have too much to lose. If the cash gets taken, that's it. And that's before we even consider what could happen to the boys.

What Adan wants is to have the money and the hostages at the same time. *Ain't going to happen, buddy*. The tension at the Tribe is at fever pitch. James keeps asking for updates but we've got no idea what is going on, as the Somali contingent is so wayward. Dick's ringing me, Kel's ringing me, Si's ringing me. I don't want to talk to anyone. It's too hard to explain as everything is changing course every thirty minutes. I just want to vomit – my gut is in spasms with nerves.

By the afternoon, K4 Qaran wants to pull out. It appears that Abdul is stirring the pot – he isn't happy with us using that operator, as it means he won't get the commission. This just confirms for us how dodgy he is. The boys head back to the general's residence overnight.

We all Skype Alto. And so begins a mammoth phone fest for Alto, talking to Musla, Adan and Nur. Musla wants this pushed along as quickly as possible. He's had a busy day today, fighting – he makes that statement sound so banal, domestic even. He is meant to have heard from Adan and Nur during the day and is surprised that more hasn't happened. He tells Alto that the gang members are young and ignorant and think if they put Nige and Amanda on the phone a cruise missile will strike them. *Watched a few too many* Rambo *films, this lot.* He will devote himself to it tomorrow. He says Adan is scared he will be killed when he gets the money. *No great loss*, I'm thinking. Given half a chance I'd like to wring his scrawny neck. You can just tell he's a little weed.

Adan's got the strops up big time when Alto speaks to him. He can't get on with Nur. We guess he's not happy that someone else is negotiating and he thinks he's going to lose his sweetener. He also can't let the gang know he has that extra deal going on so he's leaving his belly pretty exposed. He wants to know who the white man hawala recipient is. We – the families – are to blame and we must fix this; we must get the manager of Qaran hawala to call him. There will be no POL till this happens. As if that's going to happen, given it's 7 p.m. on Sunday night.

Alto calls Nur, who is chewing khat. *Great, a stoned negotiator. Pretty sure I know where the money for that came from.* Everything is 'no problem'. I'm starting to dislike this phrase almost as much as *inshallah*. He has had confirmation from the Qaran hawala that the money is there but denied this to Adan. Nur thinks as little of Adan as Adan thinks of him: 'He's an idiot and makes no sense.' *Hear, hear.*

Musla then calls us, asking to speak to Alto. Whoa, boy, does he have some translating to do tonight! It's coming in so thick and fast we're having to make decisions on the overview that Alto gives us rather than waiting for the transcripts. Once again, Alto proves to be an absolute godsend because he is able to pick up the nuances of this cast of strange characters.

Musla tells Alto that he has spoken to both Nur and Adan. Adan wants a letter of guarantee to be faxed to Qaran hawala from Jack that he will not be prosecuted after the release of Nige and Amanda. This guy is an idiot. We agree and send off something to that effect in English, like they can read it!

Monday, 16 November

The boys go to pick up the money from the port Qaran hawala and back to the general's to pick up Adan's share, which has been kept separately. They then move to the SNSA main building, where they sit and wait. While all this dithering goes on, the general has confirmed that on delivery of Nigel and Amanda, the money will be escorted to the Bakaal hawala of the gang's choice. This all has to be done by 2 p.m. as the general is then flying out of the country.

Fuck-all happens.

Nur can't get onto Adan. I have a very bad feeling. Every second hawala in Mogadishu has counted the money. When they are reporting back to JC, all Sam can hear is me yelling to them is 'Where is the money?' and not in a *Jerry Maguire* way. I'm yelling, 'Get on the fucking plane and fly out of there!' I think Lorinda is shocked that I can suggest such a thing, but from our end it feels to me like we are courting disaster.

The pilot and co. call their bluff and load the money onto the plane. Sam immediately gets a POL. He gets to speak to both

Amanda and Nigel; they sound pretty good, they're in the same house but not together. We're all having lunch together when Sam calls us and he speaks to me, Mum and Lorinda to pass on the messages from Nige and Amanda. We're all crying at the table.

During the day we have been constantly texting Musla and Adan to move them along. Adan starts sending threatening messages and texts. We make good our previous threat that we'll take US$90 000 of Adan's share off the table. We pass this information on to both Musla and Nur.

The boys get moved to another spot in MIA as they (not to mention the cash) have been in one place for too long. They stay with the Force Commander and Major Saad.

Kellie
Newcastle
Sunday, 15 November

I cannot imagine what it's like in Nairobi, sitting and waiting.

For them it's day twelve of a week-long trip and day three of the exchange. Not receiving the up-to-date information from my CMT group is the hardest part. I have stopped my life for this and now I've got nothing.

Things are moving too fast over there for updates all the time – strategies and plans change direction faster than a bullet train.

Nothing can prepare me for the 'No, not today' reply that comes through via text message.

It's too painful to talk to loved ones on the other side. I feel so deflated, I can't cope with everyday chores. Tears just roll down my face, not sobbing or crying, but the tears just come and they don't stop. They start stinging my face and then I feel them dripping off my chin and onto my clothes. My face becomes itchy and my nose is running, but I just can't stop them from coming, and all I want to do is sleep but I can't, I just keep waiting. Wating for a message of some sort that will let us know if it's over or not.

Nicky
Nairobi
Tuesday 17 November

Adan has gone quiet; we don't hear anything from him all day. We get a text from Musla, saying that Adan has threatened the Bakaal hawala and they will not deal with him.

There is a lot of messing around with the boys trying to get the deputy PM who is in Djibouti to guarantee the money is in the system. In the meantime, Adan has been into the Bakaal hawala three times, threatening them. He wants the cash released to him before the hostages.

We insist on the boys flying home without Amanda and Nigel.

This creates a last-minute intervention by another MP. He claims there are elders trying to assist and offers to go and get them. They come back to MIA with more MP elders and one other guy, who the boys are almost certain is a member of the gang. He's young and looks surly and doesn't speak any English. He doesn't appear to have the social skills or standing of others around him, so the 'elder' label doesn't fit. This lot don't want the money at MIA, they want it moved back to K4. Everything about this screams ambush – the boys have been getting intel that they're going to get jumped. It's now too late so they can't fly out to Wadjir; they return to the Bancroft location to stay overnight.

Musla send us a text that evening saying we must get rid of Adan. If only.

Wednesday, 18 November

D-day for us. We all hope desperately that someone can pull a rabbit out of a hat, but deep down know that it will be a miracle.

For the first time ever, Jack and Sam actually have an early start. The deputy commander of the SNSA has Nur and the elder MPs at MIA but not the younger Somali who the boys think is a gang member. The MPs want to move the money to K4 Qaran, not get a receipt for it, and let the gang know they can release the hostages. This is getting more ridiculous by the minute so the decision is made to leave.

Nur is shocked that we have insisted that the boys come home. He travels back to Nairobi with them and behaves like an absolute prat. They're arguing about money – what else?

When they hit the ground in Wilson, Nur goes off in a huff. This may be a problem, as we don't know what his role is or who takes over at the Mogadishu end.

The boys arrive back at the Tribe and we are all pretty despondent. I feel drained and looking around everyone else is the same. We've all had a bit of a cry – we've all got puffy faces. In sheer desperation I get totally smashed. I drag Jack, Sam and JC kicking and screaming with me.

'I know it feels like a setback but you did the right thing. The general told the boys that if they got out of the Dish unharmed and with the cash it would be a successful mission,' JC says. I'd assumed things were getting unsafe the longer they were there, but it was alarming to find how close they had come to endangering themselves. As sad as we were about calling them back, we made the right choice.

We now have a good relationship with General Hassan, and the boys think that working with the general is the way to get them out. I like the sound of this. It's someone with a bit of responsibility on the ground with some input. I head off to bed knowing I will be nursing a hangover the next day but at least I'll be in the mood to feel bad.

Thursday, 19 November

We discover that the ransom amount has gone up to US$600K. That was put on the boys when all the MPs arrived. It's okay, because we've told Adan that money has been taken out of his amount as he took too long. What he doesn't know is that it's going to the kidnappers.

Nur also calls us, saying he's under a lot of pressure from the generals to get this sorted. And Adan is now out of the picture. Well, he's still putting his two bobs' worth in, ringing us and sending nasty text messages that we don't answer. Nur wants to know if we're still interested in finishing this. As if we weren't. So he confirms with the elders that we want to continue.

All in all it's a very sad day. We're worn down. 'Miserable' doesn't do the job at all.

Friday, 20 November

We need to go home. We have to get this sorted. I have a family at home in Australia and I just can't stay here any longer.

James calls me – he wants to meet and discuss a few things.

That gives me a nasty knot in my stomach. I feel like the ham in the sandwich and I know this is not going to be a fun conversation. But before I catch up with James, there's a meeting with Nur to get through.

I'm guessing Nur's going to be pretty stroppy. Lorinda and I tell him we must leave, we can't stay here waiting forever.

'No, no, you cannot go,' Nur says. He tells us that he has done this before, that he's also working on the French case, which is very difficult. He tells us that they had the money taken twice before the first French man was released. *Thank god we got Sam and Jack out.* Looks shoot across the table everywhere. The thought of being this close and having to go home to Australia empty handed – no money and no Nigel – brings the sting of bile to my throat.

Nur says Adan is no longer in the picture. 'He is running scared for his own life,' he says, grinning broadly. I find the smile ingratiating. His teeth are rotten at the back.

So Nur wants to go with Jack to take the money in a diplomatic pouch to Mogadishu on a commercial airline, where they will meet the MPs and elders. They will then set out to the K4 Qaran, where the money will be counted and held but it will not actually go through the system. I don't know why; I assume that way it won't incur extra charges and fewer people will know it's in-country.

This idea is a little off to me, like most money dealings in Somalia. Nigel and Amanda would be brought to K4 and Jack would take them back to the airport under protection of the general's forces. I'm thinking, *this is madness. How are we going to get the diplomatic bag through the airport?* Nur seems to think it will not be checked because it's a diplomatic bag. I think there's no way that it *won't* be checked.

I'm incredibly apprehensive about the money being confiscated as it's leaving Kenya. You can't move vast sums of money on your person in and out of Australia and I find it impossible to believe it's not the same here.

Back at the Tribe, the talk with James is every bit as awkward as I envisioned. We have pretty much run over our allocated budget for being here. He also slightly admonishes me for not heeding his advice that perhaps we have flown over to Nairobi too early in the proceedings – he'd indicated that it often takes a while to get released after the initial settlement price. The whole do-as-I-say-not-as-I-do advice from the government really shits me. I wish they would just leave me alone so we can get this done. Things have gotten pretty tense between the Australian government and AKE. James is asking me for a run-down as to what is happening.

Hey, James, I don't provide the intel, I'm just a negotiator.

As it turns out, my wish is about to be granted. James and the vast majority of AFP and defence personnel are moving out. Dad also wants to go home, he's finding it too difficult. He hates being in a foreign country and he's missing everyone, the grandkids especially.

Mum doesn't want to fly home only to have to come back again when Nige is released – she decides to go stay with friends in the UK. The government has confirmed that they will not pay for a return flight for either Mum or Dad.

The Tribe is going to cost a fortune if we stay on, so we start to make enquiries as to where else we can stay. I'd love to book into a backpackers but alas, not enough privacy for calls and negotiations. It's a tricky one because the government wants us out as it's so expensive, and it's personally costing us a fortune because we're paying to have the boys and JC here. But while we *are* here the Australian government can keep tabs on us.

Saturday, 21 November

Mum and Dad both head off. It's pretty flat and saddening for me. The homesickness is overwhelming. While it's been hard managing their expectations, it's a lot harder to explain what happens if things go wrong and they're not around to see the process.

We meet with Nur again, and – surprise, surprise – he's having some difficulty organising the diplomatic bag. He suggests that we might be able to get a government letter from Canada or Australia. He suggests Australia is more likely.

I can't believe how calm JC is about it. It doesn't faze him that it's all so fluid and I don't know how he manages to sift through all the bullshit so well.

Nur suggest that perhaps we fly the money back in with Sam and Jack. Then his phone rings and Nur has a fifteen-minute phone call in Somali, which he then translates for us. He has just spoken to General Noor who has just been summonsed to an emergency meeting at the US Embassy tomorrow, and he may be joined by General Hassan on his way back from Rome. There will now be a delay going into the Dish.

Nur is really enjoying treating us to this bit of information, like we are his minions. He's pretty full of himself – I just hope he can get the job done. I have to admit there is a little naysayer sitting on my shoulder suggesting that he's not up to the task. This is heightened by the fact that he tells us that he doesn't want to complete the exchange without General Noor or Hassan being present.

Nur also helps us send what I think of as a suck text to Musla thanking him for his assistance, for what its worth. According to Nur, Musla has put up US$60K to pay for looking after Nigel and Amanda and it's gone on for long enough. He wants his money back.

Later on that evening Nur calls and says that the MPs still want to go ahead with the exchange tomorrow and he and the general want to wait until the general is in country.

He wants us to send a letter to the MPs saying that we are having difficulty flying the money out of Kenya on an Africa express flight, which is the reason for the delay.

We send texts to that effect to all the numbers he has given us.

Sunday, 22 November

The day starts with threatening texts from Adan. He also rings but we don't answer his calls. He is pissed off. He now knows that he's been cut out of the deal and that everyone knows he had his own side deal going on.

Nur insists that Adan has no influence on those who are holding and guarding Nigel and Amanda. He's on the run, in hiding.

General Noor is in Nairobi till Wednesday morning, arriving in the Dish at 9 a.m. He suggests we set up the exchange for Wednesday or Thursday. *Inshallah*.

No! Not *inshallah*! I'm close to rage over this bloody fix-all excuse. Nur pats my hand benevolently.

All of us jump on him and verbally wrestle with him to make it Wednesday. Everything shuts at midday on Thursdays, and Friday is prayer day so nothing will get done.

JC decides to butter up Nur by inviting him and General Noor to lunch on Tuesday.

When Nur drops into the Tribe later, he tells us that the MPs keep ringing him, wanting him to hurry the exchange. Well, hello, it's not us holding things up. Nur suggests that the money go into Qaran hawala here in Nairobi, and be receipted to General Noor or perhaps himself in Mogadishu.

427

He calls later that night to say that he and General Noor would love to come to lunch on Tuesday.

Kellie
Newcastle
Monday 23 November

I've been on auto pilot, just getting on with daily life. I work at the shop, I pick up kids, I cook, and I pick up Geoff from the airport. He has come home and is staying with us. He looks old and ashen and he's trying to hold back tears when he sees me in the concourse lounge at the airport. It's heartbreaking to see a once strong, fit man look so broken. Heather has gone to stay with friends in the UK, so she can go back quickly when Nige gets out.

Geoff mopes around our house, trying to act like he is okay. We are all acting. No one is okay, we're all walking around in a daze. We all had our hopes pinned on Nigel being out by now.

Nic calls to tell me they are going in again. We decide that we're not going to tell any family members what's going on, in case this goes pear-shaped again.

Nic and I made the executive decision to task John Chase, and some family members held it against us when things went bad. It's just a symptom of the pressure we're all under, but the backlash is getting to us.

Nicky
Nairobi
Monday 23–Tuesday 24 November

It's Jacinta's fourteenth birthday and I'm half a world away. I'm eternally grateful that our friends and Si organise a party for her.

My world over here is a mess of calls and meetings and plans constantly changing. Everyone we're dealing with seems to have their own agenda while ours is quite simple. We just want to get Nigel and Amanda out. And we're so close.

Nur calls from Mombassa and says that the MPs want the money to go through yet another different hawala. JC suggests we stick with the cash going in country with Jack and Sam. Unbeknown to Nur, one of the reasons for this is that we've been trying to insure the money against theft. The guys themselves are covered by the company if they're taken, but if the money is stolen, that's it for us. The ridiculous thing is that insurance companies won't recognise the hawala system, but they think it's okay to have two guys lugging backpacks of cash through Mogadishu. There's a considerable cost involved, needless to say.

JC decides Nur needs to go back into the Dish with the boys on Friday to meet up with the general's flight. Nur tells JC that if the money goes through his preferred hawala today, then Nigel and Amanda can be brought to the MIA when the Daallo Airlines flight gets in in the morning.

JC has to take the cash into Eastling. We've been warned not to go there – half of displaced Somalia lives there. There is huge animosity about the Somali refugees from the local population. JC says that the place is more like a war zone than a slum. There are potholes that you could lose a car in and it's filthy.

JC wants to get in and out quickly, so of course the money-counter breaks and the cash has to be counted by hand. All of the Dish must know that the cash is going in, but JC has to contact the MPs to let them know, officially. It's quite a farce.

The money is being sent for Nur to be the pick-up recipient.

Nur scams another US$8K for 'security'. He has us over a barrel, and so we agree that he will get it when he meets the boys in the Dish. He also hits us up for Kenyan shillings for cab fares.

The boys and the pilot leave for Wadjir a second time. I'm just as scared for them and try, unsuccessfully, not to cry. There's even more emotion involved this time – we've all felt the pain of an unsuccessful retrieval and we know that there's the possibility of it happening again. But if they're not successful this time, we can't stay here and keep trying over and over. I admonish myself for the negative thinking but I can't help it.

Adan has gone to ground. Maybe it's a case of 'ding dong, the witch is dead'. I gleefully hope so. As soon as we dare to mention this, right on cue he starts texting and he's got all the right information about the hawala. We ring Nur to try to work out how the leak can be so massive. We find out that the gang has been informed that the money is coming and that one of the members must be in contact with Adan. All of us are apprehensive about him having this knowledge. I mean, we have shafted him and he is no longer getting his money so I'm pretty sure he would be up for some nasty sabotage. He keeps ringing into the night.

Wednesday, 25 November

Mum is flying back from the UK tonight. It feels a bit premature but she wants to be here when Nigel gets into Kenya, and she can only mark time in the UK for so long. We all hit the area in front of JC's room and wait for the calls to come in from the boys.

The boys let us know they have met up with General Sharif. He doesn't appear to be as powerful as Mohammed Sheikh Hassan or General Noor but they're going to work with what they've got.

The rest of the MPs arrive at 10 a.m. and then Nur finally gets in on the Daallo flight, which is late.

The day drags on. We're all tense, waiting for the reports that come back from the boys every thirty minutes. They sound increasingly frustrated. I have no idea where the money is. Is it safe? I'm starting to nag them, I know. I'm knitting to try to keep my hands occupied so I don't tap a hole through my sternum.

The boys ring and tell us they are getting stonewalled. Everyone over there stops to pray and eat and bugger-all else gets done. At the end of the day, Nur finally arrives alone, looking like a dog with his tail between his legs. There is great farce about how the gang and the hawala are staggering the release of funds over a couple of days to ensure that everyone who is owed money gets their share.

This is infuriating – I'm enraged. 'It's got nothing to do with us who pays whom after the deal is done!' I'm screaming this at the boys. I also want to know where the fuck the money is. 'Whoa, calm down,' Sam says. 'I've got the receipt so no one else can collect it.' He must be well over hearing my whinging, bitching, nagging voice down a tinny telephone line – I'm well over it myself. Nothing more happens so the boys pack up and head back to Bancroft camp at the airport.

We've all moved downstairs to where the Canadian consular staff are waiting. All of us feel flat. We've been invited to the Australian Embassy for dinner. I want to discuss what's going on with the plane bill as the pilot normally gets paid before he goes. Lorinda doesn't want to go to dinner; she wants nothing to do with them. JC has to debrief with the boys, so I suck it up and head off to the embassy.

I plan on having a few as I want to be as hung-over as possible so it can't hurt any worse when Mum gets in. Within half an hour of meet-and-greet – I've not even finished my first drink – JC calls.

'We got them.'

'What?'

'We've got them. We have Nigel and Amanda.'

'Ohmigod ohmigod ohmigod.' I stumble, arms held out in front of me. I can't breathe, I'm sucking in great mouthfuls of air. I'm crying hard, so hard I can't speak.

'They've got them,' I squeak, pushing the words out. Everyone folds around me, hugging me.

JC's still on the line.

'Okay, there are a few hurdles. The boys aren't with them. Lorinda has spoken to Amanda. Get back here and you can call Nigel.'

'What what do you mean, the boys aren't with them? Where are they?'

'Just get back here and we can go through it all.'

I can't get in the car fast enough. A woman from the embassy passes me great handfuls of hot barbecued food in alfoil to take with me.

JC goes over what has happened. They are holed up for the night at the Sahafi Hotel. I am swinging between exultation that they are out and gut-twisting fear that some other group could storm the hotel and take them, especially now that the news has hit the wire. My phone has gone nuts with people ringing to see if it's true – it's on morning news back home in Oz.

I finally get to speak to Nige at the hotel and tell him to keep quiet, and then I realise I've scared him by telling him he's not really safe. *Stupid, stupid, stupid.* Then I try to calm him down.

I hope he gets some sleep tonight but I bet he won't. Jack and Sam are hopeful of getting them to the airport at first light but the

Somalis are not known for their early starts.

We crack open ridiculously expensive champagne to celebrate. The first bottle is on JC. I quash the fear that we are pre-empting the celebrations. We scoff down the alfoiled food.

Nigel
The Rat Hole
Wednesday, 25 November

Wednesday starts like any normal day in captivity. After a restless night's sleep, I spend the day like most of these days, perusing my drawings, memorising my diary and reading passages of the Qur'an and the books. The heat, exhaustion and darkness leave me little option other than to sleep as part of my daily routine. The only thing I take any joy from is the two cups of tea I receive every day.

It must be just before 6 p.m. prayer when Amanda is marched past my door by a number of the boys. The sound of her chains sends a chill up my spine – something is about to happen. Then it hits me between the eyes that we are about to be handed to Al-Shabaab.

It's been nine days since talking to Sam and any thoughts of freedom have vanished. I begin throwing my things together but I don't get the chance to finish as Abdullah walks in. He orders me out the door. I try to say, 'Wait, let me get my things, what's going on . . .' but he stops me mid-sentence, barking, 'Leave them, quickly, go', as he points to the door.

I feel a great sense of loss as I leave my few possessions behind. Waiting for me in another room is Captain Yahya, and Abdullah tugs on my clothing. 'Quickly, take off everything, put these on.' Captain Yahya hands me a new shirt and jeans. Like a stunned rabbit I stand there, Abdullah barking, 'Quickly, quickly!'

I turn to him. 'How am I meant to put these on with chains around my ankles?' referring to the jeans. He ponders this for a moment before scampering out the door. Mohammad walks in moments later, his AK47 draped across his shoulder. It's so tense in here. I throw the long-sleeved shirt on, forgetting to take the singlet off but no one seems to notice.

Abdullah comes back with the keys and begins working vigorously at each of the locks on my chains with no success – months of exposure to water has rusted them solid. Captain Yahya tries to force the key and almost snaps it off. Mohammad now yanks at the chains, trying to open them with brute force. Defeated, he dashes out the door, and I use this opportunity to ask Abdullah a barrage of questions. 'What's happening? Is everything okay? Where are you taking us? What about my things?' I'm hoping to quell my ever-growing fear, my head spinning out of control. He answers, 'No talking', as he forces me to the ground in a sitting position.

Mohammad returns with a hacksaw blade in hand, and they take turns at sawing off the locks, pulling and twisting each leg into a position so as to get the correct angle. The three of them then begin conversing in Somali.

I disregard his order and say, 'Please, Abdullah, can I at least have my Qur'an?' feeling that it is somehow magically going to give me protection for what's about to take place. He says something to Captain Yahya who shakes his head. He tells me firmly, with his arm raised, 'Captain says no, no more talking.' I keep my mouth shut as I watch the sweat run down Mohammad's face as he furiously works away.

Finally Captain Yahya pulls the first chain from my ankle, but I don't register this simple freedom as I try to second-guess what the fuck is going on. Abdullah then snaps his fingers, ordering me to put on the jeans. I pull them up under my macawiis. They're swimming on me, so I tell Abdullah I need my belt, to which he shakes his head no. I drop the macawiis to the floor and show then that the jeans won't stay up. Abdullah ducks out of the room.

Mohammad orders me to the ground again as he begins working on the other lock, and when Abdullah returns, he tosses me the belt, which I slip around my waist.

After ten minutes they finally remove the second lock, and I'm ordered up and out of the room. I stand, pointing to my feet. 'Please, what about my shoes?' Abdullah races next door and brings them back and I just have time to pull them on and lace them up before Mohammad pushes me towards the door. Walking awkwardly down the short hallway, feeling as though I'm still hobbled, my balance is all over the place and my heart hammers away.

I can see Amanda in the courtyard. Some of the boys are working away feverishly at her locks. Abdullah pushes me across the courtyard and into the front passenger seat of a four-wheel drive. As I struggle to get up onto the high seat, I ask Abdullah for my Qur'an again, saying how important it is to me, but he just slams the door. I don't know why it seems so important, maybe it's because it has Ahmed's email contact in it or because it could protect me somehow if we are in fact given to Al-Shabaab.

After a few minutes I'm pulled from the car and forced into the backseat, and Amanda, the chain still around one leg, is ordered into the back with me. They take her leg, pulling it out of the car, and go to work on the lock with the hacksaw, and it seems to take about five minutes before she is finally freed from her chains. The boys rush to get into the car. Nothing makes sense. We're surrounded by guns feeling like lambs going to slaughter.

We roar through the gates and down the sandy street. My anxiety now has a red lining, made even worse with the realisation that Ahmed isn't in the car. We come into a market area with people everywhere. The headlights stretch out into the darkness. We drive a few hundred metres along a bitumen road before stopping at what looks like a fuel station, and over my shoulder I notice a car just off to the right with someone getting out of the passenger seat. They walk towards us. I'm twitchy as all fuck. We are completely out in the open and I'm terrified about who is advancing towards us, until I make out Ahmed's features. He comes to the driver's window and quickly converses in Somali. He doesn't acknowledge us and goes back to his car.

Our driver spins the car around and follows Ahmed's Subaru. We weave down the narrow streets, flying in the air as we slam through each pothole. At some point we pick up another vehicle, our car now in the middle of the convoy as we fly through the night. Finally we come to a stop opposite a petrol depot, and several men from the car behind jump into the Subaru. Ahmed then walks up alongside our windows which are slowly lowered.

He talks quickly in Somali before addressing us. Same shit, different day as he says, 'Noah, Amina, how is your situation?' Surely he can see that we are both extremely anxious? We reply in tandem, 'We're okay, where are we going?'

He replies, 'Everything is okay, don't worry', then address me directly, 'Noah, we talk about these promises you make, do we still have an agreement?' I look straight into his eyes and lie to his face.

'Yes, of course, I keep my promises.' Then he shakes my hand. He asks Amanda the same thing, and she responds exactly the same way. We take off again, ghosting Ahmed's tail-lights, and it feels like we drive for twenty minutes, again passing through the middle of a market area before hitting dense scrub. I want to believe that we are about to be released, but I trust these pricks about as far as I could kick one of them. It's quite possible that Ahmed is having one last sick joke with us.

We eventually pull up in the middle of nowhere, and it's pitch-black. My senses tell me something's not right. The boys are now outside surrounding us, their weapons drawn as though a firefight is about to erupt. Suddenly we're pulled from the car then marched across to the Subaru and pushed into the backseat. Two of the boys climb in next to us as the doors slam closed. It feels like my sphincter muscle is about to let go, I'm so terrified – we are now facing two men who I have never seen before. I'm sure we have just been handed over to Al-Shabaab.

The man in the passenger seat turns around and asks me my name. 'I'm Nigel Brennan,' I reply. Then he asks Amanda the same thing. 'I'm Amanda Lindhout,' she says. He dials a number on his mobile and begins talking in Somali. The boys exit the car, and we interlock our fingers. Amanda's grasp is so tight it feels like she is about to break my hand. With no one beside us, we start talking, though none of it makes much sense as we're both almost hysterical with fear. Amanda's rambling, asking, 'What's going on, what's happening, Nigey, where are we going?' I try to reassure her but I can't even do this for myself, and I feel like I'm going to have to slap her before she goes into a panic attack. We both start firing questions to the men in the front but they don't answer a word, which just makes matters worse.

Suddenly, the door opens beside me, and a book is flung into my lap. I can see that it's my Qur'an. We're off, just the four of us now in the car as we speed down the dirty road. We hit a T-intersection, swerving left onto a bitumen road. The driver accelerates harder as we hurtle down the road, both of us clinging to each other in terror. It feels like we travel no more than 2 or 3 kilometres before a pick-up comes out of nowhere, blocking our path. Our driver slams on the brakes, stopping just metres from impact, and there are gunmen everywhere, it seems like there are about fifty of them, all in civilian clothing, packing enormous amounts of hardware.

Amanda is hysterical, tears flowing, her words no longer computing in my head. Out of nowhere another vehicle appears alongside us, our doors are ripped open, we're pulled from the car and pushed into the backseat of the four-wheel drive opposite us. People seem to be clambering in on top of us, and we're both in meltdown, trying desperately to get some clarification about what's taking place. Amanda is clawing at me, repeatedly crying out my name.

The man beside us talking – I can see his lips moving, but my brain is in shutdown and I can't understand what he's saying. Somewhere in the haze I register that he's the spitting image of Morgan Freeman.

Suddenly it's like cotton wool has been pulled from my ears, and I begin to hear his words: 'You are safe, everything is okay, please calm down.' Before I can say anything, the car lurches forward, the pick-up truck is now out in front of us with one man anchored to the massive machine-gun hanging off the back. This man continues to talk to us.

'My name is Nur. I am a Somali MP. Please, calm down, you are safe, you are free.' I can't believe what I'm hearing, those three simple words I have waited to hear for 462 days: you are free. Tears start pouring from my eyes and I'm a blubbering mess – much to Nur's displeasure – as I let myself believe a little bit that it's actually true.

Amanda is in much the same state, in complete shock that we will no longer be treated like someone's slave, chained like an animal. Nur then says, 'Please, stop crying, you should be happy. I will try to connect you with your families.' He now has his mobile phone in hand, punching in the numbers.

He hands the phone over to Amanda, and I hear her say, 'Hello, Mum.' Lorinda's voice is just audible and my doubt vanishes – tears of joy flow freely. I try to listen to what Amanda is saying, but it's impossible. I ask Nur where they're taking us. He tells me there is a team waiting for us at the airport. *Ah, that must be where Sam is.* We suddenly stop, and all my anxiety returns instantly. I notice a massive fortified entrance, razor wire spread in all directions and guards on sentry duty looking towards us over their weapons. I get the feeling that they could open fire on us at any moment, but then I see we're in front of the Burundi AMISOM base.

We don't stop long before travelling in convoy, making our way into Mogadishu. As we go past the feeding station I point out to Amanda that we'd been there on our third day, and we also pass the road leading to the Shamo Hotel. We finally grind to a halt in K4. Everyone gets out of the car except the driver, and I feel incredibly exposed. I try to get Amanda to stay calm. As I look around to see what they're doing, gunfire suddenly erupts and bullets whiz by, and I'm so startled I almost hit the floor – I can't tell if it's our guys shooting or someone shooting at us. Everyone jumps back in the car, we do a quick U-turn, and drive about 50 metres to the doors of the Sahafi Hotel, where Nur tells us to get out. It seems we're going to have to stay here the night.

I start to tell Nur it's imperative we get to the airport, but he shakes his head and explains, 'It is not possible tonight; it is too dangerous.' I can't believe it, we're so fucking close. Is the hotel safe?

I drag my sorry arse out of the car and run through the gates. It's like being in a time warp, entering a large courtyard filled with people sitting around drinking tea and coffee. We're quickly ushered past reception and into a large formal living room. The room quickly fills up with people, and I'm on edge as I clock each of them, terrified that someone will pull a weapon. Everyone tries to talk with us at once and my head feels like it's about to pop. My throat is bone-dry, making it almost impossible to speak.

Finally Nur shoos the crowd away, telling them to give us some space as he can clearly see that we're not comfortable. I ask for water and Coke, anything to relieve my parched throat. Nur explains that there are twelve or fifteen Somali MPs staying in the hotel tonight and that it is surrounded by security and that we should feel safe, but it doesn't ease my anxiety.

Then the reality of what has just occurred slowly begins to sink in. Having Amanda next to me after thirteen months of separation is momentous and I can't stop reaching out and touching her, but I'm terrified I'm going to wake up from a dream and discover that none of this is real. We talk to each other. There's so much to say but now isn't the time for details, I'm just so happy to hold her hand. I can't help thinking how bad our speech is, we're stumbling over words as we try to answer each other's questions.

After we field questions from Nur and some of the others, they finally make arrangements for a room. We are given the option of staying in the same room, but we decide not to. We don't want to upset the apple cart, so we ask for two rooms next to each other. But the hotel is fully booked. So, not wanting to let Amanda out of my sight, we agree that I will just use my room to shower then we will reconvene in hers. We have an entourage of people escort us upstairs to the rooms, and I can't help feeling claustrophobic with all these strangers around me. I just need some space to absorb everything and have some time alone with Amanda but it looks as though that will have to wait.

As soon as we make it to Amanda's room, a phone call comes through from Sam. I tell him that we are okay and explain what happened outside the hotel. He says that they can't get to the hotel – no one is willing to take them as it is too dangerous to travel the short distance at night, but he assures me that there is plenty of security surrounding the building, and that they will be here at six in the morning to pick us up. It would be nice to have Sam here as an extra security blanket but it looks like we are just going to have to bunker down for the night.

We ask everyone to leave and give us some space. I shut the door so that it's now just the two of us, and I embrace Amanda. She seems to melt into my arms as I pull her to my chest, our emotions finally boil over as both of us begin to cry.

Amanda repeatedly says, 'We're free, Nigey, we're free.' I never want to let go. I've been longing for the touch of another human being and it warms my heart that it's Amanda. I can't believe we have both made it out alive, hand in hand just as I had envisaged all along.

The first twenty minutes together is strange; it's kind of appropriate that the two of us are locked in a small room, but I'm so happy to share this space with her. I feel like a frigid teenager, awkward and withdrawn. For so long now having been told to keep my eyes to the floor, I now find it hard to meet hers. This shyness has been forced onto me, for so long I've walked on eggshells, my self-confidence stripped from me.

Once we both feel comfortable, we give each other some time to freshen up. I head back to my room, desperate for a shower and hoping for some peaceful reflection time but it's not forthcoming. As soon as I step out of the shower there's a knock at the door.

I'm handed a phone and told that it's for me, it's Fox News and a woman asks if I know anything about the two journalists who have just been released. Stunned, I explain that I am one of them, but before she gets the chance to ask anything more I'm handed another phone. It's another media outlet wanting information, which I deflect saying I don't wish to say anything.

I'm then passed another phone, and expecting a journalist, I say hello and then hear Nicky's voice. She sounds ecstatic and it's so amazing to finally talk with her, but she puts the fear of god into me.

'You're not completely safe, not until you're out of the country, and just so you know, two French journalists were kidnapped from the hotel where you are.' I almost go into a panic attack, realising that Amanda is downstairs alone. Nic manages to calm me down by the time I hang up, but I know there's little I can do except wait. I race back down to Amanda's room.

The calls don't stop coming as the media goes into overdrive. Amanda does an interview with CTV in Canada, while I stupidly speak with a Reuters journalist from Nairobi, neither of us thinking about the consequences. Just after this Amanda speaks with her mother, who tells us to stop talking with the media, reiterating what Nicky said, that we're not safe yet and speaking out could compromise our position. Ahmed's promises come back to haunt me, and I'm sure the media will know where we are and how quickly this will transmitted around the globe. Our captors will have an ear to the radio.

It's a long night watching the clock, it seems like the longest night of my life as the minutes tick by. I'm on guard the whole time, jumpy at the slightest sound. I take two more phone calls during the night: the first from a friend in Bundaberg, which is slightly unsettling as I haven't even had the chance to speak with any of my family yet. I ask how they got this number and they tell me the ABC handed it over.

The second call I'm ecstatic to get. Talking with my brother-in-law Simon and my niece and nephews brings tears to my eyes. I have missed them all so much and the thought that I will be back with them soon is overwhelming. I'm on edge and running on pure adrenaline, I don't seem to need sleep. I watch over Amanda as she tries to get a few hours' kip.

Finally dawn breaks, and I'm desperate to get on that plane as soon as possible. It's a huge relief when Sam finally arrives with Jack. Both, I would learn, are ex-SAS and look like guys you wouldn't want to fuck with down a dark alley. Sam takes the piss out of me straightaway saying, 'I've got a can of Fosters waiting for you in the plane, mate.' I smile at the thought. They've both obviously met Nicky in Nairobi: 'Your sister is a feral bitch; shit, she can drink.' I can tell immediately it's affectionate and that they have got to know her well in a short time. They then get down to the serious side of business, explaining that the prime minister and president of Somalia have requested a meeting at Villa Somalia before we fly out. They explain that it's up to us whether we want to do it, and that there have been many people involved on the ground with our release who will be there.

Feeling that it would be a chance to say thank you to those involved, we decide to go ahead with it. So, under heavy security, we make our way down to the back car park of the hotel to the waiting vehicles. In convoy with a massive security detail, we make the short drive to the presidential palace. It turns out to be a complete circus, and we have to wait over an hour before Prime Minister

Omar Abdirashid Sharmarke is ready to accommodate us.

The boys are edgy and want to get us to the plane pronto, and we eventually get ushered into a large room that quickly fills with elders and government officials. Most of what is said during the course of discussions is in Somali and I feel a bit lost, then someone asks us if we would like to say something. Amanda doesn't feel confident and leaves it to me to thank everyone involved in our rescue.

As soon as I'm done, the boys wind things up and prepare to roll to the airport. The president is still unavailable, but the boys make the decision that we have already wasted too much time.

Again under heavy guard and in convoy, we travel at high speed towards Mogadishu International Airport, and just as we get there a phone call comes through from the president requesting us to come back as he is ready to meet with us. The boys completely brush off the idea. They want to get us on the plane. The Ugandan troops controlling the airport make it difficult, not wanting to give our vehicle access to a side gate that would allow us to drive right up to the plane. There is a furious argument between Nur and another MP in the vehicle with the Ugandan soldiers until finally they give in.

The car screams into the airfield and up alongside the awaiting Cessna. The boys bundle us into the five-seater within seconds, Jack drawing the curtains so as to shield us from the media, who are now running from the terminal towards the plane.

Everything happens so quickly. The pilot fires up the engine, which roars to life, the media are stopped in their tracks as the plane swings around and we plough head-on towards them, both Amanda and I keeping our heads down as we taxi onto the runway. Then there is complete and utter ecstasy as we bounce down the runway, the wheels lifting from the ground as we're pulled back into our seats. Everything slowly becoming miniature as we gain altitude.

When I see the breathtaking deep blue of the Indian Ocean, I know I am finally going home.

Weirdly, there's a tinge of sadness as I look down at the beautiful country below us, the waves smashing along the coastline as we track down the coast. The bitter memories of the last fifteen months are left behind for a moment, and I can't help wishing that I'd had a chance to see more of this magnificent country.

I haven't slept for over twenty-four hours, I'm running on pure adrenaline and I can't wipe the smile from my face. Sam is sitting next to the pilot and explains that we will stop at Wadjir airport, just across the border in Kenya, and that we should try to get some sleep as it will take over two hours. I'm now completely wired, talking with Jack and taking the piss out of Sam when I find out he's afraid of flying. This big tough guy white-knuckling the control stick is so hilarious.

Jack informs me that our bags and belongings are behind my seat. I pass Amanda's over, then open mine to find bags of Allen's lollies, a disposable camera, with which I start taking pictures, and a manila folder.

The folder contains letters and pictures of my family all together from last Christmas. Just seeing it, the magnitude of it all finally hits me, and tears stream down my face. I struggle to read the letters, sent with the care package, which we never received. I'm an emotional wreck. Jack hands me a handkerchief.

Amanda and I share these the things we've received from our families, and we can't quite believe that we will see them so soon. We slowly glide down onto the tarmac at Wadjir, and getting out of the plane I do a little jig, I'm so happy to be out of Somalia and in friendly territory.

We go through customs and immigration before jumping back onto the plane to make the two-hour journey to Nairobi.

I don't get an second of sleep, talking non-stop with Jack about anything and everything, even though my speech is still slow.

Then finally we begin our descent into Wilson airport in Nairobi, circling low over the game parks, and I'm almost jumping out of my skin as Jack points out the wildlife sprinting across the dry plain. On landing we taxi to a hanger, where two ambulances and a throng of government officials from both Australia and Canada are waiting for us. Amanda and I are split up, which is slightly unnerving, and we're taken to our respective consular cars. The ambulances are obviously decoys for the waiting media. A DFAT official explains that we will be transported to the Aga Khan University Hospital, where Mum and Nicky are waiting.

The cars fly out a side gate of the airport, sirens wailing as we speed through the afternoon peak hour. At one point I ask the driver to slow down, terrified that I'm going to die as he crosses a median strip to get around the traffic.

After ten or fifteen minutes of feeling like I'm in a dodgem car, we finally come screaming into the hospital. We pull up at the private entrance. I can see Nicky but I struggle to see Mum. Then as I get out of the vehicle I spy her standing in the crowd, her face full of joy but at the same time showing the strain of the last fifteen months.

I fall in to Mum's arms and at the same time pull Nicky into a three-way hug. I'm lost for words to describe the joy I feel to be in their warm embrace.

I'm introduced to a throng of people, consular officials, hospital staff and finally to Lorinda, embracing her like she is my second mother, before we're whisked upstairs.

Kellie
Newcastle
Thursday, 26 November

It's Thursday and I know the plane is going in, and should be coming out with Nige and Amanda. It's Wednesday in Nairobi, but tonight at 10 p.m. I will know if they are out or not.

Ten o'clock comes and goes and I am watching telly with my mobile next to me. Every half hour I get up to check my emails, but nothing comes through. I start texting JC but he sends a message back, 'Keep the line clear we are waiting for news'.

This is killing me.

Matt and Geoff head to bed. I want to tell them what is happening, but I don't want Geoff to be disappointed if nothing happens again. I head into the office and wait. I open up iTunes and surf the net, just filling in time and trying to empty my mind of the goings-on in Nairobi and Somalia. It's way past ten and I haven't heard a thing. 'The final countdown', a huge song in the eighties, comes on via iTunes. *You have got to be joking, the countdown has well and truly finished.* It's not happening tonight, it's too late and the plane can't leave. I go to bed with a splitting headache from crying and an empty feeling in the pit of my stomach.

Friday, 27 November

My mobile phone rings by the bed. It's 4.20 a.m. It's Nic.

'Kel, Kel, we got them.'

'You're fucking joking?!'

'No, no I wouldn't joke about this.'

I can hear people in the background, laughing and cheering, and I think this has really happened.

'Oh my god, Nic, that's fantastic. Does anyone else know?'

'No one. Can you call them? But, hang on, they're not out of Somalia yet, they will be flying out at first light.'

'Do Jack and Sam have them?'

'No, they are in a hotel with the Somali government officials who got them out.'

When I hang up, for a few selfish seconds I hold this information to myself and just let it sink it. Matt is already sitting up in bed, looking at me with the biggest smile on his face. I haven't seen that in a while.

'They've got them, they've got them, they've got them. So it's not quite finished but the kidnappers have handed them over. They are still in Somalia, I have to tell your dad.'

It's dark, the sun is yet to rise. I walk down the hallway; 462 days ago I was the bearer of the worst news any parent wants to hear and today I get to do the opposite.

In the spare room, Geoff is asleep on his stomach, facing away from the door. I gently pat his shoulder.

'Geoff, Geoff.'

He stirs and lifts his head.

'Geoff, they've got them.'

'What?' he yells through his sleepy daze, half jumping up.

'They've got them, they're out!'

He slumps back onto the bed and I can hear muffled sighs and sobs of relief coming from his pillow.

'Are you okay?'

He nods.

'I'm going to call Heather; I'll meet you down in the kitchen when you're ready.'

Heather will be getting on a plane back to Nairobi shortly so I need to let her know before she leaves.

'Hello, dear.' She sounds flat and tired.

'They've got them.'

She sounds like she is about to burst into tears. The fifteen months of anguish is released in her initial response, it's like a giant exhale. I fill her in on the little I know and she heads off to board the plane.'

I turn around and Geoff is up and dressed, Matt is making coffee and it has just gone 5 a.m. I need to phone Ham and Amy, and let them know the good news.

Ham answers. I have woken him up.

'Ham, they're out. Well, they're not out of Somalia yet, but they have been handed over and are safe.'

'Well, they're not out yet, are they? Call me back when they're out.'

I am not going to let Ham's bad mood deflate my excitement, or anyone else's. Today is an amazing day and I am going to enjoy every bit of it. It's one I will remember forever.

Matt and Geoff are online, watching the Google alerts come rolling in. I need to call Mike at KGA and get ready to head to Sydney for a press conference.

'Hi, Mike, they've got them. It's all over Google and I imagine my mobile will start ringing soon.'

'Okay, call me on the way and I will let you know the plan. Great news, Kel, well done.'

All the way to Sydney my mobile phone is going crazy. The boys from KGA were right – I need a separate mobile to call family members, Dick and Bob because my regular number is being accessed by most of the world's journalists.

I phone Dick, and Pip answers the phone and gets Dick.

'Hi, Kellie. Isn't it wonderful news?'

'I wanted to call to make sure you knew, and say thank you again.'

'Yes, I saw it on the early news, it's great news.'

'You will probably be bombarded soon by journalists, and I'm on my way to Sydney to do a press conference now, but we will talk throughout the day.'

He hands me over to Pip, who is just as gorgeous as Dick – they are both amazing people. Pip is over the moon at our news, and expresses her feelings freely. It feels so wonderful to have such great people on our side.

At KGA we get the latest run-down from Brian and Mike. There are hugs, kisses and high-fives all round when we arrive, and staff are buzzing around everywhere.

The boys give me the updated version of the press release and I practise it a few times before we head off in a taxi for the press conference in front of the art gallery. They want Matt to say a few words as well, so they bring him up to speed on what to expect.

The taxi drives through the park near the gallery, the number of reporters, TV vans and photographers is unbelievable. I feel like I might actually stop breathing. I can't lose control, not now. I've come so far under so much stress, I just need to keep it together for a bit longer. I can cry later, all the way home in the car if need be.

Brian is giving me instructions during the cab ride, but the din that occupies my brain blocks out his voice. The cab pulls up in front of the media mass, and Brian leads us over to the microphone pit, as I call it. He announces who we are and then hands it over to me.

All the confidence I had built up during practice disappears. I start to cry and can't get the words out. Matt is beside me whispering, 'Kel, it's okay, you're okay,' then someone from the pack says, 'Take a breath and start again.'

It's 10 p.m. Friday night and I am emotionally exhausted. I have seen myself on television more times than I can count. I've heard my voice on the radio and hope I don't sound like that in real life. Matt, Geoff and I are waiting for the word from Nairobi that they are on the plane and heading out of Somalia, then this ordeal will really finally be over.

At 10.07 p.m. a text arrives from Nairobi.

'Wheels r up.'

Nicky
Nairobi
Thursday, 26 November

We are up early to find out if the boys have Nige and Amanda. Sam is seriously pissed off. They had to pull in Major Saad to sort things out but they finally made it to the airport.

Then it is wheels up.

My brother is really coming home.

We all go crazy when this call comes through. Mum had arrived safely and we start letting everyone know. We Skype Si, Kel and Ham. Si was at Ange's place, which turns into the biggest party in Moore Park. Damn near every person driving past pulls in and started celebrating.

Back in Nairobi the day marches on. The boys send through another wheels-up message.

We decide to meet them at the hospital, and half an hour before landing time we all head off to gather in the family visitors' area. Richard from the Canadian High Commission calls to say they're leaving the airport. They have sent out another ambulance as a decoy.

Next call, they're at the roundabout. We all charge downstairs.

Bunched around the side entrance, we hear them long before we see them.

The consular cars come screaming in – holy shit, they're travelling fast! There is a siren too. I can see Richard grinning as the car comes screeching to a halt. I swear they laid down rubber.

Where is he? Where is he? My heart is hammering in my chest

Amanda races past. It doesn't register it's her till she's passed. Her hair is dark and in a long plait. She has glasses on which also throws me – I've only ever seen her with contacts. *Ooooooh!* 'I think to myself in a kindergarten-telltale way. The boys are going to be in so much trouble with Lorinda. They forewarned Mum and me that Nigel was thin, but they haven't warned Lorinda about how undernourished Amanda is. She was thin before but now she's scrawny.

And then I see him.

His eyes are red pissholes in the snow. The grin splitting his long bushy beard is maniacal. It's stretched right across his pale, gaunt face. His hair is really short and that's surprising – whenever he's had a beard in the past, it's been long and scruffy. And there's some definite balding going on up there.

But it's Nige and he's here and he's alive and he doesn't look too fucked up. I've got a high-pitched ringing in my head, eerily similar to the white noise that I had during the very first call, the ransom call. How weird is that? Things have come full circle.

Nige sees Mum at the door and wraps himself around her. I'm now crying hard. Not heaving sobs, but tears are streaming down my cheeks and there's no way I can stop them. I'm licking salt off my lips not knowing if it's from tears or snot.

Nige lifts his head and sees me behind Mum.

He holds his hand out and as I move towards him he gathers the fabric of my shirt at my shoulder and uses it to pull me towards him. He gathers me under his arm. He is thin, I can feel his ribs and hipbone. The three of us – Mum, Nige and me – cling to each other, crying in the doorway of the Aga Khan Hospital in a very tight embrace.

Nigel
Nairobi
Late November

Over the first few days in Nairobi I undergo a raft of medical examinations, being poked and prodded in a few tender places.

I meet more people and at times it feels like my head is going to explode, the saturation of information and sensory overload is almost too much sometimes.

I finally remove my beard, but insist that I keep my moustache – due to the fact that it's Movember – much to Mum's horror, but she's happy to see I haven't lost my sense of humour.

I can't believe what it's like to listen to music – I ask the consular officials if they would bring in some CDs, and when I'm alone in the room I put on 'My Happiness' by Powderfinger.

Listening intently to the words while I'm in the shower, I have a complete meltdown. I'm in tears, curled up in a ball on the floor almost having a panic attack, terrified that none of this is real, that I'm dreaming again.

Then I start reassuring myself that I'm truly free, that no one can hurt us anymore and that I can begin my life again.

EPILOGUE

The Money Launderer
Newcastle
2011

People ask me two things now that this 'Nigel episode' is over. The first and most obvious is how much it cost, and the second is how I am now.

The answer I give to the first question is, in monetary terms it cost approximately AUS$1.3 million to get Nige and Amanda out. It's impossible to put a cost on the emotional toll on our families.

The answer to the second is that I am so pleased it's over: it was one of the most stressful, demanding and anxiety-inducing experiences of my life. It was also the most gratifying thing I have ever done.

When Nigel returned, I gave him a card. In it, I told him that this experience had changed my life as much as it had changed his.

I have always admired those who take on foster kids, or volunteer

to care for or spend time with people less fortunate than themselves. But I always felt as if I was much too selfish to do anything
like that – spending time away from my family and my business
was something I could just never do. So I gave Nigel a card to say
thank you, not just an everyday sort of thank you but a big one:
thank you for changing my life.

What I learned about myself is that I am capable of putting
every single thing in my life to one side to focus on something, or
someone, other than myself. I put my life on hold – including my
husband, my children, my job, my friends – for my brother-in-law.

This experience has made me a better wife, mother, daughter,
daughter-in-law and sister. It has also made me a better friend. I
learned that whatever the world dishes out to you, a little bit of
positive thought and energy goes a hell of a long way. I have learned
to enjoy the 'now', to smell the coffee in the mornings, to relish
lazy mornings in bed with my children.

I have learned to appreciate the little things around me. It
doesn't matter if your house is the biggest, or your car is the most
expensive, or your clothes aren't this season's – none of this matters. What matters are the people in your life. The biggest lesson of
all is that it is greater to give than to receive, and to give someone
something and expect nothing in return, just to give, for its own
sake, is the greatest thing of all.

I am a much better person this side of Nigel's kidnapping; I am
proud of the person I have become and I am so thankful for that,
and I am so happy and grateful for my lot in life.

As for the rest of the tight five (Matt, the kids and I), we are
rock solid. Stirling started school this year and Matt could not
resist the call of the land any longer. He is back working on a
farm, where he is as happy as a pig in mud. After his shoulder

injury, he is back getting his hands dirty, working with cattle and tractors again. Gigi and Cal started a new school last year. They have really settled in and are doing brilliantly. They have made some wonderful friends and the trauma of Nigel's kidnapping seems somewhere off in the distance. The business is booming and going from strength to strength. This year we are incorporating an event-planning, decorating and management arm of the business.

We hope to set up a foundation that helps others who find themselves in situations like ours. It's something all of us feel passionately about. We want to inspire others about the power of the human spirit and the goodness that lives within us all.

The hostage
Moore Park
2011

Words cannot describe what it felt like to land in Australia – euphoric just doesn't cut it. My overwhelming happiness at being back with my family, though, was tinged with sadness. I could now see firsthand the pain that my selfishness and ambition had caused them. Their struggle for my freedom had taken a great toll, physically and mentally. Mum and Dad had aged, marriages had been strained, and family relationships were pushed to the edge.

In terms of the financial pressure, I will always be indebted to my family, friends and the other generous donors – even in the future after I've paid back their money. Something that plays on my conscience is the knowledge that the ransom which paid for my life may well be used in the killing of innocent people. It is something I will struggle with for the rest of my days.

Having been sensory deprived for such a long period, I took some time to adjust to life back home. My paranoia and feelings of over-vigilance took a while to get in check. I didn't want people to handle me with kid gloves – being treated normally, including the gentle ribbing I'd come to expect from my family, helped with the transition. I put this resilience down to my rural upbringing, my years at boarding school, and being the youngest of four siblings: I learned how to deal with piss-taking from a very early age. I also think that this is part of the Australian psyche; we see through adversity with our black humour.

Like with any defining life experience, your perspective changes. Every single one of us will face some sort of trauma or adversity in our lives; it's how we use that experience which is the making of us. Some people implode while others blossom. In my case, it has given me great strength and also revealed a few of my weaknesses. It has made me grow up and given me an infinitely more positive outlook. I hope in the future I will be able to put others' needs in front of my own, as so many people did for me.

Amanda and I keep in contact. Although it was a shared experience, we had very different journeys: she suffered far greater than I did because of the simple fact of her gender. I am so thankful that she was there with me; without her support, friendship and love I wouldn't have been able to get through the ordeal and be the person I am today. There have been times of strain between us as we have both had to come to terms with the decisions our families made. We have gone in different directions since our release, but she will always be an important part of my life, and I cherish her friendship.

I have begun working as a consultant, training journalists in managing hostile environments, hoping that my experience will save them from a similar fate to mine. And I hope to do some work in crisis management with K&R companies too. I've started public speaking, imparting my story and explaining the importance of family, friends and community – it's a simple message but without these, you really have nothing. I'm also planning to photograph Somali refugees living in Australia with the idea of touring an exhibition around the country, to expose their stories of pain and suffering – after all, that was my original intention when I travelled to Somalia. The three of us would like to set up a foundation that assists other Australians who find themselves in dire circumstances both overseas and here at home – we'd like others to benefit from what we learned the hard way.

I lost fifteen months of my life, and I'm unwilling to lose any more by dwelling on the past. Out of a horrific experience have come many good things: I am more compassionate towards others, infinitely more patient, and I have a greater understanding of the world around me. I have been given a second chance at life and I don't intend to waste it.

The negotiator
Moore Park
2011

Once Nige was safely ensconced in the Aga Khan, after he'd been fed, checked over, and his Nige-beard-ladin had been shaved off, he asked if he could watch a DVD of *The Castle*. I knew then he was going to be okay.

I also knew I was going to miss JC and the boys, but that the job was done and it was time to disband our little group. Mum was there, and it was her role to be with Nige. I was feeling incredibly guilty that I'd missed Jacinta's birthday during the first unsuccessful rescue attempt. It was time to go home.

For a little while after I got back, I felt aimless, and for a little while longer pretty pissed off about my situation. That situation being, living in a tiny two-bedroom box away from the beach with not enough cash flow to maintain farm equipment, which was hampering the growth of crops. I hit the streets to get a part-time job while we were putting this book together. Meanwhile, Si got back into the horti/agriculture side of things full time.

Many people seem surprised at the 'sacrifices' we made for our sibling. This was, and still would be, a no-brainer; I would do it for any of my brothers. I'm well aware how fortunate I am to have as brothers some of the finest men around. I would have chosen them as friends had we not been born into the same family. I hope this alleviates any guilt that Nige may still feel.

I hope my children will share equally close bonds as adults. Once, I complained to someone how unfair it was that Jacinta, who was sleeping metres from the computer, had to hear so many calls to Adan. The reply was, 'Yes, but look at what else she got from it: she saw your strength. She saw her mum take on the bad guys and win. Not many kids get to see the true mettle of their parent like that. That kid will be able to do anything because she's seen how it's done.' My friend was right, I think: that resolve does strengthen people. Even though my kids bicker, like all siblings do, I like to think this experience will have taught them the value of our family and indeed all those dear to us. And that it is worth fighting for.

A number of years ago, while we were living in middle-class suburbia, one of my kids asked whether we were rich. I explained to them that while they didn't get their every demand and whim met, we lived a comfortable life. We had jobs, food, shelter, cars, a trampoline. We were well-off by a lot of standards. I went on to tell them that Australia on the whole was very wealthy when compared to many developing countries, where as well as not having homes or food, let alone toys, kids didn't have access to doctors, and didn't go to school, especially if they were girls. In fact, I said, some were so poor their families had to sell them. After taking an enormous financial step backwards and struggling to keep afloat, if I use this as a yard stick, I realise one or two things. We have Nige back home and alive, and for lots of people the outcome isn't so fortunate. So, if wealth is relative, then we are indeed rich. You simply cannot put a price on the life of a loved one.

It took months for DFAT and the AFP to debrief us, and to this day, I have no idea what the outcomes of that debriefing were or if any policies have been changed. We have never been told. I'm not surprised or even that disappointed by this. It is what it is. Our government had parameters they couldn't and wouldn't operate outside. I just wish they had told us about them sooner. I sincerely hope that all changes before another Australian is kidnapped, which is sadly only a matter of time. To that end I am very keen, with Nige and Kell, to set up a foundation to assist Australians (and their families) who find themselves in similar situations to ours.

I've gone back to university. It's very disturbing having my kids show me how to transpose and calculate equations when it all looks like a foreign language to me. Ultimately, I'd like to study something in the field of social inequality. I've always wanted to do some sort of aid work, but Si and I decided to postpone this while the kids were little (after all, there is nowhere better to grow up than Australia). Having a solid background in horticulture might put me in good stead for some work with an overseas NGO sometime in the future. However, I think I might draw the line at Somalia.

I am an average Joe, who through sheer bloody-mindedness made something amazing happen, and I'd love to use my experience to help others. The whole kidnap experience made me realise that we're all capable of more than we think. But the next important thing I learned is that ultimately, love is mightier than any bureaucracy.

ACKNOWLEDGMENTS

There are so many people we must acknowledge, it's hard to know where to begin.

We are immensely grateful to Bob Brown, and Dick and Pip Smith, whose benevolence still overwhelms us to this day. The kindness, generosity and compassion shown by these three throughout the ordeal were beyond words. We cannot thank them enough.

Some wonderful people made Nigel's rescue possible, but none more than the team at AKE, the Crisis Management Team, Alto and the flyboy. Again, words cannot express our gratitude.

Thanks to all in the Brennan family, Aunty Alison, Naomi and Deb, Virginia and Jeff, Helen and Bert and cousins and the Jackel clan. Their support and love sustained us throughout this gargantuan task.

To all those who donated money, to those who gave support, guidance and legal advice, and to everyone who called just to tell us we were in their thoughts, we are eternally grateful to each and every one of you.

We thank all those who stealthily organised the fundraisers along with Ham and Amy, Kate, Bin and Tom, and to all those who donated at the Croppa fundraiser. At the Brisbane fundraiser Carl, Hellfire and Jane were fantastic, but there were so many more. Thank you to the Withers family for organising their own fundraiser in Sydney. Thanks to all the Moore Park crew who organised the Bundy fundraiser (and sacrificed their livers there), along with all those who bought Nigel's photo prints. Special thanks go to Jacinta and her friends, who waitressed for the grand fee of a T-shirt each.

We'd like to thank Bryce Courtenay for his guidance and encouragement. He said it would be 'the hardest fucking thing' we would do in our lives and he was absolutely on the money.

Thanks to Robert Sessions and the team at Penguin books for their enthusiasm for this story and their faith in our ability to tell it. We're especially grateful to our publisher Andrea McNamara and editor Bridget Maidment, for their patience. It has been an honour and a pleasure to work with you.

Nicky

Thanks to my immediate family – Simon and our children, Jacinta, Monty and Atticus – who survived the fifteen months of my self-exile more than admirably. In return for my absence, they provided me with love and support.

To the outer circle of my family – my parents and my other brothers, Matthew and Hamilton – and my sisters-in-law, who I am only too delighted to claim as blood. And so it ripples out to family members further afield.

Every girl needs a best friend living around the corner. Ange loves our children as if they were her own, and she has helped us in every possible way. Ange, Dennis, Ken and Alice, along with the rest of the Rocky mob, have seen all my flaws and love me anyway.

John and Erin, times of crisis create the strongest of ties; your friendship means the world to me. Will and Jack, you may not like it but you will always be my first port of call in an emergency, and for the odd piss-take.

Thanks to all my school friends who rang or turned up just as I was at my lowest ebb. Thanks to Kev and Ross and many of the

AFP negotiators, some who have made it into the book and some who haven't. While there are people like you in the force, I still have faith. Also thanks to our wide array of friends at Moore Park, who all watched over us and kept tabs on our wellbeing.

And finally to Nige, who dragged me down a road I would never have otherwise taken. It's good to have you home.

Kellie

The full list of people I could thank would take up pages, but I would like to make special mention of my family: my mum, dad, brother and sister-in-law, and, of course, my husband. The emotional support you gave me was incredible and helped me get through every day of this ordeal.

Nigel

The words 'thank you' cannot adequately convey my gratitude to those involved in my safe return home.

I know there was a cast of thousands who worked tirelessly behind the scenes for the fifteen months I was away. Many more have supported my recovery and the writing of this book since I've been home.

Thank you to my beautiful extended family and friends. Words will never express the love and admiration I have for what each of you has done. Your stubbornness and determination are the reasons I am here today. Thank you for grounding and supporting me since my return.

Thank you to Jo Dougherty and Maria Burnett for the endless hours spent debriefing and transcribing my story, for reading parts of the manuscript, and for their ongoing support and friendship.

Thank you to Brian Tyson and Michael Van Maanen of Kreab Gavin Anderson for their invaluable knowledge, support and friendship.

I'm grateful to the government officials who were involved in my case. In particular, I thank Colonel Peter Murphy, Federal Agent Detective Sergeant Michael Murray and Tim Kane for their help and support after I was released, which mentally prepared me to return home.

Thanks to my doctors – Sandra Rizzo and Desley Fraser – for their amazing support over the past eighteen months.

Finally, thank you to my co-authors – Nicky and Kellie – for their willingness to share this story, and for sacrificing time with their families to tell it. I couldn't have done it without you.

PENGUIN BOOKS

THE PRICE OF LIFE

Nigel Brennan grew up near Moree in country New South Wales. He developed a passion for photography in his early twenties and studied at the Queensland College of Art, Griffith University. He has worked as a photojournalist for APN media. Nigel is currently based in Bundaberg and works as a freelance consultant, advising companies and NGOs whose employees are sent to hostile environments.

His sister, Nicky Bonney, is married to Simon. They have three kids and run a nursery in Bundaberg. In 2011 Nicky returned to study.

Nigel's sister-in-law, Kellie Brennan, is married to Matt, and lives in the Hunter Valley with their three children. Kellie runs a busy café and gourmet catering business in the tourist town of Morpeth.